THE FOOD AND FARM POLICIES
OF THE EUROPEAN COMMUNITY

THE FOOD AND FARM POLICIES OF THE EUROPEAN COMMUNITY

Simon Harris, Alan Swinbank, and Guy Wilkinson

A Wiley–Interscience Publication

JOHN WILEY & SONS
Chichester · New York · Brisbane · Toronto · Singapore

Library of Congress Cataloging in Publication Data:

Harris, Simon.
  The food and farm policies of the European community.

  'A Wiley–Interscience publication.'
  1. Agriculture and state— European Economic
Community countries. 2. Food industry and trade—
Government policy—European Economic Community countries.
3. Agriculture—Economic aspects—European Economic
Community countries. I. Swinbank, A. II. Wilkinson,
G. (Guy) III. Title.
HD1920.5.Z8H37 1983   338.1′84   83-10462

ISBN 0 471 10261 X

British Library Cataloguing in Publication Data:

Harris, S.
  The food and farm policies of the European Community.
  1. Agriculture and state—European Economic Community countries
  I. Swinbank, A.   II. Wilkinson, G.
  338.1′, 81   HD1920.5.Z8

  ISBN 0 471 10261 X

Typeset by Pintail Studios Ltd, Ringwood, Hampshire.
Printed by The Pitman Press, Bath, Avon.

Contents

Preface

This book is intended to fill a gap in the existing range of literature on the Common Agricultural Policy (CAP). There exists, certainly, a vast range of written material on most individual aspects of the CAP, but there are few texts which aim to provide a comprehensive descriptive and analytical treatment.

The book aims to cover virtually all the important aspects of the CAP. It includes a thorough treatment of the commodity regimes, a detailed explanation of the green 'money' system, and an account of the place of agricultural expenditure in the Community Budget. There are also chapters on structural policy, and on the subject of much current concern, the impact of the Community's farm policies on Third Countries. In addition, however, the book examines the interaction between the CAP and the food industry in the Community, together with an account of the extensive European food legislation. These latter aspects are not commonly treated in texts on the CAP, despite their central importance.

Food and Farm Policies is therefore directed to the needs of a wide readership both within the Community and in Third Countries, including civil servants and politicians, businessmen in the agriculture and food industries and students in a wide range of courses. All those whose responsibilities and interests require more than a superficial acquaintanceship with the CAP, its mechanisms and effects, will find material of relevance to their concerns.

The aim has been to provide not only a description of the major features, but also to explain how the CAP has developed, and the reasons for its present form. Where economic analysis is important to an understanding of the issues, care has been taken to simplify the analysis and to explain the economic concepts used.

The Common Agricultural Policy is constantly evolving under the impetus of economic and political developments. Any book in the writing suffers from the need to provide for an arbitrary cut-off point in time, and this text is no exception. It includes the main developments in the CAP up to and including the 1982/83 price review, and provides budget data included within the Preliminary Draft Budget for 1983. Inevitably some of the detail in the text will date: nevertheless it is hoped that the exposition of the principles underlying the mass of legislation will prove of lasting value in helping those interested to cope with developments subsequent to this text's completion.

No text can be totally comprehensive if it is to remain of manageable length. *Food and Farm Policies* does not deal with forestry, fishing, or more than cursorily with State aids to agriculture; forestry, because there is as yet no comprehensive Community forestry policy; fishing because of its complexity and the fact that viii

although fish products are of importance, the details of the common fish policy are so different from those concerned with agricultural production that exclusion seemed justified; and State aids because of the paucity of reliable data.

Many people have been generous in providing comments and suggestions, and although the responsibility for the book lies wholly with the authors, our thanks are due to a large number of people from, among others, the Commission of the European Communities in Brussels, the Ministry of Agriculture, Fisheries and Food in London, the US Trade Representative's Office in Washington, the Universities of Reading (UK) and Stanford (USA), and the Grain and Allied Feed Trades Association in London.

S. Harris
A. Swinbank
G. Wilkinson

1982

Note on Exchange Rates

Throughout this text, support prices for Community farmers and amounts in the Community Budget are expressed in European currency units (ecu's). Chapter 8 explains how ecu's are made up and their uses within the Community. It may be helpful to readers, however, to give some currency equivalents for ecu's at the start, so that anyone so minded can convert figures in ecu's, as they come across them, to more readily recognizable forms.

Value of the ecu at market rates of exchange (1 ecu = x units national currency)

	Calendar years			
	1979	1980	1981	1982
Belgium (B. franc)	40.17	40.60	41.29	44.68
Luxembourg (Lux. franc)	40.17	40.60	41.29	44.68
Denmark (D. kroner)	7.21	7.83	7.92	8.15
Germany (Deutschmark)	2.51	2.53	2.51	2.38
Greece (drachma)	50.78	59.24	61.62	65.30
France (Fr. franc)	5.83	5.87	6.04	6.43
Ireland (punt)	0.669	0.676	0.691	0.690
Italy (lire)	1138	1189	1263	1324
Netherlands (guilder)	2.75	2.76	2.78	2.62
UK (pound sterling)	0.646	0.598	0.553	0.561
USA (US dollar)	1.371	1.391	1.116	0.981
Japan (yen)	300.5	315.0	245.4	243.5

Value of the ecu for Community institutional purposes (1 ecu = x units national currency)

	Value of the ecu used for the 1983 Preliminary Draft Budget	Value of the ecu used for agricultural conversions at the start of the 1982/83 marketing years
Belgium (B. franc)	44.5367	42.9772
Luxembourg (Lux. franc)	44.5367	42.9772
Denmark (D. kroner)	8.13990	8.23400*
Germany (Deutschmark)	2.42571	2.57524
Greece (drachma)	62.6003	66.5526*
France (Fr. franc)	6.18218	6.19564
Ireland (punt)	0.617501	0.691011*
Italy (lire)	1301.59	1289.00
Netherlands (guilder)	2.66265	2.75563
UK (pound sterling)	0.558500	0.618655
USA (US dollar)	1.01647	—

* Effective 29 June 1982.

Biographical Notes

Simon Harris is Group Economist and EEC Adviser for S & W Berisford plc, where he is involved in assessing the economic impact of developments on world agricultural and food commodity markets and developments in the European Community. He is the UK representative on the Bureau of the Committee on Commerce and Distribution—one of the European Commission's major consultative committees.

Prior to joining Berisford in 1974, Mr Harris was an economist with the UK Ministry of Agriculture. He was particularly involved in the government's economic assessment of membership of the European Communities prior to Britain's accession and in the discussions on the implementation of the Treaty of Accession. A graduate of London and Newcastle-on-Tyne universities, Mr Harris has written and lectured widely in the areas of the CAP and its effects (both domestic and external), and international commodity trade (particularly sugar). Major publications include *International Sugar Markets in a State of Flux* (co-author), *The CAP and the World Commodity Scene*, and *US/EEC Agricultural Trade Relations*.

Alan Swinbank is a lecturer in the Department of Agricultural Economics at the University of Reading. His teaching and research interests centre on the food and farm policies of the European Community, with a major teaching commitment to Reading's innovatory BSc in Food Science and Food Economics. He has written extensively on EEC farm and food policies, and has advised both the Food and Agriculture Organization of the United Nations and the government of Cyprus on the foreign trade implications of those policies.

Both he and Mr Harris act as Specialist Advisers to the House of Lords Select Committee on the European Communities.

A former student of the University of Reading, Dr Swinbank also studied in Canada and at the London School of Economics before spending four years working for the Commission of the European Communities. During his sojourn in Brussels he spent three years in the European Agricultural Guidance and Guarantee Fund and a year in the milk division. He returned to Reading in 1977.

Guy Wilkinson is Trade Relations Director of Express Dairy (UK) Ltd, a subsidiary of the Grand Metropolitan Group of companies, and chairman of one of the UK's main dairy trade associations. He is well placed to understand the interaction between the food industry and the national and European authorities on the one hand, and producer organizations such as the Milk Marketing Boards on the other.

After graduating from Cambridge University in 1971, he spent the next two years in the evaluation of development aid projects for the governments of Uganda and Mauritius, before joining the Commission of the European Communities in 1973, where he worked for the following seven years. During this time Mr Wilkinson spent five years in the Directorate General for Agriculture, where he was close to the formation of policy. In 1977 he became an adviser to George Thomson, then Commissioner for Regional Policy. In 1980, he joined the Central Advisory Group of the Commission where he was closely involved in the development of Commission policy on the budgetary problems of the United Kingdom.

Chapter 1

Agricultural Support and Consumer Protection in Western Economies

Throughout the Western World governments intervene in the agricultural sector in an attempt to achieve various objectives of economic and social policy; such as improving the balance of payments (by import saving or export expansion), increasing the level of self-sufficiency in essential food supplies, or preventing rural depopulation. But governments have principally intervened in the agricultural sector in order to achieve particular objectives for the farm population; such as increased farm incomes, maintenance of farm employment, and stable market prices for farm products. Many of the policies pursued have a direct impact not only on the agricultural industry at which they are aimed, but also on the industries supplying the farm sector and on the food manufacturers that purchase a large, and increasing, proportion of the output of the farm sector. In addition governments intervene extensively to control the content and presentation of foodstuffs. Less frequently governments may attempt to control or influence the retail price of food as part of general economic policies to control inflation, or of social policies aimed at improving the position of low income families. Within the European Community many of these policies, though not all, are pursued and enacted at the Community, and not the national, level. In this text attention will be paid to the form and content of such policies, their impact, and the methods employed for their implementation.

There are in essence three categories of justification for intervention in the farm sector, and two in the food sector. It will be useful to discuss these briefly;[1] but before doing so it is important to note that the classifications are not watertight and that the achievement of one objective in farm or food policy might jeopardize, or enhance, the possibility of achieving another. It is also important to note that the declared objectives of farm and food policy might well differ from those that were instrumental in generating their creation in the first instance.

1

REASONS FOR STATE INTERVENTION

Instability of market prices

Because of the nature of the farming process the volume of output tends to be highly variable. In the first place the vagaries of weather and animal or plant diseases can have a significant impact upon the quantity of produce actually resulting from any given farming operations; and in the second place the decisions of farmers may tend to result in large variations in output from year to year. Farming, in the Western economies, tends to be characterized by many thousands of small businessmen, all of whom may take investment decisions in ignorance of the intentions of their fellows. Thus if the price of a particular product is high one year, then each farmer may decide separately to increase his production for the next harvest. All these separate decisions, when considered in aggregate, conspire to produce a large increase in production which will flood the market and—unless offset by government action—drive down the price. Each farmer, seeing the price lowered, may well react by cutting back on production so that, at the next harvest, shortages will ensue. This cyclical behaviour is less of a feature of Community agriculture, because of the support mechanisms employed, than in some other Western economies where market prices can fluctuate more freely.

The instability of market prices is further aggravated by the nature of the demand for agricultural products. As prices rise then consumers tend to purchase a smaller quantity, as postulated by economists; but the nature of this response is inelastic. By this is meant that the percentage change in quantity demanded will be less than the percentage change in price. Thus a harvest shortfall of 10 per cent could result in a price rise of 30 per cent as consumers outbid each other for the reduced supplies. Equally a bountiful harvest, say 10 per cent above expectations, could result in a 30 per cent price fall.

Taken together the volume of production, and the price for which it sells, will determine the revenue (and ultimately the income) of farmers. The example of the previous paragraph demonstrates the paradox that for most basic food products, for which price elasticities of demand are less than one, total revenue will fall in years of abundant supply, while in years of short supply total sales revenue will rise. Of course all producers receive the same, or a similar, price for their produce regardless of their particular output level as they are producing homogeneous commodities. Thus if—for whatever reason—a particular producer has an exceptionally large harvest in a year of harvest failure, that individual gains handsomely, and conversely if the situation is reversed.

In the same way in which an individual farmer's income may be swollen or depleted if the peaks and troughs of his output are out of phase with those of the farm sector in general, so farmers in a particular region, or nation, may face low prices even in years of low output if produce from regions (or nations) with a more abundant harvest is freely admitted to the local market.

For reasons such as these governments intervene in the markets for farm and horticultural products. For products which can be stored the government may well enter the market during periods of peak production and purchase goods for addition to a strategic stockpile, which can then be dispersed following a penurious harvest. To a very limited extent the European Community's purchases of intervention stocks (to be discussed in Chapter 3) can be viewed in this light.[2] The reduced supply caused by stockpiling after a generous harvest tends to raise the market price; and the additional supply as the stock is released on to the market following a poor harvest tends to keep the market price down. Thus greater price stability can be achieved to the benefit, so it is said, of both producers and consumers.

There is a cost involved: that of handling and storing the product, and of the interest foregone on the capital sum necessary to fund the storage operation. There is also a potential profit: that the goods will be sold at a price higher than their acquisition cost. Neither government nor commerce can, however, accurately predict the future, nor say with certainty that a particular year's production is below, or above, trend. Joseph was very privileged in his knowledge that seven years of famine would follow seven years of plenty (Genesis, Chapter 41).

The successful operation of policies such as those outlined above would be threatened if produce were freely admitted from other countries. Thus a government which attempted to arrest a fall in the market price by buying produce for storage would find its achievements jeopardized by the free availability of cheap imports. As will be seen, the European Community has legislated to curb the flow of imports under such circumstances; and also to curb the flow of exports during periods of shortage.

The incomes of producers

Many government policies towards the agricultural sector are motivated by the belief that the incomes of farmers (though rarely those of farm workers) should be bolstered. The evidence to support the view that farmers are locked into the farming system unable to realize their assets, or redeploy their labour, and that therefore they have to accept incomes below those earned on comparable assets in the rest of the economy, is slight; although widely believed to be the case. None the less some of the older generation undoubtedly fall into this category due to their lack of suitable non-farm employment skills. On the other hand there is considerable evidence to suggest that the farm sector as a whole is in sectoral decline. By this is meant that a smaller and smaller farming population is able to supply the urban population with its food and fibre requirements. The adjustment process is undoubtedly painful for the farm sector, as for all declining sectors. Much of the pressure for income support comes from the need to moderate the pace of agricultural adjustment, in terms of the outflow of resources from farming, in order to avoid the creation of unacceptable social and political pressures.

The sectoral decline of agriculture, in terms of its importance as an employer and of its proportionate contribution to national income, is common to all Western countries. This phenomenon arises because of two opposing forces. On the one hand the size of the human stomach is limited and consequently in many developed economies the only growth in the overall domestic demand for food comes from population growth—which is, in any case, generally low. This is reflected in a low income elasticity of demand for food; any increase in expenditure tends to be used to purchase higher quality or more expensive foods with a greater processing and packaging element in the final retail price; the volume effect is very limited. On the other hand, helped by the public provision of research and advisory services, technical innovation has ensured that the supply of farm products can be expanded faster than domestic demand. As a result the normal situation faced by policy makers in Western nations is that of excess supply weakening market prices. In real terms agricultural prices tend to fall[3] and resources tend to leave the farm sector. Farm groups, not unnaturally, feel justified in their claims for farm income support.[4]

In essence what is being attempted with agricultural support policies is no more than that applied to other important declining economic sectors: a degree of adjustment assistance. For example, a Community Commissioner—Tugendhat (1980)—has defended Community industrial policy in terms directly applicable to agriculture:

> The objective of public policy must be, I believe, to ensure continued adaptation and modernization of existing industries. . . . At the same time we must take account of the social impact of these changes, helping the older industries to achieve the necessary restructuring in an orderly fashion and over a reasonable period, providing assistance for those who need retraining, and cushioning the impact of the recession on the depressed regions.

Where agricultural policy is different from industrial policy is in the extent of the support given by most countries to their farm sectors, reflecting the length of time such support has been given, the influence of the extremely well-organized agricultural lobbies, and the apparent slowness of agricultural adjustment.

The most direct way in which farm incomes could be supported would be by paying direct income supplements to particular groups of designated recipients. Rarely do governments do so, but they often give farmers preferential treatment in the assessment and taxation of income. In the European Community taxation remains a national, and not a Community, matter, although ultimately the levels and types of indirect taxation are meant to be harmonized. Already the EC countries have standardized their main consumption tax (a value added tax) and harmonized its coverage, and they are working towards harmonized VAT rates.

In their attempt to increase farm incomes governments have resorted to a number of devices which seek to reduce the costs of farm inputs, or increase the price of farm products. The extent to which the benefits from such price manipulations are retained by the farming community—and not passed on in higher land values, or usage of farm machinery, etc.— is debatable and beyond the scope of the present text. The variety of forms these various schemes can take is immense.

Some governments intervene actively in the wholesale manipulation of input prices, though this is not a major policy mechanism pursued by the European Community.[5] Such activity could, for example, involve the subsidization of fertilizers or fuels destined to the agricultural sector, or a reduced level of indirect taxation on those inputs. Equally it can take the form of subsidized credit to farmers and horticulturalists; or capital grants to aid the purchase of machinery, buildings, or land. In addition to the national activities benefiting all, or part, of the farming sector the European Community does pursue what has become known as a 'structural policy'. The aim of this policy is to adapt the fabric of the farming sector, and produce farming structures and systems which are more profitable given the prevailing economic climate. The form such aid takes is often a capital grant, or interest rate subsidy (partly financed by the Member State) to selected individuals, organizations, or governments, offsetting some of the cost of an investment programme. The apparent contradictory aims of both wishing to slow down the rate of change by support programmes, and to speed it up by structural aid, can only partially be explained by the different time scales involved.

The European Community's system of aid to the farming community is, however, characterized by its attempts to raise the price of farm produce above the levels that would normally prevail in the market. Chapter 3 is devoted to a thorough discussion of the mechanisms commonly deployed, and the associated specialist terminology. For the moment it suffices to note that the schemes commonly involve the insulation of Community markets from world markets through charges on imports and the subsidization of exports; and also the storage, processing, and sometimes destruction of unwanted produce.

Policies that seek to influence farm incomes by manipulating the prices received by farmers do have one characteristic which is worth noting: they are not selective. Thus unless special measures are taken—which in the European Community they are not—then all producers of the protected product receive the enhanced price regardless of their scale of operation or the profitability of their particular business. In fact the larger the volume of production then the greater is the benefit received by the producer. The disproportionate benefit that the Community's policies confer on larger farmers has become a matter of increasing concern. A direct income supplement could, on the other hand, be directly tailored to aid the low income, or low volume, producers; although again there are some offsetting disadvantages.

Before concluding this section of the discussion of governmental action designed to augment farm produce prices—and hopefully farm incomes—it is worth mentioning an additional alternative. If farmers and horticulturalists can be persuaded to limit their supply of produce to the market then the market price will rise and, with inelastic demand (as discussed above), total sales revenue will be increased. Under normal circumstances the farming community could not co-ordinate such collective action: it would always be to someone's advantage to increase supplies when everyone else was restricting supply. But with governmental help it can be achieved: in the United States, backed by government subsidies, farmers have limited the area planted to particular crops; in some countries, for some products, governments have legislated to create marketing boards through which all produce must be sold such that the flow of goods can be restricted; and some governments have imposed quotas on the volume of production that can be sold. All such schemes need to be backed-up by a limitation of imports. To date the quota system has only been used by the European Community for sugar, though its particular form is somewhat more complicated than that outlined above. In addition the European Community pays subsidies to encourage the formation of producer co-operatives which, in the fruit and vegetables sector, are given powers to restrict supply to the market.

The volume of production

Under this heading a number of objectives are listed, all of which have the common characteristic that they seek to influence the volume of production from home resources. It is seldom that the motives that generate these policies can be separated from other concerns of farm policy (e.g. farm incomes); or that the measures enacted to achieve the objectives can be differentiated from other food and farm legislation.

The belief that a nation, or a region, should be nearly or fully self-sufficient in foodstuffs is not one that is enshrined in the Treaty establishing the European Economic Community, except to the extent that it is necessary to ensure security and stability of supply, but it is one that has always had a strong appeal to policy makers and opinion formers in Europe. Because of the essential nature of food to our continued existence, and because of the uncertainties that are believed to exist for its future availability on world markets, the additional cost of having a greater self-sufficiency in foodstuffs is thought to be worthwhile. Lack of space inhibits a full treatment of this topic and the interested reader is referred to Ritson's recent work (Ritson, 1980). The dependence of West European agriculture on imported fuels, fertilizers and feeding-stuffs should be noted. It is not clear what form a self-sufficient farming *system* would take, when all inputs as well as output are taken into account.

Of equal emotional appeal in some quarters in the European Community, although again not enshrined in the Treaty, is the belief that a large and prosperous rural community is inherently desirable and adds to the political stability of the country. The observed tendency for the size of the farming pop-ulation to decline aggravates this belief. One way in which this policy objective can be achieved is to enhance the profitability of farming and so encourage a greater retention of population in rural areas. An alternative strategy, pursued for example by the Danish government,[6] would be to limit the size of farms and hence maintain a minimum number of self-employed farmers. In Germany the wide-scale development of part-time farming has helped maintain a larger rural population than otherwise would have been the case.

Other policies to maintain, or increase, the level of production are motivated by the fear that without such intervention the population in certain regions (notably hill and mountainous areas with poor resource endowments) would otherwise fall below the critical level capable of sustaining a local culture and the physical infrastructure (transport, shops, etc.) necessary for modern life. Large areas of land could even be abandoned. However, governments, and the European Community, have not always found it necessary to offer blanket support to the farm sector to ensure that such regions are advantaged: for example, in the European Community various measures allow headage payments to be made on cattle and sheep kept in such regions.

In the past support to the farm sector has also been advocated on the ground that an increased agricultural output will relieve pressure on the 'balance of payments' and result in an increased national income. Thus in France exports of food products are seen as the 'green oil' of the country; and in Britain the contribution that farming may or may not make to the 'balance of payments' has been a recurring theme in policy discussions.[7] These questions are rather difficult to handle in a book of this type, but will be discussed briefly in Chapter 8.

The price of food

European consumers devote between 15 and 30 per cent of their total expenditure to food (Table 1.1) and it would be understandable if they were to express a view as to a 'fair' price. Indeed, one of the basic aims of the European Community's agricultural policy, as expressed in the Treaty, is the provision of food at 'reasonable prices' to consumers. Despite the emergence of a

Table 1.1 Expenditure on food and beverages, as a proportion of private consumption in the European Community, 1979.

Country	Foodstuffs	Non-alcoholic beverages	Alcoholic beverages
Belgium	18.6	0.5	1.7
Denmark	18.4	7.6*	
France	18.6	0.5	2.3
West Germany	15.2	3.0	
Greece	28.6	0.9	3.0
Ireland†	24.8	1.4	12.3
Italy	26.7	0.3	1.9
Luxembourg†	18.9	0.4	1.7
Netherlands	16.8	0.6	2.3
United Kingdom	17.1	0.7	2.1

* Includes tobacco.
† 1978.
SOURCE Commission, 1982, p. 218 (derived from Eurostat Statistics).

Community-wide consumer grouping (BEUC—Bureau Européen des Unions de Consommateurs) it is mainly British and, to a lesser extent, German consumer groups that have expressed concern about the impact of the European Community's farm policy on the cost of food.

It is not inevitable that attempts to raise farm incomes should be reflected on an increase in the cost of food. Prior to the United Kingdom's accession to the European Community a deficiency payments system was in operation whereby, if the price received by producers for farm products was below the level guaranteed by the government, the difference (the deficiency payment) would be paid directly as a subsidy to the farmer. Although the phrase 'deficiency payment' is not acceptable terminology in the European Community some schemes—notably for beef and lamb (Chapter 5), olive oil and processed fruits and vegetables (Chapter 7)—do have similar characteristics.

Nor should it be supposed that price movements at the farm gate will be reflected in equivalent percentage changes in the retail price. All foodstuffs incur transport, wholesale and retailing costs before delivery to the consumer; and most are subject to substantial processing and manufacturing costs. In all Member States—except for the moment Greece—value added tax (VAT) applies to food; although so far at differing rates. The VAT percentage on food ranges from zero in the United Kingdom to 22 per cent in Denmark (Commission, 1982, p. 192). The Danish farmers' unions have estimated that in Denmark in 1980 only 30 per cent of the retail price of food was reflected in farm gate values; though the proportion varied considerably from product to product (Table 1.2). If Danish farm gate prices were to rise by 10 per cent, and all manufacturing and retailing margins remained constant, the retail price of food would only rise by about 3 per cent.

None the less governments within the European Community have often acted

Table 1.2 The Danish farmer's share in the retail price of food (1980—percent of retail price).

Product	%
Drinking milk	50
Butter	93
Cheese	42
Eggs	48
White bread	11
Rye bread	17
Potatoes	28
Sugar	19
Average, all commodities	30
Indirect taxation ⎫ Distribution and processing ⎭	70

SOURCE   Danish Farmers' Unions, 1981, p. 46.

to moderate, or reduce, the impact of farm price support policies on food prices. As shall be seen in Chapter 8—discussing green money and monetary compensatory amounts—the French government in 1969 so acted; as did the British government subsequently. Some governments, notably the British, have given nationally financed food subsidies in their attempt to moderate the rate of food price increases during periods of particularly rapid inflation,[8] and consumer subsidies have for some years been paid from Community funds on butter and olive oil.

Consumer protection

Governments have long been involved in legislation protecting—or purporting to protect—the interests of consumers. Such actions involve weights and measures, price displays, the listing of contents, and other rules designed to protect the consumer from unscrupulous trade practices; and rules governing hygiene, contamination and additives to foodstuffs. As the 'supermarket revolution' has progressed these measures have increased in practical importance: for an increasing proportion of our foodstuffs are prepackaged, precooked, and otherwise prepared before purchase.

One of the problems that arises from such laudable practices is that the rules have become so complex, and so particular to different markets, that they actually act to discourage international trade. Economists express this by calling such measures 'non-tariff' trade barriers.[9] Thus it is not surprising that the European Community has paid increasing attention to measures of this kind, and that in its attempts to encourage trade between the Member States it has sought to enact legislation harmonizing such measures throughout the Community. This legislation will be outlined in Chapter 12.

NOTES

1. The reader wishing to pursue at greater length the following discussion is referred to Ritson's textbook (Ritson, 1977); and Josling's review of the literature on agricultural policy (Josling, 1974).
2. It must be added, however, that the primary objective of EC intervention buying is market price support within seasons. The stocks so acquired will later be exported or diverted to other uses.
3. According to the British Ministry of Agriculture (1979), UK farm prices fell in real terms by some 1 per cent annually in the 20-year period from the mid-1950s to the mid-1970s.
4. Possibly the best recent text on the agricultural problem is Johnson (1973).
5. The European Community has become increasingly concerned about the extent, and importance, of national aids to agriculture. To date the attempts of the Community to control and rationalize national aids has been limited, but renewed policy initiatives are to be expected. The problem is outlined in Chapter 9.
6. Legislation has limited the maximum size of farm in Denmark. The Danish Agriculture Act of 1973 increased the maximum permitted size of farm to 100 ha; but in June 1978 additional legislation was passed forbidding the amalgamation of farms

10

if the total area of the farm after amalgamation were then to exceed 75 ha (Hirsch and Maunder, 1978, p. 76).
7. See, for example, the debate between Josling and Winegarten (1970).
8. The British experience of food subsidies in the mid-1970s has been reviewed in Witt and Newbould (1976).
9. Hillman has considered non-tariff trade barriers—not just those associated with consumer protection—at length (Hillman, 1978).

REFERENCES

Commission of the European Communities (1982) *The Agricultural Situation in the Community: 1981 Report*, Brussels.
Danish Farmers' Unions (1981) *Landøkonomisk Oversigt 1981*, Copenhagen.
Hillman, J. S. (1978), *Nontariff Agricultural Trade Barriers*, University of Nebraska Press: London.
Hirsch, G. P., and Maunder, A. H. (1978) *Farm Amalgamation in Western Europe*, Saxon House: Farnborough.
Johnson, D. G. (1973) *World Agriculture in Disarray*, Fontana: London.
Josling, T. E. (1974) Agricultural Policies in Developed Countries: A Review, *Journal of Agricultural Economics*, **25**.
Josling, T. E., and Winegarten, A. (1970) *Agriculture and Import Saving*, Occasional Paper No. 5, Hill Samuel and Co: London.
Ministry of Agriculture, Fisheries and Food (1979) *Possible Patterns of Agricultural Production in the United Kingdom by 1983*, HMSO: London.
Ritson, C. (1977) *Agricultural Economics: Principles and Policy*, Crosby Lockwood Staples: London.
Ritson, C. (1980) *Self-sufficiency and Food Security*, Centre for Agricultural Strategy, University of Reading.
Tugendhat, C. (1980) Keynote address to Conference on Industry and the World Economy, Newcastle-upon-Tyne.
Witt, S. F., and Newbould, G. D. (1976) 'The Impact of Food Subsidies', *National Westminster Bank Quarterly Review*, August.

Chapter 2

Decision Making and the CAP

The Treaties of Rome (1957) setting up the European Economic Community and the European Atomic Energy Community, and the Treaty of Paris (1951) setting up the European Coal and Steel Community, laid down a formal institutional framework with a set of functions and responsibilities ascribed to each institution.[1] Each Treaty established four main institutions: a Council of Ministers, a Commission (or High Authority), an Assembly (Parliament),[2] and a Court. In addition the Euratom and EEC Treaties provided for an Economic and Social Committee to assist the Council and Commission. From the beginning there was a Common Parliament and Court for the three Communities; and following the merger Treaty of 1967 a common Council and Commission. Each Treaty also laid down a set of procedures regulating the formal links between the four main institutions.

Some twenty years later, the formal system remains the same, but its practical application has changed. New bodies have come into existence, having a real authority even if no formal Treaty existence, the most notable being a European Council. Another, the Court of Auditors, was established by Treaty in 1975. Some institutions have never developed the role they were intended to have, especially the Economic and Social Committee. The powers of the Council of Ministers have grown substantially in relation to the Commission, and the working relationships between the two have never had the distinctiveness apparently envisaged by the Treaties. The European Parliament, now directly elected, has entered a new phase and may have a new and increased role to play.

Procedures have also changed and developed along with the growing complexity and coverage of Community policies. New intermediate committees of officials have grown up to manage and co-ordinate the work of the Treaty based institutions, and some of these have come to have as much influence as the institutions that they represent. The Committee of Permanent Representatives and the Special Committee on Agriculture, discussed below, filter all proposals and other material before it reaches the Council of Ministers, and in some respects replace the Ministers in all but name.

All of this has given rise to a complex and constantly shifting environment within which decisions are made on the whole range of Community policies,

11

and particularly the agricultural policy. The system is an amalgam of an original theory of checks and balances, and a dynamic political and economic reality. The complexity of the system is increased by the fact that consensus is the foundation of the whole Community construction; decisions are made on the basis of a repetitive procedure, with changes and amendments being made both as formal proposals and informal suggestions at all stages of the process. The Community edifice, and the agricultural policy as a major part of it, is almost certainly not capable of withstanding for very long the refusal of one Member State or Institution to participate in the consensus procedure. The last occasion when the system underwent a major test was in 1965 with the 'empty chair' challenge of the French Government, resolved by the elaboration of the Luxembourg compromise.[3]

Very few sanctions are provided for within the system, and the ultimate sanction available to sovereign states *vis-à-vis* their own citizens, that of force, is not available to the European Community or its Court of Justice. This reality, together with the widely differing political and economic systems of the Member States, explains much of the complexity of procedure and of Community law. It also explains the often slow and undramatic nature of Community business. But it has meant that the decision making process is potentially open to a wider range of outside influences, and for a longer period, than is normally the case with similar national legislation.

The heart of the system is, in an important sense, the Commission of the European Communities in its role as sole initiator of Community legislation. No decision having legal effect can be made without an initial proposal from the Commission. This is a power the Commission has jealously guarded over the years, although there are signs that it is being eroded. Proposals are formally made to the Council, but in reality all proposals are subject to detailed prior examination by the Committee of Permanent Representatives or, for most agricultural matters, by the Special Committee on Agriculture. Council decisions normally provide the primary legislative framework, laying down the main principles of Community law, whereas the drafting and execution of implementing legislation, which provides for the more detailed rules of application, is delegated to the Commission. The major part of the Commission's workload, and a significant part of all Community business, is related to this management function and to the implementing legislation that it requires.[4] The European Parliament and its Committees provide opinions on the draft legislation put to the Council where this is required by the Treaty, although increasingly in other areas as well, as also does the Economic and Social Committee. The European Court of Justice, meeting normally in Luxembourg, oversees the whole process of the making of Community law and its application. It is open to individuals as well as to the Member States and the Institutions, and has had a strong influence on the development of the common agricultural policy (CAP) and on the development of the institutions in recent years.

The aim of this chapter is to provide an understanding not only of the formal institutional processes in relation to the common agricultural policy, but also of the way in which proposals come to be put forward, and of the various 'windows' which may be open to interested organizations and individuals. The major part of the business of the CAP as it affects farmers, the food industry and consumers, is conducted within the Commission and its associated network of Management and Advisory Committee. Hence particular attention will be paid to this part of the overall process.[5]

For purposes of description five major steps may be identified in the operation of the agricultural policy, or indeed, of other Community policies, starting with the proposed (or draft) legislation, through decision and then implementation. In reality, the interrelationships are inextricable, but it is helpful to distinguish the following elements:

Commission—initiatory.

Council—discussion and decision.

European Parliament—advisory.

Commission—management

Court of Justice—supervisory.

THE COMMISSION

The initial impulse

Although it is true that formal legislative proposals can only come from the Commission, the initial impulse for new proposals can come from a wide variety of sources. Indeed, the ability to introduce into the Commission system new ideas, or suggested modifications to existing mechanisms or regulations, is one of the most effective points of pressure that exists. Once embodied in a formal Commission proposal, an idea develops a momentum which it could scarcely gain otherwise, no matter what its source. The main impulse in the case of national legislation derives usually from the political programme developed by governments at the time of their election. This, of course, has as yet no precise counterpart in the Community, and there is a real danger that policy becomes only a reaction to political or economic events rather than having a basis in any coherent programme. A certain programming of future activity does exist, for example in food law harmonization, but in general such an approach is less common with agriculture than in other policy areas. The agricultural policy, particularly because it is highly developed and has created a series of powerful interest groups, is particularly susceptible to this reactive approach for a very large part of its activity. Reaction to problems is a major stimulus to policy formulation, whereas new initiatives, or modifications to existing legislation deriving from an overall programme, have been rather rare.

Where new initiatives have been developed, the main impulse so far as the institutions are concerned, has very often come from the Commission and the

Court of Justice rather than from the Council or the European Parliament. In part, of course, this is the result of institutional responsibilities since part of the Commission's role is to propose solutions and to maintain a momentum in Community policy. Nevertheless, the Council of Agricultural Ministers is a highly conservative body, and the major ideas of past years have come from other sources. The Mansholt Plan of 1968, and more recently the new directions in structural policy, the proposals for Mediterranean agriculture, the changed pricing policy in the cereals sector, the series of proposals for the milk sector, the closing of the original open-ended guarantee system by the development of the idea of producer co-responsibility for expenditure on surplus disposal; all these have derived from the Commission rather than the Member States. Of course it would be wrong to suggest that such proposals are developed by Commission officials in a vacuum. They are naturally the result of exposure to suggestions, proposals, and criticisms from a variety of sources. The Commission's role is to produce a course of action which, where possible, synthesizes these into an appropriate form.

The impulse for changes in the day-to-day operation of the CAP, particularly changes to market management, to the level of aids, to export refunds, or to the operation of the intervention and support systems, come from a much wider range of sources. Trade organizations, firms and individuals, either in direct contact with the Commission or indirectly through the respective Ministries of Agriculture and Intervention agencies, are of substantial importance in providing the impulse for draft legislation.

If the initial impulse is important, so also is the timing of the introduction of ideas. The Community's agricultural year is dominated by the agricultural price review; a process which starts in October and can finish as late as June the following year. Although the management of the agricultural policy carries on throughout this period, there is an increasing tendency to link even relatively minor issues to the price review as the negotiations develop. This process normally engulfs a wide range of other policy issues in a complex series of linkages and trade-offs.[6] It can cover proposals for modifications to legislation specifically made by the Commission at the outset as a part of the 'prices package', but other issues usually are swept up and included. Indeed, it is not uncommonly the case that matters of pure management, normally the responsibility of the Commission, are decided in the context of the price review through the device of including statements of intent in the minutes of the appropriate Council meeting.

Internal structure of the Commission

Although to the non-specialist observer the Commission may present a rather uniform façade, it does, of course, like all bureaucracies, have a well-defined structure, not particularly dissimilar in its main elements to those of national administrations. Certain aspects owe more to Continental practice than to what is customary in the United Kingdom, but the particular responsibilities given to the Commission by the EEC Treaty have given it a distinctiveness due to the intention of the Treaty's authors that the Commission should have a wider role than that of being a mere civil service.

The major structural division within the Commission is between the Commissioners and their advisers (Cabinets), and the administrative departments known as Directorates General (DGs—see Table 2.1) which collectively make up the services of the Commission. The Directorates General are either policy linked or have responsibilities for other matters such as legal affairs, co-ordination, or administration.

The fourteen Commissioners (appointed by the Member States for a four-year renewable term of office) divide up the responsibility for the Directorates General between them, with several smaller Directorates General grouped under a single Commissioner. A Commissioner may well try to apply his particular personality or policy preferences to his Directorate General as would

Table 2.1

A. *List of Directorates General in the Commission of the European Communities*

DG I	External Relations
DG II	Economic and Financial Affairs
DG III	Internal Market and Industrial Affairs
DG IV	Competition
DG V	Employment and Social Affairs
DG VI	Agriculture
DG VII	Transport
DG VIII	Development
DG IX	Personnel and Administration
DG X	Spokesman's Group and DG for Information
DG XII	Research, Science and Education
DG XIII	Information Market and Innovation
DG XIV	Fisheries
DG XV	Financial Institutions and Taxation
DG XVI	Regional Policy
DG XVII	Energy
DG XVIII	Credit and Investments
DG XIX	Budget
DG XX	Financial Control

B. *Other Special Units of the Commission of the European Communities*
Secretariat General
Legal Office
Statistical Office
Customs Union Service
Environment and Consumer Protection Service
Joint Research Centre
Euratom Supply Agency
Security Office
Office for Official Publications

a Minister in a national government; however, his success is likely to be constrained by the preferences of the Member States, the personality of his most senior official (the Director General), and the effectiveness of his Cabinet. Normally Cabinets are composed of five advisers, the senior members often being drawn from the political and national background of each Commissioner or seconded from the national administration[7] with the other members being seconded from a Directorate General of the Commission.

Cabinets have considerable influence and perform an important formal and informal role in the operations of the Commission.[8] They provide a line of communication to the Member States, and are an important entry point for ideas and influence from the outside world into the policy making process of the Commission. All the weekly meetings of the Commissioners are foreshadowed by a previous meeting of the Heads of Cabinet aiming to process the agenda, to sort the essential from the inessential, and to identify the points for discussion and decision by the Commissioners. Many subjects, notably agriculture, are delegated to specialist meetings of Cabinet members responsible for the subject, assisted by officials from the appropriate Directorate General. These meetings are intended to help ensure the collegiality of Commission decisions, although in practice they tend to give particular power to the larger Directorates General, which can often succeed in pushing proposals through on grounds of urgency or technical significance that Cabinet members without specialist technical knowledge find difficult to challenge. In Commission meetings it is relatively unusual for a formal vote to be taken although it is by no means unknown. A simple majority vote would be required.

The Directorates General are hierarchically organized from the smallest unit, the division, through the level of the Directorate to the Director General himself. They tend to act in isolation, and even internal co-ordination can be surprisingly poor. The Directorate General for Agriculture (DG VI) is one of the largest in the Commission with 10 per cent of total administrative staff[9] and has always had a reputation for separateness. Indeed, its internal construction mirrors to a considerable extent the functions of the different Directorates General within the Commission as a whole. Within DG VI there are units dealing with all facets of the agricultural policy. Although such a structure should be conducive to good co-ordination with other Directorates General, the ability to keep within itself a wide range of expertise has generally enabled it to keep other Directorates General at arm's length.

The comprehensive nature of DG VI's structure has meant that the points of useful access to the agricultural policy via other Directorates General are limited. In reality, of course, many other policy areas impinge directly on agriculture; notably policies concerned with the food industry, consumer affairs, external relations, and development aid. This is not, however, always reflected in practice in the relationship of DG VI to the other Directorates General. This is particularly the case with the Directorate General for Industry. The food industry has long realized that its best hope of influencing agricultural policy lies much more in direct lobbying of DG VI than in indirect approaches via other Directorates General: even with the development of a food industry division within the Directorate General for Industry, this appreciation remains basically unchanged.

Decisions on legislation are taken either by the Commission acting collegiately at the weekly meeting, or by what is known as the 'written procedure', under which approval is deemed to have been given if no objection to a draft decision has been registered within a given time limit. Additionally, there are a large number of cases of minor legislation (though not always minor in their financial consequences) where authority is delegated to a particular Commissioner who subsequently reports to the Commission on the use made of the delegated power.

THE COUNCIL

The Treaties provide for a Council of Ministers made up of one representative for each of the Member States. In practice meetings of the Council are devoted to particular subject areas, be it agriculture, transport, or finance. The groupings of Ministers meeting in Brussels or Luxembourg reflect this fact and are termed the Agriculture Council, Finance Council, etc., as appropriate. Council meetings dealing with different topics frequently take place at the same time. Primacy is in practice, however, accorded to the Foreign Affairs or General Council. The system of the separation of Councils according to topic does lead to problems: it has, for example, often been claimed that the Ministers of Agriculture meeting in Council take decisions with financial consequences which pre-empt the decisions of their colleagues concerned with finance. On a number of occasions in recent years, and particularly in 1981 and 1982 in connection with the reform of the Community budget, the Foreign Affairs Council and even the Heads of State meeting as the European Council (see below) have attempted to deal with agricultural matters; these attempts have not generally met with great success.

The Councils are serviced by a full-time secretariat of permanent officials, independent of both the Commission and the Member States. The main task of the secretariat is to provide organization, documentation, and background material for the multitude of committees that exist to process the draft legislation before formal discussion and decision by the Council of Ministers. The presidency of the Council and of all the Committees that depend upon it is taken by each Member State in turn for a period of six months. The Council Secretariat has the important function of providing the necessary continuity of procedure and, through its legal services, of defending the rights of the Council.

The committee structure

All proposals sent to the Council from the Commission are examined in one or more committees made up of national and Commission officials, though the Commission representative does not have a vote. There are broadly three levels at which the committees operate. First, the technical committees and working parties of experts dealing with the details of proposals and their technical aspects. Second, the Treaties provide for a number of committees whose task is to examine the sectoral aspects of proposals in any field. The Monetary Committee provided for in Article 105 of the EEC Treaty, and the Trade Committee also known as the '113 committee' from its mandate in Article 113 of the EEC Treaty, are examples. Third, at the apex of the Committee system is Coreper, so called from its initials in French (Comité des Représentants Permanants) which meets twice weekly.

Coreper is composed of the Permanent Representatives (ambassadors) or their deputies, of the Member States to the European Communities, together with a senior Commission representative. Coreper passes proposals to the other committees for analysis, and reserves more important issues for itself. It is responsible for preparing the agenda of Council meetings, and will itself take a range of decisions, leaving only the need for formal confirmation by Ministers. Coreper has developed into the central element in the decision-making process to which Ministers delegate the greater proportion of decisions.

The Special Committee on Agriculture (SCA)

Coreper does not deal with agricultural questions unless there is a clear double policy interest.[10] Instead these are handled by a sub-committee of the Agriculture Council, consisting of permanent officials from the Member States[11] and known as the Special Committee on Agriculture (SCA). The SCA reports directly to the Council of Agriculture in the same way as Coreper reports to all other Councils. As with Coreper, all agricultural proposals from the Commission come first to the SCA, which will either pass them to the Council after discussion, or more likely, will refer them first to a technical working party for detailed examination. The Commission representative is always present to explain and defend the proposals, and to represent the Community interest. It is in this sense that the Commission is sometimes known as the 'eleventh Member State'.

If the SCA can agree on a particular piece of draft legislation, then it will only require confirmation by the next Council regardless of its Ministerial composition. Such items are known as 'A' points and require no further discussion. Other proposals, known as 'B' points, will be put to Agriculture Ministers either for guidance on particular aspects or for overall discussion and decision. The SCA does not normally vote, and a representative may come under considerable pressure to fall in line if it is felt that a point is of too technical a nature to go the Ministers. The process from receipt of a proposal from the Commission to its formal adoption may take anything from ten days in the case of an uncontroversial proposal to many years in other more complicated, controversial, or less urgent cases.[12]

In the course of discussions both in the technical groups and in the Special Committee, proposals may be modified substantially. The Commission will normally accede to this process, and will indeed take an active role in suggesting amendments and in finding a compromise formula, provided that the changes are compatible with what it considers to be the spirit of the original proposal. When in the SCA the Commission refuses to change particular elements of a proposal, the issue will go to the Council in the same way as would an objection raised by a Member State. An objection by the Commission can, however, have more force than that of a Member State in certain circumstances. If the Commission refuses to change its proposal, the Council requires unanimity to make a modification; and the Council cannot itself initiate a proposal.

Although the Commission retains its right of proposal throughout the Council process, in the normal operation of the working groups there is considerable informality in the making and accepting of modifications, so long as the changes are acceptable to the Commission. The Treaty seems to have envisaged a rather more formal structure; the Commission would present its proposed legislation worked out in considerable detail, and leave the Council to accept or reject. In practice, such a system could hardly have worked and Commission officials are closely concerned with every stage of discussion in the Council.

It is probably fair to say that in recent years the SCA has, unlike Coreper, become less effective and less useful even in its own domain. Whilst it undeniably clears away much technical discussion from the Ministers, it has suffered increasingly from an inability to relieve Ministers of the burden of decision-making even in matters of lesser importance. This is in part a consequence, and in part a cause, of the similar difficulties which the Agriculture Council finds in reaching decisions. Nevertheless, discussions at the level of the SCA are very important as a major point of access for interest groups in achieving changes in proposed legislation. Of course, the extent to which this is possible will depend upon the accessibility of national Governmental structures, and this varies markedly between different Member States.[13] It will also depend upon the relative strength of bargaining position and the degree to which officials are permitted to exchange agreement on a particular point for satisfaction on another. The Special Committee on Agriculture is the earliest stage in the whole Council process where final decisions are taken. These may be on matters of a mainly technical nature, but it is often precisely these that are of most interest to industry and trade. The process of discussion at this level can be extremely protracted, with a subject being passed repeatedly backwards and forwards between the SCA and its technical groups.

Majority voting

The great majority of Council legislation on the Common Agricultural Policy is based on Article 43 of the Treaty, and may in theory be decided in the Council on the basis of qualified (weighted) majority voting. In practice a vote in the Council is very rare, so that inevitably the work of the SCA is directed towards achieving compromises which can be unanimously accepted by all ten Member States. This takes time and tends to favour the development of comprehensive package deals in Council negotiations.

In May 1982 a majority vote did take place which attracted much public interest. During the winter of 1981–82 the British government had been seeking concessions on the UK's future net contributions to the Community Budget, to follow on from a temporary agreement which had covered the years 1980 and 1981 (see Chapter 13). However, agreement had not been forthcoming: partly due to the complexity of the issues at stake, and partly because of the resentment felt by certain other Member States over Britain's negotiating tactics. In 1980 Britain had threatened to veto the 1980–81 farm price increases unless a deal on the Budget were agreed, and now in 1982 threatened the same tactics over the 1982–83 farm price review. Additional complicating factors were that the 1980 Budget agreement had, unexpectedly, proved to be rather more beneficial to the United Kingdom than had been envisaged—and the other Member States wished this to be taken into account in the 1982 agreement—and that Britain's new Foreign Secretary, following the resignation of his predecessor, was preoccupied with the UK dispute with Argentina over the Falkland Islands.

Roy Jenkins, a former President of the Commission, commented:

> We thought that the veto on agricultural prices was a secure weapon with which to force a Budget settlement. But although 'linkage' is an old Community device, employed by us on the same issue in 1980, and by others on other subjects, the vital national interest point had never been explicitly used in this way before. (Jenkins 1982, p. 14.)

Other Member States, including France, argued that there were two issues: the farm price package and the Budget negotiations. On the former Britain was in agreement with the details of the package proposed, consequently a point of vital national interest was not at stake and hence the Luxembourg compromise could not be invoked. Encouraged by the Commission, the Belgian presidency of the Agricultural Council proceeded to a vote, and sixty-two regulations covering the 1982–83 farm price package were each implemented by majority vote; Denmark, Greece, and the United Kingdom refused to take part.

The British press saw this as an abandonment of the Luxembourg compromise which jeopardized Britain's relations with the EC (and those of Denmark and Greece as well). As yet it is too early to judge what the long term effect will be. Rather than changing the whole basis of decision-making within the Council, however, the events of May 1982 are likely to have a subtler impact on the balance of consensus and compromise that characterizes Council decision-making. The Luxembourg compromise will undoubtedly remain, though Members will be more careful about invoking its use on issues that are not recognized by the other States as being of vital national interest, and in retrospect the majority vote of May 1982 will be viewed as an isolated, but significant, event.

THE EUROPEAN COUNCIL

There are no Treaty provisions establishing the European Council, but none the less this body has an important role in putting together extra large package deals, or breaking the deadlock of discussion in the Council. Three times a year the Heads of State or Government, together with the President of the Commission, meet as the European Council. Some of these meetings have produced few concrete results, but others have established new priorities and outlined the framework for new or amended policies. As the European Council has no legal status within the Treaty, the package deals assembled within this forum are not legally binding. It is incumbent upon subsequent meetings of the Council to enact the necessary legislation, and this has sometimes resulted in Council members having rather different views on the framework of the decision previously concluded by their Prime Minister or President.

THE EUROPEAN PARLIAMENT

The European Parliament has a number of formal roles assigned to it within the institutional structure of the Community. With the Council it constitutes the Budgetary Authority of the Community and has specific powers and responsibilities in relation to the Budget. It is called upon to deliver opinions on draft legislation submitted by the Commission to the Council; it is able to pass resolutions on any matter it considers to be important, although these do not have any binding force; it may pose written and oral questions to the Commission and the Council; and it may dismiss the Commission *en bloc*. In practice these powers are less formidable than they seem at first sight, although the Parliament has, particularly since its direct election in 1978, shown itself adept at extending its role and powers into new areas.

The Parliament has 434 Members, drawn proportionately from the different Member countries. Members are directly elected for a period of five years, although a dual mandate with national Parliamentarians is still permitted. Within the European Parliament, members are organized in political groups across national lines, although on many issues a national pattern of voting may be observed. United Kingdom MEPs are at present either part of the European Democratic Group or of the Socialist Group.

Each month for one week the Parliament meets in full session in Strasbourg or Luxembourg. Its working programme is decided upon by the Parliamentary Bureau, composed of representatives of the political groups; the Bureau agrees upon the distribution between political groups and nationalities of the chairmanship of the 15 specialist Parliamentary Committees and of other office-holders. The formal business of the Parliament is conducted through this network of Committees which report to the monthly meetings of the full Parliament. Each major subject area, including agriculture, is represented through a Committee, which has two major responsibilities; to produce draft opinions on proposals for Council legislation and, often as part of the same document, to draw-up draft resolutions for the full Parliament. These draft documents are prepared by a 'rapporteur' who is a member of the Committee concerned and, for proposals of major importance, is appointed by it on the basis of balance between political groups, or for familiarity with the subject matter in matters of less political significance. Thus the draft report of the Committee on Agriculture on the Commission's proposals 'on the fixing of prices for agricultural products and on certain related measures (1981/1982)' was drawn up by Mr G. Ligios, an Italian MEP of the Christian Democrat Group. His draft report considers different elements of the Commission's proposals, calls upon the Parliament to reject some aspects, to modify others, and to accept others. The draft is normally drawn up after the Committee has heard evidence from Commission officials or from other sources. It is then put to the Committee on Agriculture by vote; if adopted, it is sent to the full Parliamentary session for debate along with reports from other Committees dealing with the same set of proposals.

The Commission is not obliged to modify its proposals in line with Parliamentary opinions, nor is the Council required to accept them. In practice the Commission will frequently modify technical aspects of a proposal, but will not normally accept modifications which upset what it considers to be the balance of the proposal. Nevertheless, the Commission has, particularly since the direct elections, made a special effort to co-operate with the Parliament, and now forwards some proposals for Council legislation to it, even where this is not technically required under the Treaty. A 1980 judgement of the European Court of Justice[14] has potentially opened the way to further powers for the Parliament by ruling that the Council of Ministers may not adopt legislation without a Parliamentary opinion where this is required under the Treaty of Rome. Thus the Council may override an opinion, but it may not act in the absence of one.

In addition to the drafting of opinions on draft legislation, Parliamentary Committees may produce reports on their own initiative on any subject they consider to be of interest or importance. Individual Members of Parliament may put written questions to the Commission or Council, and may also put oral questions during question time during full Parliamentary sessions.

The budgetary responsibilities of the Parliament are defined by reference to the division of expenditure between 'obligatory' and 'non-obligatory' items. Broadly, those elements of expenditure which are considered to derive directly from Treaty obligations, notably CAP expenditure, are classified as obligatory. Other items, notably Regional and Social expenditure, are classified as non-obligatory. The Parliament has very limited powers over the former, but rather more extensive powers where the latter are concerned. Much effort is expended each year in the classification of expenditure into one category or the other.

The responsibilities and powers of the Parliament seem therefore to be quite extensive. In practice they are much less so, not only because the Council is not obliged to abide by Parliamentary opinions, but also because extensive areas of legislation are never put to the Parliament at all. This is the case for the whole range of Commission management legislation under the CAP and in other areas. This represents a very major part of total Community legislative activity, discussed below, and of budgetary expenditure. The Parliament may attempt to question Commission officials, and it does have certain powers over the major items in the Budget. Whilst it remains true that the Parliament has little formal control over the day-to-day management decisions and the expenditure which results from them, the Commission has co-operated with the Parliament in attending Committee meetings and in providing regular documentation. In addition, the Parliament has used the argument that an action by the Commission must be shown to be consistent with the budgetary provision, to question the Commission about its management of the Common Agricultural Policy.

The Parliament is constantly attempting to extend its powers, particularly within the agricultural and budgetary domain. No attempt will be made to consider in detail recent efforts by the Parliament to extend its budgetary powers; but two aspects may be noted: the rejection of the 1980 General Budget of the Communities, and the attempts, successful in the 1981 budget, to bring some small part of the agricultural expenditure within its ambit. For this purpose Parliament used the device of transfers from the obligatory items of the agricultural chapters to the non-obligatory reserve chapter 100. Apart from the extension of its budgetary powers, the Parliament has strongly criticized, and sought to limit, the cases where the Council can decide without formal Parliamentary approval.

The Parliament has a significant role to play in the development of Community legislation, and its position and responsibilities are likely to grow over the years. Apart from its formal institutional role, the Parliament and its Members are increasingly able to have access to Commission and to national officials, and to influence decisions at the stage before they are formalized into draft legislation.

THE COMMISSION IN ITS MANAGEMENT ROLE

The Commission's management role accounts for by far the major proportion of its activities in all sectors, and particularly within the Common Agricultural Policy. This management role covers not only the innumerable tasks associated with the preparation of proposals, the collection and presentation of statistical data and the monitoring of management information, but also very considerable legislative activity. Except in a number of specific areas where the Commission has been given a direct management role by the Treaty of Rome—competition policy, national aids—it is the Council of Ministers which is given the power to decide upon Community legislation, if necessary after receiving the opinion of the European Parliament. In practice, however, the Council restricts its decision making to matters of principle, of political importance, or where the setting of a primary legislative framework is concerned. It delegates to the Commission in accordance with Article 155 of the Treaty the preparation and adoption of secondary legislation which sets out the detailed provisions for the way in which

Council decisions are to be implemented; furthermore, the Council leaves the Commission to take such periodic decisions as may be necessary for the modification of prices, refunds, coefficients, and subsidies in the day-to-day management of the different agricultural product markets.

It is clear that without such a division of labour between Council and Commission, the former would rapidly be swamped with a mass of detailed legislative proposals with which it is not equipped to deal. In 1979 for example, the Commission adopted some 1500 regulations through the Management Committee procedure described below.[15] This is not, however, merely a matter of administrative convenience. Member States recognize that if the managed markets of the Common Agricultural Policy are to be operated successfully, then rapid decision-making is essential. Not only would it be difficult to convene meetings of ten Member States sufficiently rapidly; but in addition, in the absence of regular use of a majority voting system in the Council, it would be very unlikely that agreement could be reached within the limited time available. The different interests would be too strong to be solved other than by the traditional Council means of delay and compromise. These require more time than is available. Member States have therefore always accepted the need to maintain a clear procedural distinction between primary and secondary legislation. Even during the period of the 'Empty Chair' crisis in 1965, for example, when France boycotted all meetings of the Council, the Commission's Management Committees continued to function.

Of course, certain management decisions can have very significant political and budgetary repercussions and the Council may feel unable in these circumstances to leave the Commission entirely free to make its own management decisions. Certain techniques have been developed for such cases, notably the use of restricted sessions of the Special Committee on Agriculture, or of undertakings and declarations of intent given by the Commission to the Council. This latter technique has become increasingly used, not least in the context of the annual price negotiations, and risks a blurring of the traditional separation of responsibilities. In interpreting Council and Commission decisions, it is important to go beyond the text of the legislation adopted and to examine the record for declarations of intent as these will be a guide to the Commission's future policy.[16]

The European Parliament has fully appreciated the importance of the Commission's management powers as well as the fact that its legislation is not subject to Parliamentary opinions; the Commission is not required to seek an opinion to the same extent that the Council is. Whilst the Parliament has always favoured the separation of the Commission's management powers from those of the Council, it has also sought to bring them within its own purview.[17] The Commission has in recent years responded to these pressures by defending its management policies before Parliamentary Committees, and by accepting that the Management Committee system should not be extended into new areas outside the Common Agricultural Policy. It is also worth noting that the Court of Auditors has seen it as part of its responsibilities to comment on the Commission's management of the CAP, and this has provided the Parliament with a further means to call the Commission to account.

Management Committees

The Management Committees are statutory bodies, whose existence is prescribed in the basic regulations setting up the major commodity regimes. For example, Article 25 of Regulation 2727/75 setting up the common organization of the market for cereals specifies that 'a Management Committee for Cereals ... shall be established, consisting of representatives of the Member States and presided over by a representative of the Commission'. There are separate management committees for twenty different products including cereals, sugar, and dairy products, which each meet on a weekly basis; for other products, where the nature of the market regime requires less frequent modifications, the Management Committee may meet as infrequently as once or twice per year. This was the case for example for flax and hemp and for plants in 1979. An idea of the comprehensiveness and complexity of the system can be gained from the mere fact that in 1979 there were 456 meetings of Management Committees, an average of two per working day.

The Management Committee meeting usually brings together some two to three officials per delegation from the Ministry of Agriculture in each Member State under the chairmanship of a senior Commission official. Officials from other Ministries or from the national Intervention Agencies may also attend. The discussions are of course confidential, although a summary of the outcome is usually given by Commission officials. The degree and manner in which national officials collaborate before and after meetings with their own industrial and trade circles, varies a good deal. In the United Kingdom the responsibility for the implementation of legislation lies with a number of different bodies; with the Ministry of Agriculture, the Intervention Board for Agricultural Produce (IBAP), and HM Customs and Excise. The boundaries of responsibility overlap to some extent; however, IBAP is largely responsible for the intervention system and for exports. Customs and Excise, by virtue of its historic role, tends to take the lead in matters concerning imports. The Ministry of Agriculture has the formal policy role. These arrangements differ in many respects from those of other Member States and are often considered to give rise to a lesser degree of co-ordination between the public authorities and the food industry than in the rest of the Community.

Decisions by Management Committees are of fundamental importance to food processors and traders; those with direct impact on producers are more usually taken at the level of the Council. Decisions at Management Committee commonly operate directly on the processing industry to provide an indirect effect on producer incomes. It might be thought therefore that the interests of the food industry should be well represented; in practice this is not necessarily the case despite the fact that matters of commercial importance are often involved. For example, export tenders for sugar and cereals are decided every week by the Management Committees.

At each meeting the Committee will have before it an agenda drawn up by the Commission[18] and previously circulated. This will consist partly of draft legislation on which a decision is to be taken, partly of drafts at an earlier stage for discussion only, together with a wide variety of other matters concerning the collection of statistics, the assessment of the market situation for the products covered by the particular Management Committee, or of the interpretation of existing legislation. In the case of draft legislation, the Commission will put forward a draft, listen to and take part in the discussion, and then put the proposal to the Committee for an opinion by vote.

The Management Committee does not have the power to reject or accept draft legislation proposed by the Commission. Hence its vote concerns which of three alternative opinions will be given: an opinion in favour; an opinion against; or an absence of opinion. The vote is taken on the basis of a weighted majority (Article 148 of the Treaty of Rome) with the following weightings being given to the different Member States:

France, Germany, Italy, United Kingdom	10 each
Belgium, Netherlands, Greece	5 each
Ireland, Denmark	3 each
Luxembourg	2

The total vote is thus 63, and the qualified majority is set at 45 votes, thus preventing the four large Member States from achieving a positive or negative opinion over a combination of the smaller. A positive opinion is given when 45 votes are cast in favour, a negative opinion when 45 votes are cast against, and an absence of opinion results in all other cases. Whatever the outcome, the Commission is entitled to go ahead with its proposals, and in the case of a positive opinion, or in the absence of an opinion, it will almost always do so. In the case of a negative opinion, the Commission can go ahead, or it may defer for up to one month. In either case, it must inform the Council of Ministers, who have the power to override the Commission's decision within a month.

Negative opinions are very rare; there were none in 1979 out of 1,451 votes taken, and even an absence of opinion occurred in only 97 of these votes. This apparently successful outcome is the result of care by the Commission in drafting its proposals and in accepting modifications before a vote as it has an interest in ensuring that the system works. It is also due to rather deft footwork in judging in advance, and from the chair, what modifications are necessary to suit which combination of Member States. The number of unanimously positive opinions is quite low, demonstrating that management decisions could not easily have been taken by the Council. Following a vote, the Commission will consider the proposal within its own internal procedures described earlier. It is possible, though it would be unusual, for proposals to run into opposition within the Commission after a vote in the Management Committee. If a modification of substance is then to be made, the proposal must pass again before the Management Committee. In all cases, however, the legislation does not have full legal effect, until its publication in the *Official Journal of the European Communities*. There have been occasions, however, when the food industry has acted on the basis of a favourable opinion from the Management Committee, but has been subsequently embarrassed because the proposal was not accepted by the Commission. This occurred in June 1981 when the aid for skimmed milk in casein was increased, the delay in decision occurring because the written procedure was blocked by one or more Cabinets.

In addition to the product Management Committees, there are ten other specialist Committees to which relevant draft legislation must be submitted for opinion. The procedures are not precisely the same in each case, and three groups may be distinguished. For the following specialist Committees, the procedures are the same as for the product Management Committees:

Standing Committee on Agricultural Structures

Community Committee on the Farm Accountancy Data Network

Standing Committee on Seeds and Propagating Material

European Agricultural Guidance and Guarantee Fund (FEOGA) Committee

Standing Committee on Agricultural Research

The following committees are somewhat different. If the Committee fails to approve the measures within three months of the date on which they were submitted to it, the Commission adopts the proposed measures with immediate effect:

Standing Veterinary Committee

Standing Committee on Feedingstuffs

Standing Committee on Plant Health

Standing Committee on Zootechnics

Finally, the procedure for the Standing Committees on Agricultural Statistics and for Agricultural and Forestry Tractors falls between these two procedures.

Matters related to the use of monetary compensatory amounts and 'green' conversion rates within agriculture are dealt with on an *ad hoc* basis through what is known in Brussels as a horizontal Management Committee. This is due not to the position of the delegates, but to the fact that their responsibilities touch on numerous product sectors. Other Committees of a statutory nature exist outside the CAP, but whose deliberations are very important to it. In particular, these include the Committee on Origin, the Committee on Common

Customs Tariff Nomenclature, the Standing Committee on Foodstuffs, and a number of others relating to trade questions.

For completeness it should be mentioned that the Commission has powers to adopt legislation without submitting proposals to the Management Committee, notably in cases of great urgency or where a purely mechanical calculation is in question, and for example, changes in import levies will not normally be submitted to a Management Committee. However, in such cases the Commission has to report to the appropriate Management Committee as to how its powers have been used.

Advisory Committees

The Management Committees described above are statutory bodies which the Commission is obliged to consult. However, it has also long felt the need to be seen to draw on expertise and opinion beyond that available from officials in the Management Committees. In order to achieve this, but within a formal framework, the Commission has encouraged the formation of Advisory Committees parallel to the product areas for which Management Committees exist.

These committees have no formal powers and act in an advisory capacity to the Commission only. They do not vote, and their constitutions and membership are decided upon by the Commission. Two aspects of their structure should be noted. First membership is restricted to individuals representing trade or industrial bodies organized at the European level.

The second aspect relates to the formal structure of the Advisory Committees. Their membership ranges from 28 to 48 members, of which usually 50 per cent are representatives of producer organizations, 25 per cent to trade and industry, with the remaining 25 per cent allocated to trade unions, consumer groups, or other interested parties. It can be seen from this that the range of interests represented can be extremely wide, and full agreement is only likely to be reached on the basis of the most general policy issues.

The development of these Advisory Committees at the European level has a number of particular advantages for the Commission; it ensures that the arbitration of different national viewpoints takes place at one remove from the Commission itself; it enables the Commission to be seen to have consulted interests in all Member States; it ensures that the viewpoints expressed are general rather than particular, and that the strength with which they are put forward is necessarily diluted to take account of differing national considerations. The Advisory Committees do have a useful role to play, but it is probably one which is of more use to the Commission than to the individual companies from which are drawn the national delegations to the European organizations which are actually represented on the Advisory Committees. Nevertheless, the individual who sits on the Advisory Committee will have a unique carte d'entree to the Commission, and will be able to keep particularly close to the development of policy.

Co-responsibility group

This is a specialist advisory group in the dairy sector, set up in 1977 in connection with the legislation providing for the co-responsibility levy. Article 2.1 of the regulation requires the Commission to consult the European Farmers' Union (COPA) on the level of the levy. At the same time the Commission committed itself to consult the Advisory Committee for milk and milk products on the spending of funds derived from the application of the co-responsibility levy. The Co-responsibility group was set up as part of the arrangements for consultation of the Advisory Committee.[19] Although its responsibilities are limited to the dairy sector, it is an unusual committee in two respects; first its existence derives from political agreement rather than from legislative act; second it is consulted on specifically financial and budgetary questions, a policy area which is normally reserved to the Commission, the Council and the European Parliament which together constitute the Budgetary Authority of the Community. Such involvement was a major concession to the producer organizations which make up the co-responsibility group.

It is not possible to describe in detail the multiplicity of means by which the Commission receives and disseminates information in the course of its management activities. As an organization it is surprisingly accessible to the outside world, probably more so than is the case with most national civil services. Many producer, trade, and industrial organizations maintain an office in Brussels to ensure that their direct interests are kept in view, and to receive and pass back information. There is little doubt that there is commercial advantage to be gained by early information on decisions taken or policy directions likely to be followed. The major difficulty confronting those who are affected by the Commission's management of the CAP lies largely in two contradictions which are constantly faced by the Commission.

First, for any given management decision, a far wider range of considerations needs to be taken into account than would ever be the case at the national or trade level. On the face of it, the decisions to be taken—selling prices of products from intervention, acceptability of tender offers, costs to be taken into account in establishing processing margins—are those faced by managers in industry and in national civil services. However, the Commission in making these decisions must bear in mind not only the 'objective' elements, but also those relating to the institutional, political, and budgetary consequences across the range of Member States. This inevitably means that decision making is slower than it would otherwise be, but more importantly, it is less predictable to those who are most directly concerned by the decisions taken. The second contradiction relates to the fact that the Commission is a civil service, but is in many cases required to act as a commercial organization. The difficulty is particularly acute for surplus products, where market prices tend to be firmly at the level of the intervention price, and where surplus disposal schemes must be directly managed by the Commission. The Commission has tried to escape from this dilemma by widening the gap between target and intervention prices, by abolishing price regionalization, or by establishing levels of export refunds and other aids through tender systems, all of which are intended to give more scope to market mechanisms.

EUROPEAN COURT OF JUSTICE

The Court of Justice is the final legal arbiter in matters of European legislation. Articles 164 to 188 of the Treaty of Rome provide its basic powers, and these are exercised through ten judges initially appointed by Member States, though subsequently quite independent of them. The Court is able to receive cases from individuals, from companies, from Member States, and from Community institutions, notably, in practice, from the Commission under the procedures laid down in Articles 93 and 169 of the Treaty.

The Court sits in Luxembourg. Its deliberations are prepared by the Advocate General, a Court official who is responsible for the collection of evidence and for presenting a first view of the merits of the case in question.

The Court has no powers to enforce its judgements against Member States; it can only declare a particular course of action incompatible with Treaty obligations. It has no powers to impose fines or sanctions of any other kind.[20] The position of the Court thus rests upon the same consensus that supports the very existence of the Community. In fact, no Government has yet been prepared overtly to refuse to accept a Court ruling; although in certain recent cases (relating to tachographs in the case of the United Kingdom and to sheepmeat in the case of France) there has been a tendency to say 'will comply but not yet'.

The Court has been of very considerable importance in the legal and constitutional development of the Community, and has continually pushed forward the frontiers of the Community's competences and not least in respect of the Common Agricultural Policy. A number of major cases in the agricultural sector may be quoted to illustrate both their relevance to different Community Institutions, and for the case law they established.

The Charmasson case concerned the national regulations governing the import into France of bananas. The Court, in its judgement of December 1974 (Case 48/74), laid down two rulings which are of importance in limiting the powers of Member States to regulate trade even where no common organization of the market yet exists. It ruled that although a national market organization could continue to operate in the absence of a Community regime, it may not be such as to impair the operation of free intra-Community trade. The case also defined what constituted a national market organization, and stated that a simple quota system was not permitted.

Isoglucose. A number of references to the Court arose out of the Commission's proposals for the common organization of the isoglucose market in 1977. That which is of particular interest derives from the adoption by the Council of Ministers of an amending regulation (itself the result of an earlier Court ruling) based on Article 43 of the Treaty of Rome, but without waiting for an opinion of the European Parliament. The Council claimed that the matter had been urgent and that the Parliament had been asked for an urgent opinion. The Court ruled (Case 138/79 of 29 October 1980) that Parliament's opinion was required to enable adoption of legislation by the Council, and that the present text was, therefore, invalid. This ruling seems to give the European Parliament the significant new power that it can withhold its opinion and thus prevent the adoption of legislation.

Compulsory Incorporation of Skimmed Milk Powder in Animal Feedstuffs. This Council Regulation (563/76) was intended to help dispose of the Community's substantial stocks of skimmed milk powder. It provided that the use of vegetable proteins, whether imported or domestically produced, was subject to the prior purchase of a certain quantity of skimmed milk powder from intervention stocks. In Case 114/76 on 5 July 1977 the Court ruled that the Regulation 'constituted a discriminatory distribution of the burden of costs between the various agricultural sectors . . . and could not be justified for the purposes of attaining the objectives of the CAP'. The Regulation was thus declared null and void.

Cassis de Dijon. This case (Case 120/78 of 20 February 1979) concerned the import into Germany of a French fruit liqueur with an alcohol content below that specified as a minimum level by the national German legislation. The Court held that the national legislation constituted a measure having an effect equivalent to quantitative restrictions on imports, and hence was illegal. The significance of this ruling, which was confirmed in subsequent rulings, lies in its consequences for the process of harmonization of national legislation. The Cassis case established that national food standards legislation cannot be used to prevent intra-Community trade unless related to 'public health, fiscal supervision and the defence of the consumer'. As a result the need for harmonized European standards has been much reduced.

These cases illustrate the very wide impact that Court rulings can have on Community practice and policy.

NOTES

1. The policies described in this text all derive from the EEC Treaty; for convenience, this is subsequently referred to as the Treaty of Rome.

2. The original Treaties establishing the ECSC, EURATOM, and the EEC use the phrase 'European Assembly' rather than European Parliament. On 30 March 1962 the EEC Assembly adopted the style 'European Parliament'. Since then, and more especially since members became directly elected in 1979, the phrase European Parliament has become the normal style. See House of Lords (1978).

3. The developments which led to the Community's most serious constitutional crisis on 30 June 1965, and its outcome in the Luxembourg Compromise, have been described in detail by Mayne, 1968. The crisis arose in a formal sense from a package of three measures put to the Council by the Commission. These related, first to proposals made on the financing of the CAP in the interim period between the expiry of the existing arrangements on 30 June 1965, and the beginning of the single market originally intended to commence in 1970. Secondly, the Commission had made proposals on the development of the Community's Own Resources in the form of including industrial customs duties in addition to the agricultural levies; and thirdly, it had proposed an extension of the powers of the European Parliament over the Community budget. It was this latter element which was at the heart of the French difficulties, although the nominal excuse was the failure to agree on the FEOGA financing arrangements by midnight on 30 June 1965. At that hour the French Foreign Minister left the Council and his empty chair remained vacant for the next seven months. In fact at lower levels Community business did continue with French participation, but clearly the French abstention from the Council was crippling.

The resolution of these problems was found in January 1966 at Luxembourg. The Luxembourg Compromise dealt with the powers of the Commission (the Commission itself was not present at the meeting), and with the question of majority voting in the Council. The compromise in practice established the principle that a Member State may not be outvoted on a matter which it declares to affect its vital national interest. The precise wording of the compromise is, however, not clear and states only that 'the French delegation considers that where very important interests are at stake, the discussion must be continued until unanimous agreement is reached'. The next phrase, however, adds that 'the six delegations note that there is a divergence of views on what should be done in the event of a failure to reach complete agreement'. Nevertheless the compromise enabled the Community's normal working to be resumed, albeit on the basis of a fundamental change of attitudes within the Council, and also of the place of the Commission in the pantheon of Community institutions.

4. The legislation adopted by the Council and the Commission on the basis of the EEC Treaty takes three forms; both Institutions issue regulations, directives, and decisions. Regulations are binding and are directly applicable in all Member States; thus they do not require implementing national legislation and in fact have precedence over any existing national legislation. Most of the price support measures of the CAP are based upon Council and Commission regulations. Directives are binding in the sense that a specified result must be achieved, but the national authorities are free to choose the appropriate national legislation to achieve the directive's objectives. Much of the food law harmonization programme, and structural policy for agriculture, is based upon directives. Decisions are binding upon the legal entity to whom they are addressed; hence it is by decision that the Commission would notify successful tenderers for export refunds. These three legislative acts are published in the *Official Journal of the European Communities* on a daily basis. Thus the Council Regulation on the common market organization of the market in cereals is Regulation (EEC) No. 2727/75 of the Council of 29 October 1975 and it was published in the *Official Journal of the European Communities*, volume 18, No. L181 on 1 November 1975; in this text this is abbreviated to Reg. 2727/75: OJ L181. This is quite adequate to locate the regulation, as the regulation number itself indicates the year of publication.

5. This chapter is not intended to provide a comprehensive guide to the Community's institutions as such; for texts covering these aspects see, for example, Noel (1979), Erridge (1980), or Sasse *et al.* (1977). Particular parts of the decision making process are referred to in other studies; for example, Edwards and Wallace (1977), Economic and Social Committee (1980), and Morgan (1976).

6. This process is discussed further in relation to the level of agricultural support prices set at the annual review, see Chapter 3.

7. Generally those Cabinet members specially drawn from a Commissioner's country of origin will not be permanent Commission officials. Hence when their Commissioner's term of office ends, they may leave Brussels with him.

8. Cabinets of personal advisers to a Minister are standard Continental political practice. In the UK and Ireland, however, this is not the case and Ministers have to make do with advice from their permanent civil servants. The private office has a different and largely organizational function.

9. Commission answer to written Question 1560/79, OJ C110.

10. Public health and veterinary matters are an exception, however, as they are dealt with directly by Coreper.

11. The UK representative is based in Brussels, the German and French representatives travel weekly from Bonn and Paris.

12. In cases of urgency, however, and provided a Council is meeting at that time, a Commission proposal can be made, adopted, and implemented within 24 hours.

13. There has historically been a much closer institutional interrelationship in France and the Netherlands for example, between civil service, industry, and producers, than in the UK.

14. The judgement in Case 138/79 of 29 October 1980 on isoglucose referred to later in this chapter.

15. In the second half of the 1970s the proportion of total Community legislation accounted for by agricultural matters was over four-fifths. Nearly all of this would have been concerned with market support operations.

Number of Community Legislative Acts

	1976	1977
1. Total	4229	3865
of which:		
2. Agricultural legislation	3543	3210
3. Row 2 as percentage		
of Row 1	83.8	83.2

SOURCE Commission answer to written Question 588/78, OJ C282.

16. Unfortunately this advice is difficult to follow for outsiders as the Council's Minutes are not published. Generally, however, important declarations are leaked to the Press.

17. National Parliaments of the Member States, in their examination of proposals for Community legislation, also are unable to look at proposals under the Commission's Management Committee procedures.

18. Member States have the right to put forward their own points for inclusion on Management Committee agendas.

19. The details of this consultation are provided for in a letter of 27 July 1977 from Commissioner Gundelach to Mr Cafarelli, at that time President of COPA.

20. Although the suggestion has been made recently that the Commission might be able to withhold reimbursement of FEOGA expenditures from Member States where national aids have been illegally paid to farmers.

REFERENCES

Economic and Social Committee—General Secretariat (1980) *Community Advisory Committees for the Representation of Socio Economic Interests*, Saxon House: London.

Edwards, G., and Wallace, H. (1977) *The Council of Ministers of the European Community and the President in Office*, Federal Trust: London.

Erridge, A. (1980) *Decision Making in the European Community—an Exercise*, Civil Service College: Ascot.

House of Lords Select Committee on the European Communities (1978) *Relations between the UK Parliament and the European Parliament after Direct Elections*, Session 1977–78, 44th Report, HL 256, HMSO: London.

Jenkins, R. (1982) 'How Britain Turned a Blind Eye to Community Solidarity and Missed the Budget Boat', *The Guardian*, 7 June.

Mayne, R. (1968) *The Institutions of the European Community*, European Series No. 8, Chatham House/PEP: London.

Morgan, A. (1976) *From Summit to Council: Evolution in the EEC*, European Series No. 27, Chatham House /PEP: London.

Noel, E. (1979) *The European Community: How it Works*, Office for Official Publications of the European Communities: Luxembourg.

Sasse, C., Poullet, E., Coombes, D., and Deprez, G. (1977) *Decision Making in the European Community*, Praeger: London.

Chapter 3

Price Support in the European Community

THE ESTABLISHMENT OF THE COMMON AGRICULTURAL POLICY

The Treaty of Rome

The Treaty establishing the European Economic Community specified that one of the tasks of the new Community shoud be 'the adoption of a common policy in the sphere of agriculture' (Article 3). Article 39(1) goes on to say,

The objectives of the common agricultural policy shall be:
  (a) to increase agricultural productivity by promoting technical progress and by ensuring the rational development of agricultural production and the optimum utilization of the factors of production, in particular labour;
  (b) thus to ensure a fair standard of living for the agricultural community, in particular by increasing the individual earnings of persons engaged in agriculture;
  (c) to stabilize markets;
  (d) to assure the availability of supplies;
  (e) to ensure that supplies reach consumers at reasonable prices.

This paragraph of Article 39 is probably the most quoted section of the whole EEC Treaty, and it is tempting to devote considerable space to an analysis of its contents. However the utility of such activity is open to question and the reader, if so inclined, is invited to refer back to this paragraph if, later in the exposition, some aspects of policy seem to conflict with the objectives of Article 39— objectives which are common to the agricultural policies of most developed countries. Nor is it only in the Community that conflicts arise between the policies followed and the stated objectives: any list of 'desirable' objectives tends to contain contradictions. How, for example, is a 'fair' standard of living for farmers to be reconciled with consumers buying their food at 'reasonable prices'?

None the less, two points need to be made before moving on. First, attention should be drawn to the first word of indent (b) which has been described as the most neglected word in the Treaty. This says that the farm income objectives are to be achieved by increasing productivity and ensuring rational resource use in the farm sector. Second, it should be noted that the drafting of Article 39 in 1957 did not in itself create the common agricultural policy (generally known as the CAP). It was not until the mid-1960s that the definitive form and shape of the CAP crystallized: at a time when Third Countries (i.e. non-member countries) had lost their opportunity to influence its development in international trade negotiations. Although the Treaty is a supremely important legal text in determining what can, and cannot be done, it is to an analysis of the CAP itself, as defined in the multitude of subsequent legislation, that attention should be devoted.

The need to devise a common policy on agriculture can be viewed at two levels. There is first a view that free trade in manufactures would not be possible without equalizing the conditions under which food is produced and traded because of the importance of food prices in determining wage levels. This argument, however, has always looked rather thin as there is no obvious and direct relationship between food prices, the proportion of consumer spending going on food, and national wage levels. A deeper motive for 'doing something about agriculture' probably arose from an implicit trade-off between Germany and France. France was not going to enter into free trade in manufactures unless free trade applied also in agriculture where she had a comparative advantage over Germany. Germany, although already a major industrial power after the devastation of the Second World War, had still an important agricultural sector which it was not going to sacrifice.

The Stresa Conference

Recognizing that the agricultural policies of the six signatories of the EEC Treaty differed in many respects and that the construction of a common policy for agriculture would present formidable difficulties, the Commission was instructed to convene a conference of the Member States to consider the problems (Article 43). The conference was held at Stresa, in Italy, between the 3rd and 12th July 1958 (Commission, 1958a). Following the conference, in its first report on the activities of the Community, the Commission outlined its views on the problems of agricultural policy (Commission, 1958b, pp. 67–72).

The Commission considered that the central problem facing agriculture was 'the disparity existing between the level of income in agriculture and that in other sectors of the economy' (Commission, 1958b, p. 67). In constructing a CAP the Community would have to bear in mind its political and economic interest in maintaining its trade relations with Third Countries: 'This fact alone prohibits the Community from becoming a self-sufficing entity' (Commission, 1958b, p. 68). But 'Apart from its trade aspects, the common policy for agriculture covers two main fields: market and price policy and policy for improving the structure of agriculture' (Commission, 1958b, p. 69). The market and price policy dominated the CAP from the first and dictated the Community's trade policy in farm products. The Community has never succeeded in establishing a vigorous and effective structural policy (if indeed such a development were possible): the haphazard and limited collection of legislation which deals with structures in the agri-food sector will be discussed in Chapter 9.

At this early stage the Commission, understandably, was not in a position to produce its blueprint for agriculture; but was none the less aware of the problems facing the awaited CAP. Thus the Commission noted that it would 'serve no useful purpose to ask for improvements in the structure of agriculture if prices were at the same time fixed at a level which enabled even those enterprises to cover their expenses, which owing to their inferior structure were producing at high costs'. (Commission, 1958b, p. 70).

The problem which has dogged the CAP throughout its history was already apparent.

> In the past, attempts to increase agricultural incomes have been based on the too one-sided principle of increasing production. True, this has led to a marked increase of productivity per worker, especially as there was a simultaneous decrease in the number of persons occupied in agriculture. However, the increase in production has led to new difficulties on the markets. In view of the fact that production of the major products is increasing more vigorously than consumption, surpluses are appearing on the various markets and their disposal is causing serious difficulties and worries. (Commission, 1958b, p. 70).

The main factors influencing the development of the CAP

To document the political intrigues and setbacks that marked the evolution of the CAP throughout the 1960s and 1970s would be a fascinating, if involved, study.[1] It is not the intention to attempt such a task here, but it is hoped to indicate the major achievements and decisions. This is because an understanding of how the CAP operates today, and of the reasons why it displays certain features, can best be gleaned from a brief historical review.

A number of events have had important influences. First, the existence of national price support schemes and the political necessity to establish free trade within the Community in farm products, meant that decisions on Community-wide price support mechanisms, and the level of price support, had to be made quickly. Second the pressing need to enter trade negotiations with the outside world, within a general climate of trade liberalization, meant that decisions had to be reached as to which products were of importance to European agriculture, and where concessions could be made. It is likely that the pressures imposed upon the fledgling organization and its small but idealistic staff by the need to participate in the almost continuous round of GATT negotiations[2] in the first half of the 1960s helped produce the Community's inward looking and defensive views about the CAP that many outside commentators claim to discern today. Chapter 11 deals with the Community's external trade arrangements and their development under Third Country pressures.

A third factor influencing the evolution and character of the CAP was the debate over finance. What aspects of common policies should be financed, and how should the necessary income be raised? At the time of writing the Community is undergoing yet another financial crisis that has important implications for the farming community. These matters are discussed at greater length in Chapter 13. A fourth important influence on the farm and food policies of the Community was the first application for membership by Denmark, Ireland, and the United Kingdom in 1961; their subsequent accession in 1973; the traumas involved in Britain's renegotiation of her membership (1974/75); and, more recently, the accession of Greece (1981) and the applications for membership received from Portugal and Spain. The final factor which was of importance was the world commodity price boom of the early 1970s: this led the architects of the CAP to believe that EC price levels were not grossly out of line with world market prices, that access to the world market could not guarantee security of supplies, and that the maintenance of price stability to consumers within the Community was an important achievement of the CAP.[3]

Given the pressures and burdens of work laid upon the Community's institutions because of the factors outlined above, it is perhaps not surprising that a comprehensive policy has yet to be achieved. Effort has been devoted to liberalizing intra-Community trade in farm products and, to a lesser extent, in processed foods; little energy has been left to tackle the so-called structural problems of European agriculture or to harmonize and control the various national aids which affect the cost and availability of resources to agriculture and the food industries.

The CAP dates from 1962 when the first regulations governing produce markets were introduced. On 14 January 1962, after a marathon session of the Council of Ministers, agreement was reached on the mechanisms by which the markets for six products (cereals, pigmeat, poultrymeat, eggs, fruit and vegetables, and wine) were to be regulated. It was at this meeting that the system of variable import levies (discussed below on pages 47–48), so characteristic of the CAP, was decided upon. On 1 August 1962 the market systems for cereals and the cereal-based livestock products came into being, and the 'chicken war' began (see also Chapter 11).

The 'chicken war' arose partly because of the inconclusive nature of the Dillon Round. One of the purposes of that negotiating round was that Third Countries be compensated for the trade diversionary aspects of the EEC's formation. But in the case of agriculture the EC members were, at the time of the negotiations, trying to resolve their internal disputes as to the form the CAP should take and consequently felt unable to make concessions on products of importance to European agriculture that could affect the form the CAP would subsequently take. Hence at the closure of the Dillon Round in March 1962 the Americans still had 'unsatisfied negotiating rights' with respect to agricultural trade, and in their eyes these rights were jeopardized by the introduction of the CAP, and in particular the poultrymeat regime, in August of that year.

However, there were a range of agricultural products which at the time seemed of little importance to EC agriculture, and on which the EC felt able to make concessions. Consequently the EC entered into GATT bindings on oilseeds, manioc, and sheepmeat which subsequently have caused embarrassment to the Community.[4] The EC's attempts to disengage itself from GATT bindings on manioc and sheepmeat are discussed in later chapters.

The three principles of the CAP

It is the Commission's view that the decisions of 1962 established 'three fundamental principles', or pillars, on which the market and price policies of the CAP are based. These are:

> the principle of the *unity of the market* which has been implemented through the gradual harmonization of farm prices in Member States; the principle of *Community preference* implemented by a system of variable levies and the common customs tariff; the principle of *financial solidarity*, which was reflected in the setting up of the European Agricultural Guidance and Guarantee Fund. (Commission, 1975, paragraph 12, emphasis added.)

It is not difficult to recognize the logic of the three principles, or to understand the reluctance of CAP supporters to compromise in their execution; but the implementation of the principles has been notoriously difficult to achieve.

The EC is a customs union, and one of the purposes of establishing a customs union is to encourage trade between partner countries at the expense, if necessary, of trade with Third Countries. It is the clear intention of the EEC Treaty that the customs union should extend to agriculture (Article 38) and hence the concept of 'Community preference'. None the less in implementing its policies for various products (notably fruit and vegetables, and wine—see Chapter 7), and in granting trade concessions to countries in the Mediterranean Basin (see Chapter 11), the EC has been accused by some Member States of not fully respecting the concept of Community preference. Nor did the traditionalists accept with equanimity the preferential treatment afforded New Zealand dairy products, or sugar from selected less developed countries (both discussed in depth in the appropriate chapters), following the United Kingdom's accession to the Community in 1973. To foreign suppliers it is the concept of Community preference, epitomized in the variable levy, that is the most objectionable part of the CAP.

The concept of financial solidarity involved two elements: the first that expenses incurred as a result of the policy should be financed by the Community, and the second that income generated by the policy should be regarded as part of the income or 'own resources' of the Community.[5] On paper this statement looks innocuous enough, but in practice many of the major battles between the Member States (and, indeed, the institutions of the Community) have centred on finance. However, further discussion of this issue is deferred to Chapter 13.

It is less easy to understand the logic of market unity. It obviously stems from the idea that with no barriers to trade between the partner countries, and under competitive market circumstances, then the price for any particular product would tend to be the same throughout the Community. Between localities price differences would exist, but the price gap between the region with the highest prices and that with the lowest prices could never be more than the transport costs between the two centres. The market price would be determined competitively and farmers would specialize in those branches of production in which they had a cost advantage, while high cost producers (whether small or large farmers) would go out of production. However, this is *not* the outcome the CAP sets out to achieve.

Market prices are administered, not competitively determined, and they are set at such a level that even high cost producers can earn a living. Within the CAP prices no longer have the limited role of bringing about an efficient allocation of resources and production; the implications for the incomes of farmers of that outcome are judged to be unacceptable. CAP prices are manipulated to engineer an increase of revenue flows (and hopefully income) to the farming community. There seems to be no good reason to suppose that this objective will be achieved more successfully with common, rather than regionally differentiated support prices—particularly if the income objective has a regional (or national) element.

The achievement of common prices for cereals, cereal-based livestock products, and oilseeds on 1 July 1967 was hailed as a marked success, because it represented a considerable acceleration of the timetable laid down in the EEC Treaty.[6] However, this was to prove a shortlived triumph. The unity of common support prices was broken only two years later with the devaluation of the French franc and revaluation of the German mark in 1969 (see Chapter 8). Common prices have never since been achieved.

The initial level of prices

The original common support prices were related to existing support prices in the national support regimes of the original '6'. The common prices were set within the range of the national support prices, the major element of political bargaining lying in the decision as to whereabouts in the range they should be fixed. Generally German support prices were at the top end of this range and French and Dutch at the bottom (Table 3.1).

In some cases—cereals, sugar beet and grain-fed livestock—the common prices were established at a level midway between the highest and lowest national prices: for other products, in particular for dairy products, the eventual compromise lay towards the upper end of the range.

The resulting common agricultural policy was more protectionist than the sum of the previous national policies for several reasons: (i) the high-price countries fought for comparatively high prices in order to avoid farm income problems; (ii) the range of products covered by protectionist measures was widened in some countries because special protectionist interests in individual countries were

Table 3.1   Relationship of national support prices by commodity to their overall average, for the original '6'. (Data for 1960/61).

	Wheat	Barley	Milk	Eggs	Cattle	Pigs
			(% of average level)			
Belgium	100	90	99	97	96	86
France	85	82	100	96	87	110
West Germany	107	132	103	111	102	115
Italy	118	106	103	115	118	95
Netherlands	89	91	95	80	97	94

SOURCE   Tracy (1964, p. 327).

extended to Community-wide protection; and (iii) the supply-control policies, previously practised in exporting countries, were abandoned in the face of the opportunities provided by the Community's market and were replaced, in effect, by a policy of export push by developing the dormant potential of their agriculture. (Heidhues *et al.*, 1978, p. 7.)

The principal cause of this outcome, according to Priebe *et al.* (1972) was the German success in preventing major income drops for its farmers. Zeller reports that despite the price restraint advocated by the Commission and the French government, the compromise erred towards the high German price levels (Zeller, 1970). Warley (1967, p. 18) points out, however, that there were several trade-offs between the '6' whereby, for example, France had to accept a higher level of farm prices in order to get strengthened Community preference, while Italy's price for accepting the commodity regimes for the northern agricultural products was a greatly strengthened fruit and vegetable regime and increased Community support for olive oil and oilseeds.

These initial pricing decisions have never seriously been threatened as, each year in the price review (discussed below), price increases are agreed based upon the existing price levels. However, from time to time the Commission has tried to coax the Council into a re-examination of the price levels—an early example being the Mansholt plan.

The Mansholt Plan

Long before the breakdown of the common pricing system in 1969 the Commission had become increasingly worried about the form and direction the CAP had taken. This disquiet was crystallized in December 1968 with the publication of a document which has since become known as the Mansholt Plan (Commission, 1968a.)[7] Sicco Mansholt was then Commissioner for Agriculture; his verve is still respected by Commission officials today, among whom rests the lingering view that if only the proposals of the Mansholt Plan had been implemented the ills of the CAP could have been cured. In this document the Commission expressed its view that:

> market and price support possibilities alone cannot solve the fundamental difficulties of farming. These policies are subject to narrow limits; if those are exceeded markets will be disorganized and the costs to the Community will be intolerable, without any effective improvement for the farming population. (Commission, 1968a, paragraph 16.)

It was the Commission's belief that the Community could, and should, actively intervene to achieve a substantial restructuring of the layout, organization, and size of farms—the envisaged structural policy which had proved so elusive an ideal throughout the 1960s.

It was believed that if the farming population could be helped to retire, retrain, or adapt their holdings into 'modern agricultural enterprises' then the market and prices policy of the CAP could be amended such that less emphasis would be placed on the income needs of marginal producers. Whether the plan's proposals were realistic or not it suffices to note that they fell on stony ground. It was not until 1972 that rather limited initiatives were taken on structural policy (see Chapter 9); the market and prices policy of the CAP still dominates Community activity.

Before leaving the Mansholt Plan it is worth recording its view that, because of the productive capacity of European agriculture, the area of agricultural land would have to be reduced. Specifically the plan proposed that between 1970 and 1980 the area devoted to agriculture should be reduced by at least 5 million hectares, the major part being turned over to forestry (Commission, 1968a, paragraph 105). This would have represented about 7 per cent of the agricultural area of the then six Member States. For the record it can be noted that the total agricultural area of the nine Member States declined by 0.5 per cent per annum in the period from 1968 to 1978.

The Commission was not alone in believing that the farmed area should be reduced. In France, the following year, the Vedel Commission suggested that an even more marked reduction in the French agricultural area might be necessary.[8] With the renewed concern for the availability of foodstuffs for the poor peoples of the world, such suggestions today sound rather off-key. However, while keeping a low profile, the Commission has maintained an interest in fostering a Community forestry policy. The most recent proposals were made in 1979 (for an outline and discussion, see House of Lords, 1979) but the topic is not pursued further here.

Other Commission initiatives

Despite the fate of the Mansholt Plan the Commission has kept arguing the case for CAP reform.[9] The first attempt at wholesale reform of the CAP, after the Mansholt Plan, came with a document entitled *Improvement of the Common Agricultural Policy* (Commission, 1973). This was produced partly because it was felt that the accession of the UK, with its different traditions of farm support and the greater emphasis placed on consumer interests, would prove a likely catalyst in effecting change. The Commission's proposals raised themes which have echoed down the years since:

(i) to alter the ratios between CAP support prices so as to better reflect economic realities;
(ii) for farmers to bear some of the cost of surplus disposal;
(iii) for greater flexibility in the organization of the different commodity support regimes;
(iv) for an improvement in forecasts of CAP expenditure.

The surge in world commodity prices in 1973 took the pressure off CAP reform, however, as the pressing possibility of food shortages became a factor in world discussions—as in the 1974 World Food Conference held in Rome—and little came of the Commission's proposals apart from some technical changes.

The next step followed the change of Government in Britain in 1974. The new Labour government asked for a renegotiation of the UK's terms of entry, laying particular stress on CAP reform (British Government, 1974). During the period the renegotiations were underway the Commission was asked to prepare a stocktaking of the CAP, and this was duly transmitted to the Council and European Parliament in February 1975 (Commission, 1975). Despite Britain's preoccupation with the CAP, agriculture was not a key issue in the final renegotiation terms at the Dublin meeting of the European Council in March 1975, although there was agreement to the continuation of New Zealand butter imports. The suspicion must remain that high world prices for cereals, sugar, and animal feed proteins in 1973 and 1974, from which European consumers were partially protected by export taxes and import subsidies, had made the CAP appear less protectionist, and had blunted criticism. Thus evaporated another opportunity for reform of the CAP; and the 'Stocktaking', like many Commission documents before it, sank into oblivion.

CAP reform proposals at the end of the 1970s were triggered by the increasing difficulties with the Community Budget, for CAP expenditure had been growing faster than the rate of growth in resources available for the Budget. Thus the Commission (1979) produced a document entitled *Changes in the Common Agricultural Policy to help balance the markets and streamline expenditure*. In these proposals the Commission was concerned to modify the CAP to save it from the growing criticism over the surpluses it was generating, and the increased pressure to reduce expenditure arising from the Budget situation. Hence the main proposals were devoted to moving closer to market balance for milk and sugar—the two major surplus sectors—and with making producers bear more of the cost of surplus disposal.

The parting shot of the four-year term of office of the Commission led by Roy Jenkins was a document entitled *Reflections on the Common Agricultural Policy* (Commission, 1980). In it the Commission put forward the idea of a new, fourth, principle in the operation of the CAP. This 'co-responsibility principle' was that 'any production above a certain volume to be fixed, taking into account the internal consumption of the Community and its external trade, must be charged fully or partially to the producers' (p. 18). The point of the principle was that the Community's Budget could no longer maintain an open-ended funding commitment, no matter what the level of Community agricultural production. Hence the development of various measures in the early 1980s whereby producers became liable for funding a part—varying according to commodity—of the costs of 'surplus' disposal.

A new emphasis came in 1981, with the *Commission Report on the Mandate of 30 May 1980* (Commission, 1981a), in which the Commission admitted for the first time that the gap between Community support prices and world levels would have to be narrowed.[10]. These more recent proposals are discussed in the chapters dealing with the current operations of the CAP.

THE MARKET AND PRICE POLICY

The diversity and complexity of the measures the CAP deploys to support and augment the prices received by farmers is immense. Every product, or product group, is affected by a set of legislation specific to that product and, although many of the measures display common features, the permutations by which they are combined and the terminology (Table 3.2) by which they are described

Table 3.2   Terminology used for CAP institutional support prices.

	Desired market return	Minimum market price at which intervention mechanisms operate	Minimum entry prices for imports from Third Countries
Cereals	Target	Intervention/ Reference	Threshold
Rice	Target	Intervention	Threshold
Pigmeat	Basic	Buying-in	Sluice-gate*
Poultrymeat and eggs	—	—	Sluice-gate*
Milk and milk products	Target	Intervention	Threshold
Beef and veal	Guide	Intervention/ Buying-in	Formula based on the relationship of the market price to the guide price.
Mutton and lamb	Basic	Intervention	—
Sugar	Target	Intervention	Threshold
Wine	Guide	Activating	Reference
Fruit and vegetables	Basic	Buying-in/ Withdrawal	Reference*
Olive oil	Production	Intervention	Threshold
Oilseeds	Target	Intervention	—
Raw tobacco	Norm	Intervention	—
Dehydrated fodder	Guide	—	—

* To which import levies (the livestock products) or import duties (fruit and vegetables) must be added.

differ from product to product. Nevertheless, it will be convenient at this stage to describe the instruments commonly used, as in later chapters (Chapters 4 to 7) this material will be drawn on to give a more detailed picture of the commodity regimes. Central to the philosophy of the CAP is the concept that the producer should receive his reward from the price paid in the market for his produce, rather than from direct income supplements or payments related to numbers of livestock kept, or crop areas grown.

The main institutional support prices

The terminology used for the main CAP institutional support prices varies between commodity (Table 3.2). The archetypal commodity market regime—that for cereals—uses three such prices.

Target prices. These represent the return that it is desired that producers should receive on their sales. In other words target prices represent the levels which domestic market prices should attain. However, target prices as such do not have any practical market significance because they do not trigger policy actions. Their significance lies in the fact that they are the reference point from which the other institutional support prices are derived.

Threshold prices. These represent minimum entry prices for imports from Third Countries, and are defined to apply at Community frontiers with the rest of the world. They are set at such a level that target prices cannot be undercut by Third Country imports. To ensure this threshold prices are calculated from target prices taking account of internal distribution costs. Threshold prices represent the 'ceiling' for EC internal market prices under normal circumstances. Above these levels Third Country supplies are relatively freely available; should EC domestic market prices show signs of rising significantly above threshold prices then world supplies will be drawn in.

Intervention prices represent minimum market prices ('floor' prices). National intervention agencies have an obligation to buy, at intervention prices, Community produce offered them—but only for those products which are eligible for intervention support.[11] Hence, under normal circumstances market prices should not fall below this minimum level, although the price received by the farmer will reflect the intervention price as adjusted for the quality of the farmer's produce, the costs of handling and transport from farm-gate to intervention store and, if necessary, of processing before delivery to intervention.

Thus there is a price band which defines the range within which domestic market prices are free to fluctuate, while being maintained above world market prices. The bounds of the price band are set by the Community's institutional support prices. The ceiling on domestic market prices is set by the institutionally determined minimum import prices at which Third Country supplies are allowed to ·enter the EC. Conversely, the floor is set by the institutionally determined minimum market prices at which governments have a commitment to intervene to prevent market prices dropping any further. For most commodities the minimum import price is some 20 to 30 per cent above the minimum domestic market price. These levels are generally, but not always, above world levels.

The economics of CAP price support[12]

To help in understanding the effects of these price support measures, a simple economic model is valuable. In Figure 3.1 the Community is considered as an importer: still the situation for maize, 'hard' breadmaking wheat, rice, olive oil and—depending on the stage reached in its production cycle—beef. In Figure 3.3 the EC is considered as a net exporter: the situation for common wheat, barley, wine, sugar, and dairy products.

In Figure 3.1 the curve DD shows the EC's demand schedule for a commodity in which it is in deficit over the range of prices shown. The lower the price the greater the quantity consumed; conversely the higher the price the less is consumed. The curve SS shows the EC's domestic supply schedule. This shows that

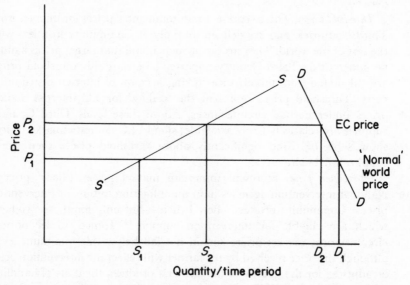

Figure 3.1 An imported product. P_1 is the 'normal' world market price, P_2 is the EC support price (or price band), S_1 is domestic production at world price P_1, S_2 is domestic production at supported price P_2, D_1 is domestic demand at world price P_1, D_2 is domestic demand at supported price P_2, $D_1 - S_1$ are imports at world price P_1, and $D_2 - S_2$ are imports at supported price P_2.

Note: To avoid unnecessary complications in the presentation the effect of the EC's policy on the world market price has been ignored. This point will be taken up in Chapter 11.

the higher the price the more will be produced domestically. The gap between the two schedules on the figure indicates that the EC is a net importer of the commodity being considered as it is producing less than its consumers demand at the price levels shown.

The 'normal' world market price is represented by the price line P_1. At that price, were there no barriers to entry for Third Country production, Community producers would supply quantity S_1 and consumers would demand quantity D_1. The excess of demand over supply $(D_1 - S_1)$ would be met by imports.

If the authorities were to enact legislation such that P_2 became the price paid by consumers and received by producers, what would the implications be? Production would become more profitable and supply would expand from S_1 to S_2: clearly a preferred position for producers. However, the higher price would lead consumers to cut back on their purchases of the product (from D_1 to D_2): clearly a less preferred position for consumers. And the volume of imports would fall from $S_1 D_1$ to $S_2 D_2$ to the detriment of producers in Third Countries. This is the situation in the Community where the support price band is normally set above world levels. As a consequence the Community's self-sufficiency in agricultural products has risen significantly since the CAP's creation.

Import mechanisms

How can domestic market prices be kept up (at the level represented by P_2) when supplies from the world market are available at the lower price P_1? The method adopted has been to tax imports as they come into the Community. In Figure 3.1 the import tax is represented as the unit difference between the prices (i.e. P_2 less P_1), while the revenue raised by the tax is the unit rate of tax times total imports.

The Community uses three principal types of import taxes: these are import duties, countervailing charges, and variable import levies. Import duties (or tariffs) may either be specific as a fixed charge of say £10 per hectolitre imported, or *ad valorem* where a constant percentage of the import price is charged as a tax, for example 26 per cent in the case of imported corned beef. In so far as the EC uses import duties in the agricultural and food sector, the duties are generally *ad valorem*.

Clearly, however, the application of an import duty is not sufficient to ensure that where minimum entry—or threshold prices—apply, represented by P_2 in Figure 3.1, these levels are always achieved. If the price were to fall on world markets, then the duty-paid import price would also fall. Hence, for the major CAP products where such minimum entry prices are set (Table 3.1) countervailing duties or variable import levies are applied.

Although both these latter policy mechanisms have similar implications for the level and stability of the EC price level they have rather different consequences for foreign suppliers. Two examples might help to clarify the difference. For cereals the world market price is monitored on a daily basis and—broadly speaking—the import levy of the day is based on the difference between the lowest recorded world market price quotation and the threshold price. Any foreign supplier of the same grade of grain at higher prices would be at a competitive disadvantage on the EC market, because the same levy is payable on all imports whether high or low priced.

Contrast this with the reference price system applied to certain types of fruits and vegetables. Provided the landed price is greater than, or equal to, the reference price then the only import charge payable is an import duty: the minimum import price thus being the reference price plus the duty (see Figure 3.2). If, however, the foreign supplier has a landed price less than the reference price, a countervailing duty will be payable *on produce from that supplier*. Consequently no foreign supplier has an incentive to price at less than the reference price because that will trigger the application of countervailing duties against itself.

In the first example (import levy and threshold price) the level of domestic prices determines domestic demand and supply and hence the share of imports. Competitive pricing by foreign suppliers cannot increase the overall import share, but can increase the proportion of imports coming from the lowest cost foreign supplier. In the second example (reference price) again the share of imports in the domestic market is determined by domestic price support mechanisms when foreign producers could supply the EC market at less than the reference price. However, in this instance the lowest cost foreign producer cannot expand its share of the import market at the expense of higher cost producers if their costs in turn are still less than the reference price.[13] In other words, under the levy mechanism, the competitive ranking among Third Country suppliers of the same quality product is unchanged, whereas with the reference price system all Third Country suppliers able to supply at the reference price or less are put on an equal basis.

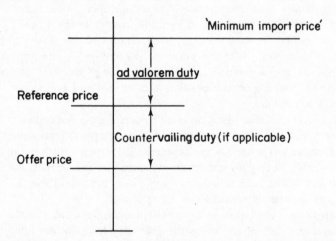

Figure 3.2   The reference price system for certain fruits and vegetables.

Support mechanisms on the domestic market

Although import controls are always a necessary feature of a price support policy—otherwise cheap imports would erode the high prices—they will only be a sufficient mechanism when the region has a net import requirement for the product concerned. For the EC as a whole, and for many regions within the Community, this is not the case for many products. Hence additional support mechanisms are necessary. In Figure 3.3, within the price range under consideration, supply (SS) exceeds demand (DD). The policy mechanisms seek to remove the excess of supply over demand at the desired EC price level of P_2. In EC jargon this quantity is often referred to as a surplus.

The major internal market support measure is the availability of intervention buying at some level close to the target price. Although only a single line (P_2) is shown in the figure this may be taken as representing the price band as discussed earlier. Hence support buying is available by the national intervention agencies at this level; the quantity needing to be bought-in being the excess of production over consumption (S_2 less D_2) at the administered price levels. There is, however, a problem of knowing what to do with intervention stocks. Occasionally some can be resold to the domestic market, and some may be sold at a cheaper price to selected groups or for specified purposes. Much has to be

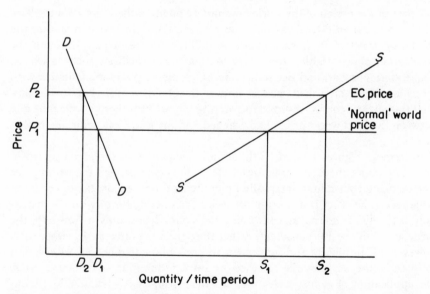

Figure 3.3 A product in 'surplus'. P_1 is the 'normal world market price, P_2 is the EC support price (or price band), S_1 is domestic production at world price P_1, S_2 is domestic production at supported price P_2, D_1 is domestic demand at world price P_1, D_2 is domestic demand at supported price P_2, $S_1 - D_1$ are exports at world price P_1, and $S_2 - D_2$ are exports at supported price P_2.

Note: To avoid unnecessary complications in the presentation the effect of the EC's policy on the world market price has been ignored. This point will be taken up in Chapter 11.

exported, and it has been found that the budgetary costs are lower if the trade undertakes the responsibility to export direct rather than exporting products which have previously been bought into intervention.

Export refunds

In terms of Figure 3.3 the quantity to be exported is the difference between D_2 and S_2. It is obvious that the Community will not be competitive as a seller on world markets, however, until the gap between its internal prices and world levels can be bridged. This difference is paid as a subsidy to traders when they export the product from the Community. The Budget cost of this exercise is represented by this quantity times the unit difference between P_2 and P_1—the necessary unit export subsidy rate. Like the variable import levy, the export subsidy (known as an export refund)[14] can be varied to bridge the price gap however large or small. Provided the necessary Budget funds are available, any quantity of production can be disposed of on the world market, driving other suppliers from the scene.

Export levies and import refunds

For part of the period of the world commodity boom in the years 1973 to 1975, when world prices exceeded Community levels, the EC acted to maintain the insulating effect of its border measures.[15] This was principally through the application of a variable export levy for major commodities such as wheat, maize, barley, sugar, and rice to prevent EC domestic prices rising in line with the movement of world prices above threshold levels. For one commodity—sugar—the EC resorted to granting import subsidies to bridge the gap between the level world prices had reached and the lower EC domestic market prices.

In terms of Figures 3.1 and 3.3 the situation would be represented by a world price line above the Community level. The EC acts to prevent the world price signals being transmitted internally by applying a unit export tax to cover the difference. The effect is as for import levies (described above) with the insulation of the EC's internal market being the policy focus, only in this case the 'beneficiary' is the EC consumer, rather than the EC producer. In either case, however, EC producers and consumers are responding to different price signals to those on the world market, as they are insulated from it. In domestic terms, the application of export levies reverses the normal CAP transfer from consumers to producers. When export levies are in operation, their effect is to prevent the EC's internal market prices rising to world levels. In effect, producers are subsidizing consumers.

Deficiency payments

Although the archetypal CAP regimes work through raising market prices, for certain commodities systems of direct payments to producers are employed instead. Using Figure 3.1, the effects of a deficiency payments system can be shown. Suppose the objective of the policy is to give producers the guaranteed market price P_2. The variable import levy (buttressed if necessary by domestic market intervention) can be used to achieve this objective. Alternatively the authorities, whilst guaranteeing the producers a total price of P_2, could allow the product to be freely imported and bought and sold at price P_1. The taxpayer would then be called upon to make up the difference $(P_2 - P_1)$, between the guaranteed price and the realized market price, to the producer in the form of a direct subvention or deficiency payment. The producer, confident of receiving a total return of P_2, would produce the quantity S_2, but consumers would have the advantage of consuming the quantity D_1 at price P_1.

As with the variable levy the deficiency payment is variable and would fall to zero if the realized market price rose to P_2. The subventions paid under the CAP to oilseed producers have this characteristic. There are in addition payments to producers which are fixed irrespective of variations in the world market price.

CAP PRICE SUPPORT IN MORE DETAIL

From the foregoing description of target, intervention, and threshold prices it should not be inferred that the mechanisms deployed, or the impact on the market, are the same for all products; or even that they apply to all products. But it does serve as a useful base for a more detailed description of the CAP. Table 3.3 presents in summary form the main provisions of CAP price support—including the measures currently in force, and those proposed for potatoes and agricultural alcohol.

The existence of an intervention or withdrawal price means that under some market circumstances the authorities will acquire produce for addition to their intervention stocks. Sometimes a change in market circumstances can be foreseen which will allow the resale of the product on to the market at a price at least equal to the intervention price. More frequently, however, the authorities have no such opportunity and they must, perforce, resort to a number of stratagems to reduce their intervention stocks or limit the quantities delivered into intervention. Implicit in this idea is that other markets, either domestically or internationally, must be made as attractive to producers as is intervention. Internally the Community has subsidized the sale of products to certain individuals (e.g. old age pensioners) or processors (e.g. skim milk for incorporation in animal feed, or butter in ice cream or bakery products) who would otherwise be unable or unwilling to purchase. For some products the Community subsidizes private storage in the hope that the market price will have risen by the time the product comes out of the store.

In addition to, and sometimes in place of, these provisions, direct aids are in some instances given to producers. The items listed in column (i) of Table 3.3 are such a miscellany that it is difficult to categorize. It includes aids received by producers in disadvantaged regions (to durum wheat producers, and the

Table 3.3 Summary of Main CAP instruments to support prices.

Product (a)	Import controls		Export aids		Internal measures		Consumer/ processer subsidies (h)	Direct producer subsidies (i)
	Conventional tariffs applicable (b)	Variable levies (c)	Refunds (d)	Food Aid (e)	Support buying (f)	Private storage (g)		
Cereals	—	Yes	Yes	Yes (mainly wheat)	Obligatory	Intervention 'B'	Starch, beer, glucose	Durum wheat
Rice	—	Yes	Yes	Yes	Obligatory	—	Starch, beer	—
Pigmeat	—	Yes, plus additional levies	Yes	—	Possible	Yes	—	—
Poultry and eggs	—	Yes, plus additional levies	Yes	—	—	—	—	—
Milk and milk products	—	Yes	Yes	Butteroil, skimmed milk powder	Obligatory	Yes	Wide range: animal feed, food manufacturers, consumers	Subsidy on skim fed to animals on farm
Beef and veal	Yes	Yes	Yes	Discussed	Obligatory	Yes	Consumers	Variable premia. Headage payments
Mutton and lamb	—	Yes, but subject to a 20% maximum rate	No, but provision exists	—	In certain regions at certain times of year	Yes	—	Headage payments and variable premia
Sugar	—	Yes	Yes	Yes	Obligatory	Yes	Chemical industry	—

		Countervailing duties			Preventive distillation		Distillation	
Wine	Yes	Countervailing duties	Yes	—	Yes	Yes	—	—
Agricultural alcohol	Yes	—	Proposed	—	—	—	Proposed	Proposed
Fruit and vegetable	Yes	Countervailing duties	Yes	—	Yes	—	Aids for processing and marketing	—
Olive oil	—	Yes	Yes	—	Obligatory	Yes	Consumption and processing	Yes
Oilseeds	Yes	Possible compensatory levy	Yes	—	Obligatory	—	Production aid claimed by processers	—
Tobacco	Yes	—	Yes	—	Obligatory	—	Purchaser premiums	—
Peas and field beans	Yes	—	—	—	—	—	Incorporation and production aids	—
Dehydrated fodder	Yes	—	—	—	—	—	Processing aids	—
Potatoes	Yes	Countervailing duties proposed	Proposed	—	—	Proposed	Starch fodder	—
Seeds	Yes	—	—	—	—	—	—	Yes
Silkworms	Yes	—	—	—	—	—	—	Yes
Fibreflax and hemp	Yes	—	—	—	—	Yes	—	Yes
Cotton	Yes	—	—	—	—	—	Production aid	—
Hops	Yes	—	—	—	—	—	—	Yes

headage payments on cattle and sheep under the hill farming directive); payments to former milk producers to cease production; an income supplement to olive producers which is invariant to current output; flat rate payments to seed producers; deficiency payments on oilseeds; variable payments to fruit and vegetable processers, and various payments to sheepmeat producers.

All of these items taken together form the common policy on markets and prices; but their variety is such that it is difficult to describe and analyse the CAP as a single entity, both with respect to the citizens of the Community and those of Third Countries. Chapters 4 to 7 will be devoted to a further extension of this pandora's box, while in Chapter 8 the additional complications of green currencies and monetary compensatory amounts are discussed.

Conflict between the commodity regimes

The foregoing discussion has pointed to the diversity of support mechanisms used within the CAP, and the emphasis placed on the stability of support prices. As a prelude to subsequent chapters it is opportune to comment on the probable consequences of these features of the CAP which have contributed to the cumbersomeness of the policy.

The emphasis on price stability has resulted in a lack of adaptability in the individual commodity regimes. They have not reacted sufficiently quickly to changing market circumstances, either domestically or internationally. In Chapter 11 it is pointed out that the lack of reaction to changing international market circumstances very probably aggravates the instability of international prices. But even taking a more parochial view, the tendency for output to outstrip demand—most notably for sugar and dairy products—leads to many complaints about the cost of EC surpluses.

The stability of prices has led to conflicts between the support regimes, and the difference in the treatment of particular products has compounded the problems. Thus when wheat production exceeds the demand for wheat as a bread grain the excess has to be fed to livestock. When intervention prices for common wheat were higher than for other grains (as they were in the past), then expensive denaturing subsidies had to be used to dispose of the surplus. If cereal substitutes can be more freely imported into the Community than can cereals themselves—which is the position because of concessions made in the Dillon Round of GATT negotiations—then livestock producers will tend to switch from cereals to cereal substitutes in their animal feed rations.

The GATT concession on oilseeds, whilst 'threatening' the cereals regime as noted above, also caused problems in the marketing of milk products and olive oil. Thus the protein rich meal from soya is a cheap competitor to skim milk powder in pig feed; and the vegetable oil, in the form of margarine, competes with butter. Considerations such as these have led to many appeals, from Community farming circles, for the taxation of competitive products. These, and other examples will be discussed in the following chapters.

THE ANNUAL PRICE REVIEW

Timing of annual review

Once the initial levels for common support prices had been set, the Community had to regularly review their levels. This commitment is included in the basic Regulation governing each commodity support regime. Under normal circumstances common support prices are reviewed annually in a composite package which covers all the commodities included in the CAP.

Originally this review was meant to occur well before the new prices came into effect so that farmers had time to adjust their investment and production decisions. Thus the basic Regulation for the cereals regime says that the intervention price for common wheat shall be fixed before 1 August of each year for the marketing year beginning during the following year (i.e. a year's advance warning). In the basic Regulation for beef the guide price for cattle is to be fixed before 1 August of each year for the marketing year beginning during the following calendar year. In practice the Community has never kept to this timetable, apart from the first years of common prices. From 1969 onwards these target dates have been missed.[16] Currently price proposals tend to be submitted at the beginning of December and to be agreed the following spring—often with immediate effect for the dairy and beef sectors and only a four-month gap before implementation in the cereals sector (i.e. after sowings for that season have been completed).

Indeed, since November 1973 it has been the Commission's policy (Commission, 1973) to delay its price proposals to the end of the calendar year preceding the beginning of the next marketing year so as to have more up to date information available to it when making its proposals. The effect of this shortening of the price fixing timetable is to delay the effect of any alterations in support price levels and ratios on production levels and patterns to the next but one marketing year, thus making it more difficult to exert any immediate effects.

Consultations in the review

These annual price proposals are only made by the Commission after consultations with various interests. One of the UK fears when negotiating for entry into the Community in 1971 was that the right of farmers to be consulted before the proposals were made (which applied in the UK under its existing system of agricultural support), would be diluted in the Community context. The Community allayed these fears by pointing out that 'before, during and after the drawing-up by the Commission of . . . the price proposals, contacts take place with the professional agricultural organizations organized at a Community level', and that contacts were also maintained 'with industrial, commercial and trade union circles and with consumers'. The UK accepted that the existing review had 'the intention to have effective and meaningful contacts in particular with producer organizations operating at a Community level'.[17] Although the Commission has accepted the importance of consumer interests, their weight in the price-setting process will always be less than that accorded to producer interests until the structure of the Council of Agriculture Ministers changes. This, however, can only occur as individual Member States come to terms with the development of the consumer lobby.

Factors affecting the Council's decisions on support prices

Although it is the Commission which makes the prices proposals each year, it is the Council of Ministers which takes the final decisions as to the levels of support prices. The factors which the Commission takes into account include the results of the 'objective method',[18] the Community's general economic situation, the situation on overseas markets, and in particular the market situation for the main commodities. The Commission has felt itself increasingly constrained by the persistence of 'surpluses' and the Budget costs of their disposal. Generally the Council has only been able to reach agreement on the basis of a higher rise in common prices than proposed by the Commission (Table 3.4).

There are various reasons for this development. First, there has been the increased difficulty which the EC has experienced in taking decisions of any sort, let alone decisions as complex, because of differing national interests, as those related to CAP support prices. While the factors leading to a slowing in the Community's decision-taking ability are several, and not necessarily obvious, the result has been to make the annual price fixing meetings the occasion for settling all the major outstanding CAP policy matters in one composite package. In consequence the agenda becomes burdened with many issues not directly related to the setting of farm prices, and the level of prices itself becomes a negotiable item in the construction of an all-embracing package which settles many issues at once.

Second, there has been the re-emergence of a degree of national control over farm prices in the second half of the 1970s, in particular, because of the effect of the agri-monetary system in allowing individual Member States to set the conversion rates to be used for converting common prices into their national currencies. A detailed discussion of the green conversion rate system cannot be attempted here, but must be deferred to Chapter 8. The then President of the European Commission, Roy Jenkins (1978), characterized the situation at that time as 'when national prices in francs, lira and pounds are affected more by green devaluations and revaluations than by the common prices, there is a process of re-nationalization of the CAP'.

The agri-monetary factor led to an upward pressure on Council price decisions because of its asymmetric bias. For countries with depreciating currencies there was the ability to award price increases in national currencies to their farmers through devaluations of their agricultural conversion rates. Hence these countries (typically Italy, the UK, Ireland, and France during the 1970s) were to an extent indifferent to the level of common prices. Whereas for countries

Table 3.4 Commission price proposals and council price decisions. (Average percentage increase in support prices expressed in units of account for all CAP commodities).

	Commission proposals for common prices	Council decisions for common prices
1974/75*	7.2 + 4.0	8.8 + 5.0
1975/76	9.0	9.6
1976/77	7.5	7.7
1977/78	3.0	3.9
1978/79	2.0	2.1
1979/80	0.1	2.1
1980/81	2.4	4.8
1981/82	8.0	9.4
1982/83	9.0	10.4

* A second round of price fixing took place in October 1974.

SOURCE House of Lords (1982, p. xvi.); and *The Economist*, 22 May 1982, p. 75..

with appreciating currencies (typically Germany, the Netherlands and, in the early 1980s, the UK) the effects were reversed: any change in their agricultural conversion rates led to a drop in their national farm prices. Hence, if their farmers were to receive an annual price increase this had to come from the common prices agreed by the Council. Consequently it was in their interest to argue for a larger common price increase than proposed by the Commission.

Because of the complexity of the package that has to be constructed each year there are opportunities open to a Member State wanting a particular decision for a minor commodity, of interest mainly to itself, for holding-up agreement on the entire package until it achieves its wish. This third reason for Council price decisions tending to be higher than Commission proposals might be described as the lowest common denominator factor—that is, agreement is only ever secured on the lowest common denominator which all Member States can accept. In price-fixing terms this means that Member States argue for price increases in commodities of particular interest to themselves, and as a quid pro quo, will accept increases for commodities of more importance to other Member States.[19]

NOTES

1 Various authors have dealt briefly with the development of the CAP in the 1960s (e.g. Warley, 1967; Butterwick and Neville-Rolfe, 1968; Marsh and Ritson, 1971; Tracy, 1982) and there have been various studies of the political development of the Community. However, a definitive account of the struggles to establish the food and farm policies of the Community is still lacking.

2. The General Agreement on Tariffs and Trade (GATT) is the major international forum within which trade issues are negotiated and agreements policed. As a consequence of the formation of the EEC it was expected that intra-EEC trade flows would develop in preference to, or even in place of, trade between EEC members and

other countries. For this the other GATT signatories were entitled to compensation. One of the aims of the Dillon Round (1960–1962), named after C. Douglas Dillon, Under-Secretary of State in the United States administration, was to negotiate this compensation. The Kennedy Round (1964–1967) failed in its objectives of liberalizing international trade in agricultural products, but was more successful in manufactures. For an invaluable review, see Warley (1976).

3. Some commentators might add a sixth factor: the upheavals of the international monetary system and the subsequent introduction of border taxes and subsidies (known technically as monetary compensatory amounts—MCAs) in intra-Community trade. Although this development was not unimportant, it could be argued that its significance lay in the fact that MCAs relieved unresolved disputes over the level of support prices, particularly after the first enlargement of 1973. These issues are discussed in Chapter 8.

4. A GATT binding is a formal commitment, by the country or region concerned, not to increase the tariff (or further restrict the access conditions) unless agreed within the GATT forum; and entered into presumably in exchange for some concession in another aspect of trade policy by another GATT signatory.

5. The Community's own resources are defined in Chapter 13.

6. The Treaty specified that there would be a twelve-year transitional period (extending to 1 January 1970) divided into three four-year stages.

7. COM (68) 1000 actually comes in six parts. However, it is Part A (together with its statistical annex—Part B) entitled *Memorandum on the Reform of Agriculture* that has always attracted most attention and which is still worth reading today, though copies are few and far between. Part A is in English translation. Specific proposals were also made to deal with the emerging surplus in the dairy sector (Part C), the first in a long succession of such documents.

8. (Ministère de l'Agriculture, 1969). Under one scenario the area of cultivated land in France would have had to fall by a third. For an English language summary of the Vedel Report by the Commission's rapporteur, see Bienayme (1970, pp. 11–25).

9. See, for example, Commission (1973), (1975), (1980), and (1981a). These documents together with the Mansholt Plan are the working documents cited in this text which are worth seeking out, despite the difficulties involved.

10. The Commission's proposals were further elaborated in another policy document of October 1981 (Commission, 1981b). The Community's budgetary problems, and the background to the Mandate document, are discussed in Chapter 13.

11. The commitment varies from product to product. For some, such as most cereals, the obligation is open ended; whereas for other products the commitment is more circumscribed. Thus for sugar only production within the maximum quotas is eligible, while for sheepmeat intervention is only available in certain regions at certain times of the year.

12. The following is a simplified analysis of agricultural policy in the style popularized in Europe by Josling (Josling, 1969).

13. The description of the reference price policy mechanism in the text has been simplified. Some additional features are introduced in Chapter 7.

14. In Community eyes the export refunds are not export subsidies as such, as they are only meant to be large enough to enable Community exporters, buying domestic production at high internal prices, to compete on world markets. In other words the difference between domestic and world prices is being refunded to exporters.

15. For a commentary on the Community's reaction to the 1972/74 world commodity boom, see Harris (1975). In 1980 world sugar prices were again in excess of domestic support levels.

16. For a list of dates of Commission price proposals, and Council decisions, see Ries (1978, pp. 183–193).

17. 'Declaration on the system for fixing Community farm prices', *Official Journal of the European Communities*, Special Edition of 27 March 1972.
18. The information used in the 'Objective Method' calculations is described in Veer (1979). For an analysis of the issues raised by the 'Objective Method', see Swinbank (1979).
19. For a full discussion of the process of fixing agricultural support prices in the Community, see Harris and Swinbank (1978).

REFERENCES

Bienayme, A. (1970) 'The Vedel Report proposals for the reform of French agriculture', in Federal Trust, *Current Agricultural Proposals for Europe*, London.

British Government (1974) *Renegotiation of the Terms of Entry into the European Community*, Cmnd. 5593, HMSO: London.

Butterwick, M., and Neville-Rolfe, E. (1968) *Food, Farming and the Common Market*, Oxford University Press: London.

Commission of the European Economic Community (1958a), *Receuil des documents de la Conférence Agricole des Etats Membres de la Communauté Economique Européenne à Stresa du 3 au 12 Juillet 1958*, Brussels.

Commission of the European Economic Community (1958b) *First General Report on the Activities of the Community*, Brussels.

Commission of the European Communities (1968a) *Memorandum on the Reform of Agriculture in the European Economic Community*, COM (68) 1000, Part A, Brussels.

Commission of the European Communities (1968b) *Mesures a moyen terme pour différents marchés agricoles*, COM (68) 1000, Part C, Brussels.

Commission of the European Communities (1973) *Improvement of the Common Agricultural Policy*, COM (73) 1850, Brussels.

Commission of the European Communities (1975) *Stocktaking of the Common Agricultural Policy*, COM (75) 100, Brussels. This was published in *Bulletin of the European Communities*, Supplement 2/75, Brussels.

Commission of the European Communities (1979) *Changes in the Common Agricultural Policy to help balance the markets and streamline expenditure*, COM (79) 710, Brussels.

Commission of the European Communities (1980) *Reflections on the Common Agricultural Policy*, COM (80) 800, Brussels.

Commission of the European Communities (1981a) *Commission Report on the Mandate of 30 May 1980*, COM (81) 300, Brussels.

Commission of the European Communities (1981b) *Guidelines for European Agriculture*, COM (81) 608, Brussels.

Harris, S. (1975) *The World Commodity Scene and the Common Agricultural Policy*, Centre for European Agricultural Studies: Wye College.

Harris, S., and Swinbank, A. (1978) 'Price Fixing under the CAP—Proposition and Decision', *Food Policy*, **3**.

Heidhues, T., Josling, T., Ritson, C., and Tangermann, S. (1978) *Common Prices and Europe's Farm Policy*, Trade Policy Research Centre: London.

House of Lords Select Committee on the European Communities (1979) *Forestry*, Session 1979–80, 6th Report, HL 28, HMSO: London.

House of Lords Select Committee on the European Communities (1982) *Guidelines for European Agriculture and the 1982–83 Farm Price Proposals*, volume 1, Session 1981–82, 10th Report, HL 101, HMSO: London.

Jenkins, R. (1978) Speech given at the opening of the Royal Agricultural Show, Stoneleigh, UK, 3 July 1978.

Josling, T. E. (1969) 'A Formal Approach to Agricultural Policy', *Journal of Agricultural Economics*, **20**.

60

Marsh, J. S., and Ritson, C. (1971) *Agricultural Policy and the Common Market*, PEP/Chatham House: London.

Ministère de l'Agriculture (1969) *Perspectives à long terme de l'Agriculture Française 1968–1985*, Paris.

Priebe, H., Bergmann, D., and Horring, J. (1972) *Fields of Conflict in European Farm Policy*, Trade Policy Research Centre: London.

Ries, A. (1978) *L'ABC du Marché commun agricole*, Fernand Nathan and Editions Labor: Paris and Brussels.

Swinbank, A. (1979) 'The Objective Method, A Critique', *European Review of Agricultural Economics*, **6**.

Tracy, M. (1964) *Agriculture in Western Europe—Crisis and Adaptation since 1880*, Jonathan Cape: London.

Tracy, M. (1982) *Agriculture in Western Europe—Challenge and Response 1880–1980*, Second edition, Granada: London.

Veer, J. de (1979) 'The Objective Method', *European Review of Agricultural Economics*, **6**.

Warley, T. K. (1967) *Agriculture: the Cost of Joining the Common Market*, PEP/Chatham House: London.

Warley, T. K. (1976) 'Western Trade in Agricultural Products', in Shonfield, A. (ed.), *International Economic Relations of the Western World 1959–1971*, Vol. 1, Oxford University Press: London.

Zeller, A. (1970) *L'Imbroglio agricole du Marché Commun*, Calmann-Levy: Paris.

Chapter 4

The Cereals/Livestock Complex

In this chapter, the support mechanisms for cereals, pigs, and poultry are discussed. At first sight such an arrangement may seem strange. In terms of CAP support regimes, however, it is a logical link as pigs and poultry are regarded as processed cereals, and their support regimes are linked to that for cereals.

CEREALS

Importance of the regime

The support regime adopted for cereals is important in two major respects. First, cereals are a major cost component for the livestock industries. For modern intensive pig and poultry production, compound feedingstuffs (which consist principally of cereals) may account for over two-thirds of total production costs. For dairying and beef production, because of the use of extensive production systems based on grass, the cost of compound feedingstuffs and of cereals fed in unmixed form are not of such crucial importance, although they are still a major cost item, particularly for some producers. Taking the compound feedingstuffs produced in the EC as a whole, cereals accounted for just under 40 per cent by weight of the total ingredients used at the end of the 1970s (Commission, 1982a, p. 413). If the cereals fed in an uncompounded form to livestock were also taken into account, however, then the proportion by weight of the feedingstuffs used in animal feed accounted for by cereals rose to over 70 per cent (Commission, 1982a, p. 410).

The second major reason for the cereal regime's importance is that cereal production occupies a significant proportion of the EC's total agricultural land area. In 1975 in the then nine Member States cereals were grown on almost 60 per cent of the arable land, or 30 per cent of the total land area used in agriculture (Commission, 1980a, p. 284). Thus the level of price support given to cereals is an important factor in determining support price levels for other arable crops.

It is also important to note that the cereals regime was the first CAP support system to be adopted. Hence it was the first regime to be worked-out in depth. The arrangements adopted served as a model for the other products for which full support regimes were to be used. Not only was the type of regime adopted for cereals important, but also the level of support prices set. Because of German fears (due to the electoral significance of its small cereal growers at that time) the decision was taken to set a common price level toward the top of the range formed by the Member States' individual national cereal support prices. The consequence was that the support prices for the major livestock products and other arable crops had to be set at a level high enough to compensate.[1]

Economic Significance

Cereals are produced throughout the Community, but because of the wide span of latitude covered by the Member States, different cereals are grown in different parts. Thus maize cannot be grown economically in the north and successful production is restricted to Italy, Greece, and parts of France. Conversely, rye production is restricted to the north of the Community—principally Germany and Denmark, although a significant volume is grown in France. The pattern of production is shown in Table 4.1.

Despite their significance as a basic food, as a cost item for livestock production and as a crop grown throughout the EC, cereals are of smaller importance in the total value of agricultural production than might have been expected. This reflects the predominance of livestock production in Community agriculture. In 1980, all cereals (including rice) accounted for just under 13 per cent of the total value of agricultural production. By contrast the largest single livestock item—dairy products—accounted for almost 20 per cent (Commission, 1982a, p. 174) and livestock products as a whole—dairy, meat, eggs— accounted for some 56 per cent. In comparing cereals and livestock it should be noted, however, that not all cereals are counted in the total value of agriculture, as a significant proportion are consumed on the farms of production and never enter into commerce. The Commission (1980b, p. 59) estimated that about a third of EC cereal production is consumed in this way. In France about a quarter of cereal production is consumed on the farm of origin and in Germany about half (Commission, 1980b, p. 59).

The most important cereal type—in terms of the proportion of the value of agricultural production in the Community as a whole—is wheat. In 1980 it accounted for 7.2 per cent, followed by barley (3.2 per cent), and maize (1.7 per cent). The wheat grown in the EC does not on its own produce 'strong' flour suitable for use in the production of the type of bread favoured in the UK, hence the continued EC imports of North American wheats with relatively high protein contents suitable for producing these flours. Nevertheless, because of improvements in the quality of wheat grown in the EC and advances in baking technology, such imports have tended to drop. Some durum wheat is grown also, principally in Italy and destined for pasta production.

Table 4.1 Cereal production by Member States as a proportion of EC '10' total (1980). (Percentage).

	Greece	Germany	France	Italy	Netherlands	Belgium	Luxembourg	UK	Ireland	Denmark
Wheat	5.3	13.1	39.7	21.9	1.6	1.7	0.0	15.0	0.4	1.2
Rye	0.0	79.7	7.5	0.7	1.7	1.3	0.1	0.8	0.0	8.2
Oats	2.9	25.4	36.6	3.9	5.3	2.3	0.2	14.5	2.1	6.7
Barley	2.0	19.2	29.3	1.1	0.9	1.8	0.1	28.5	4.2	12.9
Maize	8.0	3.7	59.9	28.3	0.0	0.0	0.0	0.0	0.0	0.0
Rice	6.3	0.0	2.1	91.6	0.0	0.0	0.0	0.0	0.0	0.0

Note: EC '10' total equals 100.0.
SOURCE Commission (1982a, p. 176).

Coverage

The basic cereal support mechanisms were introduced in 1962,[2] and allowed a five-year transition period during which existing national support prices were to be harmonized. Unified common support prices throughout the Community came into effect on 1 July 1967.[3] Products covered are:

(a) The whole grains (common wheat, durum wheat, barley, maize, rye, oats, buckwheat, millet, canary seed, grain sorghum, 'other' cereals);
(b) Wheat and rye flour, groats and meals;
(c) First stage processed cereal products ('worked' cereals and cereal meals and groats, malt, gluten, cereal residues), starch (including starch containing roots), and glucose.

Budget Cost

Spending on the cereals regime has always been one of the most significant items in the total cost to the Community Budget of agricultural market support: in the late 1960s/early 1970s, cereals support accounted for some 30 to 40 per cent of total spending. In the mid-1970s, with higher world prices, spending on cereals fell to about 10 per cent, before showing a tendency to rise again at the start of the 1980s—reaching 17 per cent in 1981. The pattern of spending in selected years is shown in Table 4.2, while Chapter 13 sets out a full discussion of the role of the Budget in CAP operations.

Despite the emphasis placed on the role of intervention buying in other accounts of the cereals regime, in practice spending on export refunds has always been the largest single category of spending on cereal market support and one which has tended to rise over time—reaching nearly 70 per cent in the 1982

Table 4.2 Spending on the cereals regime by the Community Budget.

	1972	1977	1982
	(Actual)	(Actual)	(Provisional)
1. Total spending on cereals regime (ua in 1972, ecu in 1977 and 1982)	908.2	629.9	2115
2. As a percentage of total spending on farm price support	40.2	9.2	15.3
3. Main cereal support measures as a percentage of total spending on cereals	100.0	100.0	100.0
export refunds	50.2	58.1	62.8
denaturing premiums	7.7	—	—
production refunds	13.1	12.2	6.9
durum wheat production aid	11.9	21.4	8.3
storage measures	17.1	8.3	22.0

SOURCES Commission (1976, p. 377; 1980b, p. 254; 1982f, p. B/164).

Budget estimate. Spending on denaturing has stopped following its suspension in 1974; production refunds on cereals used for various food manufacturing operations have tended to decline; while the cost of the various intervention storage measures has varied.

It is seldom realized that unlike the dairy or sugar regimes, levies collected on imports cover a significant proportion of the cereal regime's costs. During the 1970s between a half and three-quarters of all Budget spending on the cereals regime was covered by import levies on cereals, mainly on maize and 'strong' wheat; although it should be recognized there is not a self-contained Budget section for cereals into which the income from cereal levies flows. The revenue from cereal levies forms part of the Community's Budget as a whole (Chapter 13).

However, the progressive rise in threshold prices, relative to intervention prices, brought about by the 'silo' system (see below) had the effect of reducing demand for imported cereals from 21.6 million tonnes in 1976/77 to an estimated 13.4 million tonnes in 1981/82, with a consequent loss of import levy income.

Support Measures

General description

The cereals regime uses a wide range of support measures—as might be expected with the archetypal CAP commodity regime. What is perhaps less expected is the extent to which the original measures devised in the 1960s needed to be modified in the 1970s as it was realized that they were over-elaborate and leading to undesired results (see later discussion). A significant feature of the cereals regime, which generally escapes notice, is the extent to which its coverage reaches forward from agriculture into the processing industries—especially cereal processing (e.g. to produce flour, malt, and various cereal meals and residues) but also the production of starch and glucose. Before discussing these points, however, the basic institutional support mechanisms must be summarized.

The full range of CAP support mechanisms described in Chapter 3 apply to the cereals regime. Thus there are three principal support prices. The *target prices* are the pivot of the system. They are set for durum wheat, common wheat, barley, rye, and maize and represent the level of market prices in Duisburg that farmers should receive for their sales. Duisburg in the Rhine Valley of West Germany is the centre of what is taken to be the Community's principal deficit area. The target prices form the upper end of a price band within which market prices fluctuate, the lower bound being set by *intervention prices*. Common intervention prices apply throughout the Community, abstracting for the moment from the complications of the green 'money' system discussed in Chapter 8, and the fact that new Member States are allowed a transitional period in which to adjust their price levels to the EC's common support level.

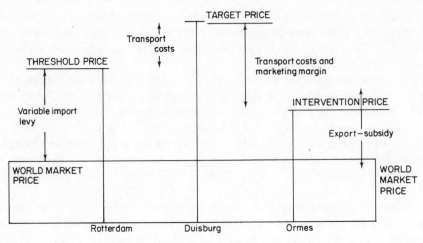

Figure 4.1   CAP price support for cereals.

Although the intervention prices apply throughout the Community their level, in relation to the target price, is nominally fixed for Ormes (the area of greatest surplus) and is lower than the target price by the cost of transport between the two centres and a 'marketing margin' (see Figure 4.1). The reader should be warned, however, that both target and intervention prices are set by the Council in response to political pressures, rather than in response to formal guidelines.

As a generalization, market prices for the main Community produced cereals, in most seasons, tend towards intervention prices because of the EC's excess of production over consumption.[4] Only for maize and 'hard' bread-making wheats, where the EC is less than self-sufficient, are market prices generally near target prices, as imports cannot undercut them. This is due to the *threshold prices* which are derived from target prices by allowing for transport costs from the Community frontier (taken as Rotterdam, the EC's main grain import port) to Duisburg. Threshold prices are set not only for the cereals for which target/intervention prices apply, but also for oats, buckwheat, millet, canary seed, grain sorghum, and the main cereal flours.

To prevent imports undercutting domestic prices, variable import levies are charged (see below) which cover the full difference between world prices and threshold prices. For the many processed products covered by the cereals regime, variable import levies are also charged, even though threshold prices are not set. Variable import levies on these processed products are set monthly by taking the import levies charged on the basic cereals, of which they are the processed form, and applying coefficients which, for example, take into account the weight loss involved in processing, and then incorporating a fixed element to protect EC processers. Such a derived method of calculation was adopted for these products as reliable world price series on which separate variable import levies can be directly calculated do not exist.

As described in Chapter 3, export refunds are granted to enable EC-produced cereals to compete on world markets. Generally the rates set are lower than for import levies (Figure 4.1) as domestic market prices are normally close to intervention prices and exporters only need refunds to cover the difference between their actual purchase prices on the internal Community market and the world market; whereas import levies cover the full distance from world prices to threshold prices which form the upper bound of the institutional support price band within which domestic market prices move. Figure 4.1 demonstrates another feature of the export refund system which again is not readily apparent. That is, the export refund is not an exact calculation, whereas that for the import levy is. This arises as the majority of refunds awarded are set by tender, and the refund rate traders are willing to bid for reflects varying market prices between different regions of the EC and traders' own supply/demand situations at the time of each tender as well as their differing assessments of the prices they can sell at on Third Country markets. As a result, it can be that the refund awarded to an EC exporter enables him to undercut other exporters in specific Third Country markets.

Regionalization and the width of the price band

The initial cereals regime provided little scope for domestic market prices to fluctuate according to market conditions. This was in part a continuation of the pre-EEC policies followed by the original '6'. The 'dirigiste' nature of these policies was reflected also in the apparent conviction that the market could not be relied upon to ensure that grain would flow naturally from surplus to deficit areas within the Community. This seems the only possible justification for the elaborate system of regionally differentiated intervention prices adopted for wheat, rye, and barley in the early 1960s. The system—known as regionalization—was adopted also for oilseeds, rice, and sugar.

The differences between the intervention prices, according to the basic cereals regulation while regionalization still applied, corresponded 'to the disparities in prices to be expected in a normal harvest under natural conditions of price formation on the market and allow the free movement of cereals within the Community in accordance with the requirements of the market'. Although this was the justification, in practice the system was based on transport costs.

There were four main classes of intervention prices (Butterwick and Neville-Rolfe, 1971, p. 69). These related to:

(i) centres (such as Duisburg and Marseilles) in the main deficit areas of the EEC;
(ii) centres (such as Rouen and Rotterdam) in the main ports;
(iii) centres (such as Chartres and Chateauroux) in the main production areas.

These three sets of centres were known as principal centres. From them

Table 4.3   Basic intervention prices as a proportion of
target prices. (Percentage).

	Barley	Common wheat	Maize
1967/68	93.15	92.94	84.96
1973/74	91.80	92.05	81.81
1974/75	87.38	90.31	81.82
1975/76	87.38	90.31	81.82
1976/77	84.18	86.18* 76.32†	81.42
1981/82	78.68	80.17* 71.67†	78.68
1982/83	78.53	79.29* 71.53†	78.53

* Wheat of minimum bread-making quality—reference price as
proportion of target price.
† Wheat not fulfilling the conditions for bread-making
quality—basic intervention price as a proportion of target price.

(iv) prices in secondary centres were derived using transport costs.

For 1971/72 there were 37 'principal' marketing centres in the original '6' and a
further 782 'secondary' marketing centres.

Regionalization was abandoned for rye in 1973, barley in 1974, and common
wheat in 1976. Since then, single flat-rate prices have applied throughout the
Community, although the number of intervention centres has been
maintained.[5] The single flat-rate intervention prices have been set at 'the lowest
derived intervention prices which would have been fixed in the Community'
(Regulation 2727/75) had regionalization still applied. Partly as a result of the
abandonment of regionalization and partly as deliberate policy, the
institutional support price band within which cereal market prices fluctuate has
been widened markedly. This can be seen from Table 4.3.

This change reflects the Community's experience that an institutionally-
determined set of intervention prices could never hope to reflect the conditions
of any particular season when small climatic differences could significantly alter
a region's net cereal balance. Consequently it gradually came to be accepted
that the system of regionalization for intervention prices probably did more to
distort than to smooth grain flows. One particular reason for this was its
rigidity. Once the system had been set up, vested interests were created to
defend the existing pattern of price relationships between intervention centres.
Hence the system could not be amended easily to take account of changes in the
cereal balance between areas.

The hierarchy of cereal support prices

When common support prices were introduced on 1 July 1967, the ratios of the
cereal support prices, one to another, seem to have been arbitrarily set and
related to the levels applying in the '6' before the EC's creation. The most

noteworthy feature was the treatment of common wheat which had the highest intervention price, reflecting the traditional view of wheat as the premier food grain, whereas the other grains had generally lower, and differing, intervention prices reflecting their main use as animal feedingstuffs.[6] It was found, however, that the relative narrowness of the gap between intervention and target prices for each cereal, together with the seemingly arbitrary relationship between the support prices for the various cereals resulted, in the Commission's view, in unnecessarily high import volumes, while too much Community grain was being sold into intervention.[7] The narrower the institutional price band for any particular cereal then the more likely it is that the peripheral, deficit, regions obtain their supplies from Third Countries rather than surplus regions within the Community. Of equal importance, was the paradoxical result that the production of maize (for which the EC had, and still has, a substantial deficit) was not encouraged, whereas the production of common wheat (for which the EC was approximately in balance) was over-encouraged. Consequently, the EC was generating surpluses of common wheat and barley, while still needing to import large quantities of maize.

The principal defects in the original system identified by the Commission were; first that the intervention price for wheat was set at too high a level (as it was premised on wheat being used for food); and second, that there was no differentiation between wheat for bread-making and wheat for animal feed. As a result high yielding varieties of wheat had been developed which were not of bread-making quality, but which were eligible for support buying at the bread-making wheat intervention price leading to large purchases of feed wheat into intervention. Thirdly, the intervention prices for the other grains did not reflect their relative nutritional values as animal feedingstuffs.

By 1973 the Commission had come to accept the need for a better hierarchy of cereal support prices and for the abolition of regionalized intervention prices: it called for changes to both in its 'Improvement of the CAP' document of that year (Commission, 1973). However, the Council took over two years to act, so that it was not until the 1976/77 season that the first stages in the rationalization of cereal prices were taken, when a single intervention price for wheat (not of bread-making quality) was introduced at the same level as that for barley. The maize intervention price was put at the same level as that for barley and feed wheat in 1978/79, while that for rye was aligned in 1982/83, see Table 4.4.

Table 4.4   Ratios of basic intervention prices; barley taken as reference point.

	Barley	Common wheat	Maize	Rye
1967/68	100.00	116.18	90.59	102.94
1973/74	100.00	109.46	86.99	101.30
1976/77	100.00	100.00	96.72	106.90
1978/79	100.00	100.00	100.00	107.14
1982/83	100.00	100.00	100.00	100.00

The outcome is the so-called 'silo' (or 'cathedral') hierarchy of grain support prices—Figure 4.2. Under this system, a single flat-rate intervention price applies for all the feedgrains throughout the Community (including wheat not of bread-making quality) with the objective of allowing market forces to set

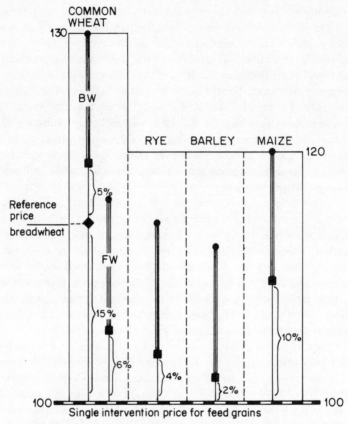

Figure 4.2 The silo system for cereal prices. ■ = market prices in surplus areas (Orléans/Ormes); ● = market prices in deficit areas (Duisburg); ═ = regionalization element (transport costs Orléans/Duisburg); BW = wheat of bread-making quality; FW = wheat not of bread-making quality.

(1) The market prices for barley, maize, rye, and feed wheat are differentiated according to their relative nutritional values.

(2) The Commission assumes that, even in surplus areas within the EC, market prices will be slightly above intervention levels: 2 per cent for barley and 5 per cent for bread-making quality wheat.

(3) The difference between the reference price for wheat of bread-making quality and the single intervention price applying to wheat not of bread-making quality is meant to reflect the lower yields of bread-making quality wheat varieties.

SOURCE   Based on Commission (1982e, p. 13).

price relativities between the grains, rather than attempting to set them institutionally. The single intervention price for feed grains provides a common floor, while the maize target price provides an effective ceiling for feed grain market prices as the EC is still a substantial net importer of maize. By providing a common floor, and at the same time widening the band between intervention and target prices, much greater scope is left for market forces to set market prices so that they reflect relative nutritional values[8] and supply/demand in any given season. At the same time, by widening the price band, the degree of Community preference over Third Country imports was increased. As a result of the new system, one of the Commission's main aims of reducing the need for intervention buying appears to have been achieved.

Denaturing and incorporation

The revised arrangements for wheat under the 'silo' system take much further the distinction between bread and feed wheats than that which applied under the original cereals regime. Although there was then a single intervention price for all wheat, denaturing and incorporation payments were granted on wheat used for animal feeding. The effect of the payments was to make wheat competitive as a feed grain. The premia were meant to compensate for the difference between the prices of milling wheat and barley. They were paid to compounders where EC milling wheat was incorporated in animal feedingstuffs. Where wheat was used by farmers direct, it was denatured with dye or fish oil to ensure it did not re-emerge on the milling wheat market.

Denaturing acquired a negative political image, however, because it was said surpluses of food grains were being created which were not going to humans, but instead were being 'wasted' in animal feed uses. During the 1973 and 1974 difficulties on the world cereals market (marked by shortages and high prices), the Community effectively suspended denaturing in February 1974 when the premium was set at zero, although the provisions permitting denaturing did not lapse finally until 31 July 1976.

Hence a major aim of the 'silo' system for wheat, in the Commission's eyes has been to 'permit the use of surplus common wheat to meet [feedgrain] market requirements, without the need for permanent intervention measures' (Commission 1979, p. 15). In other words, to allow wheat to be competitive as a feedgrain so avoiding the need for substantial intervention buying. This policy has not been as successful, up to the time of writing, as hoped originally, as more wheat than needed by EC millers has been classed as being of bread-making quality and hence eligible for the bread-making wheat support arrangements (see below) so making it uncompetitive as a feed grain.

The arrangements for wheat of breadmaking quality

The EC's main difficulty with the revised cereals regime has lain in the arrangements for wheat. While the concept of allowing feed wheat to compete in the animal feed market with the other feed grains was desirable economically, its acceptance by the Member States depended on the introduction of politically satisfactory arrangements for bread-making wheat. This was achieved by the introduction of a fourth institutional support price into the cereals regime—a *reference price* applicable only to wheat of bread-making quality and set at some 12 per cent above the common feedgrain intervention price. For its first season of operation (1976/77) the reference price operated as a normal intervention price for bread-making wheat. Since then, however, it has operated (and still operates) as an indicator of the need for special intervention measures for the rest of the year. Starting with the 1981/82 season, however, the reference price was split to give a lower level for wheat of minimum bread-making quality and a higher level for wheat of average bread-making quality.

The EC's ability to have a separate institutional support price for wheat of bread-making quality depends crucially on the ability to distinguish reliably such wheat. Millers have always applied commercial criteria which have been flexible enough to vary according to the quality of a particular season's harvest. The Commission had a more difficult task as it had to devise objective tests which could be applied equally throughout the EC. Hence, almost by definition, the tests could not easily be made flexible and thus could not take into account millers' subjective judgements as to the acceptability of a particular grain sample given the circumstances of that season. In the end, a mechanical test of 'dough machinability' was introduced:[9] a wheat sample which fails this is ruled not to be of bread-making quality and hence ineligible for support at the reference price. A difficulty has been that the EC produces some 42 million tonnes of wheat capable of meeting the standards (applicable at the time of writing) governing bread-making quality, whereas the EC uses not more than half this quantity for bread-making. The result is to discourage its use for animal feed and to increase the Budget cost of subsidizing its export.

Special intervention measures

Special intervention measures may be introduced for wheat of bread-making quality to support market prices at the reference price. These can take the form of any, or all, of the following:

(a) Storage payments by intervention agencies to private holders, so that grain is held off the market (commonly known as Intervention B). This is similar to the private storage arrangements frequently applied under the EC's support regimes for the livestock products and wine;

(b) As above, but giving intervention agencies the right to buy the grain at the expiry of the storage contracts;

(c) Buying by intervention agencies at the reference price (i.e. normal intervention, commonly known as Intervention A). This has happened in the first three months of each season since 1977/78, but such intervention is not automatic and has to be specifically agreed by the management committee procedure each season;

(d) Buying by intervention agencies through tenders.

The necessity for the use of these measures is decided upon by the Commission, on a season-by-season basis, under the management committee procedure. The normal intervention arrangement for feedgrains is that intervention buying is always available. By contrast, the measures for bread-making quality wheat are not continuously available. Before they can be used, there has to be specific authorization—normally for a limited period.

Special intervention measures may apply also for feedgrains. The provisions are very general: basically 'any operation which avoids risks of heavy sales into intervention is eligible to be approved . . .'. (HGCA, 1979, p. 44). Measures which have been used have included the payment of a slightly higher price for grain than the normal intervention price so as to forestall a market collapse, paying to private traders the financial costs of storage, moving grain to other areas of the EC with a transport subsidy, and making the seasonal scale applied for storage more attractive.

Monthly increments

In order to ensure an even flow of grain on to the domestic market throughout the year, a system of monthly increments is applied to threshold, intervention, reference, and target prices. This system is designed to ensure that market prices rise during the season, due to the monthly increases in institutional support prices, by enough to cover the costs of storage. In effect, grain which is harvested in two to three months of the year is made available without hiccups in its supply throughout the rest of the year, while carry-over payments are available generally at the end of each season, so that grain can be carried into the following season despite the drop in intervention prices at its start because of the seasonal scale.

Import levies

In Chapter 3, the operation of import levies and export refunds was explained in outline. For the calculation of import levies in the cereals sector the EC has a sophisticated system for collecting, on a daily basis, the world prices on which the levy calculation is based. Although the procedures followed are reasonably objective, elements of judgement are involved. In practice, this means that in all cases of doubt the Commission will err on the side of caution and the levy, as set, will probably be larger than necessary. The procedure followed is:

(a) The daily collection of world prices on the basis of c.i.f. offers to the EC. 'The number of quotations received is in the region of 80 for wheat, 22 for oats, 4 for buckwheat, 9 for rye, 17 for barley, 60 for maize, 20 for millet, 21 for sorghum and 7 for canary seed . . . only one quotation is adopted for each cereal; this is a matter for judgement'. (Commission, 1979, Annex III, p. 5).

(b) If the Commission does not feel the offers reported to it are representative of world prices, it has discretion to synthesize world prices on the basis of prices at the main US markets (Chicago and Kansas City) plus prevailing internal US and trans-Atlantic freight and insurance rates.

(c) Because the levy calculation is based on the lowest 'representative' price for each type of cereal c.i.f., world prices have to be corrected to a standard quality basis Rotterdam (Table 4.5). This entails two sets of corrections. First, offers to other EC ports have to be brought to a Rotterdam basis by adjusting for freight rate differences between ports. Second, and more importantly, 'in order to make the qualities, grades, categories or varieties of imported cereals comparable with the Community standard quality, coefficients of equivalence have been created, which are added to or deducted from the c.i.f. price of a given cereal'. (Commission, 1979, Annex III, p. 2). These coefficients—which basically represent observed historic market price differentials—were originally set in 1967 and revised in 1971. That they have been unrevised for so long 'may have led to distortions in the prices of imported cereals' (*Agra Europe* undated, p. 10–09).

(d) World prices have to be converted to European currency units (ecu's) for the final part of the levy calculation. For this step, special conversion rates are calculated which relate market rates of exchange for Third Country currencies to ecu's via the central rates of the Community currencies fully participating in the European Monetary System (EMS). These conversion rates are reviewed weekly and modified if necessary.

Table 4.5 Example of the calculation of the variable import levy for common wheat.

1. Imported wheat type	Soft Red Winter 2	Hard Winter 2 Ordinary	Dark Hard Winter 2 (13.5%)	Northern Spring 2 (14%)
2. C.i.f. price in US dollars/tonne (ex-Rotterdam)	157.00	152.00	153.00	159.00
3. Coefficient of equivalence in ecu/tonne	(–4.54)	(–10.89)	(–13.61)	(–15.12)
in dollars/tonne	–6.06	–14.54	–18.18	–20.20
4. Corrected c.i.f. price in dollars/tonne (2–3)	150.94	137.46	134.82	138.80
5. Exchange rate applicable from 25 April 1979 for converting world market price data in dollars to ecu	1 US dollar = 0.748741 ecu			
6. C.i.f. price in ecu/tonne	113.00	102.93	100.96	103.94
7. Threshold price in ecu/tonne	199.94	199.94	199.94	199.94
8. Levy in ecu/tonne			98.98	

Note: Lowest offer price underlined.
SOURCE Commission (1979, Annex III, p. 14).

(e) After the lowest representative world price for the EC standard quality for each cereal has been calculated (Table 4.5), it is deducted from the Community's threshold price to give the unit import levy to apply for the following 24 hours starting at midnight.

Problems of the import levy calculation

Despite the thoroughness of its import levy calculation, the Commission has reservations about the system's operation. In particular, it fears that exporters to the world market may work together to manipulate world prices against the Community. Thus the Special Committee of Inquiry (Commission, 1979, Annex III, p. 7) referred to 90 per cent of the world market being 'controlled by a small number of multinational companies which virtually determine world prices', and claimed that this domination had tended to increase which 'could become a source of concern'. Subsequently, however, the Commission (1982c, p. 22) appears to have qualified its reservations by pointing out that inter-governmental transactions and open tenders accounted for 'a large part' of world trade in cereals and stating that it believed 'competition between commercial operators is such as to prevent the formation of artificial prices'.

The Commission also knows that, despite its best efforts, cereals can (and do) enter the Community—after import levy has been paid—at under the threshold prices. There are three principal reasons for this.[10] First, currency fluctuations have been wide enough and erratic enough at times to allow traders to buy cereals at significantly more favourable exchange rates than those used by the Commission in its import levy calculation—with the result that cereals may be saleable at a cheaper price, in ecu terms, than that assumed by the Commission for the import levy calculation.

Second, although the Commission carefully discovers spot and forward cereal prices for the purpose of setting levies, it cannot discover traders' actual costs. For example, a trader may have been able to buy grain and/or freight more cheaply than the official market quotations. By skilful use of the futures markets at particular times, a trader in effect can cheapen his physical purchase price. As Debatisse (1981, p. 34) points out 'The combination of purchasing/sales operations, transport, exchange and hedging frequently enables items to be sold at a lower price than that at which they were purchased, while still making a profit'.

Third, the Community needs to import cereals, particularly 'strong' North American wheats for the bread grist and maize for industrial purposes. The user industries need to be assured of a regular flow of supplies throughout the year based on forward contracts. For this purpose, the industries must know in advance the price they will have to pay for their imported raw materials, of which as much as half may be represented by the EC import levy. Sales to processors commonly therefore are made on a 'levy-paid' basis, i.e. the seller is responsible for the levy. To make this possible the Community allows importers to fix the levy in advance. Some 80 per cent of cereal import licences have the levies advance fixed (Commission, 1979, Annex III, p. 5). This facility, when world cereal prices are dropping, can be used to ensure that the grain pays a lower levy than that prevailing on the day of import, and hence enters the EC under the threshold price.[11] Such opportunities arise only infrequently and the Commission can (and does) protect itself against this by suspending the advance fixing facility when it considers that world market prices (e.g. because of uncertainties about harvest prospects, or exchange rates) are fluctuating abnormally. Such suspensions tend to cause a furore among traders, but the Commission considers its primary duty is to ensure that undue advantage is not taken of the pre-fixing facility.

The mechanics of advance fixing are relatively simple. Traders, when applying for an import licence, may specify that the rate of import levy is to be that in operation on the day of application. For most of the grains, these licences have a 45-day validity. If the trader has timed his application correctly, then by the time he declares the grain to EC Customs officials, the world price will have dropped and a higher unit import levy will be applicable than that fixed on his licence. The importance of this facility may be judged from the fact that there is a market in advance fixed licences among traders.

Although grain may (and does) enter the Community at under threshold prices, in practice the discounts tend to be relatively small—normally not more than (say) US $5 a tonne. Discounts are not larger because the traders' ability to cheapen their purchase prices is limited, and because traders will not wish to undercut EC domestic market prices as this reduces their profit margins. Further, the high protein North American wheats suitable for making 'strong' bread-making flours can never enter under the threshold price for wheat because the EC system of coefficients ensures that they face an import levy significantly larger than that on EC standard quality wheat.

Export refunds

In Chapter 3, the EC's use of export refunds to enable it to compete on world markets was discussed. Some of the more specific issues involved with export refunds in the cereals sector are elaborated here. As a general point, the Commission increasingly tends to use export refunds to dispose of excess EC grain early in the season as it finds this cheaper than taking grain into intervention—paying storage charges—and having to export the grain anyway with an export refund later in the season (HGCA, 1981). However, the Commission does not follow a consistent policy in this respect, for example because it is deterred by low world prices and thus the cost of refunds from encouraging exports (as was the case in 1982) or by budgetary constraints at the end of the financial year.

For cereals the EC uses two systems for fixing export refunds. First, there is a system of standing rates of export refund which are available at all times, and second a system of weekly export tenders. The use of export tenders in the cereals regime was not developed widely until 1976. Since then, however, tenders have become the main method for setting refunds: it was estimated that by 1979 more than 70 per cent of wheat and barley exports were with export licences awarded at the tenders, rather than with licences taking the standing rate of refund (Commission, 1979, Annex III, p. 8). As a complement to its proposals for Long Term (multi-annual) Agreements for the supply of agricultural products to Third Countries (discussed in Chapter 11), the Commission has proposed, however, an increased use of standing refunds to give it a greater capacity to control the volume of exports to specific destinations.

Every week, after consulting the management committee, the Commission must fix the standing refund. Its procedure as set out by the Commission (1979, Annex III) was as below. More recently the method for fixing export refunds has been less precise as the Commission has been very concerned to ensure that the standing refund rate is below that set at the tenders.

(a) Find EC f.o.b. prices in the most competitive export areas—Rouen for common wheat; the UK for barley early in the season; and France for barley later on.

(b) After corrections for national price differences because of the green conversion rate system, conversion to US dollars at the going rate of exchange.

(c) EC prices (f.o.b. in US dollars) are then compared with f.o.b. prices in US dollars offered by other exporters—principally the USA and Argentina. 'The average difference represents the potential refund, but is only a guide. At this stage it serves only as a yardstick' (Commission, 1979, Annex III, p. 10).

(d) The differences in US dollars are then converted to ecu's using the average dollar/ecu exchange rates calculated for import levy purposes.

(e) The unit export refund rates are then set for each cereal as 'somewhere around the average of the differences between the prices calculated, having due regard to quality factors and to the market appraisal by the management committee' (Commission, 1979, Annex III, p. 10).

(f) The rates of export refund are differentiated by destination to take account of the differing freight costs involved in reaching them. For this purpose, Third Countries are divided into seven zones, although some countries—Malta, Switzerland, and Yugoslavia—are treated individually and may have specific refund rates set. (Often refunds are not set for all zones, but only for 'nearby' destinations, e.g. Switzerland and Scandinavia, or for countries where there is a specific trading need for a short period, e.g. Africa south of the Sahara.)

(g) As with the import levies, advance fixing is also allowed for export refunds which may be set for the current month plus two months ahead. As with advance fixed import levies, correctives are set taking account of any major divergence between spot and forward prices.

For refunds set at the export tenders, the procedures are very different. First, tenders may not be held throughout the cereal year. During the period that tendering is permitted (the length of which will vary according to season) the tenders are held weekly. Traders bid through their national intervention agencies who pass the bids on in an anonymous form to the Commission. The bids are then ranked by the Commission with the cheapest bids (i.e. those wanting the smallest rates of export refund) at the head of the list. The Commission compares the bids with its own estimate of what unit refund rates are necessary. It will accept bids only up to this level, or up to any quantity bar it may be operating if the total of accepted bids has reached such a level before the Commission's maximum potential rate of refund is arrived at. The refunds awarded at the tenders are open market ones valid for anywhere in the world, although there is a provision to restrict exports to particular countries or zones. During the US embargo on grain sales to the USSR at the beginning of the 1980s, the zoning system was used to hold separate tenders for Eastern Europe and to exclude the USSR from any of the tenders.

The Commission likes the export tender system as it allows greater control over the volume of EC exports. Also, it generally proves cheaper to the Community Budget than the standing refund system as traders are competing against each other to secure export licences. An advantage for traders of the tender system is that the licences have a longer period of validity—month of issue plus four months.

Export levies

When world prices are near to or above EC threshold prices, the system is reversed and export levies are fixed. Traders, instead of bidding for export refunds, bid for levies. Unlike import levies, export levies are not fixed according to a set formula, but are set at levels sufficiently high in order to ensure an 'orderly' domestic cereal market. The effect of the levies is to prevent EC domestic prices from following upward trends in world prices. Up to the time of writing, export levies for cereals have been only applied in 1974 and 1975.

Cereal surpluses and the problem of cereal substitutes

Traditionally the EC has been a net importer of cereals. 'However since 1960, apart from the exceptional years of 1975 and 1976 when the harvests were very poor, Community production has been going up more rapidly than consumption' (Commission, 1979, p. 12). As a result the EC's degree of self-sufficiency for all cereals rose from some 85 per cent at the time of the EC's first enlargement, to over 100 per cent at the beginning of the 1980s (see, for example, Table 4.6).

Between the individual cereals, however, the position differs widely. For maize the EC has been, and is likely to remain, a substantial net importer, particularly of maize for industrial purposes (such as the manufacture of starch/glucose and distilling). By contrast, for common wheat and barley the

Table 4.6   EC cereal self-sufficiency ratios. (Percentage).

	Total Wheat	Barley	Maize	All cereals
1956 to 1960 average	90	84	64	85
1973/74	104	106	56	92
1978/79	110	112	59	96

SOURCE   OECD (1974, p. 29), Commission (1977a, p. 212; 1982a, p. 222).

EC had a growing surplus during the 1970s. Thus in 1980/81, the Community, while importing some 11 million tonnes of maize and 3 million tonnes of 'strong' bread-making wheats, was itself exporting 11 million tonnes of common wheat and flour and between 5.5 and 6 million tonnes of barley.

For 1980/81, EC total cereal production reached 124 million tonnes. In its 'Guidelines' report, the Commission (1981, p. 26) suggested that in the absence of any changes in the cereals regime, production would reach 135 million tonnes by 1988. With usage for human consumption at best static, any increase in domestic usage had to come from the animal feedingstuffs sector. Yet, again according to the 'Guidelines' report, 'In the absence of any change in import conditions and relative prices, future additional demand for animal feed would be covered by imported substitutes rather than by Community cereals, and the increase in the Community's cereal production would therefore have to be exported . . .' (Commission, 1981, p. 26). As with other commodities, the spur to change has been the implications for the EC Budget. Were the Commission to be correct in its forecasts, then the Community would be faced with a significantly larger expenditure on export refunds in the cereal sector as the more cereal substitutes imported, the more cereals would have to be exported.

The background to this sombre outlook is that EC usage of so-called cereal substitutes[12] has expanded markedly following the growth of the EC's animal feed compounding industry, the development during the 1960s of computer techniques for minimizing the cost of compound animal feeds, and the increased availability of cereal substitutes on world markets at prices which made them attractive for inclusion in compound feeds relative to the EC's high domestic prices for cereals. Between 1975 and 1979, the proportion of cereals in EC-produced animal feeds dropped from 44 to 39 per cent.[13] By 1980, compound feeds were using some 14 million tonnes of cereal substitutes, as against 73 million tonnes of cereals as such (Commission, 1981b, p. 26).

Until 1981 the Commission had insisted on regarding the 'problem' of cereal substitutes as one which could only be solved by increasing the controls over their entry into the EC. In its proposals for 1982/83 CAP support prices, however, the Commission made a direct link between control over substitutes and the level of EC cereal prices compared with world prices. The Commission justified the application of controls over the import of cereal substitutes as being a temporary measure necessary only until EC cereal prices were closer to world levels and hence cereal substitutes were less competitive within the EC. For most of the products in question—brewers' and distillers' residues, maize gluten feed, fruit residues, and sugar beet pulp—the EC applies a nil rate of import duty bound in GATT. For manioc (perhaps the most widely known substitute) the EC applied up to 1982 a variable import levy up to a maximum yield of a 6 per cent tariff, also bound in GATT; while for cereal residues variable import levies apply—although it is claimed that the coefficients for deriving these are out-of-date and produce import charges which are too small.

For manioc the EC had negotiated 'voluntary' export restraints with the principal Third Country suppliers by 1982 whereby the Community was prepared to continue to apply a 6 per cent tariff on its imports from them, provided the volumes imported were restrained within agreed quota limits. For imports above the quota levels, however, the EC would apply a full variable import levy based on that for barley. It took the Community a long time to negotiate the quota arrangements as, its import tariff being bound in GATT, it had to negotiate with the countries affected: the quota restrictions could not be applied unilaterally. For 1982 up to 1984 inclusive, the quotas were agreed at almost 6 million tonnes—of which 5 million tonnes were earmarked for Thailand, half a million for Indonesia, 370 000 tonnes for China, and the rest (90 000 tonnes) for other GATT members (principally India and Brazil). For 1985 and 1986, although the total quota level at almost 6 million tonnes was unchanged, the levels earmarked for Thailand were reduced by half a million tonnes to allow for increased exports from, principally, Indonesia. To compensate Thailand for the limitation on the size of her manioc exports, the Community agreed to provide assistance for rural development and crop diversification projects.

On maize gluten the Commission also proposed in 1982 that there should be introduced a quota to control the growth in imports. The quota was to be set at 3 million tonnes—the then level of imports. The USA, however, objected very strongly to any limitation on her potential export volumes as maize gluten sales (which nearly all went to the EC) were a vital factor in the economics of the maize wet milling industry. Furthermore the GATT binding on maize gluten imports had been secured in the Dillon Round of GATT negotiations to provide compensation to GATT members for the CAP's creation and the likely trade diversion effects which would result. Hence, the binding on maize gluten was politically a particularly sensitive one for the USA. None the less, the Commission proposed that negotiations should be opened in the GATT, under Article XVIII, on the basis that continued increases in the EC's imports of maize gluten were disrupting its internal market for cereals and that compensation would be offered for restricting them to a level of 3 million tonnes annually.

For the residues of cereal milling, the Community altered in 1982 the coefficient used for calculating the import levy on bran with the effect of raising the levy charged. The EC could do this with comparatively little difficulty as there was not a GATT binding on the level of import charge to be applied.

Reform of the cereals regime

It was not until its 'Guidelines' document (Commission, 1981) that the Commission was prepared to accept that many of its difficulties with the cereals sector, and particularly with cereal substitutes, arose because domestic prices were set at too high a level. In the 'Guidelines', however, the Commission made a narrowing of the gap between EC and world prices for cereals its key proposal for reform. To this end, it suggested that over a period of years, EC cereal support prices should be lowered relatively to those in its principal competitors: it suggested that US domestic support prices for cereals would form a suitable reference point.

The Commission saw this approach as being helpful in four important respects:

(a) That the cost to the Budget of the cereals regime would be cut;
(b) That the EC tendency to surplus creation would be reduced;
(c) That demand for cereal substitutes would be lowered as domestically produced cereals became more competitive in price;
(d) That a relative lowering of cereal support prices would, in turn, make it possible to lower livestock support prices.

Quantitative limits were also proposed by the Commission for the volume of domestic cereal production that would be eligible for price support. It was suggested that a long-term production objective should be set of 130 million tonnes for total EC cereal production in 1988 and that for the intervening years interim targets should be set. The figure for 1988 was based on the EC maintaining its 1980 export volume and meeting all additional demand for cereals in animal feed from domestic production, rather than from imported cereal substitutes. When domestic production in any one year exceeded the target for that year, then—according to the Commission's proposal—intervention prices in the following year were to be cut.

The Council of Ministers in its decisions on 1982/83 CAP support prices adopted the Commission's proposal for production thresholds and set a level of 119.5 million tonnes of EC cereal production for 1982/83 (excluding durum wheat). It took two other decisions, however, which reduced the potential impact of the production threshold concept. The first was that a three-year average of production would be looked at, rather than just a single year's, so that only if the average of production in 1980/81 to 1982/83 exceeded the 119.5 million tonne threshold was the 1983/84 intervention price to be reduced. The second decision was that the threshold should be increased to the extent that imports of cereal substitutes exceeded 15 million tonnes.

The cereals regime and the processing industries

The EC's processing industries are affected by the cereals regime through its control over the ease (or otherwise) with which imports can enter the Community, and exports be made from the Community. Additionally, for the manufacture of certain products, production refunds are available.

The first stage processing industries are those producing a product based on one cereal where normally a change in its nature is not involved (e.g. cereal meals, groats, 'worked' cereals, flour). Import levies are charged on Third Country imports of these products. The levies consist of two elements: a so-called fixed component[14] representing a protection margin for the processer plus a so-called variable component, set monthly, based on an average of the first 25 days of the previous month's import levies for the basic cereal from which the product is derived. For exports, broadly speaking, refunds are set in the same manner as the variable component of the import levy. One peculiarity of the export refunds is that those for malt, because of the long-term nature of the trade, may be valid for up to 12 months when advance-fixed as against the current month plus four which applies for the licences on most other processed cereal products. A development in 1981 was that the export of spirit drinks was brought within the coverage of the cereals regime so that an export refund could be paid on the export of whisky to cover the higher cost of EC barley used in its production as compared with the price it was available to Third Country distillers. This provision was included in the cereal regime as agreement on an EC ethyl alcohol regime was still blocked.

The products, on the manufacture of which production refunds are available to ensure their competitiveness with Third Country imports, are:

(a) Starch[15] manufactured from maize, common wheat, broken rice, wheat flour, and potatoes;
(b) Glucose manufactured from maize groats and meal by the 'direct hydrolysis' process;
(c) Quellmehl used for bread-making and manufactured from maize, common wheat, and wheat flour;
(d) Groats and meal of maize and broken rice used for brewing.

The level of and relationship between these refunds has represented a constant source of difficulty for the Commission. In 1975 the production refunds for quellmehl manufacture and for the manufacture of groats and meal for brewing were withdrawn, but were reinstated by a judgement of the European Court in 1978. The major problems, however, involve starch manufacture.

There have been a number of changes—or proposed changes—in policy which have destabilized the industry. For example, in recent years the Commission has:

(a) Amended the original system by abolishing the system of supply prices[16] which applied up to 1975,
(b) Attempted to abolish the subsequent system of production refunds (without supply prices) over the two years 1977/78 and 1978/79,
(c) Proposed the abolition of production refunds for starch in food uses, but

their retention for starch going to non-food uses (Commission, 1977b), and

(d) At the beginning of the 1980s, pledged itself to make new proposals for reform.

Aid for starch manufacture was introduced originally as a means of enabling EC starch manufacturers, using CAP products as raw materials, to compete with synthetic substitutes available from the petrochemical industry. Subordinate reasons concerned the need to provide aid for starch potato growers (strongly concentrated in one region in North Holland) and the need to ensure a balance between the starches produced from different agricultural raw materials. Subsequently the Commission has wanted to scrap the system—in whole, or in part—because starch manufacture is regarded as a basic manufacturing industry having little in common with farming, while the refunds involve a cost to FEOGA and there is a feeling that domestic production subsidies should not be available for an industry mainly using imported raw materials (i.e. maize). The House of Lords (1977, p. vi) commented on the perverse fashion in which the starch arrangements had operated, as they felt that no policy continuity had been given the industry.[17]

The Commission (1982d, p. 19) explained some of the difficulties it faced in revising the arrangements for starch. It pointed to the need for any new arrangements to deal with the 'very difficult problems' of competition from starch and starch products imported from Third Countries at a low or nil import charge, the need to ensure a balance between the treatment given different sectors of the starch industry, and the possibility that the starch aid arrangements might have to be extended to products other than starch.

Durum wheat production aid

For durum wheat there is a fixed rate *production aid* paid per hectare sown. The aid, however, is only available to producers in economically disadvantaged areas (mainly in Greece and Italy). It is only available for durum of the requisite varieties and 'qualitative and technical characteristics establishing that pasta made therefrom is not sticky when cooked' and thus suitable for pasta production. These provisions were introduced following a large increase in the area of durum unsuitable for pasta production in France.

POULTRYMEAT AND EGGS

General Comment

The regimes for poultrymeat and eggs both came into operation on 1 July 1967. They may be considered as essentially one unified regime which happens to be expressed in two basic regulations.[18] The regime is closely linked to that for cereals, and for many purposes poultry and eggs are regarded as 'processed cereals'. There are no internal market support measures for eggs or poultrymeat. Because of the cyclical nature of poultry production, and the self-correcting nature of the market mechanism, it has always been felt by EC policymakers that it would be unwise to attempt to put a permanent 'floor' in the market through intervention because of the risk of building up large stocks extremely fast. This thinking has undoubtedly been reinforced by the increasingly 'industrial' nature of modern egg and poultry production—very far removed from the social problems of small farmers.

Economic Importance

Neither eggs nor poultry are very important in terms of EC agricultural production—thus poultrymeat provides just over 4 per cent of the value of final agricultural production in the EC and eggs about 3.5 per cent. Among the Member States there are wide divergences in the importance of their poultry industries. In only the UK is production, as a proportion of the total value of agricultural production, in double figures (at some 12 per cent). Italy, the Netherlands, Belgium, and France have industries whose percentage contribution to their countries' agricultural production is between 7 and 10 per cent.

Egg production is highly concentrated in terms of agricultural enterprises, so that, for example, holdings with more than 10 000 layers account for over half of the production in most EC countries and almost three-quarters in the UK and the Netherlands (Commission, 1982b). For poultrymeat, production is very concentrated in the northern countries of the EC with over 90 per cent of production coming from holdings with more than 10 000 birds. This is less so in France, Italy, and Greece where more traditional forms of production and marketing (drawn birds) are still important.

Budget Cost

Because of the lightly structured support regimes applied for eggs and poultry and because, relative to its production, the EC exports only a small amount (although these exports are very significant in world terms) the combined cost to the Budget of support for eggs and poultry is less than one per cent of total spending on market support. What Budget spending there is—estimated at 84 million ecu in 1981— is all on export refunds for sales to Third Countries.

Support Measures

The principal CAP policy instrument used for the protection of EC poultry/egg producers is the *basic import levy*. Because there is little international trade in poultry products, the levy is not calculated as the difference between world prices and an EC threshold price. Instead it is calculated on the basis of correcting for the difference between EC and world cereal prices (cereals being the single largest cost item for poultry production), plus a margin of protection.

Specifically the levy is made up of two components:

(a) For the quantity of feedgrains required to produce a kilo of poultry product, the difference between their cost on world markets and within the EC is calculated quarterly;

(b) To this is added the protective element set at 7 per cent of the sluice-gate price (see below) for the previous year. This element is calculated annually and applies from 1 August in each year.

Although the formulation of the basic levy, at first sight, seems reasonable taking into account differences in cereal costs and applying only a small margin of protection, in fact the system is more protective than it appears because of the working assumptions built into the calculations.[19] Both the basic levies and sluice-gate prices are multiplied by coefficients to get corresponding rates for egg products and poultry cuts.[20]

The basic levy, as revised quarterly, has to be paid on all imports. There is provision, however, for an *additional import levy* to be charged on offers to the EC which are below *sluice-gate prices*; the sluice-gate price being the computed cost of production with the feed ingredients costed at world market prices. This provision, to apply additional levies, is used regularly as a normal part of the poultry regime. Unlike basic import levies which may be estimated in advance, as a precise formula is used, additional levies are set by the Commission at whatever level it judges to be necessary and may only be paid by one country. Hence they are not forecastable. For countries which have agreed not to allow their offer prices to fall below sluice-gate prices, additional levies are not charged.

Sluice-gate prices are set quarterly paralleling the basic import levy calculation:

(a) The cost of the feedgrains in a prescribed ratio is calculated at world prices for the previous six months;

(b) A fixed allowance is added for transport costs;

(c) To this base cereal cost is applied a standard feed conversion ratio to get the cereal cost per kilo of product;

(d) A standard amount is then added covering the cost of other non-cereal feed elements and general production and marketing costs.

Export refunds are available from time to time to enable EC exporters to sell on the world market certain 'traditional' exports and, as a short term measure, to aid exports in times of EC oversupply. In principle, the refunds cover the difference between domestic market prices and world prices of cereals. The EC had, however, become a more regular (and more significant) exporter to world markets at the end of the 1970s. As a result poultrymeat was one of four commodities subject to a US complaint to GATT in 1982 about the EC's use of export refunds to take an inequitable share of world markets.

PIGMEAT

General Comment

In its support mechanisms the pigmeat regime[21] goes farther than that for eggs and poultrymeat in that it also provides for a measure of internal market support. It is still, however, a relatively lightly structured regime because of the cyclical nature of pig production, coupled with the self-correcting nature of the market mechanism and the fear that a more heavily structured regime would lead quickly to large surpluses. As with eggs and poultry, pigmeat is regarded as a processed cereal.

Economic importance

In terms of the value of EC agricultural production pigs account for some 12 per cent, and about 40 per cent (by weight) of meat production. In terms of geographical location production is concentrated in the areas bordering the North Sea and the English Channel, as well as in Northern Italy. In 1980 about 30 per cent of the value of EC production was in Germany, 16 per cent in France, and between 10 and 12 per cent each in the Netherlands, Italy, Denmark, and the UK.

As with poultry production, there is a trend to specialization, although it has not gone so far. Between 1977 and 1979, the number of farms with over 200 pigs increased by some 11 per cent, while farms with less than 50 pigs dropped by 14 per cent. To some extent what appears to be emerging is a dual structure with a sector of modern, specialized, highly intensive pig units at one extreme (where the majority of pigs will be), and at the other extreme farms with a few pigs which are kept principally for home use. The Commission (1982b, p. 154) points to a slower rate of decline in farms with only one or two pigs, as against those with between three and fifty pigs.

Budget cost

In 1981, spending by the EC Budget on pigmeat amounted to 155 million ecu, equal to some 1½ per cent of total spending on CAP market support. Around four-fifths of spending on pigmeat goes for export refunds, and the remainder on private storage aids.

Support measures

The regime covers not only live pigs, but also pig carcasses and cuts (in chilled, frozen, salted, dried, or smoked form), lard and unrendered pig fat, processed pigmeat products (including canned pigmeat and sausages), and pig offals. The full regime came into operation on 1 July 1967. The marketing year for support prices starts annually on 1 November.

As the Community is approximately self-sufficient in pigmeat, measures restricting imports would be insufficient on their own to maintain domestic market prices. Support for the internal market comes principally from three policy measures:

(a) A system of sluice-gate prices and import levies on Third Country products prevents the undermining of the Community market from outside;
(b) Export refunds are introduced as a means of removing supplies from the Community market which otherwise would have a price-depressing effect;
(c) Aids to private storage schemes are introduced to remove from the Community market temporarily surplus supplies of pigmeat.

One general feature about the regime's policy measures is that they tend to be used in a countercyclical manner to neutralize, at least to some extent, the pig production cycle. Thus, both export refunds and private storage aids are not always available; rather they are used when the Commission, after consulting the pigmeat management committee, feels them to be necessary.

The basic price and intervention

The only institutional price set is the *basic price*. The factors to be taken into account when fixing it are the level of sluice-gate prices and 'the need to fix this price at a level which contributes towards stabilizing market prices without, however, leading to the formation of structural surpluses . . .'. In concept the basic price is equivalent to the target and guide prices of other CAP regimes—i.e. it represents a desired level of market prices to be received by producers.

Theoretically the basic price is supported by intervention buying which may be introduced when market prices on representative markets[22] are below 103 per cent of the basic price. The introduction of intervention buying is not mandatory: it has not been used since 1971. In the event of intervention buying being introduced, however, a buying-in price may be set anywhere in the range 78 to 92 per cent of the basic price.

In practice, the use of *aids for private storage* has evolved to become the only measure operating domestically to support market prices. The Commission prefers that commercial interests should withhold supplies from the market rather than the public intervention agencies. It is felt that firms will have a greater interest in maintaining the quality of stored pigmeat, and will be better able to judge when supplies can be released on to the market without depressing prices.

The aids are available as and when considered necessary for particular types of pigmeat. Firms applying for the aids have to agree to store the pigmeat for a stipulated length of time—anything from three to five months—depending on what has been decided by the Commission following the management committee procedure.

Trade arrangements

The pigmeat regime's policy measures directed towards trade with Third Countries parallel those for eggs and poultrymeat. Thus, all imports have to pay a *basic import levy* which is calculated quarterly in two parts:

(a) an amount equal to the difference between EC and world prices for cereals—to offset the difference in feed costs (on the debatable assumption, however, that pigs have an all-cereal diet);
(b) an amount equal to 7 per cent of the EC's calculation over the previous year of the world cost of production—justified as a margin of protection for EC producers.

The basic levy is set for pig carcasses, and coefficients are used to derive the levies for pigmeat cuts and products.

As is the case for poultry, the EC calculates the world cost of pigmeat production, known as the *sluice-gate price*.[23] Imports which are offered to the EC at below this level attract a *supplementary levy*. This represents the difference between the offer price and the sluice-gate price. It is set by the Commission and generally applies to a few countries for particular pigmeat items. Countries which have agreed to observe the sluice-gate price are exempted from the charging of supplementary levies.

Export refunds are decided by the Commission through the management committee procedure and they are set taking into account world prices for pigmeat and the differential between Community and world cereal feed prices. In practice refunds are available for most products for export; they can be varied by product or destination[24] as the need arises.

NOTES

1. The issues concerned with the setting of the initial level of support prices were discussed in Chapter 3; for further discussion see Priebe *et al.* (1972).
2. Regulation (EEC) No. 19/62.
3. Regulation (EEC) No. 120/67, since superseded by Regulation (EEC) No. 2727/75.
4. In fact, market prices below intervention levels may exist. Traders may, if they wish, sell at a lower price and, within limits, will prefer to do this rather than: (i) face the risk of having the cereals that they have offered to intervention being rejected on quality grounds and then having to remove them from intervention stores at their own cost, and (ii) wait for payment from the intervention agency.
5. According to the UK's Home Grown Cereals Authority (1979, p. 40) intervention centres 'are located in regions having an appreciable production of cereals which substantially exceeds local demand either regularly or occasionally, but must also have adequate storage facilities and transport connections for taking over and disposing of sufficiently large quantities of cereals. There is provision ... for centres

to be determined elsewhere on the basis of either substantial storage facilities or because of a special importance as a market for cereals, but only where their facilities permit the assembly and disposal of substantial quantities of home-grown grain'. At the beginning of the 1980s, the number of centres was 662 for common wheat, 139 for rye, 429 for barley, 355 for durum, and 127 for maize.

6. Although, of course, some rye has traditionally been used for breadmaking, while both barley and maize are used in various food products.

7. Sales to intervention of common wheat were 1.268 million tonnes in 1973/74 and 2.057 million tonnes in 1974/75, despite Community cereal prices being relatively high following the dramatic rise in world cereal prices due to the short world crops of the early 1970s.

8. To an extent relative nutritional values can vary between seasons owing to variations, for example, in nitrogen and fibre contents.

9. For a description of the 'dough machinability' test and a detailed account of the minutiae of the cereals regime, see HGCA (1979).

10. Debatisse (1981, pp. 34–40) describes in some detail the various methods by which grain may enter the EC at under threshold prices. This analysis is developed further in Debatisse (1982).

11. The Commission does, however, apply premiums to adjust for any decline in world prices expected at the time the licence is taken out. These premiums are related to futures prices and hence cannot fully cover world price movements in so far as spot prices on the day of import differ from the earlier futures prices for that time. The skill of traders in deciding when to advance fix is illustrated by an event in January 1982 when licences for 1.24 million tonnes of maize (out of an estimated EC annual requirement of some nine million tonnes) were taken out in just two days when levies were at their lowest level for the month. See *Agra Europe* (1982, pp. M/3–M/4) for a full explanation of the considerations involved.

12. The term 'cereal substitutes' is misleading, although it is the customary term for many products which may be used as alternatives to cereals in compound animal feedingstuffs. The products in question are not in any sense inferior to cereals: they have different nutritional characteristics. They include manioc (also known as cassava or tapioca), cereal residues (e.g. brans, sharps, wheat offals, and grain screenings), brewers' and distillers' residues, maize gluten feed, fruit residues (principally fruit pulp), and sugar beet pulp. Oilseed cakes and molasses are frequently referred to as cereal substitutes. This is a misnomer as oilseed cakes are principally protein sources, while molasses act as a binding agent for compounds and as a sweetener.

13. See evidence from the Grain and Allied Feed Trades in House of Lords (1981). This report discusses the issues raised by the Commission's cereal substitute proposals.

14. Actually this element is a rate of *ad valorem* import duty—normally 7 per cent.

15. Except where the starch is used subsequently for isoglucose production.

16. Under the original starch system, introduced in 1967, supply prices were set which were the prices at which it was desired the starch industry should get its raw materials. When the supply prices were first set they were approximately at world levels. Production refunds were paid to the industry to cover the difference between the threshold prices and the supply prices.

17. This House of Lords report examines the issue of whether (or not) the starch industry should be given aid.

18. Regulation Nos. 2771/75 and 2777/75.

19. Thus: (i) EC cereal prices are taken as being threshold prices whereas, in practice, domestic market prices may be significantly lower; (ii) world cereal prices are defined as for the cereal import levy calculation and hence represent the lowest prices to be found—which obviously not all other poultry producers in the world can achieve; (iii) the feed rations assume 100 per cent cereal content, whereas partial

substitution with non-cereal ingredients developed widely in the EC during the 1970s; and (iv) the feed conversion ratios expressing how much feed is needed per kilo of poultry product are out-of-date and ignore the technical progress made in the EC's poultry industry.

20. These coefficients may also be an additional source of protection where they are seriously out-of-line with modern conditions. Thus, one of the USA's few agricultural concessions from the EC in the Tokyo Round of GATT negotiations was the decision to modify the coefficient applied to the calculation of turkeymeat cuts which the US claimed had been set at such a level as to effectively bar US exports from the EC market.

21. Regulation No. 2759/75.

22. Representative market prices for each country are collected weekly. They are weighted together to give an EC average known as the Reference Price.

23. Average world cereal prices (from the cereal import levy calculation) are taken together with specified cereal rations and feed conversion ratios to give the cost of grain to produce certain pig products. A 15 per cent allowance is added to allow for feed components other than grain, and a fixed amount to allow for general processing and marketing costs.

24. During the second half of the 1970s, until the issue was resolved as part of the Tokyo Round of GATT negotiations, refund rates on pigmeat products to the USA were held down to avoid triggering the application of countervailing duties by the USA.

REFERENCES

Agra Europe Limited (undated) *CAP Monitor*, Tunbridge Wells.

Agra Europe Limited (1982) *Agra Europe*, Issue dated 5 February, Tunbridge Wells.

Butterwick, M., and Neville-Rolfe, E. (1971) *Agricultural Marketing and the EEC*, Hutchinson: London.

Commission of the European Communities (1973) *Improvement of the Common Agricultural Policy*, COM (73) 1850, Brussels.

Commission of the European Communities (1976) *The Agricultural Situation in the Community: 1975 Report*, Brussels.

Commission of the European Communities (1977a) *The Agricultural Situation in the Community: 1976 Report*, Brussels.

Commission of the European Communities (1977b) *Report on Starch Products in the Community and the Starch Production Refund*, COM (77) 363, Brussels.

Commission of the European Communities (1979) *Report Concerning the Guarantee Section of the EAGGF, Cereal Sector*, Vol. I and Annexes, COM (79) 686, Brussels. (A Report by the Special Committee of Inquiry set up to examine the possibilities of fraud or irregularity in the administration of EC Budget funds.)

Commission of the European Communities (1980a) *The Agricultural Situation in the Community: 1980 Report*, Brussels.

Commission of the European Communities (1980b) *The Agricultural Situation in the Community: 1979 Report*, Brussels.

Commission of the European Communities (1981) *Guidelines for European Agriculture*, COM(81) 608, Brussels.

Commission of the European Communities (1982a) *The Agricultural Situation in the Community: 1981 Report*, Brussels.

Commission of the European Communities (1982b) *Report from the Commission to the Council on the Situation of the Agricultural Markets—1981*, COM(81) 822, Brussels.

Commission of the European Communities (1982c) Answer to Written Question No. 1596/81 in the European Parliament, *Official Journal of the European Communities*, C85, Luxembourg.

Commission of the European Communities (1982d) Answer to Written Question No. 1185/81 in the European Parliament, *Official Journal of the European Communities*, C24, Luxembourg.

Commission of the European Communities (1982e) *Les Mecanismes de l'Organisation Commune des Marchés Agricoles—Produits Vegetaux*, L'Europe Verte 189, Brussels.

Commission of the European Communities (1982f) *Preliminary Draft General Budget of the European Communities for the Financial Year 1983*, COM(82) 200, Vol. 7, Brussels.

Debatisse, M. (1981) *EEC Organisation of the Cereals Market: Principles and Consequences*, Centre for European Agricultural Studies: Wye College.

Debatisse, M. (1982) *Cerealexport*, Atya Edition, Paris.

Home-Grown Cereals Authority (1979) *UK Grain Marketing Arrangements under the Common Agricultural Policy*, HGCA: London.

Home-Grown Cereals Authority (1981) *Weekly Digest*, Vol. 7, No. 46, HGCA: London.

House of Lords Select Committee on the European Communities (1977) *Starch and Seeds*, Session 1977–78, 9th Report, HL 48, HMSO: London.

House of Lords Select Committee on the European Communities (1981) *Imports of Cereal Substitutes for use as Animal Feedingstuffs*, Session 1980–81, 42nd Report, HL 270, HMSO: London.

OECD (1974) *Agricultural Policy of the European Economic Community*, Paris.

Priebe, H., Bergmann, D., and Horring, J. (1972) *Fields of Conflict in European Farm Policy*, Trade Policy Research Centre: London.

Chapter 5

Grassland Based Livestock

The livestock sector can conveniently be divided between those enterprises which are traditionally grassland-based, notably beef, dairying, and sheep, and those such as pigs and poultry which are based on more intensive systems. For CAP purposes these latter are considered as a form of processed cereals and have therefore been dealt with in the previous chapter.

Taken together, beef, dairy, and sheep represent some 37 per cent of the value of EC agricultural production. Apart from their major importance as by far and away the largest single sector of Community agriculture, the grassland based livestock enterprises are of particular importance for two further reasons. First, a substantial proportion of farms within the Community include these enterprises: over 60 per cent in all Member States (except Italy) in the case of beef, and over 50 per cent in all Member States (except Italy and the United Kingdom) in the case of dairying. Second, dairying is very often a farmer's main cash enterprise,[1] particularly in the upland and peripheral regions of the Community. It is this second factor, combined with the fact that over 70 per cent of dairy farms have less than 15 cows, that has made the milk sector the most difficult to reform of all the CAP commodity regimes.

The close linkages between the dairy and beef sectors in terms of the inputs required and the output produced, create a further complication for the Commission in its management of the two markets. Thus much of Community beef production is based on fattening calves from the dairy herd, and on the slaughter of cull dairy cows.

MILK

Economic significance

The size and importance of the Community's dairy industry are shown in Table 5.1.

The salient features of EC dairy production include first, that whilst the total number of dairy cows remained constant at about 25 million during the 1970s, yields increased significantly—by some 1.2 per cent annually over the two decades from 1960. Nevertheless, there remain wide differences in yield between

Table 5.1   Importance of dairying (1980).

Member State	Percentage of value of dairy production in EC	Percentage of value of agricultural production in each Member State	Liquid milk yield (kg/head)
Germany	23.9	23.0	4552
France	24.3	16.7	3544*
Italy	12.2	10.4	3362
Netherlands	11.4	27.8	5023*
Belgium	3.0	17.5	3847
Luxembourg	0.2	43.3	3994
UK	14.6	22.5	4757
Ireland	3.5	32.3	3234
Denmark	4.9	25.4	4846
Greece	1.9	8.1	1851
EC '10' Total	100.0	19.2	4004*

* Figures for 1979.
SOURCE   Commission (1982a, pp. 174 to 177 and 361).

the highest in the Netherlands at 5023 kg/head, and the lowest in Greece at 1851 kg/head, with thus a considerable potential for production to increase.[2] Taken together with the increasing proportion of milk delivered to dairies,[3] milk availability increased steadily to 97 million tonnes in 1981—giving rise to a substantial surplus over demand. Community consumption of dairy products as a whole stabilized in the late 1970s so that by the beginning of the 1980s self-sufficiency ratios for butter and skimmed milk powder had reached some 125 per cent and 135 per cent respectively.

France and Germany are the EC's major dairy producers, with nearly half of total Community milk production. The importance of milk to the agricultural economy is greatest, however, in Luxembourg, Ireland, and the Netherlands; it is not difficult to understand the political significance of milk in these countries, nor in the EC as a whole, with almost a fifth of the value of agricultural production coming from milk.

Budget cost

Dairy sector expenditure has for many years been the major item in the Community Budget, taking some 40 per cent of total FEOGA Guarantee Section spending during the 1970s. At the beginning of the 1980s the proportion was much lower at some 30 per cent. (Table 5.2). This was largely due to higher price levels on world markets—in part due to the co-operation between New Zealand and the EEC to raise world prices—and thus lower levels of expenditure on export refunds. The dramatic nature of the change in the level of spending on export subsidies can be gauged from the following progression: 1565.0 million ecu (1978), 2087.9 (1979), 2745.9 (1980), 1727.9 (1981), and

Table 5.2   Spending on the dairy regime.

		1981 (Actual)	1982 (Provisional)	1983 (Estimated)
1.	Total spending on dairy regime (million ecu)	3184.3	4054.0	3950.0
2.	As a percentage of total spending on farm price support	29.5	30.2	28.6
3.	Main dairy support measures as a percentage of total spending on dairy	100.0	100.0	100.0
	Export refunds on dairy products	54.3	54.5	48.2
	Aids to encourage consumption of skimmed milk and skimmed milk powder	36.3	31.2	34.6
	Storage costs for butter (both private and intervention)	6.7	10.1	7.9
	Consumption aid for butter	6.7	4.3	6.7
	Measures to encourage milk consumption	7.4	6.4	7.6
	Revenue from co-responsibility levies (treated as negative expenditure)	−15.0	−10.1	−13.1

SOURCE   Commission (1982d, p. B/211).

2208.0 (1982). The drop of 1000 million ecu between 1980 and 1981 is unprecedented and explains the reduction in the total cost of the dairy regime, as well as having helped to avert the collision between spending on CAP market support, and Budget Own Resources, which had seemed inevitable in 1981 or 1982.

Another reason for the apparent drop in the proportion of FEOGA Guarantee Section spending going to dairy is because the Commission in its Budget presentation chooses to enter the revenue raised from the co-responsibility levy on dairy producers as 'negative expenditure', rather than include it in the Budget's general revenue total. The result is that the apparent drop in the significance of dairy expenditure is overstated. (This treatment of the dairy co-responsibility levies contrasts with that for sugar producer levies which are treated as part of general Budget revenue.) Gross expenditure on dairy support can be calculated by disallowing the co-responsibility levy revenue as in Table 5.3.

Coverage

The first Regulation, No. 13/64, setting out the fundamental provisions of the dairy regime, was agreed in February 1964. This provided for support arrangements to apply during the transitional period during which prices within the then six Member States were phased together. The full regime, with common prices throughout the Community, came into force on 29 July 1968 with the

Table 5.3 Gross dairy expenditure (million ecu).

	1977	1978	1979	1980	1981	1982 (Prov.)	1983 (Est.)
1. Dairy expenditure as recorded in Budget	2924.1	4014.6	4527.5	4594.0	3184.3	4054.0	3950.0
2. Co-responsibility levies	24.1	156.1	94.2	222.9	478.5	410.0	519.0
3. Gross dairy expenditure (1 + 2)	2948.2	4170.7	4621.7	4816.9	3662.8	4464.0	4469.0
4. Percentage of FEOGA Guarantee Section spending:							
(a) As rendered in Budget	42.8	46.3	43.4	40.7	29.5	30.2	28.6
(b) Actual	43.2	48.1	44.3	42.7	32.5	32.3	31.2

SOURCE Calculated from Commission (1980a, p. 230; 1981a, p. 402; 1982d, p. B/211).

adoption of Regulation 804/68 by the Council. The regime has two objectives over and beyond the usual aim of free trade within the Community; first to ensure a satisfactory income for milk producers, and second to find a balance between supply and demand for milk and dairy products. The regulation seeks to 'stabilize markets and to ensure a fair standard of living for the agricultural Community concerned'. The attempt to reconcile the former with the latter has proved to be the major preoccupation of the management of the dairy regime, and the lack of success has given rise to the major problems of structural surplus associated with it. The price mechanism alone has been quite unable to achieve both objectives, and has in practice been used in an attempt to ensure producer income at the expense of market balance.

The main products covered are:

(a) Fresh, preserved, concentrated, or sweetened milk or cream,
(b) Butter, cheese, and curds,
(c) Lactose and lactose syrup,
(d) Milk-based compound feedingstuffs.

In principle, the dairying year runs from 1st April to 31st March, but in practice the annual farm price review is rarely completed by this date and so *ad hoc* extensions of the dairying year have to be agreed.

Support measures

The fundamental aim of the dairy sector is to support the level of returns to milk producers at the level of the *target price* for milk. This is set for milk of 3.7 per cent fat content delivered to the dairy, and represents not a guaranteed price, but one which milk producers should be able to obtain on average for all milk sold to dairies. In practice the target price is supported through the purchase of butter, skimmed milk powder, and certain types of cheese by the national intervention agencies on the one hand, and through a complex system of subsidies for consumption, production and export, on the other.

Intervention prices for butter and skimmed milk powder (SMP) are set at a level which, taking account of processing costs and yields, should ensure that the milk producer achieves the target price for milk. As in other product sectors, intervention purchasing is open ended, although since 1977 the Commission has tried to keep intervention stocks of butter and skimmed milk powder to low levels by the greater use of export refunds and consumption subsidies. This has been a major feature of the management of the regime since SMP intervention stocks rose to record levels in 1976 (see Table 5.4). Since then the cost, both politically and financially, has been recognized and, as in the cereals and sugar regimes, much greater reliance is placed on market management through exports. There has also been a change in the direction of policy relating to skimmed milk powder away from the purchase of SMP into intervention, and towards the subsidization of liquid skimmed milk on the internal market to

Table 5.4   Intervention stocks on 1 April in years shown. (1000 tonnes).

	Butter*	Skimmed milk powder
1974	97	123
1975	46	437
1976	118	1182
1977	148	885
1978	160	779
1979	294	503
1980	292	156
1981	41	144

* Public and private storage.
SOURCE Commission, *The Agricultural Situation in the Community*, annual reports for years 1976 to 1981.

avoid the costs of drying and handling SMP. The Commission has proposed the suspension of intervention for milk powder at certain times of the year as the continuous availability of intervention 'has created an artificial demand satisfied by dairies which no longer produce for the market' (Commission, 1981b, p. 34). So far, however, the proposal has not been adopted.

To illustrate the relationship between the intervention prices for butter and SMP on the one hand and the target price for milk on the other, an example of the 1982/83 support prices is given below (Table 5.5). For the purpose of calculating this relationship, which is examined by the Commission each year in the context of the annual price fixing, a manufacturer's margin is calculated from data provided by the processing industry; this includes the cost of manufacture, packaging, and transport to an approved intervention store,

Table 5.5   Calculation of the intervention milk price equivalent (IMPE) for 1982/83 (in ecu/100 kg except where otherwise stated).

	Butter		SMP
Intervention price	349.70		146.23
Less manufacturer's margin	26.94		21.82
Raw material value of product	322.76		124.41
Product yield from 1000 litres of milk (in kg)	22.973		11.00
Raw material value (milk of 3.7 per cent fat and 8.7 per cent non-fat solids)	14.05		11.31
Intervention milk price equivalent (IMPE whole milk) 3.7 per cent fat, delivered		25.36	
Fat/solids non-fat ratio in IMPE	55.40%		44.60%
Target price liquid milk		26.81	
IMPE/target price ratio, expressed as a coefficient		0.946	

together with technical yield factors. Through this calculation the Commission is enabled to keep the intervention prices for butter and SMP in line with the milk target price, but it has also allowed the Council and Commission to depress the real return to milk producers by failing to make an adequate adjustment to the manufacturer's margin. Over time the relationship between the two intervention prices has been varied to influence relative production levels and sales to intervention of butter and skimmed milk powder. In 1968, the first year of operation of common prices, the solids non-fat (SNF) contribution to the intervention milk price equivalent was only 28.6 per cent (MMB, 1978, p. 25). However, in the early 1970s, the high price of butter led to marketing difficulties and so the decision was taken to increase the SMP intervention price at a faster rate than that for butter. This in turn made the retention of skim on the farm unattractive, and contributed to the marketing difficulties of skimmed milk powder.

The IMPE is not, however, an institutional price and dairies may well in practice pay lower prices to producers, particularly in the over supplied market which has existed for many years in this sector. It can be seen that the system is intended to leave a gap between target and intervention prices of some 5.5 per cent, within which band market prices are intended to find their own level.

In addition to intervention, subsidies are payable on some milk products (butter, certain cheeses) put into private store. *Private storage aid* for butter is intended to smooth out the seasonality of milk production. It is available in the summer months to allow purchase of dairy products, which will be stored for sale in the winter months when production is lower.

The *threshold price* provides the basis of control over the price at which dairy products enter the Community. Conceptually the threshold price is the external equivalent of the target price, set with the aim of preventing Third Country imports from undercutting the target price within the EC. Variable import levies are charged as the difference between world (taken as being the lowest representative offer) prices and threshold prices. Because of the diversity of milk products, the Community categorizes them into 12 groups with a threshold price for a 'pilot product' in each group and a levy set for the pilot product. The import levy for other products (known as assimilated products) is derived from the appropriate pilot product. The effect of the import levy/threshold price system is to prevent the c.i.f. levy-paid price of any product being less than its threshold price. In practice the system means that only where special concessions are made can dairy products enter the Community.

Special import regimes

The normal import regime has been modified to permit the entry of butter in the case of New Zealand and specified cheeses in the cases of New Zealand, Canada, Austria, Finland, Romania, Switzerland, Bulgaria, Hungary, Israel, Turkey, Cyprus, and Australia on favourable terms. The arrangements for cheese were negotiated in both GATT and bilaterally; they provide for minimum c.i.f. import prices and special reduced import levies.

The arrangements for New Zealand originated in Protocol 18 of the UK Accession Treaty, which provided for the import in 1973 of 165 000 tonnes of butter, and 68 580 tonnes of cheese at special rates of levy: reducing to 138 000 and 15 000 tonnes respectively in 1977. The provisions for butter had been twice extended at the time of writing, with lower quantities each time (down to 92 000 tonnes in 1982 and 87 000 tonnes in 1983). The present arrangements remain until 1983. These provisions for New Zealand were a central element of the terms required by the United Kingdom when negotiating her entry to the Community, because of the importance of agriculture in the New Zealand economy, her traditional position as a major supplier of dairy products to the UK and the difficulty of finding alternative markets. The arrangements have frequently been the subject of much political controversy in the Community and have been used as a bargaining counter against the United Kingdom on a number of occasions in negotiations in the Council of Ministers.

Export refunds

In order to enable the Community to compete on world markets, export refunds are granted, which in principle are equal to the difference between Community market prices and average world prices. Consequently it is generally the case that export refunds are less than the import levies as these are related to threshold prices (which normally exceed Community market prices) and to lowest offer prices rather than to average world prices.

In order to provide some stability for exporters, the export refund may be fixed in advance. Prefixed export refunds are valid for a six-month period, except in the case of the United States market where the period is 30 days. The availability of prefixation has given rise to problems for the Commission's management of the market since it uses the number of prefixations as a guide for the level of the refund. However, exporters will prefix the refund in anticipation of changes in its level, or that of the MCA, leaving the Commission unable to control the quantity of product to be exported.[4] This has been of particular concern in the case of butter exported to the USSR[5] where the Commission has encountered major political difficulties because of exports to that country, and difficulties over its ability to control the quantities. As a result the Commission has taken the power to introduce a five-day waiting period, during which applications for prefixed refunds on butter and skimmed milk powder can be examined and applications refused. In addition it has been proposed that refunds for butter and skimmed milk powder be awarded by a tender arrangement similar to that applying to cereals and sugar.

The level of the export refund may be differentiated by destination, although the Commission has tried to limit the extent to which this happens. Since 1968 for Austria and Switzerland, and since 1979 in the case of Spain, the Community has agreed not to undercut their national minimum import prices set for cheeses, and consequently the export refund is lower for these destinations. In the case of the USA, where imports of most dairy products are governed by quotas, the Commission has had to exercise considerable restraint to avoid the imposition of countervailing duties. No refund is fixed for skimmed milk powder to this destination.

Management of the world market

There has been a switch in emphasis towards an increased use of export refunds and a decreased use of intervention buying by the Commission in its management of the market. This change has been basic to the management of both the internal Community dairy market, and also of the world market. In the latter case the Commission has gone to considerable lengths in conjunction with New Zealand to maintain the level of world market prices, particularly for skimmed and whole milk powder, but also for cheese and butter. The means to achieve this have been through market price understandings in GATT, exchanges of information on prices, export volumes and stocks and cuts in the level of EC export refunds wherever possible. Regular meetings take place between Commission and New Zealand officials in order to ensure a co-ordinated management of the world market.

Food aid

Provision exists within the legislation for the supply of butter (primarily in the form of butter-oil) and SMP to international organizations and to developing countries on a bilateral basis as part of the Community's Food Aid programme. Originally the programme was seen as a means of disposing of part of the Community's surplus production of these products; gradually, however, the Community has moved away from this concept towards a longer term programme no matter what the internal supply situation. The commitments in 1981 were at 150 000 tonnes of SMP and 45 000 tonnes of butter-oil. See also Chapter 11.

Measures to reduce the dairy surplus

The structural 'surpluses' of the dairy regime have proved to be deep-seated and difficult to reduce in extent. The EC has tried many schemes to reduce the scale of the surplus but it has proved extremely difficult to reduce production.

Measures to increase demand

A plethora of measures has been devised over the years to prevent a recurrence of the excessive accumulation of intervention stocks that occurred in 1976 and 1977 and to maintain a balance between the quantities disposed of on external and on internal markets. These measures take a number of different forms, but all aim to reduce the end-product price to different categories of consumer: general consumer subsidies; subsidies to specific categories of consumer; subsidies to industrial users; other disposal measures.

The Commission has from time to time shifted its emphasis from the internal to the external market and from one type of scheme to another, depending upon the nature of the pressures from the Member States and from public opinion. For example, intervention stocks of butter reached a peak of 591 000 tonnes in 1979, whilst stocks of skimmed milk powder reached a peak of 1.34 million tonnes in 1976. Up to 1982 stock levels declined continuously as the emphasis was shifted to increased levels of exports and to other types of disposal measures on the internal market. Since 1982, however, Community butter and SMP stocks have started to rise again under the influence of further milk production increases and saturated world markets.

(a) Disposal schemes for skimmed milk

With the increasing availability of skimmed milk and skimmed milk powder, it has been essential to develop further, subsidized market outlets. These are based on three principles: the separation of different markets at different prices; the encouragement of liquid skimmed milk uses to avoid the costs of drying; and the need to apply a rate of subsidy to bring the price of skimmed milk down to that of competing products, notably of vegetable proteins. The Community makes use of three subsidy schemes to ensure that liquid skim is not manufactured into unwanted skimmed milk powder. An aid is given when liquid skim is used for calf feeding, and a slightly higher aid for feeding other young animals. Similarly an aid is given to manufacturers of casein from liquid skim.

Of the skim and milk powder manufactured only about 15 per cent can be sold commercially at the full intervention price. In 1981 '60 per cent was sold as feed with a 45 per cent price reduction for calf milk replacers and the rest was exported' (Commission, 1982b, p. 129). A particular feature of the mid-1970s had been the special sales of intervention SMP, and subsidies on freshly manufactured powder, to make the product competitive with soya in pigfeed. The success of the other disposal measures meant that at the turn of the decade these latter measures were unnecessary.

(b) The protein deposit scheme for skimmed milk

Other schemes have been attempted at various times, of which the protein deposit scheme is perhaps the best known. In 1976 under this scheme, which was subsequently declared to be invalid by the European Court of Justice, animal feed compounders were required to pay a deposit on imported vegetable proteins. These were released only on proof of purchase of an equivalent quantity of skimmed milk powder from Community intervention stocks. The aim of the scheme was to reduce intervention stocks by 400 000 tonnes. There was a strong international reaction to the scheme.

(c) Subsidy schemes for butter

As for skimmed milk, a variety of schemes exist for the subsidization of butter consumption in different markets. The most important of these are the general consumer subsidies which have been payable on all butter consumption since 1979, and charged 75 per cent to FEOGA. Not all Member States have made use of this possibility and at the time of writing, Denmark, Ireland, Luxembourg, and the United Kingdom were the only users. (In the United Kingdom, FEOGA pays the full subsidy cost.) In addition short term schemes at very high rates of subsidy have been operated over peak consumption periods (principally the so-called 'Christmas' butter). These schemes are considered by the Commission to be extremely expensive per tonne of additional butter consumed since the rate of substitution of subsidized for unsubsidized butter is very high.

In addition to the general consumer subsidies, the Community operates a variety of specific schemes for reducing the cost of butter to the food industry (ice cream and baking); to the armed forces; and to non-profit making institutions. In 1981 186 000 tonnes of butter were used in these ways, down from the peak of 297 000 tonnes in 1979, but still accounting for 12 per cent of total butter sales.

(d) School milk

In 1977, the Community introduced a range of subsidies on milk (whole, semi-skimmed, and skimmed) and dairy products consumed in schools, to expand the market and encourage young people into the habit of drinking milk. Co-responsibility levy funds are said to finance the school milk subsidies.

(e) Proposals for taxes on vegetable oil consumption

A continuing strand in thinking about the CAP has been the clash between fats of animal origin (i.e. butter) and of vegetable origin (i.e. margarine). The Commission has asserted, at times, that the duty-free entry accorded to Third Country oilseeds in the EC has meant that margarine—manufactured from the oils produced from these oilseeds—was given an unfair price advantage in the Community's domestic market over butter. Consequently, it is said, one way of increasing butter consumption would be by taxing the ingredients used for margarine manufacture so that margarine's competitive edge, derived from the differing treatment of oilseeds and milk, would be reduced.

Indeed, in 1964 the Council of Ministers resolved to levy a tax on vegetable and marine fats and oils for human consumption, whether of EC or imported origins. The intention was to use the revenue from the levy as a means of reducing the Budget cost of CAP support measures for oils and fats, while improving the demand for butter. The Commission (1964) made a proposal to this effect; it repeated the need for such a proposal in the Mansholt Plan (1968, p. 15), and made a further proposal (1976). That these proposals have not been translated into decisions, at least up to the time of writing, is a tribute to the tenacity of the opposition from the oilseed crushing industries and margarine manufacturers in Germany, the Netherlands, and the UK concerned to preserve the markets for their production of vegetable oils.

Measures to reduce supply

The Council of Ministers has at various times experimented with different methods of controlling or reducing supply, but has always been reluctant to act directly to reduce producer prices in absolute terms. None the less, there was some reduction in their real value at the end of the 1970s, associated with the same general phenomenon for all farm products.

(a) Co-responsibility levies

This approach to the problem of controlling the increase in milk production was part of a package of measures introduced in 1977. Co-responsibility levies were introduced at a flat rate of 1.5 per cent of the target price for 1977/78. They were reduced to 0.5 per cent in 1978/79, raised to 2.0 per cent in 1980/81, and to 2.5 per cent in 1981/82 and reduced again to 2.0 per cent in 1982/83. In this form the levy has been charged at a flat rate on all milk delivered to dairies, with exemptions for farms in the mountain and hill areas and a reduction of 0.5 per cent in less favoured areas. The extent of the exemptions has always been a contentious issue as Member States have sought to protect their own milk producers from the effects of the levy. The revenue derived from the levy has been used to fund schemes for the promotion of exports, for milk publicity campaigns, and for research into new products as well as funding FEOGA expenditure on various subsidy schemes.

There have been many criticisms of the flat rate levy, of which the most cogent have been first, that the Council of Ministers has tended to pass the levy on to the consumer by raising support prices whenever the levy is increased; secondly, that the levy does not directly increase consumption in the way that a support price reduction would; and thirdly, that it is merely a revenue raising device which avoids control by the European Parliament. Nevertheless the levy seems to have become an established part of the Community's armoury in the dairy sector.

In 1980/81 and again in the following year, the Commission proposed a more powerful version of the levy to be paid on any increase in milk deliveries over a reference quantity, at a rate which would recover the cost to public funds of disposing of the additional quantities. In 1980/81 this was estimated to necessitate a levy equivalent to 84 per cent of the target price. However, despite commitments made in 1980/81, the Council has twice baulked at introducing what has come to be known as the 'supplementary' or 'super levy'. In 1982/83 the Council abandoned the super levy approach in favour of a declaration of its willingness to take direct measures through the intervention price, should deliveries exceed certain threshold levels.

(b) Conversion schemes

A number of schemes have been introduced to encourage dairy farmers either to convert to beef or sheep production or to go out of production altogether. These include the herd conversion and cow slaughter schemes of 1969, the beef conversion scheme of 1974, and the non-marketing and herd conversion schemes of 1977. The cost effectiveness of these schemes is at best uncertain and there is reason to believe that the subsidies merely went to producers who would in any event have left the dairy sector. (See also Chapter 9.) The schemes have now been ended.

(c) Investment aid limitation

The Commission has repeatedly sought to reduce the level of investment aids provided in the dairy sector. The Community's provisions for structural aid investment do not apply to the dairy sector, and there are severe limits on the products for which investment aids are given under the Community's marketing and processing improvement scheme (Regulation 355/77). More recently the Commission has proposed that all national aids be ended.

(d) Other measures

From time to time the Community has experimented with other ideas; in 1980/81 the Council adopted a regulation providing aid for suckler cows in an attempt to encourage non-intensive methods of dairy farming. In the Guidelines document (Commission, 1981b, p. 30), a special levy was proposed for milk from 'intensive' farms—defined as being those delivering more than 15 000 kg of milk per hectare of forage. These moves may be viewed as part of a Commission attempt to reduce the milk surplus by reducing the extent of intensive milk production based on bought-in concentrates. The special levy proposal foundered on opposition from the Netherlands and the UK, in particular.

Proposals for reform

The past ten years have each seen proposals by the Commission aimed at mastering the milk surplus. The Council of Ministers has, as regularly, rejected or watered down these proposals to the point where they have lost all effectiveness. The importance of the dairy sector in the agricultural economies of the Member States and the social needs of the peripheral regions where livestock farming is virtually the only possible activity, have accounted for the reluctance of the Council to adopt measures having any significant effect.

In the five years from 1977 to 1982 repeated attempts were made to introduce measures based on the concept of co-responsibility. The Council has repeatedly made commitments for succeeding years which in the event have never been fulfilled. In 1982 the Commission has gone back to earlier proposals to moderate the rate of increase in intervention prices according to the rate of increase in milk deliveries in the preceding year. The idea of variable intervention prices is not new, and has in the past been linked to the level of intervention stocks of butter and skimmed milk powder. The control of intervention price increases to 'prudent' levels has been a constant theme in past years. In general it is fair to say that years in which this has been successful have been followed by years in which the loss in previous years has been made good, either directly through common price increases, or through manipulation of green rates of exchange. Apart from these more direct approaches, a variety of schemes have been introduced and phased out based on conversion of herds away from milk; these have been described earlier.

In practice the only path left open has been to find new means of disposing of the increasing quantities of milk available. Prior to 1976 stocks of butter and particularly skimmed milk powder were built to very high levels. This policy was subsequently abandoned, largely because of the harmful political consequences, in favour of market segmentation policies based on direct consumption subsidies for animal feed or human consumption in the case of butter. In 1982 as stocks of skimmed milk powder began to build up again, pressure has mounted to re-introduce subsidized animal feed schemes which had been temporarily dropped whilst stocks remained low. In addition export levels have risen and the Community has significantly increased its share of total world trade in dairy products.

There is a limit to the extent to which these openings can continue to be exploited, particularly in the case of exports. This fact, together with the increasing pressures on the Community Budget, may give rise to renewed attempts to limit deliveries particularly through the price mechanism. Nevertheless the political strength of the dairy sector remains as strong as ever and dramatic measures should not be expected.

Liquid milk marketing arrangements

The operation of the internal market

Free trade within the Community exists as yet only for dairy products. For liquid milk, restrictions remain because of different national legislation in the Member States governing milk hygiene. Since the unified dairy market came into effect, the Commission has made a number of attempts to achieve free trade in fresh milk. It succeeded at a relatively early stage in gaining agreement on Community quality standards for fresh milk, although the final provisions did not come into force until 1977. However, the Commission's proposals on health and hygiene had remained before the Council of Ministers for over a decade up to the beginning of 1982. This had not prevented the development of a considerable trade in fresh milk between certain Member States, notably from France and Germany into Italy. In other cases, however, restrictions remained in force; the United Kingdom enforced licensing regulations which had the effect of preventing the import of fresh, UHT, and sterilized milks, although not of UHT cream or flavoured milk. The Commission challenged the UK regulations in respect of UHT milk in 1981. The European Court of Justice ruled in 1982 that the UK measures were excessive and therefore illegal.

Minimum fat content

With regard to whole milk, Member States have had to choose between the marketing of standardized or non-standardized milk on their own territory. Standardized milk can have milk fat added or removed, to produce a standardized product. The United Kingdom and Ireland have chosen non-standardized milk for their own dairy needs, and are able to refuse entry to standardized milk of less than the average fat content of their own production.

The treatment of marketing boards

One of the contentious issues at the time of the UK's accession to the EC was the treatment of its milk marketing boards which were long established, having been founded in the 1930s. The boards buy nearly all milk sold off farms and sell it on to the processers. The issue of the boards' future was not settled until 1978. In that year Article 25 of Regulation 804/68 was modified to provide that 'a Member State may be authorized to grant to an organization representing at least 80 per cent of the number and at least 50 per cent of the production of the milk producers ... (a) the exclusive right to buy from producers ... (b) the right to equalize the prices paid to producers'. Further conditions related to the maintenance of a relatively high level of liquid milk consumption in the United Kingdom compared with the rest of the Community.

This political decision was reached against a background of concern on the part of other Member States that the Milk Marketing Boards would use their monopolistic position and price pooling policy as a means to undercut the price of imported dairy products.

BEEF

Economic significance

Beef production takes place on over half of the farms in the Community (although the number of farmers having cattle for beef production dropped consistently during the 1970s at about 4 per cent annually): production comes either from specialized beef herds or more often from dairy herds. Beef production contributes some 16 per cent of final agricultural production in the Community. There are wide variations between individual Member States, however; in Ireland and Luxembourg beef production accounts for 36 per cent and 29 per cent respectively of final agricultural production, whereas in both Italy and the Netherlands, the figure is as low as 11 per cent. Two factors are of particular significance; first, over 80 per cent of cows are from dairy or dual purpose herds, and there is therefore an inescapable link with measures taken in the dairy sector.[6] Secondly, consumption has remained relatively static in the recent past, whilst production has risen. As a result the rate of self-sufficiency in the Community has grown steadily from 94 per cent in 1978, to 98 per cent in 1979 and

103 per cent in 1980. This increasing degree of over-supply is attributable in part to the gradual lengthening of the 'upswing' or surplus periods of the cattle cycle; and in part to the inroads that other meats, notably pig and poultry, have made into total meat consumption. The more rigid and formal nature of the beef support system compared with those for pigs and poultry has undoubtedly been a contributory factor.

During the 1970s, production increased at an annual rate of 2.4 per cent, while consumption grew at 1.7 per cent. For the 1980s, however, the Commission's forecasts indicated a worsening imbalance: 'In the absence of any change in the existing policy, production is forecast to grow at an average of 1.5–2.0 per cent . . . Consumption of beef . . . is forecast to grow rather slowly at 0.7 per cent a year.' Furthermore, 'The Community can expect to remain a net exporter of beef in the coming years. . .', (Commission, 1981b, p. 31).

Coverage

The single unified common market regime for beef and veal was brought into effect on 29 July 1968, with the adoption of Regulation 805/68, after a transition period of three and a half years during which prices in individual Member States were gradually aligned. Subsequently major modifications were made to the regime in 1972, when 'permanent' intervention was introduced, and again in 1977 with significant changes to the import regime following a period in which import licences had been suspended.

The regime covers the following categories:

(a) Live cattle and calves,
(b) Beef and veal, fresh, chilled and frozen, salted, dried, or smoked,
(c) Beef offals, fresh, chilled, frozen, salted, dried, or smoked,
(d) Preserved, processed and canned products containing beef and veal or beef and veal offals,
(e) Beef and veal fat.

The marketing year runs from the first Monday in April to the eve of that day in the following year.

Budget cost

Table 5.6 below shows expenditure on different items for selected years between 1976 and the preliminary draft budget estimates for 1983.

With the exception of 1975 and 1981, when beef expenditure was particularly high, spending on the beef and veal regime has remained around 10 per cent of total expenditure. In the years 1977 to 1979 spending was at about 6 per cent whereas in the years 1980 to 1982, it had risen to around 12 per cent. Within these totals, expenditure on export refunds rose from a fifth to nearly 60 per

Table 5.6 Spending on beef.

	1976 (Actual)	1979 (Actual)	1981 (Actual)	1982 (Prov.)	1983 (Est.)
1. Total spending on beef and veal (million ecu)	615.9	748.2	1,436.9	1,415.0	1,283.0
2. As a percentage of total spending on farm price support	11.0	7.2	13.3	10.5	9.3
3. Main beef support measures as a percentage of total beef and veal expenditure	100.0	100.0	100.0	100.0	100.0
Export refunds	21.7	36.1	57.4	55.7	58.7
Intervention and private storage	56.5	55.8	27.4	29.2	22.5
Slaughter and other premiums	21.8	8.1	15.2	14.8	18.8

SOURCES Commission (1980b, p. 254; 1981a, p. 413; 1982d, p. B/216).

cent, whilst intervention spending fell from 56 per cent to under a quarter of the total.

Support measures

For each marketing year the Council of Ministers fixes two internal support prices. The first is the *guide price*, which is fixed for live animals and calves and is intended to take account of various considerations including future trends in beef and veal production and consumption as well as the market situation. The guide price represents the desired average price on the Community market for all quantities sold during the marketing year.

As with all the main CAP support regimes, this market price objective is supported by an *intervention price* which is set at 90 per cent of the guide price. The intervention price has assumed a greater importance in the beef regime than originally intended. Initially intervention buying was conceived as being a discretionary part of the regime; since 1972, however, intervention buying has formed a permanent part. In addition, the raising of the guide price by 65 per cent between 1971/72 and 1976/77 meant that market prices were raised to levels which consumers were not prepared to pay. Consequently intervention buying had to play a more significant role in supporting market prices through its function of providing a floor to the market. As a result there was a large build-up in intervention stocks between 1974 and 1976 and again in more recent years (Table 5.7).

Although the intervention price is fixed for live cattle, in practice intervention applies only to meat from certain types and qualities of livestock for which

Table 5.7 EC beef intervention purchases. (tonnes).

1973	23 000
1974	465 000
1975	414 000
1976	362 000
1977	260 000
1978	227 000
1979	330 000
1980	410 000

SOURCE Commission (1982b, p. 150).

buying-in prices are fixed. For example, from the beginning of the 1981/82 marketing year the Commission restricted intervention buying to meat from male animals. Subsequently the Commission further restricted the availability of intervention buying support by making only forequarters eligible from the beginning of the marketing year until July and hindquarters from November to the end of March. A principal aim of this restriction on the availability of intervention was to reduce the Budget cost of beef support.

The derivation of buying-in prices is complex. It starts with the fact that certain national grades and categories of livestock are specified for each Member State for Community price reporting purposes. Some of these livestock categories are selected as being eligible for intervention. For these categories buying-in prices are determined by applying to the Intervention Price various

Table 5.8 Calculation of the UK buying-in price for a specific livestock category—Steers M forequarters.

		ecu/100 kg
1.	EC intervention price (1982/83) for adult cattle	176.66 (live weight)
2.	Adjusted by market price coefficient of 0.95 for steers (category M)	167.827 (live weight)
3.	Converted to dead weight using killing out percentage of 54.4	308.506 (dead weight)
		pence/kg
4.	UK upper* buying-in price for beef carcasses converted at green rate	190.86 (dead weight)
5.	Adjusted by the market price coefficient of 0.80 for forequarters, straight cut at 20th rib	152.69 (dead weight)

* Upper buying-in prices are linked directly to the cattle intervention price by the specified coefficients and killing-out percentages. Lower buying-in prices also exist for Grade B animals which are set as a fixed amount below the upper buying-in prices.

coefficients. (These coefficients were meant originally to reflect the differing market conditions and prices existing between the Member States.) In turn these buying-in prices—for particular qualities of carcass decided by the individual Member States—are converted into actual prices by the use of killing-out percentages, i.e. the yield of carcass meat from the live animal. Table 5.8 above shows the derivation of the buying-in price for forequarters of steers (category M) for the UK between May and August 1982.

Support buying

Under the provisions for support buying, national intervention agencies are obliged to purchase specified categories of beef at the relevant buying-in prices, providing the appropriate price conditions have been met. In 1978 the permanent intervention system was modified to take into account the relationship between national *reference prices* (the observed average market prices for finished cattle of the specified categories) and the upper buying-in prices in each Member State. Thus where for any Member State its reference price for any particular category remains below 100 per cent of its buying-in price for two weeks, the Commission is obliged to reintroduce support buying for the category in question in the country concerned. Where a country's reference price remains at between 100 and 102 per cent of its buying-in price for three weeks, intervention buying of the category concerned may be suspended through the Management Committee procedure. (In the Republic of Ireland, however, where beef production is particularly important to the economy, intervention buying is not suspended unless its national reference price rises above 85 per cent of the Community guide price.) If the reference price is above 102 per cent of the buying-in price for a particular category in any Member State, then the Commission may suspend purchases of the category concerned without first consulting the Management Committee.

Meat bought into intervention is subsequently released on to the market through one of three types of disposal scheme. First, there is a permanent fixed price sale of bone-in beef. All bone-in beef which has been bought in before specified 'release dates' is normally available at these prices. Second, there is a tender arrangement for boneless beef on a weekly basis; and third, a fixed price sale for boneless beef. Apart from these, special sales are held occasionally under exceptional circumstances.

Private storage aid

In addition to intervention buying, there is heavy reliance on *private storage aids* to reduce the pressure on intervention. As in other regimes, a subsidy is available to traders to hold meat of specified categories off the market for limited periods of time—usually up to six months. The level of the storage aid may be fixed in advance or determined by tender. From the Commission's point of view private storage aid has a number of advantages: it is more flexible than intervention buying as there are fewer restrictions governing the meat categories which may be covered; and it tends to be cheaper for FEOGA since the product remains the property of the trader, and consequently is better cared for than publicly stored beef. In a sense the system of private storage aids may be looked on as a pre-intervention stage as the Commission introduces it when market prices are under pressure, but have not yet fallen to intervention levels.

Premium schemes

Since 1975, there has been a cattle slaughter premium[7] and a calf premium. The slaughter premium is operated only by the UK, whilst Italy, the Republic of Ireland, and Greece pay the calf subsidy—as a payment on any calf of six months age and born in the relevant 12-month period. To emphasize the exceptional nature of these subsidies, the Council renews them annually as part of the price review and, in addition, FEOGA pays only part of the cost, the remainder being borne by the countries implementing them. The slaughter premium is payable as the difference between the average weekly market price in the UK, and a target price fixed according to a seasonal scale by the British government, but which on an annual basis may not exceed 85 per cent of the guide price. In addition, the amount of the premium may not exceed a fixed amount per head of cattle, and is deducted from the buying-in price when intervention buying operates in Britain. The result of the system is to give greater latitude to UK market prices to move freely to reflect seasonal fluctuations in cattle marketings and consumer demand, without imposing a rigid floor in the market with intervention buying at too high a level. In turn, consumers benefit from the periods of lower market prices permitted under the system.

There is also a premium for maintaining suckler cows, introduced in 1980/81, whereby producers who undertake not to sell milk for a 12-month period and to keep their suckler cows for at least six months, can receive a subsidy per cow. The aim of the subsidy is to help the incomes of specialist beef rearers without incidentally increasing those of dairy producers. In its proposal for the 1982/83 price fixing the Commission stated that it would try to develop a single premium scheme for specialist beef holdings which would be 'a more uniform direct aid to producers' incomes . . . (which) would enable prices to be adjusted in future years in such a way as to maintain consumption'. (Commission, 1982c, p. 99.) The Commission is particularly worried about the sensitivity of beef consumption to price rises.

Under the provisions of the hill farming Directive (discussed in Chapter 9) hill livestock compensatory allowances are paid in some Member States on hill cattle and sheep. A final series of premium schemes, as mentioned in the dairy section above, have related to efforts to reduce the EC dairy surplus by persuading producers to switch to beef production. These schemes have had only limited success and, at the time of writing, all have been ended.

Measures to improve consumption

In 1974 and 1975 there was a scheme for subsidizing beef consumption by old age pensioners through the granting of beef 'coupons'. On a consistent basis intervention stocks of beef are made available at special prices to welfare organizations.

Import levies

Following three years of over-supply and low market prices during which time all import licences were suspended under the operation of the safeguard clause (July 1974 to March 1977), the beef regime's import measures were reviewed and strengthened in 1977. The purpose of the changes was to find a balance between an adequate degree of protection to Community producers, and the need to import beef to satisfy political and GATT obligations. Under the revised system, the Community applies a 20 per cent *ad valorem* duty on Third Country imports, plus a variable import levy calculated as the difference between a monthly average of the c.i.f., duty paid price for imports (in three main categories) and the Community guide price. The nominal import levy arising from this calculation is, however, further increased (reduced) when Community domestic market prices are below (above) guide prices according to the following scale—Table 5.9.

'Special measures' may be taken when domestic market prices are at exceptionally high levels. Thus, in 1972/73 EC import duties on beef and veal were suspended, the levies having already fallen to zero.

Table 5.9　Calculation of the actual rate of import levy applied according to the relationship between the Community reference price and the guide price.

Community reference price† as a percentage of the guide price	Actual rate of levy to be applied as a percentage of nominal import levy
Greater than 106%	nil
104–106	25
102–104	50
100–102	75*
96–100	100
96–98	105
90–96	110
Less than 90%	114

* The levy for frozen beef may be fixed between 75 per cent and 100 per cent of the basic levy.
† A weighted average of the national reference prices.

Concessionary import regimes

As a result of the relatively high level of import levies, imports under the normal levy/duty system are scarcely possible. At different times the Community has come under pressure to provide for specified quantities of imports on concessional terms, with regard to the levy in particular. These pressures have arisen in the context of GATT negotiations, and also of the need to meet certain external policy requirements, notably with regard to the ACP countries under the Lomé Convention and Yugoslavia. As a result, by 1982, there were no less than nine special import arrangements. The importance of these special arrangements can be judged from the fact that of an average total import of beef into the EC of some 475 000 tonnes (1978 to 1980) annually, all but 15 per cent came in under these arrangements. Consequently the policy for beef is quite unique among CAP commodity support regimes—no other product for which import levies normally apply has conceded such liberal import concessions.

(a) *GATT quotas*. There are five different quotas which have been negotiated within the GATT at different times. The most important of these relates to the quota on a levy free, but full duty basis, for the import of 50 000 tonnes (boneless beef equivalent) of frozen beef—this quota is known as 'the GATT quota'. It is allocated between the Member States according to their historic importance as importers of Third Country beef. For 1982, Italy and the UK took just under 30 per cent each, while at the other extreme Ireland's share was 0.1 per cent.

Two quotas relate to the import on a levy free and reduced duty basis of 43 000 head (in total) of live cattle of Alpine and mountain breeds. These mainly go to Italy and West Germany for fattening.

The two remaining schemes are of more recent origin, having been introduced in 1980 as a result of the Tokyo Round of GATT negotiations. The first relates to the import of 29 800 tonnes of fresh, chilled or frozen beef of high quality (known as 'Hilton' beef) from the USA, Canada, Argentina, Australia,

Table 5.10   Manufacturing beef balance sheet calculation for 1983.

	(1000 tonnes bone-in equivalent)
EC production	1026.0
Use from intervention stocks	46.0
Imports under the ACP quotas	6.9
Imports under the GATT quotas	4.1
Total supplies	1083.0
Total requirements	1143.0
Balance to be imported	60.0

and Uruguay; these imports are free of variable levy, but pay full customs duties. Finally, a small quota of 2250 tonnes of buffalo meat from Australia is imported on a levy and MCA free basis, mainly going to Germany.

(b) *Balance sheet arrangements.* For manufacturing purposes, the Commission calculates each year the quantity of beef which the Community will need to import each year. For 1983 the balance sheet was calculated as shown in Table 5.10. In 1983, therefore, the Community allowed the import of 60 000 tonnes of beef for manufacturing at nil or reduced levy, but full customs duty.

The balance sheet is operated on a quarterly basis with would-be importers applying for licences for quantities between 5 and 1500 tonnes each, and the licences being allocated pro rata with the total tonnage applied for as compared with the quantity to be distributed. Provision also exists within the scheme to link (known as 'jumelage') the right to a licence with the purchase of an equivalent quantity of beef from intervention.[8] However, use of this provision has not been made since mid-1979. The manufacturing balance sheet arrangements are extremely important as meat manufacturers consistently have claimed that they cannot obtain sufficient quantities of manufacturing grades of beef at an economic price from EC domestic production. There are strong grounds for accepting the manufacturers' claims as the Commission have always done the balance sheet calculations in as conservative a fashion as possible to restrict the volume of imports allowed-in. As a result of the Tokyo Round of GATT negotiations Third Country suppliers have to be consulted on the size of the imports to be permitted, but this change seems unlikely to make the Commission markedly more liberal in the calculation.

A further balance sheet type arrangement (known as the Young Animals' Balance Sheet) exists under which the Council agrees an annual estimate of imports of young male cattle needed for fattening. In 1982, the quota was fixed at 235 000 cattle at reduced or nil levy rates, but with customs duty payable. In practice this has tended to be taken up by traditional trade into Italy.

(c) *Yugoslavia.* Provision exists for the import of some 50 400 tonnes annually of 'baby beef' from Yugoslavia at half levy but full customs duty rates, provided that the EC market price is at least 98 per cent of the guide price. Yugoslavia is meant to charge a higher price for its beef exports to offset the levy reduction.

(d) *ACP.* Under the Lomé Convention, the Community allows imports from certain ACP States to enter duty free, and with reduced levies, within quotas. Only four States—Botswana, Kenya, Madagascar, and Swaziland—had such quotas which are renewed on an annual basis. For 1982 the quota for these four countries totalled 30 000 tonnes (boneless equivalent) of frozen beef on which a reduced levy of only 10 per cent of the actual variable import levy was charged, provided that the remaining 90 per cent was charged in the country of origin as an export tax. In effect the governments of these countries are enabled to take for themselves most of the market premium from sales in the Community as compared with the world market.

During 1982 these arrangements were extended to Zimbabwe on its accession to the Second Lomé Convention. An additional annual quota of 8100 tonnes of boned or boneless beef and veal was allocated to Zimbabwe under the same conditions as for the four other ACP beef exporters. Zimbabwe stated that the revenue from the tax on exports that it would be charging would be 'used to meet national priorities in the livestock sector, where these relate to smallholder production'.

Export refunds

Export refunds are payable on exports of cattle, beef, and veal. They take account of the current world market situation, the state of the EC market, and, in actual practice, of political considerations. Export refunds may normally be prefixed.

The EC at the beginning of the 1980s, on the upswing of its own cattle production cycle, emerged as a major exporter to world markets. Traditionally the EC had been a net beef importer. Thus in the mid-1970s the EC was importing a net quantity of some 200 thousand tonnes annually (including live cattle imports). By 1980 this had switched to a net export of almost 300 thousand tonnes. As a result the EC export share of the world market rose from around 15 per cent to a quarter. It should not be surprising that a swing of this magnitude in the EC's net trade position, and its emergence as a major exporter to world markets, led to considerable friction with other more traditional exporters to the world market—in particular, Argentina and Australia.

MUTTON AND LAMB

Until 1980, when the basic sheepmeat regime was introduced[9] each Member State operated its own national arrangements subject only to application of the Common Customs Tariff. In the Community of Six where, with the exception of France, production and consumption were at low levels compared with other meats, this did not much matter. However, with enlargement, the UK, Ireland, and Greece brought to the Community substantially higher levels of production and consumption, based upon quite different support systems. In the UK, a deficiency payment system was operated, enabling consumer prices to be kept down, and allowing for the import of substantial quantities of frozen and chilled lamb from New Zealand.[10] France, however, operated a support system based on high prices to both the producer and consumer. This was buttressed by a protective system of variable import levies and licences, the latter being suspended when market prices dipped below a threshold price.

Thus in determining the basis of any common organization of the market, the Commission had to recognize first that the United Kingdom and France accounted for some 77 per cent of total production; second that these Member States had quite different approaches to market support; third that the CCT duty was bound in GATT at 20 per cent and fourth that any future arrangement would have to come to terms with the dominant position of New Zealand

Table 5.11   Sheep and goat meat consumption and production by Member State.

Country	Consumption of sheepmeat as a percentage of total 1979 meat consumption (%)	Average annual sheepmeat consumption 1979 (kg/head)	Share of agricultural output 1980 (%)
Greece	n.a.	n.a.	6.7
France	4.1	4	2.6
United Kingdom	10.1	7	3.5
Italy	n.a.	1	0.8
Ireland	10.5	8	3.3
Denmark	0	0	0.0
Netherlands	1.4	1	0.7
Belgium/Luxembourg	2.3	2	0.2
Germany	1.1	1	0.2

SOURCE   Commission (1982a, pp. 174 and 221).

on the UK market. For example, in 1977 New Zealand accounted for some 53 per cent of lamb and mutton consumption in the UK (New Zealand Meat Producers' Board, 1978, p. 10); this proportion subsequently declined, partly as a result of the increase in production in the UK following the introduction of the new regime.

These difficulties led to a mutual acceptance of the status quo throughout the transitional period following UK, Irish, and Danish entry into the EC. At the end of that time, in December 1977, the Irish government decided that the French market offered potentially important opportunities for exports, and announced that action would be taken through the European Court unless the French system were modified. The French and Irish authorities came to a bilateral agreement which permitted Irish products access to the French market on a preferential basis. Since this agreement excluded the United Kingdom, it complained in its turn to the Commission. There followed an acrimonious period culminating in a judgement by the European Court in September 1979 that the French import arrangements were not compatible with its Treaty obligations.

The Commission put forward revised proposals for a common organization of the market in March 1979. Agreement was reached in May 1980, with the new regulation coming into effect in October of the same year.

Coverage

The basic regulation providing for a common organization of the market in sheepmeat and goatmeat covers the following categories:

(a) Live sheep and goats,
(b) Fresh, chilled or frozen sheepmeat and goatmeat,
(c) Fresh, chilled or frozen sheep and goat offals,
(d) Sheep and goatmeat and offals, salted in brine, dried or smoked,
(e) Prepared and preserved sheep and goatmeat and offals,
(f) Unrendered fats of sheep and goats.

Wool is not covered by the market organization as it is treated as an industrial product. The marketing year runs from the first Monday in April until the end of the previous day in the following year.

Budget

Table 5.12 shows the level of FEOGA expenditure in the four years of operation of the sheepmeat regime. It can be seen that expenditure settled at about 200 million ecus, with the major expense arising from the payment of premiums.

The market organization

The regime is distinctive among CAP support regimes in providing Member States with an option to choose between different support mechanisms—intervention buying or variable premiums—a choice which results from the previous arrangements in the UK on the one hand, and France and the Continental Member States on the other. Four main groups of support measures are provided for:

(a) Intervention buying and private storage aids;
(b) Variable premiums in place of intervention buying;

Table 5.12   Spending on the sheepmeat regime by the Community Budget.

	1980 (Actual)	1981 (Actual)	1982 (Prov.)	1983 (Est.)
1. Total spending on sheepmeat regime (million ecu)	53.5	191.5	224.0	237.0
2. As a percentage of total spending on farm price support	0.5	1.8	1.7	1.7
3. Main sheepmeat support measures as a percentage of total spending on sheep	100.0	100.0	100.0	100.0
Export refunds	—	—	—	—
Premiums	100.0	100.0	87.1	92.8
Private storage	—	—	12.9	7.2

SOURCE Commission (1981a, p. 420; 1982d, p. B/219).

(c) Annual premiums;

(d) A levy mechanism at the Community frontier, together with 'voluntary' restraint agreements with the main Third Country suppliers.

The price framework which defines these measures is described below.

The price structure

The basic price. Each year the Council fixes a basic price for fresh or chilled sheep carcasses, supposedly taking into account for this purpose:

(a) The situation on the sheepmeat market in the current year, and the prospects for production and consumption;

(b) Sheepmeat production costs;

(c) Past experience.

The basic price, which is seasonally adjusted[11] on a weekly basis throughout the year, is intended to take account of normal seasonal variations in the Community market. In practice, of course, the EC price-fixing procedure applies a nearly uniform percentage price rise to all institutional support prices, as explained in Chapter 3. There is very little differentiation between commodities.

The representative market price. The representative market price is calculated for fresh or chilled lamb carcasses on a weekly basis throughout the year, and is determined by the weighted average of prices in a series of markets within each Member State. It is the relationship between the basic price and the representative market price which determines whether private storage aids or support buying should be introduced or variable premiums paid.

Intervention prices. The intervention price is set at 85 per cent of the basic price; it is adjusted seasonally with the basic price. A derived intervention price is set for Ireland because it is a 'surplus' region some way away from its markets in the rest of the EC. Member States may choose between introducing intervention buying and the variable premium in any given year. Intervention support is, however, conditional on the introduction in the Member State in question of a carcass classification system intended to limit buying-in to those categories of sheepmeat which will provide the strongest market support.

Intervention buying may normally only operate between the 15 July and 15 December in any year, and then only if both the Community representative price is below the weekly intervention price, *and* the representative market price in the region in question is below its intervention price.

Private storage aids. As a first line of defence in market support, the regime provides for the payment of private storage aids when the representative market price falls to less than 90 per cent of the basic price. Rates of aid may be fixed in advance or set by tender.

The guide price and the variable premium

Where a Member State has decided to opt for the use of variable premiums, rather than for intervention buying, a *guide price* is fixed at the same level as the intervention price, that is at 85 per cent of the basic price.[12] Should the average market price for certified carcasses fall below the guide price, then a variable premium is payable as the difference between the two. This system is, of course, reminiscent of the former UK deficiency payments systems, and is at present operated only in Great Britain. The existence of the two support mechanisms in parallel would normally be expected to give rise to distortions in trade within the Community, particularly, for example, in trade between the UK and France. To avoid this a 'clawback' system is operated in the form of a charge on exports from Great Britain to other Community countries and Northern Ireland, equal to the amount of the variable premium. It was because of the level of smuggling from Northern Ireland to the South that, in 1982, the support system for Northern Ireland was harmonized with that of Ireland, rather than with that in the rest of the United Kingdom.

The reference price and the annual premium

In addition to the variable premium and to intervention buying, for a transitional period to 1984 producers may also be eligible for a further income support premium, designed to compensate producers for any loss they may have suffered from the introduction of the market organization. This annual premium is calculated as the difference each year between a *reference price* and the annual average market price in each of the seven regions into which the Community is divided.[13] The reference price for each region is set on the basis of the same criteria as the basic price; however, it is intended that by 1984/85 there should be a single reference price throughout the Community, and an adjustment is made each year to bring this about.

The annual premium is calculated in the following manner for each region:

(a) The difference between the reference price and the average market price (based upon the average of the representative market prices throughout the year).
(b) Multiply by the total production of sheepmeat in the previous year to give a total gross value for the annual premium.
(c) Deduct the amount of the variable premium paid, if any, during the year to give a total net value.
(d) Divide by the number of ewes recorded in the region, to give the annual premium per ewe.

In addition to the variable and annual premiums, a further compensatory premium is available to producers within the areas covered by the less favoured areas Directive.[14] However, the Community pays only 25 per cent of the expenditure on this premium.

The total return to the producer in regions applying variable premiums is therefore the sum of:

(a) The price obtained from the market;
(b) The variable premium paid on certified sheep and lambs slaughtered;
(c) The annual premium and, in areas of the less favoured areas Directive, a further compensatory premium, paid on the basis of the number of ewes in the breeding herd.

In the other areas producer returns are the sum of:

(a) The price obtained from the market;
(b) The annual premium and, in the less favoured areas, the further compensatory premium.

TRADE MEASURES

Imports

From the outset it was clear that the high level of imports of chilled and frozen lamb from New Zealand would be a central element in the negotiations for a common organization of the market. The original EC duty on imported sheepmeat was subject to a GATT binding at a maximum level of 20 per cent: to achieve an unbinding would have proved extremely expensive and politically difficult. At the same time, however, means had to be found to prevent the import of large quantities of New Zealand frozen or chilled lamb from destabilizing the sensitive and highly priced markets of Ireland and France. The Community chose to negotiate Voluntary Restraint Agreements (VRAs) with the major exporting countries, whereby they agreed to restrict their exports to the EC to predetermined levels. In return for Third Country exporters agreeing to accept VRAs, the Community agreed to limit the import levy to the equivalent of a 10 per cent customs duty in respect of live sheep and fresh, chilled, or frozen sheepmeat from these countries. Another feature of the VRAs is that the countries operating them have agreed—for a transitional period—to limit their exports to 'sensitive' regions of the Community to traditional levels. Ireland and France are at present regarded as sensitive markets.

At the time of writing the import quantities agreed under VRAs were almost 320 000 tonnes carcass weight (bone-in equivalent weight).

Imports from countries not having VRAs may only take place up to maximum annual quantities of 100 tonnes fresh or chilled sheepmeat, 100 tonnes frozen and 100 live animals for the year. For these quantities the reduced 10 per cent levy rate is charged. Other imports of sheepmeat from non-VRA countries are not permitted, even against payment of full levy. Imports from

Table 5.13   List of VRAs for sheepmeat.

Exporting country	Fresh, chilled, or frozen meat	Live sheep
Australia	17 500	
New Zealand	245 500	
Argentina	23 000	
Uruguay	5 800	
Bulgaria	1 250	2 000
Czechoslovakia	800	
Hungary	1 150	10 050
Poland	200	5 800
Iceland	600	
Austria		300
Romania	75	475
Yugoslavia	4 800	200
	300 675	18 825

Note: For Spain and Chile import quotas were still applicable until their VRAs had been negotiated.

Algeria, Morocco, Tunisia, and Turkey are admitted levy free or at a reduced levy rate because these countries had preferential duty concessions before the sheepmeat regime came into effect.

The VRAs also provide that should the EC ever apply measures to restrict imports, these will not apply to imports under the VRA quotas. The volume of exports to the EC is monitored by the exporting countries issuing export licences and the EC being prepared to issue import licences when these export licences are presented, and not otherwise.

Exports

There is provision for the payment of export refunds in the regime. But as part of the negotiations with Third Countries over the sheepmeat regime's introduction, the EC agreed that export refunds would not operate 'except at prices and on conditions meeting existing international obligations and in line with the Community's traditional share of the world export trade'. This phraseology was included in many of the VRAs as part of the EC's commitment when they were being negotiated.

Review of the market organization

The Commission will report to the Council of Ministers on the functioning of the regime as a whole by 1 October 1983. There is also a review procedure for each of the Voluntary Restraint Agreements. For example, that with New Zealand remains in force until 31 March 1984, but is to be reviewed before that date. It will continue after March 1984, 'subject to each party having the right to denounce it by giving one year's notice in writing' (Hickey, 1982, p. 69). New Zealand's commitment to restrict the flow of exports to the 'sensitive' markets of France and Ireland is contained in a separate exchange of letters. It is also valid until 31 March 1984, 'after this time there will be no restrictions on exports to these markets other than the VR Agreement'. (Hickey, 1982, p. 69). Presumably New Zealand will then seek to supply the highest price market—the ensuing market chaos is not difficult to foresee.

NOTES

1. Ries (1978, p. 157) has expressed this point very clearly: 'For more than two million European farmers, the weekly or monthly payments from the creameries have the same significance as the salary cheques from employers to their employees.' (Authors' translation.)
2. In 1950 average yields in the EC were 2500 litres per cow per year; by 1980 they averaged 4100 litres. But as Ries (1978) has said there is no reason why the average yield should not continue to rise when the best yielding cows are managing 10 000 litres annually.
3. 90.5 per cent of production in 1978, as against 60 per cent 20 years earlier.
4. According to *Agra Europe* (1981, p. 19), when the Commission initially offered an export refund of 160 ecu/100 kg for butter in 1981, 60 000 tonnes of export licences were booked 'within minutes almost of this booking facility' being opened.
5. It is understood that one reason the EC had to develop butter sales to the USSR was because of an understanding reached with New Zealand whereby the EC agreed not to expand its exports into markets which New Zealand was trying to develop as part of its diversification away from the UK market.
6. The interdependence between the EC's beef and dairy regimes is aptly illustrated by the Commission's own comment on the setting of beef guide prices. 'For its part, the pricing policy seems to have come off the rails from the moment the Community believed it could steer milk production towards meat production by substantially raising the guide price for adult bovine animals' (Commission, 1977, p. 10).
7. The slaughter premium scheme is of more significance than the calf premium scheme as it represents a dilution of the CAP principle of market prices underpinned by intervention buying as the principal method of support. The British Government has characterized the beef support system as applied in the UK as a *dual* system combining both variable slaughter premiums and intervention buying (House of Lords, 1978, p. 1).
8. As an entitlement to import beef at reduced levies is a profitable facility for the licence holders, the jumelage (or 'twinning') arrangements represent an attempt by the Commission to extract for the EC Budget some of the profit involved. When the jumelage arrangements applied potential importers had to bid for intervention beef at a quarterly tender in competition with other meat traders. The Commission saw the jumelage arrangements as a method of disposing of intervention beef stocks more quickly as its other disposal methods had not prevented a build-up of stocks.
9. Regulation 1837/80.
10. EC imports of lamb and mutton from New Zealand were 243 000 tonnes (1978), 229 000 tonnes (1979) and 198 000 tonnes (1980) (Commission 1982a, pp. 396/397). These imports accounted for 85.4 per cent of total EC imports and 23.6 per cent of total EC sheepmeat consumption on average over the three years 1978 to 1980.
11. The peak is in April, the trough in October.
12. The Commission has proposed the reduction of the guide price to 80 per cent of the basic price.

13. Prior to 1982 there were six regions, but then the UK was split in two. The regions are:

Region 1	Italy
Region 2	France
Region 3	West Germany, Benelux, Denmark
Region 4	Ireland
Region 5	Great Britain
Region 6	Northern Ireland
Region 7	Greece

The reference price in regions 2 and 7 is, in practice, fixed at the same level as the basic price. It is at this level, augmented as necessary at the annual price reviews, that all regional reference prices will be harmonized in 1984. This involves a reduction in the level in region 1, but an increase in all other regions.
14. Directive 75/268/EEC. This is discussed further in Chapter 9.

REFERENCES

Agra Europe Limited (1981) *Agra Europe*, Issue dated 3 July, Tunbridge Wells.

Commission of the European Economic Community (1964) *Proposition de dispositions concernant l'institution d'une taxe sur les matières grasses arrêtées par le Conseil en application de l'article 201 du Traité*, COM (64) 492, Brussels.

Commission of the European Communities (1968) *Memorandum on the reform of agriculture in the European Economic Community*, COM (68) 1000, Part A, Brussels.

Commission of the European Communities (1976) *Proposal for a Regulation (EEC) of the Council concerning a charge on certain oils and fats*, COM (76) 537, Brussels.

Commission of the European Communities (1977) *Amendment of the Common Organization of the market in Beef and Veal*, COM (77) 220, Brussels.

Commission of the European Communities (1980a) *The Agricultural Situation in the Community: 1980 Report*, Brussels.

Commission of the European Communities (1980b) *The Agricultural Situation in the Community: 1979 Report*, Brussels.

Commission of the European Communities (1981a) *Preliminary Draft General Budget of the European Communities for the Financial Year 1982*, Vol. 7A, Brussels.

Commission of the European Communities (1981b) *Guidelines for European Agriculture*, COM (81) 608, Brussels.

Commission of the European Communities (1982a) *The Agricultural Situation in the Community: 1981 Report*, Brussels.

Commission of the European Communities (1982b) *Report from the Commission to the Council on the Situation of the Agricultural Markets—1981*, COM (81) 822, Brussels.

Commission of the European Communities (1982c) *Commission Proposals on the fixing of prices for certain agricultural products and on certain related measures (1982/83)*, COM (82) 10, Vol. 1, Brussels.

Commission of the European Communities (1982d) *Preliminary Draft General Budget of the European Communities for the Financial Year 1983*, COM (82) 200, Vol. 7, Brussels.

Hickey, B. C. (1982) 'New Zealand's Voluntary Restraint Agreement with the EEC,' in Clough, P. W. J. (ed.), *EEC Sheep Industry Perspectives and Implications for New Zealand*, Centre for Agricultural Policy Studies, Massey University, New Zealand.

House of Lords Select Committee on the European Communities (1978) *Beef and Veal*, Session 1977–78, 11th Report, HL 63, HMSO: London.

Milk Marketing Board (1978) *Skimmed Milk Powder in the EEC—Developments and Prospects*, MMB: Thames Ditton.

New Zealand Meat Producers' Board (1978) *A Common Sense Approach to the EEC Sheepmeat Market*, London.

Ries, A. (1978) *L'ABC du Marché Commun Agricole*, Editions Labor: Brussels.

Chapter 6

Arable Breakcrops

In this chapter a disparate group of crops has been covered under the heading of 'arable breakcrops', although conventionally this term is applied to those crops (principally potatoes, oilseed-rape, sugar beet, and temporary grass) used specifically in otherwise entirely cereal crop rotations to control the build-up of cereal diseases and pests. It is convenient, however, to cover all the non-cereal arable crops grown outside the Mediterranean parts of the EC, even though some of these are specialist items grown in their own right. Consequently this chapter covers the CAP support regimes for protein and fodder crops, sugar, seeds for sowing, and that proposed for potatoes. In addition the support mechanisms for hops are discussed.

The regime for sugar is the most important of those covered in the chapter, and is the only one expanded to the same extent as those for the other major CAP commodities.

SUGAR

Economic significance

The first peculiarity of the sugar regime[1] is that it covers two different farm crops producing sugar (sugar beet and sugar cane) and one industrial product (isoglucose) producible potentially from a number of different agricultural crops. At the farm level, sugar beet is the important item within the EC, accounting for some 2.7 per cent of the value of final agricultural production and taking about 2 per cent of the farmed area. For virtually all the EC countries, the proportion sugar beet forms of final agricultural production is close to the average, apart from Greece (where it is only about 1 per cent) and Belgium (where it reaches nearly 5 per cent).

The EC's leading sugar producer is France with about 30 per cent of total production, followed by Germany and Italy with about a fifth each. France is the only EC country where sugar cane is also grown, in the French Overseas Departments[2] of Réunion and Guadeloupe. Production of sugar from cane is relatively limited (about 320 thousand tonnes at the beginning of the 1980s) and tending to drop.

In a world context the EC, taken as a single entity, is the largest producer, accounting for around 15 per cent of world production. It is also the world's second largest exporter of sugar after Cuba, and the largest exporter to the world market when Cuba's tied trade, with the Socialist bloc countries under Special Arrangements, is excluded.

The EC would undoubtedly be a significant isoglucose producer, based principally on starch from maize except that, ever since the technology for producing isoglucose became widely available in the early 1970s, the EC has rigorously controlled its production. As a result actual levels of EC isoglucose production are low, compared with those reached in Japan, Canada, and the USA, and will remain so until the sugar regime is altered in this aspect.

Community support regime

The basic sugar regime came into operation on 1 July 1968, after a five-year transition period. It covers:

(a) Beet and cane sugar; 'other' sugars excluding lactose and glucose;
(b) Sugar beet and sugar cane;
(c) Isoglucose;
(d) Molasses.

Budget cost

Spending on sugar varied between 3.5 and 10 per cent of total Budget spending on agricultural market support during the 1970s, in line with the fluctuations of the world sugar market. Principal cost items are the storage cost subsidies and export refunds (Table 6.1.)

Table 6.1   Spending on the sugar regime by the Community Budget.

	1981 (Actual)	1982 (Provisional)	1983 (Estimated)
1. Total spending on the sugar regime (million ecu)	767.4	1223.9	1531.0
2. As percentage of total FEOGA Guarantee Section spending	7.1	9.1	11.1
3. Main sugar support measures as percentage of total sugar regime spending	100.0	100.0	100.0
export refunds	53.3	64.3	68.1
storage cost subsidies	44.9	34.2	30.4

SOURCE   Commission (1982c, p. B/171).

The cost of the sugar regime is to a large extent covered by the revenue raised by the two sugar levies. These are not mainly import levies, as with the cereals regime, but levies charged to EC producers. This is because there are only minimal quantities of non-preferential imports of sugar from Third Countries, whereas there are substantial quantities of cereal imports from Third Countries. The two sugar producer levies raise revenue to cover respectively the cost of export refunds used to dispose of excess sugar on the world market and the payment of storage cost subsidies. In years when the revenue raised by the producer levy is insufficient to cover the cost of export refunds, the uncovered amount is carried over to the following year.

One peculiarity of the funding of export refunds, is that the cost of exporting a quantity equivalent to imports from the ACP states is met from the Budget. As a result, producer levies are somewhat lower than they otherwise would be if they had to cover this cost.

Support measures for sugar

General comment

The sugar regime differs in several important ways from the standard CAP commodity regime.

   (i) From its inception, the commitment to support domestic production has not been open-ended, but limited to production within the production quotas (see below).

  (ii) As an integral part of the regime, there is a major access commitment for third countries in the guarantee of a place on the Community market for ACP sugar.

 (iii) As with milk products, intervention buying support is based on the processed product (i.e. raw and white sugar), rather than the farm product (i.e. sugar beet and sugar cane).

It is paradoxical that a support system with important features suggested by those seeking to reform other CAP commodity regimes (e.g. the use of production quotas and a guaranteed access for Third Country supplies) is also one with the highest degree of over-supply and one where trade relations with other suppliers to the world market are particularly difficult because of the EC's reliance on export refunds to dispose of surplus quota sugar on world markets, and the fact that production outside the quotas (i.e. 'C' sugar) is not directly controlled. It is the total size of EC exports which concerns other suppliers, and not just the total of quota sugar exported with export refunds. The other problem that arises is not so much with the concept of production quotas and ACP access, but that these taken together exceed EC consumption.

The regime has two further features which render it unique. First, it has to cover the same product—sugar—produced from two different plants, one (sugar beet) a product of temperate zone agriculture, and the other (sugar cane) a product of tropical agriculture. This brings in its train difficulties as the processing industry differs according to which plant is handled, and has differing cost structures as a result. Second, its coverage has been extended to take in isoglucose; sugar's principal competitor in many industrial applications. As a result the regime is closer to one for sweeteners, rather than just sugar as its title suggests.

The structure of institutional support prices

The support system for sugar has a fuller range of institutional support prices than normal in CAP support regimes because it has to cover both farm and processed products. The key price is the *basic price* which represents the price farmers will receive for their beet[3] in years when producer levies are not necessary (i.e. when world prices are high in relation to EC domestic prices). As such levies are necessary normally, the Community also publishes *minimum prices* for beet which takes these levies into account. To ensure that farmers receive a minimum return, the beet factories are compelled to offer these prices at least, in their annual contracts with farmers.

In order for such a stipulation to be feasible, however, provision has to be made for the beet factories. Consequently, they are eligible for support buying at the *intervention prices* on all their sugar produced within the maximum production quotas (discussed below). White sugar intervention prices are set annually by taking the basic price for beet and adding freight and processing costs for the beet. For example, in 1982/83 the relationship between the beet and sugar prices was calculated as in Table 6.2.

A modified form of regional differentiation (known as regionalization) still applies for white sugar intervention prices and minimum beet prices. Thus the levels in Italy, the UK, and Ireland are higher than in the rest of the EC because these countries were traditionally deficit areas.

Table 6.2   The derivation of the white sugar intervention price from the basic beet price (1982/83). (Ecu/100 kg white sugar).

(a)	Basic beet price	39.32*
(b)	Implicit cost of sugar content of beet†	30.25
(c)	Factory processing margin	19.35
(d)	Beet freight costs to factory	3.59
(e)	Sub-total (b + c + d)	53.19
(f)	Less receipts from molasses sales	1.78
(g)	Intervention price white sugar (e − f)	51.41

* Ecu per tonne beet.
† Calculated assuming 16 per cent sugar content beet and the Community standard extraction rate so that one tonne of beet yields 130 kg white sugar.

In turn an intervention price for raw sugar is set by calculating backwards from that for white sugar, by allowing for a hypothetical[4] processing margin for beet factories processing raw to white sugar, the resulting weight loss and the transport costs involved in supplying raw sugar. EC production of raw beet sugar, however, is negligible (at about 1 to $1\frac{1}{2}$ per cent of its production of white sugar).

A final comment on intervention prices is that, despite their elaborate structure, intervention buying very seldom occurs. The EC's principal mechanism for disposing of its surplus sugar is its well developed system of export refunds (although these apply only to quota sugar: in 1981/82 exports of quota sugar were only about half of total EC exports). This ensures that the surplus is not visible within the EC as a sugar 'mountain' because it is exported to the world market.

The white sugar intervention price also serves as a base for the setting of the *target price*. This is set at a level 5 per cent above the intervention price, with the band between the two forming the main parameters within which domestic market prices normally fluctuate. In turn, from the target price is calculated the *threshold price* for white sugar which serves as the minimum import price for Third Country imports.

Production quotas

Production quotas were introduced as a temporary measure when the sugar regime came into full operation in 1968. The fundamental reason for their introduction was to protect those areas of relatively inefficient production in the Community which could have been expected to reduce or cease production had quotas not been used, but instead a lower support price set. The Commission (1973a, p. 5) estimated that it would have been necessary in the mid-1970s to lower prices by 25 per cent to get an adequate control over production if quotas were not to be used, in which case 'sugar production in the French Antilles could disappear; production in Réunion and Italy would fall very sharply as would production in several Northern regions of the Community'. Such results were politically unacceptable and production quotas seem likely to remain a permanent part of the regime, subject only to a nominally quinquennial[5] review of their level.

These reviews relate to the basic quotas (termed 'A' quotas) which are set by country, with national governments allocating them by factory. The Commission has tried to obtain the authority to allocate the quotas directly to factories but, as governments tend to regard their country's 'A' quota as national property, it has been refused. This nationalistic attitude to the 'A' quotas has meant that at the reviews of their level, governments have insisted that they can only be increased or remain unchanged, but not reduced as the Commission proposed at both the 1974 and 1980 quota reviews. (It is noteworthy, however, that at the 1980 quota review the British government was willing to accept a cut

Table 6.3   Production quotas for the Third Quota Period (1981/82 to 1985/86). (Sugar in tonnes, white value. Isoglucose in tonnes, dry matter).

	Sugar	Isoglucose
'A' Quotas		
Denmark	328 000	—
Germany	1 990 000	28 882
France (Metropolitan)	2 530 000	15 887
France (DOM)	466 000	—
Greece	290 000	10 522
Ireland	182 000	—
Italy	1 320 000	16 569
Netherlands	690 000	7 426
Belgium	680 000	56 667
UK	1 040 000	21 696
EC '10'	9 516 000	157 649
'B' Quotas		
Denmark	96 629	—
Germany	612 313	6 802
France (Metropolitan)	759 233	4 135
France (DOM)	46 600	—
Greece	29 000	2 478
Ireland	18 200	—
Italy	248 250	3 902
Netherlands	182 000	1 749
Belgium	146 000	15 583
UK	104 000	5 787
EC '10'	2 242 225	40 436
Maximum Quotas ('A' and 'B')		
Denmark	424 629	—
Germany	2 602 313	35 684
France (Metropolitan)	3 289 233	20 022
France (DOM)	512 600	—
Greece	319 000	13 000
Ireland	200 200	—
Italy	1 568 250	20 471
Netherlands	872 000	9 175
Belgium	826 000	72 250
UK	1 144 000	27 483
EC '10'	11 758 225	198 085

Note: Luxembourg does not produce sugar or isoglucose.

in the UK's production quota provided the other Member States were willing to accept equivalent cuts—they were not.)

In the first two quota periods (1968/69 to 1974/75 and 1975/76 to 1980/81) an element of flexibility used to be available in the specialization quotas (termed 'B' quotas). These were calculated for the Community as a whole as a percentage of the 'A' quotas—a percentage which was reviewed, although not necessarily changed, annually. In the third quota period (1981/82 to 1985/86), however, the 'B' quotas were set equal to the average of each country's three best years 'B' quota sugar production in the second half of the 1970s, subject to a minimum 10 per cent 'B' quota. As a result of this change, both 'A' and 'B' quotas are fixed for the duration of the third quota period—subject to a single review before the last two years of the period—and any element of annual flexibility in their level has been lost. The quotas for the third quota period are given in Table 6.3.

It shows a misunderstanding of how the production quotas have evolved to say that they have been unsuccessful in controlling EC production, which rose, for example, almost 60 per cent from 1973/74 to 1981/82 in part due to rapid technological progress. The aim of the quotas has been one of limiting the quantity of production eligible for EC market support, while allowing the EC's less competitive areas for sugar production to maintain their industries. In the first quota period the 'A' quotas were related to historic production levels. As part of the Community's over-reaction to the 1974 world sugar shortage, however, 'A' quotas were raised by almost a fifth and the Maximum Quotas ('A' + 'B') were raised 40 per cent, at a time when, it turned out, consumption was dropping. In the third quota period, although maximum quotas were cut marginally, the 'B' quotas were reallocated towards the countries which had the best history of filling them. As a result the quota system, as it has evolved, has institutionalized a considerable degree of overproduction. For example, by 1982/83, EC sugar consumption had dropped to around 9.5 million tonnes of white sugar equivalent (w.s.e.), as compared with maximum quotas of 11.76 million tonnes and actual production of some 14 million tonnes.

Production outside the maximum quotas is termed 'C' sugar. It is ineligible for EC price support and has to be sold on world markets without export subsidy. There is no restriction on farmers producing 'C' sugar, subject only to the willingness of processers to take the extra beet. The planned production of 'C' sugar, through plantings intended specifically for it, becomes a marginal calculation depending on a view of future world prices. As 'C' sugar cannot be produced, however, until the maximum quotas have been filled first, actual levels of 'C' sugar production are—to an extent—a residual depending on annual weather and disease fluctuations and their effects for yields.

Producer levies and co-responsibility

Commission documents dealing with reform of the CAP have come increasingly to emphasize the principle of co-responsibility, i.e. that producers should contribute towards the cost of disposing of surplus production. This principle has progressed furthest in the sugar regime. Indeed, from the time when common sugar prices came into operation in 1968, the sugar regime has employed producer levies. In the first two quota periods (that is, up to and including 1980/81) the maximum unit rate of levy that was chargeable on 'B' quota sugar production was an amount per tonne of sugar equivalent to 30 per cent of the white sugar intervention price. The levy did not apply to 'A' quota production as this was meant to be close to domestic consumption, and therefore presumed not to be in surplus. The funds raised by the levy helped meet the Budget cost of export refunds. In so far, however, as in any one year the cost of refunds was larger than the sum of the levies collected, the difference was met from the Budget.

In the third quota period (from 1981/82 to 1985/86) producers are meant to cover the full Budget cost of export refunds, apart from the cost of exporting a quantity of sugar equivalent to Lomé Convention imports which is charged to the Budget and not passed on to producers. The maximum unit levy chargeable to producers is 2 per cent of the white sugar intervention price on all their within quota (i.e. 'A' plus 'B') production, plus a further 30 per cent on their 'B' quota production. In years when these levies do not cover the full cost of export refunds, the deficit may be carried over to the following year and an extra 7.5 per cent levy charged on 'B' quota so giving, in that year, a maximum unit charge of 39.5 per cent of the intervention price. If the revenue raised is still insufficient to cover the total cost of export refunds, the accumulated deficit is rolled on to the following season with the implicit hope that, at some stage in the third quota period, world prices will turn up because of the sugar cycle so that the unit cost of export refunds drops.

The burden of the producer levies is split 60:40 between growers and processors. Equivalent producer levies apply on isoglucose production.

Storage cost subsidies and consumers

In both the cereals and sugar regimes there is the difficulty—in Community eyes—of seasonality of production as against the need for a constant supply throughout the year. For sugar the solution adopted was the creation of a system of storage cost subsidies, which are paid monthly to cover the average cost of storing sugar. As a result, inventory holders rely on the subsidies to cover their running expenses involved in storage, rather than on a rising domestic market price during the season. The storage subsidies are financed by a levy on all sales by beet processors and refiners of DOM sugar. The application of the storage levy/subsidy system for ACP sugar has been suspended to 1985/86. The levy revenue goes into a fund which year-on-year is self-balancing, with the following season's storage levy rate being set to reflect the surplus/deficit on the previous season.

As the levies are payable on all sales, apart from those into intervention, the minimum domestic market price in the EC is the white sugar intervention price plus the storage cost levy, as in so far as this level (known as the *effective support price*) is not achievable from the market it will pay producers to sell into intervention. With the rise in interest costs at the beginning of the 1980s, however, and the increase in stocks being held due to depressed world prices, the storage cost element in EC domestic market prices had become a noticeable feature at around 10 per cent. Noticeable enough for consumer and sugar user interests to start objecting to the system.

Alternative uses for sugar

Because of the lack of scope for finding extra domestic markets for sugar, the EC has not generated a major programme for subsidizing consumption as has happened with the dairy regime. The only equivalent programme is one for granting production refunds on sugar used in the chemical industry and is designed to make sugar competitive with starch produced from cereals. This programme has operated since the sugar regime's creation, except during the sugar shortage years in the mid-1970s when it was suspended. Undoubtedly, however, other schemes would be introduced were technical advances to open up important new markets; indeed the sugar regime makes provision for such developments.

Isoglucose

In the early 1970s the technology became widely available for the production of a substance (known as High Fructose Corn Syrup in the USA and Isoglucose in the EC) with equivalent sweetening power to sugar on a one-for-one basis, but generally available at significantly cheaper prices as it is produced as a continuation of the process of starch and glucose manufacture (based on maize, potatoes, and wheat). With the spurt to investment given by the high world sugar prices of 1974 and 1980 HFCS production became well established in countries with advanced food industries.[6]

In the EC, however, when it became apparent that starch manufacturers wanted to move into isoglucose production to help relieve their over-capacity problems and because for certain uses isoglucose was preferred to sugar syrups, the Community moved to control production. First, it withdrew the normal production refund on maize used for starch and glucose manufacture where this, in turn, was turned into isoglucose; second, the grant of national investment aids for isoglucose manufacture was banned; and third, a separate regime was introduced to control isoglucose production. (This regime was incorporated with that for sugar in 1981.)

The justification for these developments was that sugar was already in structural surplus in the EC. Consequently the production of a cheaper substitute which displaced sugar in important food and drink uses would increase the surplus of sugar. As disposing of this surplus was costly it was argued that isoglucose manufacturers should pay a proportion of this cost—an argument accepted by the European Court in 1978, although as a result of the Court ruling the planned method for applying the levy had to be altered. The outcome was that production quotas (see Table 6.3) and producer levies are applied to isoglucose manufacturers as to sugar beet processers, while variable import levies apply to imports from Third Countries. As a result, isoglucose production is constrained to 198 000 tonnes dry matter when, by comparison, in the USA production had reached over 2.5 million tonnes by 1980 and was still rising.

Import levies/export refunds

In order to prevent imports undercutting the *threshold price*, variable import levies are calculated and set daily. The same sort of calculation procedures are followed as with the import levies on cereals, so that the sugar levies cover the full arithmetic difference between threshold prices and 'the most favourable purchasing opportunities . . . on the world market'. The Commission seems to have rather more scope for judgement in setting import levies for sugar than for cereals because it has to take into account not only world market offers, but also quotations on the main world terminal markets, prices in important Third Country markets, and prices in international trade. With the EC's own surplus in sugar, plus its obligation to take in ACP sugars (see below), it is not surprising that these factors combined with the import levy system ensure that EC imports of non-ACP Third Country sugars are virtually nil.

Perhaps the most controversial aspect of the EC's sugar regime is its export refund system. This has operated successfully from the Community's point of view in that it has disposed of its entire surplus of Quota sugar on world markets despite the growth in size of the surplus. The principal method of disposal is a weekly tender at which traders bid for the quantity of sugar they wish to export. It should be remembered, however, that 'C' sugar is exported without export refund and, in 1981/82, 'C' sugar accounted for half the EC's total exports.

Under the management committee procedure, the Commission calculates the total quantity of quota sugar the EC has to export each season and then divides this target level to give an approximate weekly quantity for which it is prepared to accept bids. Under normal circumstances, traders are bidding for export refunds, and the first bid to be accepted is for the lowest unit rate of refund. The next bid to be accepted will be for the next lowest refund rate and so on, until the volume of sugar bid for reaches the weekly target. The Commission does its own calculations as to what levels of export refund are necessary to sell on world markets and uses these calculations to monitor the bids. As a consequence the weekly target is not always reached where bids are too expensive in the Commission's eyes. At other times, when bids look 'cheap', a larger volume of sugar than the target may be awarded export refunds.

There is also a system of Standing export refunds—always less than the maximum refund allowed at the weekly tenders—available at all times and designed for small export quantities of speciality sugars.

World prices above EC levels

Due to the cyclical nature of the world sugar market with long periods of depressed world prices broken by short periods of extremely high prices, there can be occasions when world sugar prices exceed EC levels. This happened in 1974 and 1975, and again in 1980 and 1981.

At such times the system is reversed so that the Community commitment to insulate its domestic market can be maintained. Thus traders, instead of bidding for export refunds, have to bid for export levies, i.e. the size of levy they are prepared to pay the EC in order to be allowed to export from it. The effect of the system is to allow the Community Budget to acquire the entire difference between domestic EC prices and world prices, and to stop domestic market prices rising in line with world prices. At times of high world prices the EC also stops charging import levies and in 1974 actually resorted to granting import subsidies to encourage the import of sugar.[7]

Arrangements for ACP sugar

A crucial constituent of the negotiation of the first Lomé Convention, signed in 1975, was the incorporation of an arrangement, to replace the access several Commonwealth countries had enjoyed to the UK market under the Commonwealth Sugar Agreement, having equivalent effect in the EC market.[8] Under the Sugar Protocol incorporated in the Lomé Convention the Community agreed 'for an indefinite period to purchase and import at guaranteed prices' some 1.3 million tonnes w.s.e. annually. The commitment for an 'indefinite period' means that even if the Lomé Convention should be allowed to lapse at some time in the future, the sugar provisions will be maintained.

The arrangement is exceptional to the character of EC trade concessions in several respects:

 (i) The Protocol is open-ended in time, whereas most other trade concessions apply only for a stipulated period;
 (ii) There is a definite guarantee for levy-free entry for a given quantity at a stipulated price. Most other trade concessions do not give a price guarantee, nor do they give a levy-free entry;
(iii) The price paid ACP sugar producers is within the price band to Community producers and hence has to be reviewed annually when the institutional support prices for sugar are fixed. This price guarantee is unique among EC trade concessions.

Generally, but not always, the *guaranteed prices* paid ACP producers have equalled the EC's raw and white sugar intervention prices. Although the ACP producers receive the same prices as EC beet farmers, their prices apply c.i.f. European ports, so that freight and insurance they have to pay themselves. The ACP producers are not liable, however, for EC producer levies.

The most significant difficulty with the operation of the Sugar Protocol has concerned the availability of adequate cane sugar refining capacity and a market for the sugar once refined. The House of Lords Select Committee on the European Communities (1980) found that the survival of the major market for

ACP cane sugar—in the UK—depended on there being a sufficient market premium in the UK to allow Tate & Lyle, the UK's only major cane sugar refiner, to cover fully its costs.

Other difficulties that have arisen with the operation of the Sugar Protocol have concerned:

  (i) The lack of 'negotiation' over the guaranteed prices: in effect the EC has laid down the prices in most years. One constraint on the EC's willingness to grant more generous guaranteed prices is its need to consider what prices the cane refiners can pay and still be viable when selling at EC internal market prices.

 (ii) The reduction in the quotas due to shortfalls (Table 6.4). The Commission has to reduce the quotas automatically if an ACP country does not fill its quota and cannot point to forces outside its control (such as tornadoes) as being the reason for the shortfall;

(iii) The ACP demand for help with freight costs to the EC.

The EC and the world market

It has been explained above that the EC's sugar production rose markedly during the 1970s: at the same time domestic consumption tended to drop. As a result the EC's self-sufficiency from its domestic production rose from 91 per cent in 1973/74 to 158 per cent in 1981/82. If account is taken of the EC's cane sugar imports from the ACP—as it should be as these imports are a guaranteed source of supply for the EC based upon an inescapable Treaty-determined obligation—then the EC's self-sufficiency rate in 1981/82 was almost 172 per cent.

Despite this there are no sugar 'mountains' in the EC, as all the surplus to domestic needs is exported to the world market, either with export refunds (if it is quota sugar) or without any refund (if it is 'C' sugar). This led to the EC share of the world market rising from 7.5 per cent in 1976 to 22 per cent in 1980.

In turn this expansion caused problems for other exporters to the world market. In 1978 Australia and Brazil launched separate complaints in GATT that the EC had used its export refunds to take an inequitable share of the world market. In 1982 these complaints were withdrawn and replaced by a single complaint supported by ten countries including Argentina, Australia, Brazil, India, and the Philippines.

The EC's reliance on the world market to dispose of its surplus sugar has meant that it found it impossible to join the International Sugar Agreement (ISA). In 1968 the nub of the EC's case against entry was that it had not been offered a large enough export quota. By 1978 the EC was claiming that the ISA should be more heavily based on the use of stocking arrangements and less on the use of export quotas. Essentially the EC's fears relate to having an external authority (i.e. the ISA) stipulate how much it may export and the unacceptability of this to some EC countries, plus its realization that stocking

Table 6.4   Preferential sugar quotas by country. (tonnes white sugar equivalent).

Quota years (July/June)	1975/76 and 1976/77	1977/78	1978/79	1979/80	1980/81	1981/82	1982/83
Barbados	49 300	49 300	49 300	49 300	49 300	49 300	49 300
Belize	39 400	39 400	39 400	39 400	39 400	39 400	39 400
Congo	10 000	10 000	10 000	4 957	4 957	4 957	4 957
Fiji	163 600	163 600	163 600	163 600	163 600	163 600	163 600
Guyana	157 700	157 700	157 700	157 700	157 700	157 700	157 700
India	25 000	25 000	25 000	25 000	25 000	0	0
Jamaica	118 300	118 300	118 300	118 300	118 300	118 300	118 300
Kenya	5 000	5 000	5 000	93	93	93	4 000
Madagascar	10 000	10 000	10 000	10 000	10 000	10 000	10 000
Malawi	20 000	20 000	20 000	20 000	20 000	20 000	20 000
Mauritius	487 200	487 200	487 200	487 200	487 200	487 200	487 200
St Kitts-Nevis-Anguilla	14 800	14 800	14 800	14 800	14 800	14 800	14 800
Surinam	4 000	3 199	4 000	2 667	2 667	2 667	2 667
Swaziland	116 400	116 400	116 400	116 400	116 400	116 400	116 400
Tanzania	10 000	10 000	10 000	10 000	10 000	10 000	10 000
Trinidad & Tobago	69 000	69 000	69 000	69 000	69 000	69 000	69 000
Uganda	5 000	5 000	5 000	0	0	0	0
Zimbabwe	—	—	5 000	—	—	6 000	25 000
Total	1 304 700	1 303 899	1 304 700	1 288 417	1 288 417	1 269 417	1 292 324

SOURCES   Regulation 3225/80 (Protocol No. 7) giving the text of the Second Lomé Convention.
Regulation 237/82 on Zimbabwe's accession to the Lomé Convention.
Council Decision 75/456/EEC of 15 July 1975 on India's sugar quota.
Notices of the Commission in *Official Journal* C112 (13 May 1978), C97 (18 April 1979), C108 (29 April 1982), and C124 (15 May 1982).

arrangements are easier for it to implement than would be export quotas.[9] However, the EC and the ISA co-operated to an extent in an attempt to control the supply of sugar to the world market in 1981/82.

The 1977 ISA expires at the end of 1984. It was widely recognized that there were important defects in its construction. The EC, in 1981, signalled its willingness to join an improved ISA. The question was whether the improvements the EC would want in a successor ISA would be acceptable to the rest of its membership, or indeed, whether all of the membership of the 1977 ISA would be able to agree on the conditions for a successor ISA in any case.

SEEDS FOR SOWING

Coverage

The support system for seeds for sowing[10] came into effect on 1 July 1972. It has since been amended several times to widen its coverage. In 1982 it covered:

(a) Rice;
(b) Leguminous seeds (field peas, field beans, clovers, lucerne, and vetch);
(c) Hybrid maize;
(d) Oilseeds (flax, linseed, hemp);
(e) Most kinds of agricultural and amenity grasses.

Economic significance

EC fodder (herbage and leguminous) seed production was about 290 000 tonnes in 1981, equal to about a quarter of world production. Denmark is the main producer of herbage seeds, followed by the UK and the Netherlands. The UK, France, and Italy are the main producers of seeds of leguminous vegetables.

Operation

For seeds for sowing, except for hybrid maize, the regime provides support through *production aids* set at different rates per 100 kg for each species. The production aids are available only for the production of seed certified as meeting stipulated quality conditions. The level of aid is set for two years at a time taking account of the domestic market situation and world market prices, although there are provisions allowing a change in the rate of aid in the second year should EC market conditions alter drastically.

Protection at the EC frontier is applied through *ad valorem* duties under the Common Customs Tariff. Seed harvested in Third Countries may be marketed in the EC only if it is equivalent (i.e. meeting comparable quality conditions) to seed certified within the Community. (The equivalence has to be established by field inspection and official examination in the Third Countries where the seed is produced, although the EC has a network of recognition arrangements with official seed certification bodies in all important seed-producing Third Countries.)

For hybrid maize for sowing, however, a *reference price* is set annually to apply at EC frontiers. This is the average of the free-at-frontier prices which obtained during the previous three years for each type of hybrid maize. When an offer from a Third Country plus the normal CCT duty (currently nil) is lower than the reference price a *countervailing charge* is levied to bridge the gap. Once fixed this charge is levied on all hybrid maize imports of that type from that country whether they come in above or below the reference price. Under a GATT binding, however, the countervailing charge may not exceed 4 per cent of the customs value.

OILSEEDS, PROTEIN PLANTS, AND FODDER CROPS

The policy for proteins

When the oils and fats regime[11] was introduced in the second half of the 1960s, it was only felt necessary to support the production of colza, rape, and sunflower seed among the oilseeds. Even for these items, relatively lightly structured regimes were adopted as, given the EC's low self-sufficiency—only 4.5 per cent for oilcakes, and 20 per cent for all protein sources used for animal feedingstuffs (Commission, 1973b)—and its large oilseed crushing industry based on imported oilseeds, this was the most logical solution. Consequently, there is duty-free entry for imported oilseeds and oilcakes under the Common External Tariff. For the processed oils, however, there are duties which quickly increase as the degree of processing involved rises in order to protect the EC's domestic crushing industry.

The shocks of the early 1970s—when world prices for protein sources for animal feedingstuffs rocketed due to the disappearance of the Peruvian anchovy crop, and the USA followed by Brazil applied export bans on their soyabeans—dramatized the EC's dependence on imports for the bulk of its protein feeds for animals. This led some EC countries to claim that it was necessary for the Community to increase its self-sufficiency levels for protein sources. To this end, the Commission (1973b) surveyed actual and potential domestic protein sources before proposing (Commission, 1973c) a series of measures to increase EC protein production for use in animal feedingstuffs. Included were measures to:

   (i) Encourage sunflower seed production;
   (ii) Make EC-produced colza and rape more acceptable by encouraging the use of low erucic acid varieties;[12]
   (iii) Introduce support measures for domestically produced soya to encourage its production;
   (iv) Help the establishment of drying plants for fodder crops such as lucerne;
   (v) Reduce the price of EC-grown fodder legumes, such as peas and beans, when used by animal feed compounders.

As a result of these proposals support systems were introduced during the 1970s for soyabeans, flax seed (linseed), castor seeds, dehydrated fodder, and peas and beans for animal feeds.

Colza, rape, and sunflower seed

These oilseeds account for about a half of one per cent of the value of final agricultural production in the EC and take around 5 per cent annually of FEOGA Guarantee Section spending. EC production of colza and rape has expanded sharply: from some 435 000 tonnes in 1966/67 to nearly 2 million tonnes in 1981/82, when it accounted for almost 20 per cent of world production. The main EC producers of rape are France, followed by Germany, the UK, and Denmark. For sunflower seed the only producers are France and Italy; nevertheless EC production has risen from some 20 000 tonnes in 1966/67 to around 305 000 tonnes in 1980/81.

For these oilseeds a relatively traditional structure of *target* and *intervention prices*[13] is employed. As, however, there is duty-free entry for imported oilseeds, the EC's domestic market prices are set by imports and hence are normally at a significantly lower level than the target prices, as 'the intervention arrangements seem to be largely irrelevant' (Parris and Ritson, 1977, p. 80).

The principal means of support is through a system of *production aids*. These aids, set at least weekly as the difference between the target prices and world market prices, are payable to oilseed crushers to ensure they take what EC supplies are offered them—in effect, the aids operate as a crushing subsidy on domestic oilseed production. Crushers can claim either the 'spot' rate of crushing aid (known as day-aid) or 'pre-fix' the rate for oilseeds to be crushed up to five months ahead. According to the Commission the pre-fixing of the aid allows the crushers to plan the bulk of their production ahead, while leaving a margin of flexibility which the crusher can fill using the day-aid according to market conditions. In order to ensure that some of the EC's smaller inland crushers were not left with negative margins, a system of correctives to the day-aid for crushing was introduced in 1980, based on the difference between the margins available on crushing rape and on crushing competing oilseeds (principally soya). The aim was to help those inland crushers who did not have access to other (mainly imported) oilseeds when the margins on crushing rapeseed become negative and hence had to shut down when this occurred. In 1982, however, the corrective was withdrawn following a massive uptake of day aid by the large crushers.

Because of the major increase in EC production of colza and rape, together with the relatively limited market demand as colza meal is not ideally suited for animal feeds, *production thresholds* were introduced in 1982/83 to limit the quantity for whose production the EC has a support commitment. For 1982/83 a production threshold was set at 2.15 million tonnes. This level will be raised annually to an expected target production level of 3.3 million tonnes in 1988. Should production averaged over the three years 1980/81 to 1982/83 exceed the 1982/83 production threshold, then the 1983/84 support prices will be reduced proportionate to the production excess.

The support measures at the frontier consist only of the Common Customs Tariff, although as discussed already the levels of duty charged escalate markedly as the degree of processing in imports rises. Thus, while imports of oilseeds enter duty free, duties rise from 6 per cent on crude oils to 15 per cent on fully refined oils. There is provision (never used so far) for the charging of Compensatory Amounts under conditions where imports are 'threatening to prejudice' the interests of EC farmers.

Export refunds are available on EC-grown oilseeds, although in practice very little use is made of them, as unit refund rates are kept below unit rates of production aid in order not to divert supplies from EC crushers.

Soyabeans, linseed (flax seed), and castor seeds

The support arrangements for these oilseeds were introduced after the need for an EC proteins policy was agreed in 1973. Thus the arrangements for soyabeans came into effect in 1974 (although they were completely remodelled[14] in 1979), while the arrangements for linseed[15] and castor seeds[16] were introduced in 1976 and 1977, respectively. For all three the basic support system is the same and based on the fact that competing oilseeds from the world market have free entry to the EC. Consequently a system involving the maintenance of domestic market prices above world levels would be difficult to operate. Instead a form of deficiency payments system is used whereby a *guide price* is set annually for each oilseed and a subsidy (*production aid*) paid to cover the difference between this price and average world prices for the oilseed in question.

For soyabeans, the aid is payable to the first buyers of EC-grown soyabeans from farmers, provided they agree to pay farmers a *minimum price*. This minimum price is set by the Council of Ministers as part of the annual price fixing. In order to verify that buyers do pay the minimum price their contracts with farmers have to be checked by the Member States' authorities. The amount of aid is reviewed when the world market price for soyabeans is determined twice monthly.

For linseed from flax grown for either fibre or seed, a production subsidy (*production aid*) is available. Where flax is grown for seed (linseed) the aid is payable to the farmer; where the flax is grown for fibre the aid may go to farmer or processer. Growers of flax for fibre (textile flax) also receive a fixed rate aid under the regime for fibre flax and hemp (see Chapter 7).

For castor seed, the *production aid* is payable to the crusher, as with rape and sunflower seed. As with the arrangements for soyabeans, crushers of EC-grown castor seeds only receive the aid provided they pay a *minimum price* to growers. As castor seed production is at an experimental stage in the EC, a launching aid was applied initially for the three seasons 1979/80 to 1981/82, subsequently extended to 1983/84.

Despite the availability of these support arrangements, EC production of all three crops is miniscule. For soyabeans the maximum produced so far was 25 000 tonnes (in 1979) as compared with imports of some 13 million tonnes in

1979/80. The same picture applies for linseed with EC production of 50 000 tonnes in 1980 as against imports of some 250 000 tonnes of linseed as such in 1980, plus 100 000 tonnes of linseed oil and over 600 000 tonnes of linseed cake. For castor seed, EC plantings were only 10 ha in 1981. Imports in 1980 were almost 34 000 tonnes of castor seeds as such and 63 000 tonnes of oil.

Special measures for peas and field beans

As part of the 1977 package of Mediterranean measures (Commission, 1977) a support system was introduced in 1978[17] for dried peas and field beans used in animal feed. This was justified as providing an alternative crop for farmers in the EC's Mediterranean regions, as well as increasing the EC's self-sufficiency in proteins. In 1982 these measures were extended to cover peas and field beans used for human consumption.

The main policy instrument in relation to peas and field beans used in animal feed is an incorporation aid paid to feed compounders, provided that they have paid to farmers a *minimum purchase price* set by the Council of Ministers as part of the annual price fixing. As with the soyabean aid, compounders have their contracts with farmers checked before the aid is payable.

The incorporation aid is set equal to 45 per cent of the difference between the EC-determined *aid activating price* and the world price for soyabean meal. The aid activating price is meant to be determined at such a level that peas, field beans, and broad beans are competitive with soya meal in animal feeds, while allowing compounders to pay farmers the stipulated minimum purchase price. An example of the calculation for April 1982 is given below:

Activating price, 418.30 ecu/tonne
soya meal

		Minimum purchase price for peas and beans	244.70 ecu/tonne
World price, soya meal	230.01 ecu/tonne	Less aid of gives	87.43
	Difference = 418.30 − 230.01	Effective purchase	159.97 ecu/tonne
	= 188.29	price to compounder	
	Aid = 188.29 × 0.45	of peas and beans	
	= 87.43		

The average world market price for soya meal, from which the aid is calculated, is determined monthly, or more frequently if market prices are volatile. When world prices are above the aid activating price no aid is payable. When world soya meal prices are below the aid activating price, the aid is payable on the quantity of EC-produced peas and beans incorporated by compounders in their animal feedingstuffs.

The Commission (1982a) proposed, and the Council accepted, that the special measures for peas and field beans should be extended to those used for human consumption. The Commission justified the extension of the system as being necessary because it had found there was a tendency for farmers to shift to alternative crops which qualified for CAP support, while competition from Third Country supplies imported at low rates of tariff had increased as the minimum purchase price had in effect raised the market price for EC-produced peas and beans.

The policy measure adopted for peas and field beans destined for human consumption is a *production aid* payable where peas and field beans are used in products destined for human consumption, or where they are sold directly in unprocessed form for human consumption. The aid is calculated as the difference between a *guide price* (set by the Council as part of the annual price fixing) and world prices for beans and peas. The aid is only payable to companies which can prove they have paid the minimum purchase price to farmers as discussed above.

Dried fodder

As part of the reaction to the increase in energy costs in 1973/74 and to the Commission's 1973 report on proteins, a support system for dehydrated fodder was introduced in 1974. This was widened to include dried fodder in 1978.[18] Products covered include:

(a) Dehydrated products: potatoes, lucerne, sainfoin, clover, lupins, vetches—and similar fodder products—dehydrated by artificial heat drying;

(b) Other products: meal obtained from sun dried legumes and proteins from green fodder.

The regime employs two policy measures. The first, a flat rate *production aid* is available on all dehydrated fodder products at two rates: the higher rate applying on dehydrated potatoes and the lower on dehydrated fodder. The second measure involves the annual setting of a *guide price* and the payment of a variable rate *supplementary aid* equal to part of the difference between it and the world price for dehydrated fodder where this is lower.

This regime has not been very successful in that production of dehydrated fodder has tended to drop. Principally this has been due to the impact of the rise in world energy prices at the end of the 1970s and the industry's heavy fuel usage for drying, plus the high capital cost of installing modern drying equipment which can use fuel more efficiently. On the one hand driers have had to pay producers the guide prices—which were set originally to give farmers a return comparable to growing wheat and have been raised in line with other CAP support prices at the annual price fixing—while on the other hand, the increases in flat rate production aid have not covered the increases in energy costs.

The Commission, however, is keen to maintain crop drying because dried fodder is, apart from rape, the main domestically produced source of protein for animal feed and is the crop with the highest yield of protein per hectare. This begs the question whether it is a sensible use of energy resources to use them for producing animal feed proteins which are abundantly available from Third Countries; the EC is, however, encouraging the development of sun dried fodder and of ways of reducing fuel usage by driers.

THE PROPOSED SYSTEM FOR POTATOES

The Commission tried throughout the 1970s to introduce a common support system for potatoes. Its last formal proposals were made in 1975 (Commission, 1975). They provided for a relatively lightly structured regime involving an emphasis on the use of common marketing standards to improve quality and the encouragement of more disciplined marketing methods through the granting of private storage aids to groups of producers. The aids to the groups were meant to encourage the holding by them of potatoes at times of depressed market prices to avoid further supplies weakening an already depressed market. Intervention buying, however, was not envisaged. At Community frontiers, in addition to the *ad valorem* duty already applied to imports, there were to be *reference prices* (operating in an analogous manner to those for fruit and vegetables—see Chapter 7) for new potatoes.[19]

In subsequent discussions within the EC, these proposals were substantially amended. One of the first casualties was the provision for private storage aids to groups of producers of maincrop potatoes. It had been the Commission's intention that at the end of the storage period the stored potatoes would be dehydrated for animal feed if a surplus still existed. Most Member States pointed out, however, that expenditure on the storage of potatoes which were likely ultimately to be disposed of in this way would be wasteful of EC funds. The Commission therefore amended their proposal to accommodate a system whereby, as soon as a serious market imbalance occurred, producer groups could choose either to dehydrate or denature surplus potatoes into animal feed and claim aid for so doing based on the technical costs of the operation.

The proposal for supporting the new potato market by means of the reference price was also expanded to include a system of flat rate aids to producers when market prices for new potatoes fell below a previously determined EC target price.

The Commission's proposals have, to the time of writing, foundered on the inability of Member States to agree on the proposed new regime. In the meantime, EC countries maintain their distinct national support systems, although there is now free intra-Community trade. There are, however, Community provisions for the marketing of seed potatoes,[20] for the granting of production refunds on potatoes used for starch (under the cereals regime) and for the production of dehydrated potatoes (under the dehydrated fodder regime).

HOPS

Coverage

The hops support system[21] came into operation on 1 August 1971. It covers:

(a) Hops (cones and lupulin);
(b) Hop powder;
(c) Vegetable saps and extracts of hops.

Economic significance

The EC, with production of about 46 000 tonnes in 1981, accounts for just over a third of world hop production. Community production has been constrained by the 1977 decision to prohibit any expansion in hop area for two years. Since this lapsed, however, there has been a small growth in area. The main EC producers are Germany and the UK. Hops account for about 0.1 per cent of the value of EC agricultural production.

Operation of the support system

A fixed rate of *income aid* is paid per hectare planted. The amount of this aid is fixed after the hops have been harvested and takes into account the EC market situation and world prices (particularly important for hops as about 23 per cent of EC production is exported to the world market). These aids are differentiated by variety to encourage production of those most desired by users, even though it might have been expected that market prices would have given an adequate differentiation. Where it is felt the area of a particular variety is too large, the aids for the variety may be lowered as a means of discouraging its cultivation and encouraging restructuring of the industry.

For imports an *ad valorem* duty applies as part of the CCT. The EC does not grant export refunds. It talks, however, with the world's other major producers about likely market trends as a means of assessing future production prospects and whether the EC should allow its domestic production area to expand.[22]

NOTES

1. Regulation (EEC) No. 1785/81, applicable until the end of the 1985/86 quota year.
2. The Overseas Departments (DOM) are an integral part of Metropolitan France, although they are outside the main area of Continental France. Included in the DOM are Réunion, Martinique, and Guadeloupe. Martinique used to produce cane sugar, but has almost ceased.
3. At a standard 16 per cent sugar content in the beet delivered to an off-farm collection centre.
4. Hypothetical as very few beet factories are left in the Community that can only produce raw sugar. Virtually all have been converted to produce white sugar in a continuous process from beet.

5. The first set of 'A' quotas applied for the seven years 1968/69 to 1974/75; the second set were meant to have applied for the five years 1975/76 to 1979/80 but because of difficulty over agreeing their replacement levels were extended for a sixth year to 1980/81. The third set of 'A' quotas applies for the five years 1981/82 to 1985/86.

6. Commercially isoglucose is available only as liquid, which is why its use is restricted to countries with technically advanced food and drink industries. For an account of its development see FAO (1977).

7. Although it is likely that the policy of granting import subsidies was introduced with an eye to the then closely debated renegotiation of the UK's EC membership.

8. For a comparison of the provisions of the Commonwealth Sugar Agreement and the Sugar Protocol of the Lomé Convention, see Harris and Hagelberg (1975).

9. For a discussion of the Community's attitude to the ISA, see Harris (1980).

10. Regulation (EEC) No. 2358/71.

11. Regulation (EEC) No. 136/66. This came into effect for olive oil on 10 November 1966 and for oilseeds on 1 July 1967.

12. Erucic acid is poisonous to livestock in levels above certain minimum concentrations. The swing to low erucic acid varieties was encouraged by altering the quality definition of rape seed acceptable for intervention so that it contained less than 5 per cent erucic acid. (Most modern varieties actually contain less than 1 per cent.) The EC pays a special premium for rape seed low in both erucic acid and glucosinolates.

13. For colza and rape, as with cereals and sugar, when the common support prices were introduced originally they were differentiated between regions, so that lower intervention prices applied in surplus areas and higher intervention prices in deficit areas, to encourage the movement of produce from one to the other. For oilseeds, the regionalization was phased out over three years so that a single EC intervention price applied from 1982/83.

14. Regulation (EEC) No. 1614/79.

15. Regulation (EEC) No. 569/76.

16. Regulation (EEC) No. 2874/77.

17. Was Regulation (EEC) No. 1119/78. This was superseded by Regulation (EEC) No. 1431/82.

18. Regulation (EEC) No. 1117/78.

19. The operation of the proposed regime was analysed by the House of Lords (1976).

20. Directive 66/403/EEC.

21. Regulation (EEC) No. 1696/71.

22. For an assessment of world conditions and the extent to which the EC area should be altered, see Commission (1982b).

REFERENCES

Commission of the European Communities (1973a) *Memorandum from the Commission to the Council on the Future Sugar Policy of the Community*, COM (73) 1177, Brussels.

Commission of the European Communities (1973b) *Report on the Community's Protein Supplies*, COM (73) 1850 Annex, Part IV, Brussels.

Commission of the European Communities (1973c) *Improvement of the Common Agricultural Policy*, COM (73) 1850, Brussels.

Commission of the European Communities (1975) *Draft Regulation Establishing a Common Organisation of the Market in Potatoes*, COM (75) 690, Brussels.

Commission of the European Communities (1977) *Guidelines Concerning the Development of the Mediterranean Regions of the Community, Together with Certain Measures Relating to Agriculture*, COM (77) 526, Brussels.

Commission of the European Communities (1982a) *Commission Proposals on the Fixing of Prices for Certain Agricultural Products and on Certain Related Measures (1982/83)*, COM (82) 10, Brussels.

Commission of the European Communities (1982b) *Commission Report to the Council on the Production and Marketing of Hops*, COM (82) 244, Brussels.

Commission of the European Communities (1982c) *Preliminary Draft General Budget of the European Communities for the Financial Year 1983*, COM (82) 200, Vol. 7, Brussels.

FAO (1977) *Commodity Review and Outlook 1976/1977*, Rome.

Harris, S., and Hagelberg, G. (1975) 'Effects of the Lomé Convention on the World's Cane Sugar Producers', *ODI-Review*, No. 2, Overseas Development Institute: London.

Harris, S. (1980) 'US and EEC policy attitudes compared towards the 1977 international sugar agreement', *Journal of Agricultural Economics*, **31**.

House of Lords Select Committee on the European Communities (1976) *Potatoes*, Session 1975–76, 32nd Report, HL 174, HMSO: London.

House of Lords Select Committee on the European Communities (1980) *EEC Sugar Policy*, Session 1979–80, 44th Report, HL 207, HMSO: London.

Parris, K., and Ritson, C. (1977) *EEC Oilseed Products Sector and the Common Agricultural Policy*, Occasional Paper No. 4, Centre for European Agricultural Studies: Wye College.

Chapter 7

The Southern Problem

The 'Southern Problem', in terms of an alleged bias in the CAP towards farmers and farm products in the north of the EC, is a development of the mid-1970s.[1] The complaints came from the two countries principally affected—Italy and France. The French government (1977, p. 4) said that a reform of the regimes for Mediterranean agricultural products[2] was necessary so that they 'would offer Southern farmers the same guarantees and future prospects as those enjoyed . . . by producers in the rest of the Community'.

The issue was brought to a head in 1977 when France and Italy refused to agree negotiating mandates for the Commission in the entry negotiations with Greece, Spain, and Portugal until they had secured the changes for Mediterranean agricultural products that they wanted. In effect, the need to agree a common position for the EC's second enlargement gave France and Italy increased leverage to secure changes in the balance of the CAP to redress what they felt to be a long-standing Northern bias, although it was claimed that such changes were necessary to offset the effects of the second enlargement.

The complaints of France and Italy

The French Government (1977, p. 5) stated that CAP regulations had failed to provide producers of Mediterranean agricultural products with 'the same guarantees, level of earnings and possibilities of expansion' as other producers. In turn this was reflected in regional imbalances in the development of agricultural incomes caused by the Mediterranean CAP mechanisms being inadequate, due to their lightly structured nature: support only being available for some products and at relatively low levels. Protection against third country imports was felt to be 'not effective enough', both because the general mechanisms were too limited, and because of the extensive import duty reductions granted to the Community's Mediterranean Associates. Furthermore, it was claimed that the proportion of FEOGA expenditure going to Mediterranean agriculture was unfairly low in relation to its importance in total Community production. Finally, it was said that the agri-monetary arrangements led to distortions in competition because of the way MCAs were operated.[3]

The Italian Government (1977, p. 1) claimed that 'an anomalous situation' had arisen because Mediterranean agricultural products were not given the same degree of Community preference as other CAP products. As a result Italian agricultural exports had not done as well in other Member States, as their exports had done in the Italian market. It was said that action was needed on structural policy to help with the development of the Community's Mediterranean regions, and in CAP regimes in order to improve 'the conditions under which the main Mediterranean products are produced, marketed, and processed and to ensure that the principle of Community preference is adhered to more often' (Italian Government, 1977, p. 4).

Both governments had important reservations about the way in which the CAP support arrangements for Mediterranean products operated. With respect to *fruit and vegetables* the French government expressed its concern about the effect a localized market imbalance might have upon prices in other Member States, because of the free-trade conditions which apply within the Community. It was said that:

> In order to prevent any such disturbances, a procedure for correcting distortions of competition should be introduced in *intra*-Community trade, to be administered by the Commission.
> The *intra*-Community offer price for every important variety of fruit and vegetables benefiting from a basic price and a purchase price . . . should lie at a minimum level determined by the purchase price plus a flat rate amount to equal the average cost of packing and transport in the Community. (French Government, 1977, p. 11.)

What, it seems, the French were proposing is that there should be a minimum intra-Community trade price for fruit and vegetables. This is an idea the Commission subsequently attempted to take-up for wine in 1978.

Both memoranda expressed concern about the operation of the reference price systems for fruit and vegetables. The Italians proposed that an existing provision in the basic Regulation should be implemented for calculating the entry prices 'so that producer prices . . . are taken into account as well as the prices of goods from third countries' (Italian Government, 1977, p. 8). This suggestion was taken up by the Commission in December 1977, but not adopted. The suggestion was raised again by the Commission in the discussions on the Iberian accession.

The Italians had three other specific proposals for fruit and vegetables:

(i) That the intervention (i.e. withdrawal) system should be extended to cover tangerines, new potatoes, artichokes, and melons;

(ii) That marketing (i.e. 'penetration') premiums should be paid on table grapes and peaches;

(iii) That the reference price scheme should be extended to cover new potatoes, onions, garlic, runner beans, walnuts, almonds, hazel nuts, carrots, water-melons, and melons.

Table 7.1 Table to compare Mediterranean products' share of spending on agricultural market support and of agricultural production. (Per cent).

	Share of FEOGA Guarantee Section expenditure	Share of value of EC agricultural production
1974	16.4	19.0
1975	16.9	18.5
1976	20.6	17.1
1977	13.5	17.6
1978	7.7	18.4
1979	12.2	18.8
1980	15.9	19.7

SOURCE   Calculated from Commission, *The Agricultural Situation in the Community*, annual reports for years 1975 to 1981.

The Commission's response was limited by the need to ensure that surpluses of Mediterranean agricultural products were not generated to match those already existing for Northern products. It was also felt that changes which would lead to major increases in Community expenditure, especially after the second enlargement had occurred, should not be conceded. The Commission accepted, however, that agricultural development in the EC's Mediterranean regions had fallen behind that in other regions, and as a result Mediterranean farmers had lower incomes than in the rest of the EC. The Commission emphasized that the problem of low incomes was part of a pattern of regional underdevelopment of which agricultural problems formed only a part—albeit an extremely significant one, as agriculture is one of the, if not the only, major sources of employment available.

There appears to be some justification also for the complaints that Mediterranean agricultural products have received a smaller proportion of Community spending on agricultural market support than their importance in EC agriculture warranted (Table 7.1). (Although there is no economic or administrative principle which says CAP expenditure should necessarily be on an equivalent basis with commodity importance).

For 1981 and 1982 the Budget appropriations give a larger share to Mediterranean products (20.1 and 21.8 per cent respectively) in part due to the large wine harvests in 1979 and 1980.

The Mediterranean Package

In 1977 the Commission (1977a, 1977b, 1977c) proposed a series of measures, which came to be known as the Mediterranean Package, in an attempt to meet the French and Italian complaints. Measures proposed were:

(a) *Structural*
   Grants to assist irrigation in Southern Italy.

Grants to improve the structure of the wine sector in parts of Southern France.

Measures to improve rural infrastructure (grants for the provision of electricity and water supplies and the building of roads).

Higher rate of grant aid under the general Community measures for encouraging the improvement of agricultural processing and marketing.

Grants for afforestation.

Help towards the creation of an agricultural advisory (extension) service in Italy.

(b) *Commodity related*

Fresh fruit and vegetables—allow the renewal of orchards, increase protection against Third Country imports, give more support to producer groups.

Wine—restructure Community production to improve its quality and reduce the size of the excess.

Fodder crops—introduce subsidies so that processed peas and field beans would be competitive against soya in animal feedingstuffs. (The fodder crops are dealt with in Chapter 6.)

Processed fruit and vegetables—introduction of subsidies for processers of Community grown fruit and vegetables so that the processed items could compete with Third Country supplies.

Most of these proposals were adopted during 1978 and, as such, represent a significant development of the CAP in its balance between North and South. It is too soon to say what effects, if any, the structural changes have had, particularly given the Italian history of slow implementation of EC structural measures due to administrative problems. The changes in commodity regimes have had significant effects, as will be seen in the discussion below.

It is claimed, however, that the disequilibrium in the CAP still exists. The argument is that the greater degree of protection afforded Northern products leads to a situation where 'the more productive and affluent regions reap a large share of the benefits of the CAP'. (Benedictis, 1981). This is an argument accepted by the Commission which believes that one of the CAP's main defects is that it has tended to increase, rather than decrease, farm income disparities between regions (Commission, 1980a, p. 8). This was picked-up in the Commission's 'Mandate' Report (1981a, p. 13) where it was suggested that one of the seven basic guidelines for the future of the CAP should be 'an active structures policy tailored to the needs of individual agricultural regions'. The Commission also argued that the problems of the Mediterranean regions of the Community needed special consideration. This led it to issue, as part of its follow-up work on the Mandate Report, a further document (Commission, 1981b) entitled 'Mediterranean programmes—lines of action'. This document is notable for recognizing that the EC funds available under its agricultural, regional, and social policies need to be used to the full and that Community and national policies need to be integrated. Implicitly the CAP was no longer expected to be a surrogate for the lack of adequate EC regional and social policies in facing the problems of the EC's Mediterranean regions. The Commission suggested that the Community's aim must be to improve incomes and employment prospects, while recognizing that alternative employment opportunities outside agriculture were very limited. It was also recognized that while incomes could be improved by intensifying production, for Mediterranean products this should not be allowed to generate structural surpluses, while for non-Mediterranean agricultural products the production possibilities were limited by 'natural and market conditions'.

The Commission indicated, in very general terms, that future proposals for Mediterranean products would include:

(a) *Structural measures*

Improvement of marketing;

Encouragement to older people to give up farming;

Direct income aids;

The development of other activities such as food processing, fisheries, tourism, craft activities and the development of new forms of energy.

(b) *Market measures*

Encouragement of substitute lines of production (including new varieties of fruit and vegetables and afforestation);

Measures to stimulate consumption;

Improved Community preference and a more effective export policy.

In particular the Commission put forward proposals—discussed below—for modifying the olive oil, fruit and vegetable, and wine regimes as part of the preparations for Spanish and Portuguese accession.

FRUIT AND VEGETABLES

Economic significance

In 1980, for the Community of '10', fruit and vegetables accounted for nearly 13 per cent of the value of EC agricultural production—with vegetables accounting for somewhat over half of this total. The Commission (1980b, p. 115) estimated that after Spanish and Portuguese accession, the proportion accounted for by fruit and vegetable production would rise to around 16 per cent, even before allowing for any increased output in the new Member States.

Between the Member States there is a wide variation in the significance of fruit and vegetable production. At one extreme are Greece and Italy with about a quarter of their agricultural production coming from these products. At the other extreme are Ireland, Luxembourg, and Denmark with under 5 per cent of their agricultural production accounted for by fruit and vegetables (Table 7.2).

Given this wide variation between Member States, it cannot be surprising

Table 7.2 Proporation of Member States' agricultural production contributed by fruit and vegetables in 1980. (Per cent).

Belgium	12.7	Greece	27.0	Netherlands	18.4
Denmark	2.1	Ireland	3.2	UK	9.3
Germany	9.4	Italy	23.7		
France	10.4	Luxembourg	2.9	EC '10'	12.7

SOURCE   Calculated from Commission (1982b, pp. 174/175).

that their contribution to the EC total also varies widely. Thus Italy is the Community's major producer accounting for over 40 per cent of both fruit and vegetable production. In the Commission's category of 'other' fruit and vegetables
(dried pulses, citrus fruit, grapes, and table olives) Italy accounts for nearly 60
per cent and Greece almost 30 per cent of the value of EC production
(Table 7.3).

Products covered

The support system for fruit and vegetables came into effect on 1 July 1968,
although there are two basic Regulations—dealing with fresh fruit and
vegetables, and processed fruit and vegetables respectively.[4] Products covered
are:

(a) All temperate fresh fruit and vegetables (excluding fresh grapes other
than table grapes, potatoes and olives) and nuts (excluding tropical
nuts);
(b) All processed fruit and vegetables—frozen, dried, canned, pickled in
various preservative solutions, crystallized, juiced, cooked as jams,
purees, and pastes.

Budget cost

Overall Budget expenditure on market support for fruit and vegetables is comparatively low at around 6 per cent. This proportion is, however, much higher

Table 7.3   Fruit and vegetable production by Member State as a proportion of EC '10' total (1980
(Per cent).

	BLEU	Denmark	Germany	France	Greece	Ireland	Italy	Netherlands	U
Fresh fruit	2.7	0.6	17.6	21.6	9.9	0.2	40.0	2.4	5.
Fresh vegetables	4.4	0.8	5.1	21.4	6.3	0.9	40.1	10.1	10
Other fruit and vegetables	0.6	0.1	0.1	7.8	29.6	0.0	58.1	0.5	3

Note: EC '10' total equals 100.0. Other fruit and vegetables include dried pulses, citrus fruit, grapes, and tab
olives.
SOURCE   Commission (1982b, pp. 176/177).

Table 7.4 Spending on the fruit and vegetables regime by the Community Budget.

	1981 (Actual)	1982 (Provisional)	1983 (Estimated)
1. Total spending on the fruit and vegetables regime (million ecu)	641.1	689.0	932.0
2. As per cent of total FEOGA Guarantee Section spending	5.9	6.3	6.7
3. Main fruit and vegetable support measures as per cent of total spending on fruit and vegetables regime	100.0	100.0	100.0
Fresh fruit and vegetables including:	34.4	32.8	33.2
Compensation to producer groups for withdrawals	16.6	13.8	16.4
Compensation to encourage processing of citrus fruits	9.7	9.2	8.4
Export refunds	6.4	8.1	6.2
Processed fruit and vegetables including:	65.6	67.2	66.8
Production aids for processers	64.4	65.9	65.8

SOURCE Commission (1982e, p. B/192).

than earlier in the 1970s when spending took only about 1 per cent of the FEOGA Guarantee Section. The principal reason for the rise was the introduction of processing premiums in 1978. As can be seen from Table 7.4 spending on processing premiums accounts for about two-thirds of total spending on fruit and vegetables, followed by withdrawal payments for fresh fruit and vegetables at about 15 per cent of the total.

Support measures for fresh fruit and vegetables

The internal support system is relatively lightly structured. It relies heavily on aids to producer groups to encourage them to control supplies and on common quality standards to stop poorer quality produce being marketed. A more heavily structured support system involving mandatory intervention buying and high levels of external protection has not been created because of the fear of generating major surpluses (and hence unacceptable levels of Budget cost) due to the characteristics of EC fruit and vegetable production. These include the perishability of most fresh fruit and vegetables (hence the difficulty of storage), coupled with wide yield fluctuations between seasons, the consequent instability of market prices, the complexity and fragmentation of marketing channels, and the wide variations in product quality both between and within seasons as well as between regions.

Two internal support prices are set annually—basic and buying-in prices—for the eleven fresh fruit and vegetable items (see Table 7.5) considered

Table 7.5 Products for which basic, buying-in, withdrawal and reference prices are fixed.

Basic, buying-in and withdrawal prices	Reference prices
Apples	Apples
Pears	Pears
Peaches	Peaches
Sweet oranges	Sweet oranges
Mandarins	Mandarins
Lemons	Lemons
Table grapes	Table grapes
Tomatoes	Tomatoes
Aubergines	Aubergines
Apricots	—
Cauliflowers	—
—	Plums
—	Cherries
—	Cucumbers
—	Courgettes

to be the most important in determining producer incomes i.e. the most politically sensitive. The support prices apply only to produce meeting the quality standards.

Basic prices. These are fixed by the Council and are meant to take account of the need to:

(i) Contribute to the support of farm incomes;
(ii) Stabilize market prices without creating structural surpluses;
(iii) Consider the interest of consumers.

In fixing these prices, the Council examines average EC domestic market prices in the preceding three years. As the House of Lords (1981, p. viii), pointed-out 'the Council has substantial discretion in fixing annual basic prices' and that 'the least controversial approach is to apply to the basic prices agreed in the previous year an agreed percentage which may vary from product to product and which has regard to the Budgetary consequences of the Council's decisions'. Basic prices do not necessarily apply for an entire year (e.g. the mandarin basic price applies for $3\frac{1}{2}$ months), nor are they fixed at a single rate but vary throughout the marketing season. Their only practical importance is that they serve as a reference point from which buying-in and withdrawal prices are set.

Buying-in prices: fixed annually by the Council at various proportions of the basic price—cauliflowers, tomatoes, and aubergines (40 to 45 per cent), apples and pears (50 to 55 per cent), the other six products covered (60 to 70 per cent). These are the prices at which, after applying the appropriate quality coefficients, national intervention agencies may intervene, once a Commission decision has been taken. In practice, however, all the EC countries (apart from Greece) have opted to allow producer groups to withdraw produce instead.[5]

Withdrawal prices: These are consequential upon the above two support prices set by the Council. They are the only internal support prices which are relevant in practice as these are the levels at which producer organizations may receive reimbursement from the Community for withdrawal operations. Producer groups may withdraw any products, at any price, but they receive compensation only for the eleven products listed in Table 7.5 at the withdrawal price. Essentially withdrawal prices are higher than buying-in prices by an amount equal to 10 per cent of the basic prices, but their detailed calculation is complicated because of adjustments for size, variety, and quality of produce as shown in Table 7.6.

Table 7.6   Example of the calculation of withdrawal prices for Golden Delicious and Cox's Orange Pippin apples in December 1982. (Ecu/100 Kg).

	Golden Delicious	Cox
Basic price	28.46	28.46
Buying-in price	14.58	14.58
Calculation		
Buying-in price	14.58	14.58
× Quality coefficient for class II fruit	×0.7	×0.7
	10.206	10.206
× Variety coefficient	×1.0	×1.2
	10.206	12.247
(a) *Large fruit* (70 mm and more for Golden Delicious, 65 mm and more for Cox) × size coefficient	×1.0	×1.0
	10.206	12.247
+ 10% of basic price	+2.846	+2.846
= withdrawal price	13.052	15.093
(b) *Small fruit* (less than 70 mm for Golden Delicious, less than 65 mm for Cox) × size coefficient	×0.7	×0.6
	7.144	7.348
+ 10 per cent of basic price	+2.846	+2.846
= withdrawal price	9.990	10.194

Withdrawal operations

As the withdrawal operations are the principal internal method of market support for fresh fruit and vegetables the extent of such actions is worth examining. For most products withdrawals seem to be relatively limited, although mandarins have had significant volumes withdrawn in most years (over 10 per cent of the crop in all but two of the six years examined in Table 7.7). As one would expect, however, given the fluctuations in crop size between years, the crop proportions withdrawn vary widely. Thus lemons have varied between zero withdrawals and 7 per cent of the crop, and apples between 0.05 per cent and 11 per cent.

The EC Member States have to ensure that supplies, once withdrawn, do not re-emerge on the commercial market. Provision is made for free distribution to charitable institutions, schools, prisons, and hospitals, in fresh or processed form; failing that they may be supplied when fresh as animal feed; or they may be processed into alcohol by distillation (peaches, pears, and apples) or into animal feed (oranges).

Quality standards

The Community's support policy is based on an elaborate system of common quality standards which restrict the marketing of 28 fresh fruit and vegetable products to qualities meeting the standards. The quality standards cover classes Extra, I, II, and III: the full range of standards are not applied to every product. These measures limit the quantities reaching markets and hence help support market prices, particularly as withdrawal operations are only available for produce meeting EC quality standards. Produce for processing or for sale at the farm gate, however, does not have to meet the standards.

Table 7.7   Proportions of EC fruit and vegetable production withdrawn. (Per cent).

	1975/76	1976/77	1977/78	1978/79	1979/80	1980/81 (provisional)
Cauliflowers	1.35	0.90	2.61	2.8	2.94	0.46
Tomatoes	2.83	0.49	0.45	0.4	3.06	1.28
Peaches	2.79	18.50	3.91	2.5	6.61	2.78
Pears	7.34	12.37	2.10	1.2	2.57	6.46
Apples	10.99	2.57	0.05	5.5	7.89	6.30
Table grapes	–	0.12	0.00	0.0	0.00	0.03
Mandarins	11.83	9.92	7.47	14.6	36.14	16.37
Oranges	2.79	16.89	1.10	6.5	0.16	4.16
Lemons	1.38	7.11	0.00	3.3	0.00	0.00

SOURCE   Commission, *The Agricultural Situation in the Community*, annual reports for years 1977 to 1981.

Producer organizations

Producer organizations play a key role in the system as it is only through them that market support occurs. Accordingly, the regime encourages the formation of producer groups by subsidizing their 'start-up' costs, by investing their activities with official sanction and by exempting them from the EC's provisions covering anti-competitive practices. Despite this encouragement, Commission (1982b, p. 261) figures appear to suggest that the proportion of fruit and vegetables sold through co-operatives is still somewhat less than for pigs, milk, and cereals. A major feature of the Commission's proposals arising from its Mandate Report were actions to improve the effectiveness of producer organizations by allowing them to extend their powers (on production and marketing) to independent growers whilst at the same time strengthening the coverage and disciplines of producer groups (Commission, 1981e).

Citrus production and production premiums

Since the beginning of the 1970s short- and medium-term measures have existed to improve the production and marketing of domestically produced citrus fruit so that it was better able to compete with Third Country imports. The short-term measures consisted of the payment of marketing premiums (known as 'penetration' premiums) to sellers of EC-produced citrus fruit when sold in other Member States. The medium-term measures consisted of a system of aids to improve the production and marketing of specified varieties of oranges, lemons, mandarins, and clementines: it was (and is) the Commission view that, in particular, the wrong varieties of citrus were being grown and that there was a lack of marketing and processing equipment. In 1982 it was decided to phase out the penetration premiums for lemons and clementines over three years from 1983/84 and the premiums for oranges and mandarins over three years from 1990/91. At the same time the citrus restructuring aids were extended to lemons and made more attractive to encourage their uptake, but limited to Italy, Greece, and Corsica.

Problems with the support mechanisms

The problems associated with these measures arise at two levels. First, at the general level of producer and consumer interests there is a feeling among producers that the support mechanisms are not effective in raising market prices and also that the level of support available for Southern products is far less than for Northern products. On the other hand, politicians and consumer interests are extremely sensitive over the accusations that the policies result in the destruction of food, and hence they will not readily countenance a permanent expansion in withdrawal operations, although apricots and aubergines have been added to the original list. Second, there have been problems with the coefficients used in calculating withdrawal prices. For example, at the beginning of the 1980s, British producers alleged that the coefficients encouraged the production of large Golden Delicious apples at the expense of the generally smaller Cox apples.[6]

The Court of Auditors (1980a) had problems with the policing of the operations of producer groups as they felt that some EC countries did not have the organized marketing systems, or the coherence of the internal market of the Netherlands on whose pre-EEC system the Community's fruit and vegetables regime was based. The Court also felt that the system of checks on withdrawn produce was a 'weak spot'. In Italy it was found that the EC quality standards were not respected for produce sold domestically, and that withdrawn products often did not meet the standards. Furthermore, it has been suggested that the large production of apple concentrate in Germany is derived in part from withdrawn apples that should not have been allowed to leak back on to the market.

When examining the operation of the penetration premiums, designed to enable Italy to overcome the costs involved in marketing in Northern Europe, the Court of Auditors (1980b) were puzzled by the fact that produce was being withdrawn in Italy when, taking account of the premiums, a better return would have been achieved by producers marketing in the rest of the Community. The Court concluded that this phenomenon was due to structural factors which encouraged Third Country imports to Northern Europe and made these markets less accessible to Italian produce.

Border protection

The EC applies *ad valorem* import duties to Third Country imports. In some cases these duties vary during the year (i.e. a seasonal calendar applies whereby the duties are highest when levels of domestic EC production are highest), while extensive duty reductions exist for EC Associates although these duty preferences vary within season. Additionally, for nine of the eleven products eligible for domestic support plus cherries, plums, cucumbers, and courgettes there is a system of minimum import prices termed *reference prices* to underpin the duties. (See Table 7.5.)

Despite the general EC rule that national import quotas on Third Country supplies are abolished, some quantitative import restrictions applied by the Member States before 1970 are still permitted. These restrictions take the form of very small import quotas or complete import bans (France and Belgium) for certain Third Country fruit and vegetable items during the seasons of domestic production.

The reference price system was outlined briefly in Chapter 3. Reference prices are fixed by the Commission: essentially they are based on average EC producer prices in the preceding three seasons but with the proviso that from one year to the next the reference price in any particular period will not be less, in ecu terms, than the price fixed for the same period the previous year; nor will it be increased by more than the estimated percentage increase in production costs.

The price of imported produce is monitored in representative markets, for each foreign supplier. From this figure is deducted the full rate of the customs duty that should have been paid. This calculation is designed to show whether or not the products from any particular country respected the reference price when imported. If the calculations show that the import price was less than the reference price by 0.6 ecu/100 kg, or more, for two successive days, or for three days out of five, then the Commission will impose a countervailing charge on all future supplies of this product from the offending country until it is shown that the reference price is respected. The countervailing charge will be fixed at the difference between the calculated offer price and the reference price. The intention, as depicted in Figure 3.2, p. 48, is to ensure that a minimum import price, equal to the reference price plus the full *ad valorem* customs duty, is respected.

There are, however, two significant consequences of the way the system is applied. First, it should be noted that the countervailing charge is not applied against the offending shipment, but rather against subsequent shipments from the Third Country concerned. This is an added inducement to the country to ensure that its export trade is under the monopoly control of a producer co-operative or marketing board, because if it is not then any shipper facing marketing difficulties in Europe might—by selling cheaply—inadvertently trigger the application of countervailing charges against subsequent shipments from that country.

Secondly it should be noted that the same calculation—market prices less the *full* rate of the Common Customs Tariff (CCT)—is performed even when the supplying country has a tariff concession in the EC. The tariff concession does not allow the country to gain a price advantage on the Community market, rather it allows the country concerned to retain a higher share of the sale proceeds.

An example might clarify all this. Suppose the reference price is 100 ecu/100 kg and the CCT a rate of 20 per cent. Then, abstracting from distribution costs, etc., countervailing charges would be triggered if the imported product were marketed at less than 120 ecu/100 kg. This would also be the case for a country which was asked to pay a preferential CCT rate of 10 per cent. When produce from two foreign suppliers is being sold at a market price of 120 ecu/100 kg, the ordinary supplier retains 100 ecu and pays 20 ecu to the Community in customs duties whereas the preferential supplier retains 109.1 ecu and pays 10.9 ecu in customs duties. (In both cases it is assumed that no countervailing charges are payable in addition to customs duties.)

Preferences are in fact granted to a number of countries around the Mediterranean Basin, and to the ACP states under the provisions of the Lomé Convention. Although the system does not allow them to undercut the minimum entry price in Europe it does allow these countries higher export earnings—provided they have marketing boards which can ensure countervailing charges are not applied—and it does, potentially, allow higher cost suppliers to continue supplying the European market who could not otherwise afford to do so. (In terms of the numerical example outlined above, any country with c.i.f. costs to Europe of 100 ecu/100 kg or less could price in the EC at 120 ecu/100 kg; the country with the tariff preferences however, could still sell at 120 even if its c.i.f. costs were as high as 109.1 ecu/100 kg.) In practice, however, the range of varieties, qualities, and methods of presentation covered by any reference price category would mean that suppliers would compete on non-price terms if the reference price became a limiting factor.

Although superficially reference prices and basic prices are based on EC market prices, in practice they have diverged increasingly, as since 1978 production costs have been taken into account in calculating reference prices, and production costs have risen faster than the increases in basic prices allowed by the Council of Ministers. Hence there is no direct relationship. Further, they may refer to different types of production. Thus the reference price for tomatoes at the beginning of the season (1 to 20 April) refers to glasshouse produce, whereas the basic price is fixed for open-air produce later in the season.

For apples, a system of 'voluntary' import quotas is applied to imports from southern hemisphere suppliers. This means the Commission attempts to agree export quantities with the suppliers which will not overburden the EC internal market and depress prices. Chile has not always been willing to accept these arrangements and twice the Commission has applied the safeguard clause to prevent the importation of apples from Chile. As a result of these actions Chile complained to GATT which reported in Chile's favour at the end of 1980,[7] although when Dutch traders tried to claim compensation from the Commission, the European Court dismissed the claim.

Export refunds

Export refunds are available for the export of some fresh fruit and nut items. To be eligible for refunds fruit has to meet at least the Community's Class II quality standard.

Support arrangements for processed fruit and vegetables

There are three schemes for helping processors of domestically produced fruit and vegetables of which only one is of major importance[8]—*the aid for processed fruit and vegetables*. This scheme was introduced in 1978 for initially a five-year period as part of the Mediterranean package. Under it, provided processers enter into contracts with producers to buy specified quantities at *minimum prices* (set by the Council) they can receive a processing aid designed to enable them to sell their production competitively with Third Country supplies on the EC domestic market.

The scheme was introduced for a limited period, and with restricted product coverage, because of the controversy it aroused. Traditionalists felt that if the existing EC measures to control the access of Third Country supplies were inadequate then the measures controlling imports should be strengthened. The alternative route, which was the one adopted, was to give some form of income support to domestic processers so that they could compete with Third Country

Table 7.8   Budget spending on the aid
for processed fruit and vegetables.

Fiscal year	Spending (million ecu)	
1979	282.3	
1980	484.1	
1981	412.7	
1982 (Prov.)	440.0*	133.0†
1983 (Est.)	436.0*	177.0†

* Tomato-based products.
† Fruit-based products.
SOURCES European Parliament (1980, p. 458); Commission (1982e, p. B/192).

supplies without strengthening import measures and raising domestic market prices. The controversy arose because it was felt that this was a departure from 'normal' CAP mechanisms which would involve heavy Budget spending and would not necessarily be effective in ensuring the ability of domestic processers to take up EC produce.

Despite the initial intentions the scheme has shown a seemingly inexorable tendency to expand in scope and cost. When introduced on 1 June 1978, five products were covered and the cost was to be 146 million ecu in a full year. Actual costs have been very much higher (Table 7.8) despite a 10 per cent cut in aid levels in 1980/81, as the quantities claimed for have been much larger than expected and a number of extra products have been added.[9] The levels of aid—despite the cut in 1980/81—were equivalent to 34 per cent of the value of the processed product and 95 per cent of the value of the tomatoes used in that year (Commission 1981c, p. 42). The Commission (1981c, p. 42) commented that 'The aid, which was introduced as a means of supplementing the incomes of producers in disadvantaged Mediterranean regions, has resulted in serious problems of disposal of the processed product'.

For Williams pears and cherries in syrup, limits on the quantities which would receive aid were set when they were added to the original list in 1980. For most of the other products the Commission proposed the introduction of fixed quantities on which aid would be given at the 1981/82 price fixing—although this was not adopted by the Council. At the 1982/83 price fixing, however, a production threshold was introduced equivalent to the use of 4.5 million tonnes of fresh tomatoes, with specific allocations for tomato concentrate and whole peeled tomatoes. It was agreed that, if the production threshold was exceeded in 1982/83, the Council would take 'appropriate measures' in 1983/84.

Border protection

The principal measure of import protection is provided by *ad valorem* import duties. Although these vary in level from product to product, and there are many duty reductions on imports from EC Associates, in general the rates are relatively high (ranging up to 26 per cent on some canned products); for products, such as many canned fruits, containing high sugar contents, an extra duty applies.[10]

Further, for the so-called 'sensitive products'[11] a system of import certificates is operated. The aim of the system is to allow the Commission to monitor the level of imports into the EC, and to consider whether the EC market can absorb the volume involved. Hence there is a five-day delay between the application for a certificate and its grant. Without a certificate imports cannot be made.

When the system was introduced in the mid-1970s it was feared that it would be used to restrict the volume of imports, as a result of Commission refusals to grant licences under the safeguard clause. The example of the three-year suspension of import licences for beef was quoted frequently. It was argued by the Commission, however, that first, once a licence was issued it could not be withdrawn and therefore the licence gave security to the importer. Second, the Commission suggested that the safeguard clause would be used sparingly—as has turned out to be the case—because of the international pressure caused by the earlier suspension of beef import licences.

The issue of import licences has been stopped only once: this was for canned mushrooms in 1978. They were not issued again until 1980 when the main Third Country suppliers entered into 'voluntary' export restraint agreements[12] which, in 1981, were replaced by import quotas.

A further measure of import protection is represented by the surveillance system applied to imports from Eastern Europe of many fruit and vegetable items. Importers are required to obtain an import document before being allowed to import—although this document does not confer a right to import. Again, the purpose of the system is to allow the monitoring of the level of imports.

Export refunds are available on sugar used in processed products exported to Third Countries. Additionally, for products not containing sugar, refunds are, in principle, available to enable EC production to be exported. In practice, these are little used—in 1982 only four products were eligible.[13]

TOBACCO

Economic significance

Tobacco production is confined almost entirely to three countries—Greece, Italy, and France—although there is a very minor production in Belgium and Germany. As an item in Community agriculture, tobacco production is unimportant: in 1980 it accounted for only 0.6 per cent of the value of EC agricultural production, but 6.4 per cent for Greece. However, it has a regional significance, being produced in some of the most disadvantaged areas of Italy and Greece and principally on a small scale with most growers having less than one hectare.

The problem with tobacco in the EC is that its production 'is mainly of varieties for which demand is limited (particularly oriental varieties) and its consumption is of varieties of which only a small quantity is produced in the Community (particularly flue-cured varieties)' (Commission, 1981c, p. 39). As a result, in 1980, EC production was approximately 256 000 tonnes, imports 470 000 tonnes and exports 70 000 tonnes. The Commission (1981c, p. 39) observed that there was not a problem of overproduction in the EC—with self-sufficiency only about 45 per cent—but there was a problem over the suitability of the varieties grown.

Products covered

The regime covers 26 varieties of EC-produced raw tobacco which are split into five classes: dark air cured, fine cured, light air cured, flue cured, sun cured. The regime for raw tobacco came into effect in 1970.[14]

Budget cost

The EC tobacco regime is relatively expensive in terms of the Community Budget, as compared with its importance in EC agriculture. The sharp increase in the level of spending between 1981 and 1982 is due to the accession of Greece (Table 7.9).

Support measures

The aim is to provide EC tobacco growers with an adequate income, while allowing tobacco manufacturers to obtain supplies from Third Countries relatively freely.

The principal support measure is a system of *premiums for purchasers*, paid to

Table 7.9 Spending on the tobacco regime by the Community Budget.

	1981 (Actual)	1982 (Provisional)	1983 (Estimated)
1. Total spending on the tobacco regime (million ecu)	361.8	627.7	668.0
2. As percentage of total FEOGA Guarantee Section spending	3.3	4.8	4.8
3. Main tobacco support measures as percentage of total spending on tobacco regime	100.0	100.0	100.0
Purchaser premiums	79.1	92.8	91.6
Intervention buying	19.3	4.0	4.8
Export refunds	1.6	3.0	3.4

SOURCE Commission (1982e, p. B/200).

buyers of EC-produced raw tobacco, designed to bring its price down to world levels and hence to provide an incentive to take all the Community's production. The premiums are calculated as the difference between *norm prices*—equivalent to target prices and set annually by the Council—and the price of Third Country tobaccos to the EC. The norm prices have to be paid to EC growers.

Intervention support buying is available: *intervention prices* are set at 85 per cent of norm prices (90 per cent up to 1981/82). However, where production exceeds average production levels in the three previous years by a stipulated amount, or where quantities bought into intervention exceed a given percentage of production, then the Commission has to report[15] on the situation for the varieties in question and make proposals for reducing intervention or norm price levels to discourage production of the variety in question. At the 1981/82 price-fixing it was agreed, for example, to lower the intervention prices for oriental varieties and Kentucky to 85 per cent of the norm price (80 per cent in 1982/83). The Commission was to review the effectiveness of the system of tobacco premiums during 1982/83.

Sales to intervention reached excessive levels at the end of the 1970s. Thus 18.3 per cent of the 1979 crop was sold to intervention, and 21.7 per cent of the 1980 crop (Commission, 1982b, p. 344). By variety, however, there was an even wider range. Of the 1979 crop, 52.4 per cent of the variety Perustitza was sold to intervention and 40.0 per cent of the variety Erzegovina.

Border protection

Ad valorem import duties apply to Third Country imports (subject to minimum and maximum specific duty levels). There is a large volume of imports, about two-thirds of which come in at nil or preferential duties (Commission, 1981f, p. 383), even where the tobaccos concerned compete directly with EC production, e.g. oriental tobaccos and Virginia and Kentucky tobaccos.

Future policy

According to the Commission (1981c, p. 39) the EC 'must reduce the production of varieties for which there is no demand on the market, in favour of conversion to varieties which can be marketed. There must also be a conversion, within the varieties grown, from the lower to the higher qualities'.

OLIVE OIL

Economic significance

Olive oil, in the context of EC agriculture as a whole, is relatively unimportant, accounting for about 1.5 per cent of the value of agricultural production.

However, olive oil is produced only in the south of the Community where it is of major importance in Mediterranean agriculture with most Italian and Greek farmers having some olive trees. According to the Commission (1982c, p. 65) roughly one million families cultivate olives in Italy, about 300 000 in Greece and 40 000 in France—with the EC total of wild and cultivated olive trees amounting to roughly 307 million and the Community accounting for 47 per cent of world production. In 1980 some 6 per cent of the value of Italy's agricultural production came from olives and olive oil and 11 per cent of Greece's.

Community self-sufficiency until 1975 was relatively constant at around 70 per cent. From then it rose steadily so that, taking account of Greek accession, self-sufficiency had reached about 95 per cent by the beginning of the 1980s.

Products covered

Products covered in the olive oil part of the oils and fats regime[16] are olives, olive residues, and olive oil—whether crude, purified, or refined. That part of the regime covering oilseeds is described in Chapter 6. The olive oil marketing year runs from 1 November to the following 31 October.

Budget cost

Olive oil is like tobacco, in that the proportion of the spending on market support is significantly larger than its importance in EC agricultural production. The principal expenditure items are the production and consumption aids (Table 7.10).

Table 7.10 Spending on the olive oil regime by the Community Budget.

	1981 (Actual)	1982 (Provisional)	1983 (Estimated)
1. Total spending on the olive oil regime (million ecu)	442.7	684.0	742.0
2. As percentage of total FEOGA Guarantee Section spending	4.1	5.1	5.4
3. Main olive oil support measures as percentage of total spending on olive oil regime	100.0	100.0	100.0
Production aid	62.0	57.0	52.2
Consumption aid	23.1	30.3	34.5
Intervention buying	11.5	6.4	6.1

SOURCE   Commission (1982e, p. B/175).

Support measures

The original regime

The arrangements for olive oil were substantially modified in 1978 because surpluses were starting to appear, and there was a major problem of fraud. The regime, as originally introduced in 1966, was not modelled on that adopted for cereals. It was felt that such a system would lead to too high an olive oil market price, in relation to the prices of other vegetable oils which could be imported from the world market at relatively low rates of import duty. Consequently, under the original system, a target market price was fixed in relation to the price of other vegetable oils, with a production aid payable directly to olive growers on their production of oil, equal to the difference between the target market price and a production target price representing the total return to be received by growers.

The problem of fraud arose because of the number of growers and crushers, and the difficulty of checking their individual claims for aid—in Italy there were over a million growers and over 12 000 crushing plants in the early 1970s. The Commission's Special Committee of Inquiry (1975) into FEOGA frauds found that in 1972 20 per cent of olive oil subsidies granted were based on fraudulent claims. The problem of surpluses arose it was felt because, as a result of the inflexibility of the single annual setting of the market target price, olive oil was not competitive with other oils and hence consumption was tending to decline and EC self-sufficiency to rise. Consequently, large quantities were sold into intervention.[17]

One way out of this worsening situation would have been to raise the price of other vegetable oils, produced from Third Country oilseeds, by increasing EC import charges. This solution was not acceptable, however, because of opposition from the EC's oilseed crushing industry which did not want to see duties increased on its raw materials; and as many of the duties in question were bound in GATT, difficult negotiations with Third Countries would have been necessary to secure their unbinding.

Consequently when, in 1978, the regime was modified, a consumption aid was introduced to make olive oil more competitive on the EC's domestic market. Furthermore, so as not to encourage an increase in production, the production aid was restricted to existing production areas.

Internal support measures after 1978

The income of olive oil producers comes from two sources: the price they can realize on the market and a *production aid*. The market price, in turn, is supported by an *intervention price* at which support buying is available to growers (not packers), but only on olive oil which has not received the consumption aid—discussed below. At the annual price fixing, the first institutional support price to be set is the *production target price* which represents the desired total

Table 7.11   EC Olive oil support prices (ecu/tonne).

	1979/80	1980/81	1981/82	1982/83
1. Production target price	2350.4	2479.7	2727.7	3027.7
2. Production aid	539.0	558.1	600.0	666.0
3. Producer selling price	1821.4	1921.6	2127.7	2361.7
4. Intervention price	1731.9	1801.2	1909.3	2179.3
5. Consumption aid	351.4	471.6	677.7	911.7
6. Representative market price	1470.0	1450.0	1450.0	1450.0

revenue to be received by growers on the oil produced from their olives, not on the olives themselves. The production aid bridges the gap between the production target price and a theoretical *producer selling price* set just above the intervention price (see Table 7.11).

When the regime was revised in 1978, the system of production aids was retained due to its 'social and political importance' (Commission, 1977b, p. 9). This aid is confined to areas which were planted with olive oil trees at 31 October 1978 (1 January 1981 in the case of Greece) in an attempt to limit the potential Budget liability. If an individual grower claims the aid it is paid on the basis of the number of olive trees harvested and average yields for the region concerned. This change in the system avoids the necessity for closely checking individual production claims as was meant to have happened under the original system, but did not judging from the level of fraudulent claims.[18] In the case of those growers (the majority) who are members of a producer organization, the production aid is paid on the actual quantity of oil produced. This change from the original system is meant to encourage the formation of producer groups which the Commission sees as being of importance, as it has claimed that owing to their absence producers have not always received the full benefit of the regime's provisions.

Prior to the change in system, the theoretical producer selling price was set at a level intended to permit olive oil to be marketed in competition with other vegetable oils. Since then, however, intervention prices (and hence producer selling prices) have been raised in line with the producer target price at the annual price fixing, and a system of *consumption aid* has applied. This aid represents the difference between the producer selling price, on the assumption that packers' purchase prices are close to this level, and a *representative market price* set as part of the annual price-fixing, although it can be adjusted if necessary during a marketing year. In principle, the consumption aid is set so as to maintain a ratio of 2.3 : 1 between the price of olive oil and the predicted price of soya oil for the following year. Since the system of consumption aid came into operation, the Council of Ministers has taken a relatively high prediction for the soya oil price as a means of containing Budget spending on the consumption aid. Thus the actual olive oil : soya oil price ratio, after allowing for consumption aid, had been around 2.7 or 2.8 : 1 up to the time of writing, although it was about 2.3:1 in the first few months after the new aid system was introduced.

The consumption aid is payable to authorized packers of EC olive oil on oil marketed in containers of less than five litres capacity. It has been paid, so far, on much lower quantities than production aid (only about half the level in Italy) indicating that—providing the production aid has been paid cor-rectly—substantial amounts of oil are consumed without going through the packers. But the uptake of consumption aid may be expected to increase as the rate paid per tonne rises over time.

As with cereals, the olive oil intervention and representative market prices are subject to a system of monthly price rises as a means of encouraging the market-ing of oil steadily throughout the year.

A refund is available on olive oil used by Community food processers to encourage them to use domestically-produced oil in canned vegetable and fish products.

Border protection

Olive oil is the only major Mediterranean agricultural product which has the archetypal *threshold price* and variable import levy system of frontier protection. The threshold price is set at a level to ensure that olive oil imports cannot undercut the representative market price.[19]

Although the regime provides for the charging of import levies equal, in the normal way, to the difference between c.i.f. quotes and the threshold price, the representativeness of world price quotes has been questioned because of the domination of the world's olive oil trade by a few large companies. Conse-quently in 1976 a system of tendering for import levies was introduced whereby importers bid against each other for the size of levy they are prepared to pay to bring olive oil into the EC. The Commission then fixes a minimum import levy and accepts bids above this level. In practice, this system has replaced the normal variable import levy system.

There are a series of preferential reductions of the levy charged on imports from the Community's Mediterranean Associates. Olive oil is one of the few products on which import levies apply where the EC has allowed concessions. In all cases, however, the levy concession is only available if the foreign supplier charged a correspondingly higher price.

Export refunds are available for exports to Third Countries. These are set at such a level as to allow EC exports to compete with Spanish oil exports. In practice, Community exports have been relatively stable for many years.

Preparation for Spanish entry

The Commission (1981d) put forward for discussion a series of measures to alter the olive oil regime in preparation for Spanish entry to the EC. It feared that if action was not taken the olive oil surplus in the enlarged Community would be about 200 000 tonnes a year (principally due to a consumption drop) and the additional cost to the Budget incurred in disposing of the surplus oil and in safeguarding growers' incomes would be some 720 million ecu. The Commission's forecast assumed that there would not be an increase in production on the basis that the production aid was restricted to existing production areas. The Commission's ideas were aimed primarily at boosting consumption by altering the price ratio of olive oil to other oils. They included, however, three ameliorative suggestions:

(a) To encourage producers to shift from olive production to other crops. However, the Commission suggested that only 'modest changes' would be possible because of the importance of olives in the regions where they are grown, and the lack of alternative crops due to the poor soil and hilly conditions under which many olive trees are cultivated;

(b) To ensure that in the new Member States the payment of production aid was limited to those areas planted before 1 November 1978, as in the Community of '9'. This measure was meant to discourage any expansion in production in Spain and Portugal prior to accession;

(c) To ensure that the transition period for Spain was as long as possible, so as to delay the impact on the olive oil market.

The three more substantial suggestions were:

(d) Whilst maintaining producer prices, to reduce consumer prices by increasing the consumption aid. The aim was to reduce the price of olive oil in relation to that of other vegetable oils to a ratio of 2:1 and hence maintain consumption;

(e) To change the import arrangements for oilseeds so as to reduce the impact on Spanish olive oil consumption of duty free or reduced duties applied by the EC on oilseed imports;

(f) To impose a 'non-discriminatory tax on consumption of vegetable oils which, in order to comply with the Community's international obligations, should apply both to Community-produced and imported vegetable oils'.

These suggestions were contentious in a number of respects. Thus the British Government challenged their whole basis by suggesting that the consumption aid encouraged olive oil to be drawn 'artificially' into commercial marketing channels (as it was only payable to packers). According to European Report (1982, p. 7) the UK said the result would be ever increasing Budget costs and little improvement to producers' returns, since much of the consumption aid would be spent on disposing of the surplus on a residual world market. The UK suggested, as an alternative to the Commission's proposals, that the consumption aid should be phased-out so that the price ratio between olive oil and other oils would be determined by the market and growers would obtain their return from a flat-rate aid per tree, irrespective of yield, plus the market price on olive oil production.

The revival of the idea of a consumption tax on vegetable oils and/or the raising of the low or nil duty rates applied to imported oilseeds was a revival of a long running theme which had previously been found in the context of plans for improving butter consumption (see discussion in Chapter 5). This time round, however, the proposal would have two desirable effects—in the Commission's eyes—in that it would raise revenue for the Budget necessary to fund the olive oil surplus, while restricting the competitiveness of imported oilseeds and so helping olive oil consumption.

The objections, principally from the UK, Germany, and the Netherlands related to doubts as to the extent olive oil consumption would be aided in fact[20] and fears about the creation of further difficulties in international agricultural trade and, in particular, the likely reaction of the USA. The US Government made it very clear that the EC's duty bindings 'on soyabeans and soyabean products were not negotiable' and that any action by the Community affecting US soya exports would lead to US retaliation.

WINE

Economic significance

The bulk of EC wine production (almost 90 per cent) occurs in Italy and France, with the remainder in Germany (7 per cent), Greece (3 per cent), and Luxembourg (0.1 per cent). For the Community as a whole, wine production accounts for a relatively small proportion of total agricultural production, but this varies according to the size of any particular year's harvest—in 1976 the level was 2.5 per cent, as against 6 per cent in 1979. For Italy and France, however, wine production is of greater significance, accounting for around 8 per

Table 7.12   EC '9' wine production.

	Yields (hl/ha)	Production (1000 hl)	Total utilization* (1000 hl)	Self-sufficiency (%)
1966/70 (average)[†]	51.7	138.4	141.8	97.6
1971/75 (average)	62.4	147.2	144.9	101.6
1972/73	54.4	127.3	143.7	88.6
1973/74	72.2	170.7	144.7	118.0
1974/75	67.5	160.3	150.2	106.7
1975/76	60.9	145.4	147.0	98.9
1976/77	61.7	148.4	140.3	105.8
1977/78	54.2	128.3	136.3	94.1
1978/79	58.9	138.3	134.2	103.1
1979/80	76.1	177.2	139.6	126.9
1980/81 (provisional)	n.a.	158.5	132.7	119.4
1981/82 (estimated)	n.a.	133.5	n.a.	n.a.

* Excludes wine distilled as a market support measure.
† EC '6' only.
SOURCES   Calculated from Commission (1980c and 1982d).

cent of agricultural production in both countries in 1977 and 12 per cent in 1979. The social importance of wine production is greater than these figures suggest because of its heavy concentration in particular regions and because vines can be grown on small farms. Thus about a third of all EC holdings have vineyards on them (Commission 1981f, p. 375).

The three most significant economic characteristics of the wine sector are:

(i) Its yield and hence production variability between years;
(ii) The tendency of domestic consumption to decline since 1974/75;
(iii) The increasing level of EC surplus production throughout the 1970s.

These characteristics are shown in Table 7.12.

Products covered

Among the EC's first Regulations was No. 24 of 1962 'on the progressive establishment of a common organization of the market in wine'. It introduced the concepts of a viticultural land register, a wine register, a wine management committee, and Community-wide statistics in order to gain knowledge of the wine market. The unified market in wine was not established until much later, however, in 1970. Aims of the regime are not only oriented towards the protection of producer incomes and bringing the wine market into balance, but also there is a heavy emphasis on improving quality.[21]

Products covered are:

(a) Grape juice, unfermented;
(b) Wine of fresh grapes and grape musts;
(c) Fresh grapes (other than table grapes) and wine vinegar;
(d) Wine lees, grape marc, piquette.

Budget cost

The proportion of the Budget spent on wine market support varies significantly (Table 7.13) with fluctuations in the size of the harvest. The large harvests in the middle and end of the 1970s can be readily identified.

Table 7.13 Proportion of FEOGA Guarantee Section spending on wine.

Year	%	Year	%	Year	%
1972	2.3	1976	2.4	1980	2.6
1973	0.3	1977	1.3	1981	4.2
1974	1.4	1978	0.7	1982 (prov.)	3.1
1975	2.9	1979	0.6	1983 (est.)	3.4

SOURCES Calculated from Commission, *The Agricultural Situation in the Community*, annual volumes for years 1975 to 1981, and Commission (1982e, p. B/198).

Table 7.14   Spending on the wine regime by the Community Budget.

	1981 (Actual)	1982 (Provisional)	1983 (Estimated)
1. Total spending on the wine regime (million ecu)	459.4	416.0	469.0
2. Main wine support measures as percentage of total spending on wine regime	100.0	100.0	100.0
Intervention storage	19.7	21.9	13.6
Distillation of wine	68.5	52.9	55.4
Compulsory distillation of by-products of wine making	0.0	8.7	7.5
Aid for grape must	0.6	8.9	7.9
Taking over of alcohol from compulsory distillation	0.0	0.0	9.4

SOURCE   Commission (1982e, p. B/198).

The main market support activities (Table 7.14) are the various distillation measures and private storage aids, although their relative importance varies with the abundance of each year's harvest and the size of the stocks already held.

Support arrangements for wine

Because of the marked fluctuations in production and quality between years, a wide range of support measures are employed. This, plus the importance of the technical detail of wine production, leads to an extremely complex regime.[22] Two support prices are fixed annually for six types of table wine:[23] these do not, in practice, apply for quality wines as demand for quality wines is strong and, if anything, tends to exceed supply. Approximately 73 per cent of EC wine production is table wine, 21 per cent quality wines, and 6 per cent other wines.

Guides prices: are fixed annually by the Council for table wines.

Activating prices: which may not exceed 95 per cent of guide prices—are fixed taking into account several conflicting factors, including the state of the market, the quality of the harvest, the need to ensure price stability without causing structural surpluses, and estimates of future conditions. The activating prices form the trigger for the various intervention mechanisms, when average market prices[24] received by producers fall below them.

The main support measures for wine producers involve *aids for storage* and *distillation.* The aim of these measures taken as a whole is 'to ensure equilibrium on the market in table wines and a *minimum guaranteed price* on the market for such wines equal to at least 82 per cent of the guide price coming into effect in the year of the harvest concerned' (Article 3a, Regulation (EEC) No. 337/79). The concept of the minimum guaranteed price was introduced in 1982 when the distillation measures in the wine regime were heavily revised as part of the preparations for Spanish and Portuguese accession.

The aim of the storage schemes is to reduce market supplies for a specified length of time by granting private storage aids to producers (either as individuals or groups) which cover storage costs and interest charges. These aids apply provided that wine is held off the market for either three months (termed short term contracts)[25] or nine months (termed long term contracts). When the provisional balance sheet at the beginning of a wine-growing year suggests that total supplies available will exceed likely demand for that year by more than four months' consumption, provision for long term contracts is introduced. In years when such contracts are available producers may enter into them only if they are signed in the two months between 16 December and 15 February.

The distillation measures were revised in 1982. The aim was to take any surplus off the market at the beginning of a season so that prices did not become depressed in the first instance and have to be raised later. The thinking here was that a greater cost to the Budget was incurred if market prices were allowed to become depressed and efforts then had to be made subsequently to raise the level of prices, as against preventing market prices becoming depressed in the first instance by removing the likely surplus before it had had a chance to have a major effect. It was felt the measures taken under the wine regime as it existed up to 1982 were ineffective in raising market prices in years of heavy surpluses while involving large Budget outlays in exceptional distillation measures taken later in the season. Up to 1982 the distillation measures consisted of:

(i) *Preventive distillation* applied when the volume of wine in store at the beginning of a season exceeded seven million hectolitres. The price the distiller had to pay the producer—termed the *buying-in price*—was equal to 55 per cent of the guide price;

(ii) Additional distillation measures (the *Guarantie de bonne fin*) for wine covered by long term storage contracts if, when they expired, market prices were still depressed. The price payable was relatively high, at the full activating price;

(iii) *Exceptional distillation* whereby producers could have their wines distilled voluntarily if other support measures were unsuccessful in raising market prices. (Such measures were necessary in 1981/82 because of the stock build-up following the large 1979 and 1980 harvests.)

From 1982, the distillation measures applied were strengthened in order to ensure that the minimum guaranteed price (at 82 per cent of the guide price) was achieved. The revised distillation measures are:

(i) *Preventive distillation* may be introduced as an early season measure—from 1 September until the opening of obligatory distillation, or otherwise, 20 January—in view of the likely size of the forthcoming harvest, or to improve the quality of wines being marketed by removing poor quality wines. The buying-in price is 65 per cent of the guide prices for each type of table wine, except in seasons when obligatory distillation is in operation, when the buying-in price is only 60 per cent of the appropriate guide prices.

(ii) *Obligatory distillation* is an innovation dating from 1982. It applies in seasons of large harvests, where total availabilities in the mid-December estimate exceed normal annual consumption by an amount equivalent to more than five months' consumption. The buying-in price is 60 per cent of the guide price for each type of table wine.

The total quantity to be distilled is such that end-season stocks are meant to be reduced to a level equivalent to between five and six months' normal utilization. By 20 January the European Commission has to state the percentage of each producer's table wine production which has to go for obligatory distillation. In order to reduce the administrative costs involved, however, small producers may be exempted up to a level equal to 8 to 10 per cent in total of the Community's table wine production.

The quantities of wine going for obligatory distillation are reduced by the quantities which have been distilled under the Guarantie de bonne fin arrangements and the quantities which have been put into preventive distillation. The interlocking of the preventive and obligatory distillation measures is significant. If producers think an obligatory distillation is likely then the more they can put into preventive distillation the better as not only are they paid more quickly, but the obligatory distillation may be averted entirely if enough has gone to preventive distillation. The basic Wine Regulation states explicitly that obligatory distillation 'shall be decided upon only if such distillation does not entail a disproportionate administrative burden'.

(iii) The *exceptional distillation* arrangements were strengthened in 1982, so that in seasons when obligatory distillation is applied, exceptional distillation is triggered automatically. In seasons when obligatory distillation is not necessary, the Management Committee has to take a separate decision on the authorization, or not, of exceptional distillation. The normal maximum quantity of wine which may go for exceptional distillation is five million hectolitres, unless the Council of Ministers accepts a higher figure.

The buying-in price for wine going for exceptional distillation is 82 per cent of the guide price for each type of table wine. Producers may put wine to exceptional distillation only when they have satisfied their obligations under obligatory distillation, should this be in operation.

(iv) The *Guarantie de bonne fin* distillation provisions for wine coming out of long term storage contracts were made permanent in 1982. At the same time the buying-in prices were set at $91\frac{1}{2}$ per cent of the guide prices for red wines and 90 per cent of the guide prices for white wines.

(v) *Obligatory distillation* was tightened-up in 1982 for wine produced from grapes normally destined for uses *other* than producing table wines. Thus it covers all wine made from table grape varieties, as well as wine made from grapes normally used for cognac production (Charentes in France) and from grapes to be dried in Greece. None of these wines are meant to be marketed and the obligatory distillation is intended to ensure they are not. The buying-in price for such wines is 50 per cent of the class AI guide price.

The introduction of obligatory distillation depended on the distillers being willing to take all the wine offered them. As part of the 1982 revisions of the wine regime, provisions were introduced to grant *aids to distillers* provided they had paid the appropriate buying-in prices for wine going for obligatory distillation. The aids are payable provided that the products obtained from distillation either have an alcoholic strength of at least 52 per cent by volume for direct sale (i.e. eaux-de-vie), or an alcoholic strength of 92 per cent for sales to the intervention agencies (i.e. as neutral alcohol). When the intervention agencies come to sell the neutral alcohol, they are meant to avoid disturbing the Community market for alcohol and spiritous beverages: in so far as this is not possible there is provision for the Community to pay for their disposal in other ways.

Thus the effect of the 1982 revisions to the wine regime spreads further than just wine producers. The result is to help the survival of a lot of inefficient distilleries which probably would have had to close otherwise.

Border protection

As with fruit and vegetables, wine imports are subject to the charging of duties under the Common Customs Tariff, although these are specific duty rates (i.e. ecu/hl) rather than *ad valorem* duties. Additionally there is a system of minimum import prices—termed *reference prices*—backed up by the imposition of countervailing duties.

Reference prices: are set annually by the Council and are based on the guide prices for wine plus the costs involved in bringing Community wines to the same marketing stage as imports.

The countervailing duties are charged on imports whose free-at-frontier offer price, plus CCT duties paid, is less than the reference price for that product. Most of the world's wine exporters, apart from the USA, have agreed not to supply the Community with wine at under the reference prices. As a quid pro quo these countries are exempted from the application of countervailing duties.

For the countries of the Mediterranean Basin associated with the EC there are a series of preferential duty reductions. Normally these concessions are limited to specified quantities. Once the quota limit for any year is exceeded for a particular supplying country then import duties revert to their full level.

The reference prices on wine are applied in a rather different way to those on fruit and vegetables, as described above, although they do perform a similar role and have a comparable differential impact on foreign suppliers. In particular two differences can be noted:

(i) Whereas customs duties have to be added on to reference prices for fruit and vegetables to determine the minimum import price, customs duties on wine are paid before the reference price comparison is made;
(ii) Countervailing charges would be applied against an offending shipment, not against subsequent shipments.

The first of the differences noted is merely one of method: as with fruit and vegetables preferential suppliers of wine are allowed to retain a higher proportion of the sale price, not charge a lower market price. The second point noted does introduce a real difference into marketing behaviour: there is less need for a supplying country's exporters to adopt a collective marketing strategy because one maverick supplier will not, unlike the case with fruit and vegetables, disrupt the entry conditions for his competitors. In practice, the fact that the control concerns invoiced prices at the border, and not actual market prices within the EC, probably means that it is easier to undercut the reference price, and get away with it, than it would be for a supplier of fruit and vegetables.

Oenological practices and wine marketing

Much of the detail of the wine regime is occasioned by attempts to improve the quality of EC wines, even though the broad aim is the support of producer incomes. As there is such a wide diversity of natural conditions under which wine is produced in the Community, its wine-producing areas are classified into six *zones viticoles* to which different institutional provisions are applied. In particular differing minimum natural alcohol strengths, according to zone, have to be achieved before enrichment is allowed for table wines to raise alcoholic strength further. Again, according to zone, the levels and conditions vary under which acidification and sweetening is permitted.

Apart from aiming to improve the general level of table wines, it is policy to increase the proportion of quality wines produced (both measures having the effect of reducing the structural surplus). The term 'quality wine p.s.r.'[26] is reserved for wines from specified regions meeting specified conditions as to grape variety, minimum alcoholic strength and wine-making practices. Although each wine producing country has its own quality terms the most famous is the French *appellation controlee*. In Germany the basic term is *qualitatswein* and in Italy *denominazione di origine controllata* (DOC).

Another important method by which the quality of EC wines is improved is the obligation placed upon producers to submit the by-products of the wine-making process to a distiller. This effectively reduces the amount of wine a producer can extract from his harvest. These by-products—marc (the residue from the pressed grapes) and the lees (the sediment deposited in the course of fermentation)—or the equivalent quantity of wine, are distilled and delivered to intervention agencies which make payments intended to cover the distiller's costs and provide the producer with a total return equivalent to that which he would have received if there had been no obligation to distil.

The Community has also detailed provisions governing how wines may be described in an attempt to ensure that the contents of a bottle are the same as described on the label. As the Commission's Special Committee of Inquiry (1978) found, however, these provisions—despite their complexity—still can be circumvented.

Control of plantings

The principal instrument for controlling the Community wine surplus has been a complete ban on the planting of new vines for table wine production; first introduced in 1976, this ban was extended to 1986 as part of the Action Programme for the Wine Sector (Commission, 1978c). As a result of the ban, the Community's wine producing area dropped from a peak of 2.53 million ha in 1976/77 to 2.44 million ha in 1979/80 (a drop of 5.2 per cent). The Commission (1982d) expect a further significant drop to come as the area of young vines (vines do not bear until their fourth year) dropped nearly 45 per cent over the same period, while the renewal rate fell to about 1.3 per cent annually, indicating a progressive ageing of EC vineyards (and an average vineyard life of about 75 years).

However, it was recognized that the EC could not ban all new plantings for ever. Further that one of the main factors in the trend to a larger surplus of wine production was that, while vine areas (before the ban on new plantings) were relatively constant, yields had grown due to the replanting of existing vineyards with higher yielding varieties and the establishment of new vineyards on soils flatter and richer than those traditional for wine production. As a result, there had emerged a large surplus of mediocre table wines—as the quality of wines from the vineyards in non-traditional areas tended to be poor.

Consequently, a principal feature of the Action Programme was the introduction of a classification of areas as to their suitability for wine production associated with differing restrictions on replanting, according to the area type. The Commission has moved also to improve its knowledge on wine-grape varieties and the average age of EC vines so that an annual assessment of the EC's wine producing potential can be made.

As part of the drive to encourage better quality wine production, the rules are less restrictive for plantings for quality wine p.s.r. production. Furthermore inducements are available, through the payment of grubbing-up premiums and conversion premiums, when land is turned over to other crops.

Improvement of demand

The Commission (1980d) has been concerned to lower the rates of excise duty charged on the consumption of wines in the non-wine producing countries of the Community, especially in the UK. With wine consumption stagnating, and even dropping in the traditional wine drinking countries, the Commission has suggested that a significant increase in consumption could occur in the non-wine producing countries if the consumption taxes, which are felt to discriminate against wine, could be brought into a ratio of 3 to 1 with the tax on beer. However, in the UK, the British government has estimated that even if wine excise duties were halved, it would lead to only a 20 per cent increase in UK consumption (House of Lords, 1979), which would be insignificant in terms of total EC wine consumption.

Preparation for Spanish entry

The Commission (1981f) made several proposals to amend the wine regime to prepare for Spanish entry to the EC. The burden of these proposals was the need to intensify the EC's efforts to achieve better balance between production and consumption prior to the Iberian enlargement, and to encourage an improvement in wine quality. In a sense the proposals represent a continuation of the measures undertaken as part of the Action Programme.

The main proposals were:

(a) The introduction of a new, early season, low-price obligatory distillation intended to remove the surplus from the new harvest at the start of the wine year;

(b) Amendment and rationalization of existing distillation measures to make them more effective;

(c) Encouragement of the use of grape must by means of a levy on sucrose used for enrichment (to increase alcoholic strength);

(d) Stiffening of the rules on replanting of vines in irrigated areas classed as not naturally suitable for wine growing. Spain would be expected to continue its pre-accession restrictions on irrigation for vines;

(e) An increase of 0.5 per cent in the stipulated natural alcoholic strength of wine, in order to discourage production of high yield, low quality varieties.

ETHYL ALCOHOL

The Commission originally made proposals for a market organization for ethyl alcohol of agricultural origin in 1972. Later these were revised completely (Commission, 1976) and amended substantially (Commission, 1979) but up to the time of writing the proposals had not been adopted. Consequently national arrangements are still being applied by the Member States.

The proposals[27] involve the reserving of certain industrial sectors for ethyl alcohol of agricultural origin. Were the proposals to be adopted, the 'reserved sectors' would include vinegar, alcoholic drinks, the pharmaceutical industry, and the perfumery and cosmetics industries during a five-year transition. These sectors would be forbidden from using ethyl alcohol produced from industrial raw materials (i.e. petrochemicals). The aim of the proposals is to maintain a market for ethyl alcohol produced from agricultural raw materials by denying significant sectors of industrial demand access to ethyl alcohol produced from petrochemicals.

The necessity for a support system for ethyl alcohol of agricultural origin is held to arise because its manufacture by distillation is a major outlet for surplus agricultural commodities, particularly wine. The distillation of wine as a surplus disposal measure, however, is not only an expensive method for producing alcohol, but also disruptive of the EC market for ethyl alcohol because of the volumes involved. It is because of considerations such as these that the Commission's proposals have made such little headway, especially as there were important synthetic ethyl alcohol producers who objected to losing part of their market.

As a result of the lack of progress on a market organization for ethyl alcohol, separate arrangements had to be made for the granting of an export refund on the cereals content of whisky as part of the cereals regime. These arrangements came into affect in 1981, despite the necessity for such provisions having been agreed much earlier as part of the UK's accession arrangements.

RICE

In most important respects the rice regime[28] is a copy of that applied for cereals (discussed in Chapter 4). Within the EC the two have tended to be treated as a pair because of Italian and French demands that rice producers should be given equivalent support to that given to producers of the other cereals.

Economic significance

Rice is grown in France, Greece, and Italy, although Italy accounts for about 90 per cent of total Community production. In terms of the value of agricultural production, rice is of minor significance, accounting for about 0.2 per cent. FEOGA spending on rice is equally limited, varying between 0.2 and 0.5 per cent.

Annual EC rice production is about one million tonnes, although it varies between 0.8 and 1.1 million with yield fluctuations. Production has been tending to decline, however, mainly due to a drop in the area sown. (Between 1978/79 and 1981/82 the Italian rice area fell 11 per cent.)

Traditionally the EC has been a net rice importer, although its domestic self-sufficiency has tended to rise. Principally it imports true long grain rice, but also some round grain rice. It exports, however, significant quantities of what is termed long grain rice (actually more akin—Mitchell (1982, p. 5)—to a medium or short grain rice) under the EC rice regime. The major reason for the two-way trade is that the rice support system does not distinguish between what it terms long grain rice and true long grain. As the European climate is not conducive to the production of true long grain rice, output of medium grain rice is encouraged instead—to the detriment of round grain rice production.

The demand, however, is principally for true long grain rice and round grain rice. Medium grain rice is not a major market. The result of the support system is to encourage the over-production of medium grain rice which has to be exported, while true long grain rice has to be imported.

Coverage

The support system covers:

(a) Paddy, husked, semi-milled, and milled rice;
(b) Broken rice;
(c) Rice flour, groats, meal, pellets, starch, and flakes.

Support measures

As with cereals, there are three main support prices: *target, intervention, and threshold*. The intervention price available to the farmer is expressed in terms of paddy (i.e. unprocessed rice), whereas the target and threshold prices are expressed in terms of husked rice.[29] The derivation of the target price takes into account not only the milling costs involved in de-husking rice, but also transport costs from Italy to the Rhine Valley in Germany and the so-called 'market component'—which is justified as providing room below prices of imported rice for market prices for domestically produced rice to respond to internal demand.

In turn, the threshold price is derived from the target price, but includes a fixed allowance as a component for protection of the EC rice milling industry.

Border protection

Variable import levies are fixed weekly to cover the difference between threshold prices and the lowest representative offer price. Because of the number of different rice varieties in world trade coefficients are used to convert world market price quotes for these varieties to the EC standard quality so that a lowest offer price can be determined. This procedure is equivalent to that applied when the Commission determines lowest offer prices for cereals on the world market. Unlike cereals, however, the rice import levies are only fixed weekly—although they can be changed during a week to take account of threshold price changes, due to the monthly increments in their level, or where world prices have altered very significantly.

Prior to 1978/79 the threshold price for husked long grain rice was some 20 units of account (see Chapter 8) higher than that for round grain rice. The USA, in particular, objected to this as it meant a higher degree of EC preference for its 'long' grain rice production and an unjustified barrier to EC imports of true long grain rice. As part of the Tokyo Round of GATT negotiations it was agreed that this threshold price differential should be phased-out in two equal stages in 1978/79 and 1979/80. It is significant that this was achieved by raising

Table 7.15   The Derivation of the target price for rice for 1982/83.

		ecu/100 kg
(a)	Intervention price for paddy rice in surplus area	290.55
(b)	Market component (11 per cent of intervention price)	31.96
(c)	Milling costs involved in de-husking rice	40.57
	Sub-total	363.08
(d)	Times 1.25 for weight loss equals derived husked rice price in Italy	453.85
(e)	Transport costs Italy/Germany	42.84
(f)	Target price for husked rice—Germany	496.69

the threshold price for round grain rice, rather than by lowering that for long grain rice.

Export refunds are available for EC rice exports. These are set both by a tender system and as fixed rates available to anyone applying for them. Mitchell (1982, p. 39) has criticized the export refund mechanisms as not encouraging growers to produce varieties for specific world markets, as the methods used for establishing refund levels enable 'firms to ignore the price signals coming from prospective third country customers'.

Other measures

To encourage holders of rice stocks to carry them over from one marketing year to the next there is an end of season *carryover payment*. During the season *monthly increases* apply to intervention and threshold prices in order to take storage costs into account. Finally, *production refunds* are paid to manufacturers using broken rice in the starch and brewing industries.

TEXTILE FIBRES

Prior to Greek accession, the Community had only two extremely minor CAP regimes covering textile fibres: these were for fibre flax and hemp, and for silkworms. In 1981, however, a potentially more significant support system was created for cotton as agreed in the Greek Accession Treaty.

Fibre flax and hemp

Although in terms of EC agriculture, flax production is of minor importance—being produced on some 10 000 farms in the Netherlands,

Belgium, and France—it nevertheless accounts for around 12 per cent of world production. The regime[30] provides for a flat-rate *production aid* to be paid per hectare of fibre flax and hemp. Additionally, when the internal market is depressed, stockholders may get EC subsidies for their storage costs through the national intervention agencies making available *private storage* contracts. Because of the difficulty in increasing flax sales in the EC, the EC is subsidizing a marketing programme.

Silkworms

EC production, at around 45 tonnes of raw silk, is negligible. The silkworms are reared principally in Italy, but also France and Greece. Despite the payment[31] of a flat-rate *production aid* per box of silkworm seed, EG production has dropped massively. In 1963 EC production was 143 000 boxes of silk seed: by 1979 this had fallen to 10 900 boxes. Since then EC production has fluctuated between 10 and 15 thousand boxes.

Unginned cotton

Cotton is not included in Annex II to the Treaty of Rome listing all the agricultural products to be covered by the CAP. Nevertheless, support arrangements[32] were introduced for cotton in 1981/82, as agreed in Protocol No. 4 of the Greek Accession Treaty.

Support is given through a *production aid* set equal to the difference between the *guide price* for unginned cotton and the world price. As there is not a world market in unginned cotton, world prices are collected for ginned cotton and the cost of ginning deducted. The aid is only payable to the cotton ginners provided they have paid the *minimum price*, set by the Council as part of the annual price fixing, to farmers. Aid is only available on a limited quantity of production, set at 430 000 tonnes for 1982/83.

Aid is also available for the creation of producer marketing groups, and for investment in processing and marketing equipment for cotton. These investment aids have to be provided for separately as, cotton not being included as an agricultural crop in Annex II to the Treaty of Rome, it is not eligible for aid under the CAP's structural policies.

NOTES

1. See, for example, the report by the Economic and Social Committee (1975) which suggested that the confidence of the Community's producers of Mediterranean products had been shaken by politically inspired import duty concessions granted to the countries of the Mediterranean Basin. ECOSOC (1975, p. 144) concluded there was need to 'restructure' the CAP for Mediterranean agricultural products.
2. For the purposes of this chapter, Mediterranean agricultural products are taken to be wine, rice, olive oil, tobacco, durum wheat, cotton, silkworms, and fruit and vegetables. Particularly in the case of fruit and vegetables this classification is

arbitrary as significant proportions of production are grown in the north of the Community. Durum wheat, although a Mediterranean product and included as such in Table 7.1, is discussed in Chapter 4. Fibre flax is included in Chapter 7, although not a Mediterranean product, as it fits most logically with the EC's other textile fibre policies.

3. The claim was that Italian exports of wine were proving very competitive within France because of the operation of MCAs. On this, see Report by the French Senate (1977).

4. The basic regime for fresh fruit and vegetables is given in Regulation (EEC) No. 1035/72 and processed fruit and vegetables in No. 516/77.

5. The Italian intervention agency once bought into intervention, in 1975.

6. See House of Lords (1981) for a discussion of these issues and a full analysis of the EC's fruit and vegetables regime.

7. The Panel of Inquiry found that 'there was a prima facie case of nullification or impairment of benefits accruing to Chile . . .' and that 'the economic interests of Chile had been adversely affected' (GATT, 1980, p. 19).

8. The other two schemes provide, (i) aids to assist the processing of lemons and some oranges through ensuring regular supplies to EC producers (introduced in 1969), and (ii) aids for the processing of pineapples produced in the French Overseas Departments (introduced in 1977). The purpose of the second aid is to offset the difference between the EC ex-factory price, and prices charged by Third Countries for processed pineapple. It is available to processers paying EC growers a minimum price for fresh pineapples.

9. In 1981 the number of products covered was raised to 12: peeled, frozen tomatoes; tomato flakes; prunes derived from plums; tomato concentrates; peeled tomatoes; tomato juice; peaches in syrup; Williams pears preserved in syrup; cherries preserved in syrup; tomato juice; dried figs; dried grapes.

10. Up to 1980 this added sugar duty (ads) was variable and based on the import levy for sugar. One result of the Tokyo Round of GATT negotiations was that this duty was replaced by a constant 2 per cent *ad valorem* duty for the products covered under CCT heading 20.06 (principally canned fruit).

11. Processed raspberries, canned mushrooms, frozen strawberries, dried prunes, tomato products, peas and beans in pod, peaches in syrup, and canned pears.

12. The use of import certificates coupled with 'voluntary' export restraints meant that the EC would only issue an import certificate where an export document had been issued by the government of the exporting couxtry.

13. Glace cherries, sulphurized cherries, pure orange juice, and processed hazelnuts.

14. Regulation No. (EEC) 727/70.

15. The last such report, at the time of writing, concerned oriental tobaccos (Commission, 1978a).

16. The basic regime for oils and fats is set out in Regulation No. 136/66. That part dealing with olive oil came into effect on 10 November 1966.

17. According to the Commission (1978b, p. 163), in both 1976/77 and 1977/78 public stocks were equivalent to 13 per cent of annual production.

18. Another move to limit fraudulent claims, is the Community's planned register of olive trees. This has, however, been under way since 1975.

19. The threshold price is set equal to the representative market price after adjusting for the costs of unloading and internal distribution for imported olive oil.

20. There are technical limitations as to the extent olive oil can substitute for other oils in food processing. This is because for many uses (e.g. biscuits, cakes, ice cream, confectionery and chocolate, and for most industrial uses of oils and fats) olive oil is unsuitable because of its particular technical and organoleptic characteristics.

21. The basic regime is set out in Regulation (EEC) No. 337/79.

22. For the best detailed account of the wine regime and the problems faced by the Community in applying it, see Commission: Special Committee of Inquiry (1978).
23. Table wines are, in effect, defined as wines other than 'quality wines produced in specified regions' for which stringent quality conditions have to be satisfied. The six types of table wine are:

Type	Degree of alcohol or character	Colour
RI	Between 10° and 12°	Red
RII	Between 13° and 14°	Red
RIII	Wines of the Portugieser variety	Red
AI	Between 10° and 12°	White
AII	Wines of the Sylvaner and Muller-Thurgau varieties	White
AIII	Wines of the Riesling variety	White

24. There is a complex system of price recording involving the fixing of *average producer prices* at each market which reports prices, and then weighting these prices to give *representative prices* for the Community as a whole.
25. Short-term private storage contracts are available when representative prices are below activating prices for more than two weeks.
26. Short for quality wine produced in specified regions.
27. For a full description of the proposals and an analysis of their effects, see House of Lords (1976) and (1980).
28. Regulation (EEC) No. 1418/76.
29. There are, in fact, three threshold prices set. These are for: husked rice; milled round grain rice; milled long grain rice.
30. Regulation (EEC) No. 1308/70.
31. Regulation (EEC) No. 845/72.
32. Regulation (EEC) No. 2169/81.

REFERENCES

Benedictis, M. de (1981) 'Agricultural development in Italy: national problems in a community framework', *Journal of Agricultural Economics*, **32**.

Commission of the European Communities (1976) *Amended Proposal for a Council Regulation (EEC) on the Common Organisation of the Market in Ethyl Alcohol of Agricultural Origin and additional provisions for certain products containing Ethyl Alcohol*, COM (76) 274, Brussels.

Commission of the European Communities (1977a) *Mediterranean Agricultural Problems*, COM (77) 140, Brussels.

Commission of the European Communities (1977b) *Guidelines concerning the development of the Mediterranean regions of the Community, together with certain measures relating to agriculture*, COM (77) 526, Vols. I and II, Brussels.

Commission of the European Communities (1977c) *Financial Consequences of the proposals for measures to assist Mediterranean agriculture*, COM (77) 674, Brussels.

Commission of the European Communities (1978a) *Commission report to the Council concerning the quantities of oriental tobacco from the 1976 harvest taken over by the intervention bodies*, COM (78) 417, Brussels.

Commission of the European Communities (1978b), *The Agricultural Situation in the Community: 1978 Report*, Brussels.

Commission of the European Communities (1978c) *Action Programme 1979–1985 for the Progressive Establishment of Balance on the Market in Wine*, COM (78) 260, Vols. I to IV, Brussels.

Commission of the European Communities (1979) *Amendment of the amended proposal for a Council Regulation (EEC) on the common organization of the market in ethyl alcohol of agricultural origin and laying down additional provisions for certain products containing ethyl alcohol*, COM (79) 237, Brussels.

Commission of the European Communities (1980a) *Reflections on the Common Agricultural tral Policy*, COM (80) 800, Brussels.

Commission of the European Communities (1980b) *The Agricultural Situation in the Community: 1980 Report*, Brussels.

Commission of the European Communities (1980c) *Report to the Council on the foreseeable developments in the planting and replanting of vineyards in the Community and on the ratio between production and utilisation in the wine sector*, COM (80) 622, Brussels.

Commission of the European Communities (1980d) *Report on the Scope for Convergence of Tax Systems in the Community*, Supplement 1/80 to the Bulletin of the European Communities, Brussels.

Commission of the European Communities (1981a) *Commission Report on the Mandate of 30 May 1980*, COM (81) 300, Brussels.

Commission of the European Communities (1981b) *Mediterranean programmes—lines of action*, COM (81) 637, Brussels.

Commission of the European Communities (1981c) *Guidelines for European Agriculture*, COM (81) 608, Brussels.

Commission of the European Communities (1981d) *Olive Oil*, COM (81) 610, Brussels.

Commission of the European Communities (1981e) *Proposal for a Council Regulation amending Regulation (EEC) No. 1035/72 on the common organization of the market in fruit and vegetables*, COM (81) 403, Brussels.

Commission of the European Communities (1981f) *Proposal for a Council Regulation amending Regulation (EEC) No. 337/79 on the common organization of the market in wine*, COM (81) 408, Brussels.

Commission of the European Communities (1982a) *Commission Communication to the Council on the Greek Government Memorandum of 19 March 1982*, COM (82) 348, Brussels.

Commission of the European Communities (1982b) *The Agricultural Situation in the Community: 1981 Report*, Brussels.

Commission of the European Communities (1982c) *Report from the Commission to the Council on the situation of the agricultural markets—1981*, COM (81) 822, Brussels.

Commission of the European Communities (1982d) *Commission report to the Council on the foreseeable developments in the planting and replanting of vineyards in the Community and on the ratio between production and utilization in the wine sector*, COM (82) 253, Brussels.

Commission of the European Communities (1982e) *Preliminary Draft General Budget of the European Communities for the Financial Year 1983*, COM (82) 200, Vol. 7, Brussels.

Commission of the European Communities: Special Committee of Inquiry (1975) *Report concerning the EAGGF Guarantee Section—Oilseed and Olive Oil Sectors*, COM (75) 37, Brussels.

Commission of the European Communities: Special Committee of Inquiry (1978) *Fourth Report concerning the Guarantee Section of the EAGGF, Wine Sector*, S/339/78, Brussels.

Court of Auditors (1980a) 'Special Report on various measures affecting the management of the EAGGF Guarantee Section', *Official Journal*, No. C 258, Luxembourg.

Court of Auditors (1980b) 'Annual report concerning the financial year 1979', *Official Journal*, No. C342, Luxembourg.

Economic and Social Committee (1975) *Study on the Current Prospects for the Agricultural Products of the EEC's Mediterranean Area*, CES 1223/75, Brussels.

European Parliament (1980) 'Final Adoption of the General Budget of the European Communities for the financial year 1981', *Official Journal*, Vol. 23, L378, Luxembourg.

European Report (1982) Issue No. 851, Brussels.

French Government (1977) *Memorandum on the Reform of Community Regulations governing Mediterranean agricultural production*, Council of the European Communities, R/1905/77, Brussels.

French Senate (1977) *Rapport d'Information sur les repércussions agricoles de la politique mediterranéene de la C.E.E. pour les régions du Sud de la France*, rapporteurs Pisani et Sordel, Session 1976–1977, Report No. 259, Paris.

General Agreement on Tariffs and Trade (1980) *EEC Restrictions on Imports of Apples from Chile*, L/5047, Geneva.

House of Lords Select Committee on the European Communities (1976) *Agricultural Surpluses and Ethyl Alcohol*, 37th Report, Session 1976–77, HL 191, HMSO: London.

House of Lords Select Committee on the European Communities (1979) *On the Progressive Establishment of Balance on the Market in Wine*, Session 1978–79, 7th Report, HL 47, HMSO: London.

House of Lords Select Committee on the European Communities (1980) *Ethyl Alcohol*, Session 1979–80, 21st Report, HL 99, HMSO: London.

House of Lords Select Committee on the European Communities (1981) *Fruit and Vegetables*, Session 1980–81, 22nd Report, HL 147, HMSO: London.

Italian Government (1977) *Memorandum from the Italian Government on the Mediterranean problems of the Community*, Council of the European Communities, R/1712/77, Brussels.

Mitchell, M. (1982) *Italy and the Rice Market in the European Community*, Report No. 15, CEAS: Wye College.

Chapter 8

Green 'Money' and Monetary Compensatory Amounts

The European Community's green 'money' system is both simple in concept, and extremely complicated in day-to-day implementation. Section I of this chapter will briefly explain the origins of the system and outline the meaning of the terms 'unit of account', 'green conversion rate' (green 'money'), and 'monetary compensatory amount' (MCA). The material that follows in Sections II and III contributes additional detail to the framework given in Section I. There is a brief history, in Section II, of the changes in the system which took place between 1969 and the inauguration of the European Monetary System (EMS) in 1979: and in Section III the system as it has operated since the introduction of EMS is discussed. In the final section the economic implications of the system are outlined.

I UNITS OF ACCOUNT AND GREEN CONVERSION RATES

The EEC, and before that the European Coal and Steel Community, found it necessary to fix certain monetary sums and record flows of funds in their budgets. Rather than use national currencies for this the ECSC first used the European Payments Union (EPU) unit of account, and subsequently the European Monetary Agreement (EMA) unit of account. Both were identical in value and equal to one US dollar.[1] In 1962 it was decided that the unit of account should also be used for the purpose of fixing support prices under the CAP. This original unit of account has been termed the gold parity unit of account.[2]

At the time all the major Western trading countries, including the original six EC Member States, participated in a system of managed currency markets such that foreign exchange rates were fixed for long periods of time. This system of fixed, but adjustable exchange rates, evolved out of meetings held at Bretton Woods, USA, in 1944 to determine future international trading and currency arrangements.[3] Participating governments, through their membership of the International Monetary Fund (IMF), agreed to maintain a fixed value in terms of gold for their currencies by means of market intervention by their central

187

banks. Although gold was formally the pivot of the system, in practice the US dollar played the central role as the premier currency in international trade at that time.

By making the unit of account equal to the dollar, the Community was able to use the official gold-based parities between Member State currencies and the dollar—as declared to the IMF—for its own purposes. Hence, when in the 1960s the first agricultural support prices were being set, it was logical for the Community to pick on the ua as the medium in which they were to be expressed.[4] It followed from the decision to use the ua in the CAP, and from the definition adopted for the ua, that CAP support prices—no matter which national EC currency they were expressed in—would be internally consistent.

This may be demonstrated as follows. Suppose that the intervention price for a CAP product was fixed at 100 ua per tonne—a price applicable throughout the EC—then to calculate the price paid by the German intervention agency it was necessary to take the deutschmark:US dollar exchange rate (at 4 D-Mark per dollar in the mid-1960s) to arrive at 400 D-Mark per tonne. A similar calculation would be performed in the other Member States, and the resulting intervention prices—expressed in national currencies—would be equal.

The process is summarized for two Member States in Figure 8.1. The rates at which units of account are converted into national currencies for the purpose of agricultural policy—in this example equal to the official IMF dollar:national currency exchange rates—are sometimes known as green conversion rates. They are now legally known as representative rates; and they are popularly—but inaccurately known—as green 'money'. The example in Figure 8.1 is internally consistent: because the green conversion rates used correspond to market exchange rates under the Bretton Woods system then the national intervention prices would be the same, in the sense that 400 D-Mark could be exchanged in the international currency markets for 493.707 FF.

When the CAP was being created, the world monetary system was based on the system of fixed exchange rates created at Bretton Woods, and the hegemony of the US dollar. It was a relatively stable world, at least by comparison with the

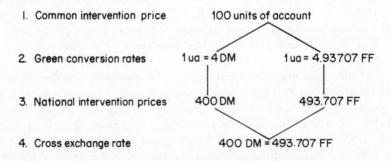

Figure 8.1 CAP price fixing for intervention products prior to August 1969.

1970s, and one where parity changes were extremely rare. Indeed, at one stage in the Community it was thought that by adopting for CAP purposes the ua based, as it was, on fixed IMF parities, future changes in the values of Member State currencies would be precluded altogether. Such a view seems ridiculous now—a case of 'the tail wagging the dog'—but at the time CAP unity was felt to be so important that it would induce, in due course, a *de facto* monetary union.

The Bretton Woods system of fixed, but adjustable exchange rates came under pressure towards the end of the 1960s as the exchange rates declared to the IMF increasingly were felt to be out-of-line with market conditions. The system made provision for parity changes which were meant to be relatively small adjustments at frequent intervals to minimize the disruption caused. In practice the adjustments were infrequent and large, and they gave rise to (and were caused by) major international capital flows. In 1969, only two years after the introduction of common prices into the CAP, changes in parity values were forced on the French and West German currencies: in August 1969 the French franc was devalued and in October 1969 the deutschmark was revalued. These parity changes marked the end of the only period when common support prices for CAP products have applied equally throughout the EC.

The devaluation of the franc meant that the dollar–franc exchange rate rose from $1 = 4.93707 to $1 = 5.55419. This had the effect of raising the price in French francs of any commodity priced in foreign currency. The French franc price of imports rose and French holiday-makers had to pay more francs for their foreign holidays (conversely, to other nationals, holidays in France became cheaper). Some franc prices—but by no means all—would have risen by as much as the price of a dollar had risen (12.5 per cent), and the others by a smaller percentage. Broadly speaking non-traded goods would (at least initially) have experienced no price change, whereas traded goods (imports and exports) would have risen in price and the extent of the price rise would have been greater (approaching 12.5 per cent) the smaller was France's role in the international trade in the product. Thus it can be seen that the whole pattern of relative prices in France would be modified; and in the absence of an agricultural policy the price of farm and food products would have been subject to change.

The French government, for a variety of reasons, decided that the French support price for agricultural products should not rise. In terms of Figure 8.1 they continued to use the unamended green conversion rate to convert from units of account to French francs, despite the fact that the official IMF exchange rate was now $1 = 5.55419 francs. Thus in line 4 of Figure 8.1 400 D-Mark was no longer worth 493.707 FF in the international currency markets, but 12.5 per cent more. One of the basic principles of the CAP—that of common support prices—had been broken.

It was not sufficient, however, for France to decide that support prices would not be increased; steps had also to be taken to stop market prices from rising. As mentioned above the intervention price (in terms of French francs) in the other Member States was now 12.5 per cent above that in France; and consequently the markets in the other Member States would provide a magnet to French produce unless the price advantage (12.5 per cent of the French support price) were taxed away. Hence French exports were subject to an export tax—now known as a monetary compensatory amount—and imports to an equivalent subsidy.

The revaluation of the mark generated a similar problem for Germany, but with different policy implications. On the international currency markets $1 US no longer bought 4 D-Mark, but only 3.66 D-Mark. Other things being equal the price of foreign goods in Germany would have fallen, in some cases by as much as 8.5 per cent; and in the absence of an agricultural policy the same would have been true for farm and food products. In terms of Figure 8.1 if the new dollar–mark exchange rate had been used in line 2 then the intervention price would have fallen by 8.5 per cent to 366 D-Mark. This was unacceptable to the German authorities and so, for the purpose of the agricultural policy, they continued to convert from units of account to marks at 1 ua = 4 D-Mark, despite the fact that this no longer corresponded to the realities of the international currency market.[5]

The German intervention price was now 9.3 per cent higher[6] than that in Italy and the Benelux countries (and considerably higher than that in France), and to maintain this price differential it was necessary to impose a tax on imports of products into Germany, and subsidize their export. The situation in late 1969 can be summarized in Figure 8.2.

In four Member States (Belgium, Luxembourg, the Netherlands, and Italy) the 'common'[7] intervention price prevailed; the price in Germany was 9.3 per cent above the common intervention price, and that in France 11.1 per cent below. On intra-Community trade with Germany an MCA was levied on imports and paid as a subsidy to the trader on exports. On extra-Community trade with Germany the same MCA was added to the import levy and the export subsidy. In the case of France the MCA was paid as a subsidy on intra-Community imports, and deducted from the import levy on imports from non-Member States. The same MCA was levied on French exports to the other Member States, and deducted from the export subsidy to Third Countries.

In terms of the simple example of Figure 8.2 the German MCA would be 34 D-Mark on all imports and exports: this can be thought of as the arithmetical difference between the intervention price applied (400 D-Mark) and that which would have been applied (366 D-Mark) had the new official IMF exchange rate been used. In practice, as will be explained in Section III, it would now be calculated by first taking the MCA percentage of 8.5 per cent (3.66 ÷ 4) and applying this to the actual German intervention price of 400 D-Mark.

The position of the French government in August 1969 was broadly that a temporary exception had to be made to the common pricing system that had begun in July 1967 because otherwise the shock to the then fragile economy, after the social disturbances of 1968, of an immediate rise in food prices would be unsupportable. Devaluations were viewed as traumatic events by all governments, and many observers; and it was believed that, unless abated, the general

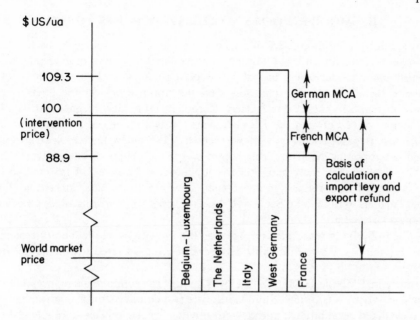

Figure 8.2   CAP pricing for intervention products—late 1969. Germany is said to have a 'positive' MCA (above the common price level) and France a 'negative' MCA (below the common price level).

rise in prices following a devaluation could erode the competitive position of the economy and lead to pressure for yet another devaluation. Consequently it was agreed that France would be allowed a two-year period of grace before returning fully to the CAP common pricing system: the gap would be halved at the beginning of the 1970/71 marketing year and eliminated at the beginning of the 1971/72 marketing year. Using the terminology which was later to be adopted, the French green conversion rate would be 'devalued' in two steps.

Germany, in the autumn of 1969 and subsequently, found it difficult to accept a cut in D-Mark prices. It has found it possible to accept reductions in the real level of price support as price increases have failed to keep up with inflation, but not in the nominal level. In other circumstances—for instance a domestic agricultural policy—a cut in nominal terms might have been possible; but to explain to German farm groups that, in D-Mark terms, EC determined support prices must be reduced has never appealed to German politicians. Thus, in 1969, Germany argued strongly that it too should be allowed a transitional period before realigning with the common level of CAP price support. The arrangements agreed for Germany were more complicated than those for France: the common prices were to be applied at the end of 1969, but for a four-year transitional period German farmers were to be compensated by direct income payments and modifications to the value added tax system.[8]

II MODIFICATIONS TO THE SYSTEM, 1969 TO 1979

Although by 1969 there were many people arguing for a change in the Bretton Woods system, and a move towards a more flexible system of exchange rate determination, there were probably few policy makers in Brussels who could foresee the exchange rate changes—and the implications for the CAP—that were to come in the 1970s. Indeed, European monetary union—with stable exchange rates between the EC currencies—was still viewed as an attainable objective. Broadly speaking, 1969 was seen by CAP policy-makers as an aberration: a temporary departure from common pricing. When, on the contrary, the 1970s showed even more marked currency movements the MCA system had to be amended and refined to meet each new circumstance. Conceptually it remained as outlined in Section I, but the operating details of the system changed frequently.

The underlying reason for change was the evolving world monetary system: the key dates are listed in Table 8.1. Several are associated with a significant change to the MCA system.

Early in 1971 the D-Mark and Dutch guilder came under strong pressure to revalue. There was a flow of funds into the two countries to take advantage of the expected revaluations; and to stem the flow the currencies were allowed to float. They appreciated on international currency markets. However, the Dutch and German governments resolved that this fact should not be reflected in the CAP price support mechanisms as it implied a fall in support prices. As in 1969 the conversion rates used by West Germany and the Netherlands for the purposes of the CAP were not consistent with the exchange rates in the currency markets, and so MCAs were re-introduced.[9] They were 'variable' because they had to be changed periodically to reflect the fluctuating value of the floating currency with respect to the fixed value of the green conversion rates. The later events of 1971: the suspension of the convertibility of the dollar into gold in the August, and the Smithsonian agreement of December meant that MCAs were introduced for all Member States as they each chose to maintain domestic price stability, rather than respect common prices, when exchange rates changed.

A major modification to the system came in June 1973 when the definition of the unit of account was changed. Prior to August 1971 the unit of account and the dollar had the same gold content—labelled the gold parity unit of account above. When the dollar-gold link was broken it was decided that the unit of account—dollar link should be maintained rather than the unit of account—gold link. Thus, with the *dollar value unit of account* as the formal pivot of the CAP pricing system, the MCA for any country depended essentially on the country's currency movement against the dollar. With the floating of the 'joint-float' currencies against the dollar in March 1973 every country had a variable MCA and a great deal of paperwork became necessary.

In June 1973 the unit of account was, in effect, redefined: instead of being linked to the dollar it was linked to the 'joint-float'. The *'joint-float' unit of account* was deemed to have a fixed value in terms of each of the 'joint-float' currencies.

Table 8.1   Monetary changes of importance to the CAP, 1971–1979.

9 May 1971	D-Mark and Dutch florin allowed to float.
15 August 1971	Suspension of dollar–gold convertibility.
17–18 December 1971	Smithsonian agreement. Realignment of world currencies involving a devaluation of the dollar, and a realignment of EC currencies against one another. Still a system of fixed exchange rates, but one involving a greater margin of movement around the central rates then adopted than did the original Bretton Woods system.
21 March 1972	A group of European—mainly EC—countries agreed to link their currencies within narrower fluctuation margins around their central rates than allowed under the Smithsonian agreement—the 'Snake'.
23 June 1972	The United Kingdom—a member of the 'Snake' but not yet the EC—allows sterling to float.
12 February 1973	Second devaluation of the dollar, and Italy leaves the 'Snake' and allows the lira to float.
19 March 1973	The 'Snake' becomes the 'joint float'. That is the exchange rates between 'joint float' currencies are fixed, but the currencies float collectively against other currencies. D-Mark revalued.
19 June 1973	D-Mark revalued in the 'joint float'.
17 September 1973	The Netherlands revalues in the 'joint float'.
15 January 1974	France leaves the 'joint float'.
11 July 1975	France rejoins the 'joint float'.
15 March 1976	France leaves the 'joint float'.
18 October 1976	Germany revalues, Denmark devalues, in the 'joint float'.
4 April 1977	Denmark devalues in the 'joint float'.
29 August 1977	Denmark devalues in the 'joint float'.
16 October 1978	Germany and the Benelux countries revalue in the 'joint float'.
9 March 1979	Formation of the European Monetary System (EMS) which replaces the 'joint float'. Link between pound sterling and Irish punt broken.

Note: The Central Bank of a country whose currency is floating does not intervene in the currency market to fix the external value of the currency; instead its value is determined by market forces.
SOURCE   Commission, 1979b, Annex A.

Thus there was a fixed MCA which only changed when the currency in question was either revalued or devalued in the 'joint-float', or when the green conversion rate for the country was 'revalued' or 'devalued'. Any country whose currency was not in the 'joint-float' had a variable MCA because the value of its currency could fluctuate markedly against the 'joint-float' currencies, and hence against the 'joint-float' unit of account. Ireland, Italy, the United Kingdom and, for much of the period, France were not members of the 'joint-float' and hence had variable MCAs.

The difference in the system prior to, and post-June 1973, can best be illustrated by an example. Suppose the international value of the dollar were to decline against all the European currencies, but that the world market price of wheat remained constant in dollar terms. In the first system all the positive MCAs would have been increased (and the negative MCAs reduced), but the levy in units of account would have remained unchanged. In the second system it would be the levy—rather than the MCA—that took the strain: the levy would increase but MCAs would be unaltered. The net effect, in terms of protection to European agriculture, was the same: EC farmers were protected from a weakening dollar whereas other EC businesses were not. (For further comment, see Josling and Harris, 1976.)

A major feature of the 1970s was the extent to which the Member States allowed CAP support prices in the different countries to diverge. The gap between the highest and lowest price was often greater than the price gap that had existed prior to price harmonization in 1967. The two 'villains' in the piece, in the sense that they occupied the two extreme positions, were West Germany and the United Kingdom. The country with the highest price level in the period under review was West Germany: the most important member of the 'joint-float'. Any adjustment towards a lower common support price was painful—despite low rates of inflation in West Germany—because it implied cuts in D-Mark prices unless offset by an increase in the common support price expressed in units of account. Thus 'revaluations' of the green D-Mark came to be associated with the annual fixing of prices, and only to the extent that D-Mark prices were not reduced. Between 1971 and the introduction of EMS in 1979 the green D-Mark was 'revalued' four times, reducing D-Mark prices by just over 7 per cent.

The United Kingdom, a country with a high rate of inflation, experienced for much of the period a depreciating currency. At times there was a reluctance to 'devalue' the green pound and hence raise CAP support prices, and, to a varying extent, food prices, in Britain. For most of the period Britain had the lowest support prices: indeed, in one bleak week in the autumn of 1976 at the depth of a sterling crisis the support price in West Germany was 60 per cent higher than that in the UK.[10]

It was not difficult to rationalize the position of the two countries. Germany, a wealthy country with a low rate of inflation and a significant number of small farmers saw its national interest in securing as high a price level as was permissible within the rules; whereas Britain, a less prosperous nation with a high rate of inflation, few people engaged in agriculture, and traditionally an importer of food at world market prices, saw its interests in having as low a price as possible.[11] The British farming interest, quite naturally, did not take the same view and protested vociferously. None the less between 1973 and the introduction of EMS in 1979 the green pound was 'devalued' seven times, raising sterling support prices by over 37 per cent. Britain's ranking in the price hierarchy was subsequently changed dramatically, with the rise in the value of sterling dating from late 1979 and the introduction of a positive MCA on British trade.

One result of the British Government's policy was the break-up of the market link between Ireland and the United Kingdom. The Irish punt had been linked to sterling for many years; when sterling was floated in June 1972 the link was maintained, and when Britain and Ireland joined the EC in 1973 they were both given the same green conversion rate. In October 1974, however, the Council of Ministers 'devalued' the green punt by a larger amount than the green pound, and so gave Ireland a higher level of price support than the United Kingdom. This gave the border between Northern Ireland and the Republic a reinforced significance because again it became profitable to smuggle agricultural produce. Prior to EC entry products had been smuggled North to benefit from UK support measures. The trade was now to the South, evading the MCAs which would otherwise have been levied. Subsequently—though not for agricultural reasons—the link between the punt and sterling was broken and the former became a member of the EMS. The appreciation of sterling in 1980 then meant British support prices were fixed at a higher level than those in Ireland, and the smugglers had to reverse the flow of produce across the Northern Ireland border.

Throughout the period the Commission maintained its insistence that MCAs should be eliminated and the unity of the market regained. It made a number of proposals,[12] all of which involved some element of automatic change in green conversion rates and none of which were acceptable to all Member States. Two issues were involved: the power of the Council to fix green-conversion rates, and the level at which prices should be harmonized.

Green conversion rates were, and still are, fixed by the Council on the basis of a proposal from the Commission. But in fact, within certain limits, a Member State indicates whether or not it wishes its green conversion rate to be amended, and if so to what extent. This doctrine has been called into question on a number of occasions—for example in 1978 when the British House of Commons instructed the Minister of Agriculture to devalue the green pound by 7.5 per cent and the Council was reluctant to comply—but it has never been seriously opposed. To date there has always been at least one Member State unwilling to cede power to the Commission to fix green rates, or to allow majority voting in the Council. The main constraint is that green conversion rate changes can only move a country's price level towards the common price level, never away from it. Hence the common price level is important both in determining an individual country's price expectations prior to price harmonization; and the level at which prices would presumably be harmonized if market unity were to be restored.

The level of the common price is determined by two factors; first the value of the unit of account in which the common price is fixed, and second the number of units of account. Hence a common price of 50 units of account, when one unit of account is worth $1, would be equivalent to $50; and would be equal to a common price of 100 units of account when one unit of account is worth $\$\frac{1}{2}$. Provided all the decision makers have this information at their disposal, and act accordingly, then the value of the unit of account is irrelevant. However, if decision makers are influenced by the distribution of MCAs then the unit of account is important, because the higher is its value, the higher the level of the common price as MCAs are eliminated. Consequently there was a lot of discussion as to whether, and under what conditions, the 'joint float' unit of account should be replaced by a lower valued unit of account which was likely to appreciate in value at a slower rate (or depreciate at a faster rate) than the 'joint-float' unit of account.[13] These discussions were terminated by the introduction, in March 1979, of EMS and the use from then onwards of the European currency unit (ecu) in agriculture.

An essential part of the compromise was the 'gentleman's agreement' of March 1979 whereby all the then Member States, apart from the UK, agreed that any new MCAs created after the agreement's inception would be phased-out over two years provided that this did not lead to a drop in support prices in national currencies for a country with a positive MCA. As a result of the UK's absence from the agreement it remains an informal understanding.[14]

III EMS AND THE PRESENT SYSTEM OF MCAs

The European currency unit

ecu

The ecu is described as a 'basket' unit, in that it consists of specified amounts of the Member States' currencies. The day-to-day market value of the ecu is determined by taking, for each currency, 'a representative market exchange rate . . . against the United States dollar' (Commission, 1979a, p. 4). A typical calculation is given in Table 8.2.

Column (a) specifies the present composition of the ecu: 0.828 D-Mark plus 1.15 French francs, and so on. The dollar equivalents of the elements of the ecu are then calculated giving a market valuation of the ecu, on the day of the example, of 1.3001831 $ US. It is then a simple calculation to obtain the value of the ecu in any world currency. It can be seen from column (d) that the D-Mark made up nearly 33 per cent of the value of the ecu; but these currency 'weights' will clearly change on a day-to-day basis as the international values of the constituent parts of the ecu vary.

The weighting system of the currencies in the ecu has a curious history. When the ecu was first defined it was given the same composition as the, now defunct, European unit of account (EUA). The EUA in turn had first been introduced into EC operations in April 1975, for certain provisions of the Lomé convention. The weighting system was 'based on a five-year average (over the period 1969–73) of the GNP and intra-European trade of the Member States, adjusted for their participation in short-term monetary support' (Strasser, 1981, p. 26). The overall value of the EUA, and hence the absolute size of its constituent parts, was set such that on 28 June 1974 it had the same value as one IMF

Table 8.2   Calculation of the daily value of the ecu.

Calculation of value on 1 December 1978

Composition of the ecu		Exchange rate against US $	Dollar equivalent of ecu	Percentage weights of national currencies in ecu	Percentage weights of national currencies in EUA on 28 June 1974
(a)		(b)	(c) = a/b	(d)	(e)
3.66	B. Frs	30.6675	0.1193445	9.2	7.9
0.217	D. Kr	5.3885	0.0402709	3.1	3.0
0.828	DM	1.9358	0.4277301	32.9	27.3
1.15	FF	4.4495	0.2584560	19.9	19.5
0.00759	£(IRL)	1.9364*	0.0146972	0.9	1.5
109	Lit	853.00	0.1277842	9.8	14.0
0.140	L. Frs.	30.6675	0.0045650	0.4	0.3
0.286	Fl	2.1035	0.1359638	10.5	9.0
0.0885	£	1.9364*	0.1713714	13.2	17.5
			1.3001831	100	100

* The dollar exchange rate supplied by London and Dublin is the number of dollars per currency unit.
SOURCE   Columns (a)–(c) (and hence (d)), Commission, 1979a, p. 5.
             Column (e), Strasser, 1981, p. 26.

special drawing right (Strasser, 1981, p. 26). Thus in Table 8.2 column (e) reflects the initial weighting given the currencies in the EUA, and column (a) reflects the absolute quantities which were necessary to give the EUA its initial value.

The ecu does differ from the old EUA, however, in that provision has been made to revise its composition. This allowed for a review at the end of the first six months operation of EMS, which produced no change, and 'thereafter every five years or, on request, if the weight of any currency has changed by 25 per cent' (Commission, 1979c, p. 95). In addition the Greek Act of Accession provides for inclusion of the drachma in the ecu basket by 31 December 1985 at the latest. None the less in 1983 the currency amounts were still those based on economic data covering the period 1969–1973.

The provisions of EMS are very complicated and well beyond the scope of this book. However, an outline of the system is necessary in order to understand the method of fixing MCAs, and the implications for MCAs of changes in EMS.[15] Eight Member States participate in the exchange rate mechanisms of EMS. At the time of writing Greece and the UK are non-participants. There are essentially two provisions. First that within certain limits participating states will keep their bilateral exchange rates fixed, and in this respect the system resembles a European 'Bretton Woods' system (see p. 187 above), or an enlarged version of the 'joint float' (see p. 192 above). The fluctuation limits are plus or minus $2\frac{1}{4}$ per cent of the bilateral exchange rates for seven of the currencies, but plus or minus 6 per cent for the Italian lira. In addition to this 'parity grid' each participating currency has a fixed rate, or 'central' rate, in ecu; if a currency's market value in terms of ecu begins to move away from its central rate by more than the 'divergence indicator' then there is a 'presumption' that that country should take corrective action. Clearly the fact that sterling is an element in the ecu, but does not participate in EMS, complicates the picture and the central bankers have devised computations which neutralize the effect of any change in the value of sterling on the market value of the ecu, and hence on the divergence indicators. But in addition to this sterling has to have a notional central rate with the ecu; otherwise the system would be incomplete.[16] Any modification of one central rate will change *all* the other central rates.

The MCA percentage

Intervention prices are fixed in ecu and then converted into national equivalents using green conversion rates (see Section I above). These green conversion rates have been amended over time, but the amendments have been designed to ensure that national prices changed as desired or—as when the ecu replaced the 'joint-float' unit of account in 1979—that national prices were not affected. Between green conversion rate 'devaluations' and 'revaluations' they remain fixed. MCAs are necessary when this price fixing process results in intervention prices in one or more Member States being set, or maintained, at a level above or below the intervention price of its partners.

The real price gap between intervention prices in the Member States will expand or narrow as real exchange rates vary, or as green conversion rates are amended. The various possibilities are summarized in Table 8.3.

The MCA gaps between the seven active participants of EMS are, to all intents and purposes, fixed for long periods of time. It is only when there is a reshuffle within EMS, when the parity grid between currencies is rearranged, that the exchange rates between the participants change appreciably. This fact is made use of in that the MCAs for the seven countries are also fixed, and are only varied when there is a change in the parity grid or when the respective green conversion rates are 'revalued' or 'devalued'. The MCA for any particular

Table 8.3   Impact on MCA gap of exchange rate, and green conversion rate, changes.

Initial MCA	Impact on MCA gap between high price and low price country of:			
	Market exchange rate		Green conversion rate	
	appreciation	depreciation	'revaluation'	'devaluation'
Positive	widens	narrows	narrows	not allowed
Negative	narrows	widens	not allowed	narrows

Table 8.4   Calculation of the UK MCA percentage for week beginning 6 April 1981.

			£0.618655/ecu			
	B. Frs/L. Frs	D. Kr	DM	FF	Fl	£ Ir
(a) UK green conversion rate						
(b) Central rate of EMS currency against ecu	40.7985	7.91917	2.54502	5.99526	2.81318	0.685145
(c) b ÷ a	65.9471	12.8006	4.11380	9.69080	4.54725	1.10748
(d) Average market rate for sterling 25–31 March 1981	77.604625	14.893413	4.733813	11.161891	5.242938	1.298541
(e) Percentage appreciation of d with respect to c $= (d-c) \div d \times 100$	15.022	14.052	13.098	13.180	13.269	14.714
(f) Unweighted average			+13.889			
(g) Franchise			− 1.0			
(h) Net UK MCA			+12.9			

country is based upon the percentage difference between that country's currency ecu central rate and its green conversion rate (following the method of calculation adopted in June 1973 for MCAs of 'joint-float' currencies).

For the eighth Member of EMS, Italy, the extent to which its currency is allowed to fluctuate against the other participants is too great to permit an irregular fixing of its MCA. Thus the MCAs for Italy and the countries not participating in the EMS exchange rate mechanisms (Greece and the United Kingdom) are 'variable' in the sense that they are calculated every week. An example is given in Table 8.4.

In calculating the British MCA it has to be remembered that the MCAs for seven EMS countries have already been fixed (even if at zero), and that central rates were used to determine those MCAs. The rather intricate calculations of Table 8.4 reflect this. For Germany, for example, for the week illustrated, the MCA was plus 3.2 per cent: the difference between a green conversion rate of 1 ecu = 2.65560 D-Mark and a central rate of 1 ecu = 2.54502 D-Mark.[17] Thus the calculations of the British portion of the MCA gap between Germany and the UK must start from the latter figure. Hence in line (c) of Table 8.4 the UK green conversion rate is expressed in D-Marks, and the other currencies, after conversion via central rates. Each day, from Wednesday to Tuesday, the market rate for sterling is noted and then averaged for the week (line (d)). The percentage appreciation of the market rate with respect to the green rate is then calculated (line (e)) and the unweighted average percentage obtained (line (f)).

A number of arbitrary deductions—known as 'franchises'—may then be applied. This was first done in 1975 when for variable negative MCAs 1.25 percentage points were deducted from the calculated MCA percentage. The main reason for this was to reduce the level of negative MCAs which were then thought to be too costly to the budget and disruptive to the agricultural policy. The franchises currently applied are: for fixed and variable negative MCAs 1.5 percentage points, and for variable positive MCAs 1.0 percentage point as in line (g) of Table 8.4. In addition there is a 1.0 percentage point franchise for fixed positive MCAs when the currency concerned has been revalued within EMS, as with West Germany. If, after deduction of the franchises the calculated MCA is greater than zero and less than 1.1 per cent it would currently be fixed at 1.0 per cent.

In Table 8.4 the MCA percentage has been calculated, to one decimal place, at 12.9 per cent. This would be the new fixing for the following Monday morning if it differed from the previous fixing by more than 1.0 percentage point. Central rate changes within EMS, and green conversion rate changes, trigger an immediate MCA modification; though green rate changes are usually timed for a Monday morning.

Sterling's impact on MCAs

If a currency should be revalued within the parity grid of EMS then not only does its value rise in relation to the other currencies, but so does the value of the ecu. The revaluation involves a formal change in the central rate of the currency primarily involved, and consequently a change in the central rate of every other ecu currency. As MCA percentages depend upon the difference between central rates and the green rates, consequently all MCAs will be modified. A revaluation of one currency within EMS will increase its positive MCA or reduce (or eliminate) its negative MCA—but not by as much as its revaluation against the other ecu currencies—but this will also act to increase the *negative* MCAs of other countries, and reduce or eliminate the positive MCAs of other countries. The opposite would happen with a devaluation within EMS.

At the time of a revaluation or devaluation within EMS the opportunity is also taken to fix a central rate for sterling more in line with market circumstances. In turn, this also changes all the other central rates and hence MCAs. A case history can best illustrate this. Immediately before the 1981–82 price fixing the Italian lira was devalued within EMS. This in itself would have triggered changes in central rates, an increase in positive MCAs, and a reduction in negative MCAs. However, the opportunity was also taken to 'revalue' the notional central rate of sterling against the ecu to reflect the fact that its market value had appreciated considerably since its notional central rate had last been fixed in November 1979. This technical correction, which had no impact in the currency markets or in the levels of farm price support in the Member States, resulted in significant changes to MCAs and ultimately affected the outcome of the 1981–82 price fixing. Table 8.5 summarizes the situation for the countries for fixed MCAs.

The 'revaluation' of sterling's notional central rate more than outweighed the devaluation of the lira within EMS. Thus the positive MCAs of the Benelux countries were eliminated, and in fact the MCA gap became negative. For Denmark, Ireland and France—none of which applied an MCA—a negative MCA would have become applicable. It should be emphasized that these changes implied a redistribution of MCAs—not a change in price levels (other than for Italy). The change in sterling's central rate had—at least initially—no *real* impact upon the system, it merely changed the point of calculation for MCAs. If, over the previous 15 months sterling's central rate had been periodically reviewed to reflect the change in the market value of sterling then the outcome would have been the same. Rather than increasing the value of the ecu gradually over time, to reflect sterling's rise in value, it was increased in a single step.

At the end of Section II (p. 196) it was suggested that the value of the unit of account might be important because it indicates the level of the 'common' price. It was certainly so in this instance because all but two Member States (West Germany and the United Kingdom) took the opportunity to devalue their green conversion rates in a move towards the common price, and this transformed what had been expected to be a long drawn out price-fixing marathon into a relatively simple affair.[18]

In fact green conversion rate changes have become a major part of the annual fixing of support prices (outlined in Chapter 3). Often a green conversion rate

Table 8.5 Impact on fixed MCAs of the changes in EMS, March 1981.

	Situation prior to the change			MCA after the change			Effect on prices of subsequent green rate devaluations† (%)
	MCA gap (%)	MCA applied (%)	Comment	MCA gap (%)	MCA to be applied (%)	Comment	
Germany*	9.80	8.8	1% franchise	7.51	6.5	1% franchise	—
Belgium/ Luxembourg*	1.80	1.8		−0.69	0	1.5% franchise	+0.69
Netherlands	1.80	1.8		−0.69	0	1.5% franchise	+0.69
Denmark	0	0		−2.54	−1.0	1.5% franchise	+2.54
Ireland	−1.35	0	1.5% franchise	−3.92	−2.4	1.5% franchise	+3.92
France	0	0		−2.54	−1.0	1.5% franchise	+2.54

* The MCA figures for dairy products in Germany and Belgium/Luxembourg were different from those shown because of an agreement at the 1980/81 annual price fixing.
† These green rate devaluations were designed to eliminate the new MCAs that would otherwise have had to be applied as a result of the March 1981 EMS changes.
SOURCE Commission, 1981, Tables 2 and 3.

devaluation has had more impact on national prices, than has the increase in terms of units of account. This phenomenon was particularly marked when there were large MCA gaps. As noted in Chapter 3, the then President of the Commission, Roy Jenkins, commented 'when national prices in francs, lira and pounds are affected more by green devaluations and revaluations than by the common prices, there is a process of re-nationalisation of the CAP' (Jenkins, 1978).

The agri-monetary factor led to an upward pressure on Council price decisions because of its asymmetric bias. For countries with depreciating currencies there was the ability to award price increases in national currencies to their farmers through devaluations of their agricultural conversion rates. Hence these countries (typically Italy, the UK, Ireland, and France during the 1970s) were to an extent indifferent to the level of common prices. On the other hand for countries with appreciating currencies (typically Germany, Belgium, and Netherlands) the effects were reversed: any change in their agricultural conversion rates led to a drop in national support prices. Hence, if their farmers were to receive an annual price increase this had to come from the common prices agreed by the Council. Consequently it was in their interest to argue for a larger common price increase than proposed by the Commission.

Commodity coverage

MCAs are not applied to all CAP products: in general the products that are covered are those for which an intervention buying mechanism is important in determining market prices, or for closely related products and for products which are of economic significance in more than one Member State. Thus eggs, poultrymeat, and pigmeat are also included because of the close links with cereals, but rice and olive oil are not because, until 1981, they had only been of importance to Italy. Fruit and vegetables, oilseeds, tobacco, seeds, hops, and silkworms are not covered because the support mechanism is less important in determining market prices; but many non-Annex II goods (see Chapter 10) are covered because of the importance of the cereal, sugar, milk, or meat ingredients. The treatment of wine has varied, and recently MCAs have only been applied by West Germany, France, and Italy.

Since 1976 it has been the general practice to implement green rate changes at the beginning of a marketing year. As marketing years run from different dates within a calendar year—the first Monday in April for milk and beef, 1 August for cereals for example—this means that more than one green rate per country, and hence that more than one MCA percentage, may be valid on any particular day.[19] This of course complicates the picture for non-Annex II goods.

Having arrived at the MCA percentage for a particular country the Commission must then calculate the actual currency sum for the particular products concerned, publish the results in the *Official Journal* and notify the national authorities. For intervention products the calculation is relatively easy. Referring back to Table 8.4: suppose there was an intervention product with an intervention price of 100 ecu per 100 kg, then its intervention price in sterling would be £618.655 per 100 kg. The MCA would be 12.9 per cent of this: £79.806 per 100 kg. However, no account would be taken of quality differences, nor—for cereals—of the monthly increases in the intervention price. For other products, where intervention does not apply, a complicated system of coefficients and adjustments must be used to determine the MCA amount to be applied.

Third Country Trade

Once fixed the MCA is applied on imports and exports, and on intra-Community and Third Country trade alike. On Third Country trade import levies and export refunds (and sometimes export levies) are also in force. As was seen in Figure 8.2, a positive MCA must be added to, and a negative MCA subtracted from, the import levy or export refund. If a negative MCA is greater than the import levy then a net subsidy is payable to traders on import; and similarly a net charge is due on export. In fact until October 1974—except for sugar—negative MCAs, whatever the MCA percentage, were not allowed to be greater than the import levy payable to ensure that import subsidies could not arise. The change in this rule benefited in particular the United Kingdom in subsequent years.

The levy or refund—before addition or subtraction of the MCA—must be the same in all Member States. If the green conversion rates were used to convert from ecu's to national currency without adjustment then clearly the levy or refund would not be the same in all Member States: a 'correction' has to be applied through the determination of a monetary coefficient at the same time as MCAs are fixed. The coefficients are in fact derived directly from the MCA percentages—in terms of the example of Table 8.4 the coefficient would be 0.871. Thus when the green conversion rate is multiplied by the monetary coefficient a conversion rate—from ecu to national currency—is obtained which approximates the central or market rate of the currency concerned with respect to the ecu.[20]

For products which are not subject to MCAs care has to be taken to ensure that the trade barriers are the same throughout the Community or trade diversions would occur. Thus levies and refunds and, for fruit and vegetables and some wine products, reference prices[21] are converted to national currencies either by applying a correction to the green conversion rate (as for the MCA products) or by using some sort of market rate.

The case of wine is unusual. Reference prices apply to table wines and certain liqueur wines. The general rule is that the green conversion rate alone is used to convert the reference price to national currencies, modified by a monetary coefficient only in those countries which apply an MCA to wine products. For liqueur wines however a 'special rate', or market rate, is used. There was an interesting exception to this: the reference price for Cyprus sherry was converted into sterling with the unmodified green conversion rate. The United Kingdom is the main market for Cyprus sherry which benefits from a reduced tariff within quota limits but subject to the reference price provisions. The net result was that when the UK's green conversion rate was overvalued in the period up to 1979, and Britain had a negative MCA, the reference price barrier was lower than it would have been had the usual provisions been applied. This was important to the Cypriots as they wished to compete on price in the UK market. In December 1980 the derogation for Cyprus sherry was abandoned, as it was no longer in their interest to use the green, rather than the market rate.

The case of Cyprus sherry is an unusual, but not totally isolated example, of the way the green conversion rate system has sometimes been used —intentionally or unintentionally—to benefit Third Countries. Notable examples are the price guarantees given on preferential sugar imports from ACP States and on butter imports under Protocol 18 into the United Kingdom from New Zealand. The price guarantees were negotiated in terms of units of account, rather than sterling, as the New Zealanders at least had desired.

While Britain had a negative MCA this system was to the benefit of the foreign supplier as it maximized the return on the permitted quantities in the British market. In the case of sugar it meant that the price guarantee was made up of the market price in the UK plus the MCA subsidy on import; for butter the MCA reduced the special levy payable.[22] With the advent of a positive MCA for Britain the situation was reversed.

In one important respect the MCA system applied to Third Country trade differs from that on intra-Community trade for, in certain circumstances, MCAs can be prefixed.[23] All commerce involves risk: in particular that market circumstances will change between the date of signing the contract and its implementation. To a certain extent these risks can be reduced by engaging in offsetting transactions in the futures markets for commodities[24] and currencies—if these exist and national law permits such activity. However, there is clearly also the risk that levies and refunds will change (reflecting both institutional and market price changes for commodities) and also that MCAs will be amended (reflecting in this case institutional price changes for commodities, green conversion rate changes, and fluctuations in currencies). Levies and refunds for some products and under specified conditions have been eligible for prefixing for some time.[25] Since April 1978 it has also been possible to prefix MCAs on Third Country trade, but only when the levy or refund is also prefixed. In the world of commerce decisions on the prefixing of levies, refunds and MCAs, the buying and selling in an unofficial market of prefixation certificates, and, at a later date, whether or not to forfeit the deposit on a certificate are of critical importance to profitability. There is, as yet no academic literature on the subject.[26]

IV   THE ECONOMIC IMPLICATIONS OF MCAs[27]

It is important to recognize that the green conversion rate/MCA system is part of the protective mechanism for European agriculture. MCAs are a necessary addition to the common level of border protection if different national price support levels are to be maintained. The levels of price support in the Member States differ because of the use of green conversion rates. To the extent that this elaborate system is successful in affecting *market* prices then the volumes of production and consumption, trade flows, and resource use; and ultimately the state of the 'balance of payments' and the level of national income will all be affected.

Thus in a broad sense the economic implications of MCAs are the same as the economic implications of any comparable system of border protection. None the less the literature has treated MCAs as a separate issue and the task of these concluding paragraphs is to briefly review the questions raised.

Location of production and efficiency criteria

One of the objectives of the CAP, as laid down in Article 39 of the EEC Treaty, is—as noted in Chapter 3—'to increase agricultural productivity by . . . (inter alia) . . . ensuring the rational development of agricultural production and the optimum utilisation of the factors of production, in particular labour'. Critics of the MCA system claim that this objective is thwarted because if in one Member State the level of price support, over a considerable time period, is higher than that in other Member States the level of production will be artificially stimulated in the higher price region. This means that specialization will not be encouraged, that is that production will not be concentrated in the low cost regions, and a potential source of gain in economic efficiency will be lost to the European economy.[28]

The basic problem with the view expressed in the preceding paragraph is not that the economics are at fault—though even this would be doubted by those who believe that the market process left to itself will not necessarily produce full employment and the optimum utilization of factors of production—but rather the implicit assumption that there is a feasible alternative policy which would lead to a better outcome. If MCAs were to be abolished all the remaining aspects of CAP support would remain, and consequently the abolition of MCAs would involve the harmonization of the levels of price support. Thus the critical question becomes: at what level are prices to be harmonized?

At the time when there was a huge discrepancy between prices in Germany and those in the United Kingdom the answer to the question was important: it was assumed that fixing a truly common price towards the top end of the range would trigger an output expansion in the low price countries which would more than outweigh the fall in production in the high price countries, as happened when the common CAP support prices were applied originally in 1967. Thus there would be a greater misuse of resources in agriculture, compared to the previous situation; and the market opportunities for Third Country producers would be correspondingly reduced. Price harmonization at the British level, by contrast, would involve a reduction in the average level of price support and so help to curb EC 'surpluses'; and lead to a gain in Community, and Third Country, welfare.[29]

In practice it is seldom the Community, let alone Third Country 'interest' that determines Community policy. National interests prevail in the Council of Ministers, and decisions reflect the fact that the gains or losses associated with price harmonization are not evenly distributed amongst the Member States. This is partly because the national mix of producers and consumers, the role they play in national policy making, and the views governments take on inflation (and its causes) and regional and national employment, differ markedly among the Member States. But it is also due to the fact that the CAP, and hence changes to the green conversion rate/MCA system, has implications for the national economy which differ from those of a similar domestic policy. The rules on financing MCAs are important in this context.

Implications for Member States

The discussion pre-empts somewhat the material of Chapter 13 (on the Community Budget) and Chapter 14 (on the 'cost' of the CAP), but a preview is warranted here. The CAP imposes a common levy or refund on Third Country trade: the levy being paid into and the refund out of the Community Budget and not the national exchequer. The MCA is either added to, or subtracted from, the common levy or refund and the net charge or payment treated as a flow to or from the Community Budget. Thus the total foreign exchange cost to an individual Member State, of importing a tonne of wheat from the world market is in effect the world market price plus the net import charge payable to the Community Budget (or less commonly minus the net import subsidy payable from the Budget). Equally the total foreign exchange receipt, to an individual Member State, of exporting a tonne of butter on to the world market would be the world market price plus the net export subsidy payable from the Budget (or, where net export levies are in operation, the world market price less the levy payable to the Budget).

On intra-Community trade MCAs are also funded by, or paid into, the Community Budget. Thus if a product is exported from a high price to a low price country the difference between the export price and the import price—the MCA—is funded by the Budget. It will be seen that the crucial difference between a Member State participating in the CAP and a country pursuing its own national, but otherwise identical policy is that in one situation the country's foreign trade in CAP products in effect takes place at CAP support price levels and in the other at world market price levels. An additional tonne of imported wheat to an EC Member State costs the world market price plus an additional payment to the Community Budget or, if bought from a partner country, a similar total sum in foreign exchange paid direct. The complications of balancing the Budget, discussed more fully in Chapter 13, modify to a certain extent the conclusions drawn here.

The particular CAP support level which is relevant to an individual country is not the theoretical 'common' level, but rather the national level after application of the green conversion rate. Thus a country's trading price will be amended if either the common ecu price level is amended *or* if the green conversion rate is changed. Consequently a proposal to harmonize CAP prices, or to 're-value' or

Table 8.6 Impact of green conversion rate changes on the national economy of an EC Member State.

	Countries that are net importers of MCA products	Countries that are net exporters of MCA products
Green conversion rate 'revaluation'	Benefit	Burden
Green conversion rate 'devaluation'	Burden	Benefit

'devalue' one or more green conversion rates, has implications for the prices at which the Member States concerned can buy and sell their MCA products.

In particular if a Member State which is a net importer of MCA goods is asked to 'devalue' its green conversion rate then, other things being equal, this would impose an additional burden on the economy. The four possible situations are represented schematically in Table 8.6.

The 'balance of payments', 'terms of trade', and level of national income

The burden[30] that is imposed on a net importer that devalues has sometimes been referred to as a 'balance of payments' cost. There have undoubtedly been semantic difficulties: Figure 8.3 attempts to clarify the situation.[31] The original level of price support is at PG_1, and after 'devaluation' of the green conversion rate (or an increase in ecu prices) this rises in national price terms to PG_2. The world market price is not specified, but is assumed to be less than PG_1. Supply of the MCA good will rise from S_1 to S_2 and demand will fall from D_1 to D_2. Imports thus fall from $S_1 D_1$ to $S_2 D_2$. Regardless of source (Third Country or EC partner country) imports used to cost PG_1 per unit; they now cost PG_2 per unit. Thus the total import cost used to be $S_1 EHD_1$ and is now $S_2 BCD_2$.

Whether or not the policy change (green conversion rate 'devaluation') has increased or decreased the total foreign exchange cost of imports of the MCA good will depend upon the price elasticity of domestic demand and supply (roughly related to the shape of D and S). If both S and D were perfectly inelastic (in the diagram they would be vertically upright) there would be an unambiguous 'balance of payments' cost of $FBCG$ (equal to $EADH$ in a redrawn diagram with S and D vertical). As one or more of S and D became more elastic the 'balance of payments' cost would fall and would become a 'balance of payments' benefit if and when $S_1 EFS_2$ plus $D_2 GHD_1$ became greater than $FBCG$. That is, when the reduction in the volume of imports and hence the saving on the total foreign exchange cost of imports exceeds the increase in the cost of imports due to their higher unit price. Ritson (1978) and Peters (1980) give additional details, but both conclude that a green conversion rate 'devaluation' can aid the balance of payments. Thus if a country is suffering from a balance of payments crisis, a green conversion rate 'devaluation' may be a policy objective

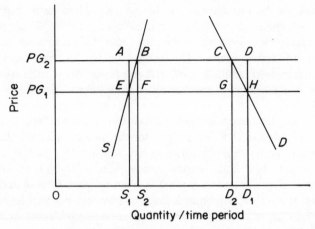

Figure 8.3   Green conversion rate 'devaluation'. S and D are
respectively the supply and demand for an MCA good.

worth considering. Even if the calculations show that there is no impact on the balance of payments of a green conversion rate devaluation, a net cost to society can still be identified. The loss to consumers can be identified as the area $PG_1 PG_2 CH$. This is only partially offset by the gain to producers of $PG_1 PG_2 BE$. The net loss to society is thus identified as $EBCH$. The bulk of this —$FBCG$—represents the additional levy payments to the budget collected on Third Country trade or the additional payments made direct to suppliers in other EEC countries. $FBCG$ might be labelled the 'terms of trade' effect[32] of a green conversion rate 'devaluation', and in practice it is often taken as a good, but slightly low, estimate of the net loss to society.

In making calculations of the cost to a country of a green conversion rate 'devaluation', before the event, analysts are unlikely to have precise estimates of demand and supply elasticities: S_1 and D_1 will (in theory) be known, as will the price change to be expected. Thus the rectangle $EADH$ may well be calculated as an over-estimate of the net cost to society of the policy change. Indeed, if S and D are assumed to be perfectly inelastic then the areas $EADH$, $EBCH$, and $FBCG$ are the same; and the net loss to society is synonymous with the 'terms of trade' effect and the additional cost to the balance of payments. The analysis, and computation, is simplified but the confusion of the reader, moving from one author to another, is compounded. Additional difficulties arise, which are not discussed here, when the analysis includes a movement in the exchange rate itself: for example, with a change in the value of the pound sterling.

A caution in Note 30 said that not all authors have accepted that a green conversion rate 'devaluation' necessarily imposes a burden on a net importer of MCA products,[33] and critics would presumably query other aspects of Table 8.6. Essentially these critics would claim that the foregoing analysis fails to portray how Member State economies sometimes operate, particularly when there is slack or unemployment in the system. Thus agricultural production could be expanded by using more efficiently the existing resources in agriculture and the ancillary industries, and by absorbing unemployed resources, at little cost to society. The increase in farm income would, via a Keynesian multiplier effect, result in a more than proportionate increase in national income that could outweigh the 'terms of trade' effect identified in previous paragraphs.

Although the circumstances—a substantial negative MCA for British agriculture—that led to this debate have for the moment altered, the questions of analysis and policy remain unanswered. Clearly the partial equilibrium analysis of Figure 8.3 might well be inadequate. However, macroeconomic analysis (the way the economy works) is open to more doubts and contested points of view than is microeconomic analysis (the way markets work); hence it is not clear how green conversion rate 'devaluations' and 'revaluations' should be analysed. What is clear, is that a green conversion rate 'devaluation' raises the level of protection to the domestic farm sector concerned and will thus be viewed with as much suspicion by the international community, as would the imposition of any other new or additional protective device.

Trade distortions

In one sense the whole of the CAP, and the green conversion rate/MCA system can be said to 'distort' trade in that the levels of price support influence supply and demand and hence import and export requirements. However, there is another sense in which MCAs distort trade, and which for the food industry is of major importance.

It is paradoxical that MCAs which are meant to remove trade distortions by compensating for differing price levels between Member States actually lead to a significant level of trade distortion themselves. Thus it has to be recognized that trading in MCA products involves significant extra costs. These costs arise in three main ways. First, there is the additional management time and expertise involved in dealing with the complexities of MCA paperwork and requirements. Second, there are costs incurred in attempting to avoid the risks of arbitrary changes which cannot be guarded against in MCA values and their effects on already existing contracts. The Commission may change arbitrarily and without warning the MCA for particular products, or the MCA percentage applied to a country in a particular week. An example of the former case was the alteration in the method for calculating dairy product MCAs in September 1977, and of the latter the temporary use of a three-week base period for calculating MCAs in March 1978.[34] Although the introduction of advance fixing for MCAs in Third Country trade has removed some of these risks, this is not the case in intra-Community trade, and hence these risks still apply in full. In order to quote a forward fixed price the trader has to include a cost element in his price to cover any conceivable MCA change. It is not surprising that the costs and risks involved with trading MCA products are such that they constitute a significant barrier to the involvement of small companies in trading outside their national frontiers.

Of potential benefit to some firms, but at the cost of the Community, are the rather strange trade flows that have sometimes materialized to take advantage of distortions in the MCA system. The Special Committee of Inquiry, in its investigation of the cereals sector, reported on one such instance (Commission, 1979d, Annex II, p. 21). Hulled maize was exported by a company located in one Member State to its subsidiary located in another Member State. MCAs were charged on export from the first, and on import into the second, Member State. The subsidiary processed the hulled maize into meal and flour, and shipped back the products to its parent company in the first Member State. Because of the inconsistencies in the MCA system, the MCA payments collected on the processed products were greater than the MCA originally charged on the basic product. In 1977/78 alone, almost 10 000 tonnes of maize entered into this 'carousel' trade.

NOTES

1. The ua was defined as equal to 0.88867088 grammes of fine gold, which in turn meant that, at this parity, there were 35 ua per troy ounce of gold. As the official price of gold at this time was US dollars 35 per ounce, it followed that one ua equalled one US dollar.
2. Swinbank (1978, p. 46). Strasser (1981, p.25) calls it simply the 'parity unit of account'.
3. See Scammell (1967) for further details.
4. It should be emphasized that the ua is not a currency. Hence that CAP support prices, although expressed in ua, have to be converted to national currencies before they can be applied.
5. The description of the events of 1969, given here, is an edited—and somewhat modified—version. The purpose is to explain the terms 'unit of account', 'green conversion rate', and 'MCA'; for a reliable history, see Irving and Fearn (1975).
6. The intervention price should have fallen by 8.5 per cent to 366 D-Mark, so by keeping it at 400 D-Mark it was 9.3 per cent higher than it would have been.
7. Despite the fact there have not been 'common' support prices in the CAP since August 1969 most sources, and this book, continue to refer to the 'common' price meaning that level of price which applies in a country having no MCA.
8. In fact it was not until 1980 that a minor vestige of the VAT concession was phased out (House of Lords, 1979, p. 84).
9. Regulation 974/71 of 12 May 1971 which reintroduced MCAs is still the legal basis for the MCA system.
10. As measured by the MCA percentages for the two countries at the time.
11. See Heidhues et al., 1978, or Ritson and Tangermann, 1979 for further discussion.
12. The first major set of proposals (Commission, 1976) involved the automatic adjustment of green rates every six months (for countries with a negative MCA) or 12 months (positive MCA) to align green rates with the average exchange rate of an 18 month reference period. These proposals were then recast in looser form (Commission, 1977b) so that the existing MCA stock was to be phased out over seven years, while new MCAs were to be eliminated each year at the annual price fixing. There was a proviso, however, that in no case would a country be required to change its green rate by more than 5 per cent in any one year.

13. See Commission, 1977a. For further discussion, see Swinbank, 1978, Chapter 4, and Swinbank, 1980b.
14. There is no official text outlining the agreement. For details, see *Agra Europe* (1979).
15. For more detail, see *The Economist*, 17 March 1979, pp. 74–75. The main documents involved are to be found in Commission (1979c).
16. If eight of the nine currencies have a fixed central rate in terms of ecu, and one ecu is composed of a fixed sum of nine currencies, then the central rate of the ninth currency is also fixed.
17. The gap was actually 4.2 per cent as determined by the calculation:

$$1 - \frac{2.54502}{2.65560} \times 100$$

From this was deducted a 'franchise' of one percentage point.
18. For an example of the pessimistic forecasts made prior to the event, see Swinbank, 1981.
19. The practice of staggering the date of entry into force of a new green rate has been extended to apply between marketing years. Thus in France the green conversion rate used for pigmeat for the 1978–79 marketing year was that which was to apply for other products in their 1979–80 marketing years. The effect was to improve the feed/pigmeat price ratio for French pig producers—a precedent which if widely adopted would render totally meaningless the fixing of 'common' prices. Another example was when, in 1979, Germany and the Benelux countries delayed the implementation of their new green rates for their dairy sectors as a means of maintaining an extra margin of protection for their dairy producers. Member States have varied the applicability of MCAs: in 1975 the UK stopped granting MCAs on imports of eggs as a means of preventing imports of French eggs which were depressing an already weak British egg market. In 1975 Germany maintained its MCAs on the import of wine as a measure of import protection when MCAs for wine were being eliminated by other Member States.
20. For those Members of EMS with fixed MCAs to which no franchise is applied the conversion rate obtained will be equal to the central rate.
21. Reference prices were discussed in Chapter 3.
22. For further discussion see Swinbank (1980b).
23. The regulations refer to 'advance fixing'.
24. A good description of the operation of futures markets for agricultural products is given in Tomek and Robinson (1981).
25. Advance fixing (prefixing) means that a trader, upon provision of a bank guarantee or the lodging of a small deposit, obtains a certificate listing a specified quantity of product and a specified levy or refund—usually the levy or refund applicable on the day the prefixing certificate is taken out. If the import or export transaction is not carried out within the specified period (say 6 months) then the deposit is forfeited. It can often be less costly to a trader to forfeit his deposit than to use a prefixing certificate with an adverse levy or refund rate.
26. Debatisse, Dumas, and Yon (1980) do, however, discuss the prefixing of levies and refunds in a slightly different context.
27. The next few pages, through to the heading 'Trade Distortions', may be omitted by the general reader.
28. In Chapter 14 a more careful attempt is made to specify the 'cost' or 'benefit' of the CAP in terms of resource use and allocative efficiency.
29. Ritson and Tangermann (1979) concluded that 'there are some grounds for supporting a movement to common prices which involves comparable decreases in high price countries to the rises in low price countries' (p. 138). This is because 'taking a "Community view" of economic welfare, the gain from a price cut in a high price

country should exceed the loss associated with the equivalent price rise in the low price country'. (Ritson and Tangermann, 1979).

30. Not all authors would accept that in all circumstances 'devaluation' by a net importer does impose a burden.

31. The authors believe the following presentation is defensible but recognize the theoretical problems raised. If S and D are specified for a single MCA good then devaluation will change the price of other MCA goods and rock the partial equilibrium foundations of the analysis. If S and D are specified for all MCA goods again the partial equilibrium foundations are shaky and in addition it is not clear how total quantity is to be specified. None the less both Ritson (1978) and Peters (1980) have used partial equilibrium analysis to discuss not only a green pound 'devaluation' but also sterling depreciation.

32. Peters (1981) points out that this might be confusing. The policy described, leading to a reduction in import demand, might be expected to result in a fall in the world market price. Hence the Community would obtain its imports of the goods at a cheaper price. This would, strictly speaking, be known as a terms of trade effect. However, a fall in the world market price would result in an increase in the levy and a gain to the Community Budget from which the country concerned might indirectly benefit. The direct impact on the country concerned is a worsening in its terms of trade.

33. See, in particular, Dickinson and Wildgoose (1979) and a commentary by Swinbank (1980a).

34. Both examples taken from Commission (1979b), Annex A. This table contains many other examples.

REFERENCES

Agra Europe Limited (1979). *Agra Europe*, Issue dated 9th March, Tunbridge Wells.

Commission of the European Communities (1976) *Communication on Longer-Term Measures in the field of Monetary Compensatory Amounts*, COM (76) 600, Brussels.

Commission of the European Communities (1977a) *Report on the use of the European Unit of Account in the Common Agricultural Policy*, COM (77) 480, Brussels.

Commission of the European Communities (1977b) *Proposal for a Council Regulation relating to the fixing of representative rates in agriculture* COM (77) 482, Brussels.

Commission of the European Communities (1979a) Communication on the calculation of the equivalents of the ecu and of the European unit of account by the Commission, *Official Journal of the European Communities*, C69, pp. 4–5.

Commission of the European Communities (1979b) *Economic Effects of the Agri-Monetary System (updated versions 1979)*, COM (79) 11, Brussels.

Commission of the European Communities (1979c) *European Economy*, No. 3, July issue, Brussels.

Commission of the European Communities (1979d) Special Committee of Inquiry *Report concerning the Guarantee Section of the E.A.G.G.F., Cereal Sector*, COM (79) 686, Brussels.

Commission of the European Communities (1981) *Proposal for a Council Regulation amending . . . Regulation (EEC) No. 878/77 on the exchange rates to be applied in agriculture*, COM (81) 172, Brussels.

Debatisse, M. L., Dumas, B., and Yon, B. (1980) *Controlling EEC External Trade by Open Market Operations*, paper A-803, Institut de Gestion Internationale Agro-Alimentaire: Cergy, France.

Dickinson, S., and Wildgoose, J. (1979) *A Framework for Assessing the Economic Effects of a Green Pound Devaluation*, Government Economic Service Working paper No. 23, London.

214

Heidhues, T., Josling, T. E., Ritson, C., and Tangermann, S. (1978) *Common Prices and Europe's Farm Policy*, Trade Policy Research Centre: London.

House of Lords Select Committee on the European Communities (1979) *EEC Farm Prices, 1979/80*, Session 1978–79, 19th Report, HL 127, HMSO: London.

Irving, R. W. and Fearn, H. A. (1975) *Green Money and the Common Agricultural Policy*, Centre for European Agricultural Studies: Wye.

Jenkins, R. (1978) Speech given at the opening of the Royal Agricultural Show, Stoneleigh, UK, 3 July 1978.

Josling, T., and Harris, S. (1976) 'Europe's Green Money', *The Three Banks Review*, No. 109, London.

Peters, G. H. (1980) 'The green pound—a simplified expository analysis', *Journal of Agricultural Economics*, **31**, 113–120.

Peters, G. H. (1981) 'The green pound—a short analysis of upvaluation', *Journal of Agricultural Economics*, **32**, 219–223.

Ritson, C. (1978) 'A note on the green pound and the balance of payments', *Journal of Agricultural Economics*, **29**, 337–340.

Ritson, C., and Tangermann, S. (1979) 'The economics and politics of monetary compensatory amounts', *European Review of Agricultural Economics*, **6**, 119–164.

Scammell, W. M. (1967) *International Monetary Policy*, 2nd Edition, Macmillan, London.

Strasser, D. (1981) *The Finances of Europe*, Office for Official Publications of the European Communities: Luxembourg.

Swinbank, A. (1978) *The British Interest and the Green Pound*, Centre for Agricultural Strategy: Reading.

Swinbank, A. (1980a) 'A note on the green pound and the national economy', *Journal of Agricultural Economics*, **31**, 253–256.

Swinbank, A. (1980b) 'European Community Agriculture and the world market', *American Journal of Agricultural Economics*, **62**, 426–433.

Swinbank, A. (1981) 'The Outlook for British Agriculture', in University of Reading, Department of Agricultural Economics and Management, *Farm Business Data 1981*, pp. 50–53.

Tomek, W. G., and Robinson, K. L. (1981) *Agricultural Product Prices*, 2nd edition, Cornell University Press: Ithaca and London.

Chapter 9

Structural Policy

As indicated in Chapter 3 there is some confusion over the term 'structural policy'. It can mean all things to all men, and usually does; and there has been little evidence until recent years to suggest that the Community has attempted to define and formulate a coherent policy dealing with 'agricultural structures', other than Mansholt's ill-fated proposals of 1968. None the less a good deal of Community legislation does purport to deal with 'structural policy', and in this chapter the more important measures in force will be outlined. The major unifying theme is that these measures are partly financed by the guidance section of the European Agricultural Guidance and Guarantee fund (FEOGA—discussed in Chapter 13).

As a prelude to the main subject matter of the chapter, the first section will outline some of the main characteristics of European agriculture.

THE STRUCTURE OF EC AGRICULTURE

Despite the masses of data available it is often surprisingly difficult to make meaningful comment on the structure of EC agriculture. This is so for three reasons: (i) the difficulty of interpretation of the data presented; (ii) lack of relevant data; and (iii) timeliness in presentation of data. When all three factors are juxtaposed—as with measures of farm income—the problems are virtually insoluble. It should also be emphasized that European agriculture is characterized by a rich diversity of farming systems, business sizes, and profitability; and that the national averages given below of necessity mask that diversity.

The difficulties noted above are compounded in the present instance because of a desire to present comparable data showing the evolving nature of EC agriculture over the past two decades. To do so figures have been extracted from a number of sources, and they should be viewed with caution. The principal source of data on European agriculture is a series of publications from the Statistical Office of the European Communities (Eurostat). In addition the Commission itself publishes an annual review on 'The Agricultural Situation in the Community' (e.g. Commission, 1982) which contains a mass of statistical information. Useful secondary sources are the periodic publications of

Table 9.1 Land area and use (1977, 1000 hectares).

	B-L	DK	F	FRG	IR	I	N	UK	EEC '9' Total	%	G	P	S	EEC '12' Total	%
Area devoted to:															
Arable	860	2 637	17 265	7 497	985	9 235	829	6 921	46 229	30.7	3 020	2 990	15 630	67 869	30.5
Permanent crops	28	11	1 571	515	2	2 971	35	65	5 198	3.5	990	585	4 974	11 747	5.3
Permanent pasture	777	279	13 074	5 205	4 770	5 275	1 196	11 403	41 979	27.9	5 255	530	10 750	58 514	26.3
Forest and wood	702	499	14 558	7 216	308	6 315	310	2 057	31 965	21.3	2 618	3 641	15 500	53 724	24.1
Other	915	811	8 100	3 978	824	5 609	1 011	3 731	24 979	16.6	1 197	1 418	3 100	30 694	13.8
Total land area	3 282	4 237	54 568	24 411	6 889	29 405	3 381	24 177	150 350	100	13 080	9 164	49 954	222 548	100
Percentage change since 1961–65 in area devoted to arable and permanent crops and pasture	−8.5	−5.5	−6.9	−6.6	+4.7*	−14.9†	−9.8	−6.8	−7.9		+4.1‡	−15.6§	−5.0	−6.8	

* In Ireland there has been a marked increase in permanent pasture (+590 thousand ha) and a fall in arable (−329 thousand ha) and 'other' land (−380 thousand ha).
† In Italy arable area has fallen by 3 456 thousand ha and 'other' land increased by 2 741 thousand ha.
‡ In Greece all categories of land use have increased but 'other' land has fallen by 438 thousand ha.
§ In Portugal arable land has fallen by 742 thousand ha and 'other' land increased by 281 thousand ha.
SOURCE FAO (1979, Table 1). (Some of the data are unofficial FAO estimates.)

Table 9.2 Percentage share of agriculture in gross national product at factor cost, and in total employment.

	Percentage share in GNP at factor cost			Percentage share in employment*			
	1968	1978	1980	1958	1968	1978	1980
Belgium	4.9	2.7	2.3	9.4	5.6	3.2	3.0
Denmark	7.7	5.4	4.4	15.9	12.8	8.8	—
France	7.5	4.8	4.2	23.7	15.7	9.1	8.8
Germany	4.4	2.5	2.0	15.7	9.9	6.5	6.0
Ireland	18.8	17.3	—	38.4	29.4	22.2	19.2
Italy	9.9	7.8	—	34.9	22.9	15.5	14.2
Luxembourg	4.6	3.1	—	17.9	10.0	5.6	6.6
Netherlands	6.9	4.5	—	12.6	7.9	6.2	4.6
United Kingdom	—	2.3	2.1	4.4	3.5	2.7	2.6
EC '9'	—	4.0	—	—	12.0	8.0	7.4
Greece	—	—	15.0†	—	—	32.0†	30.3†
Portugal	—	11.9‡	—	—	—	29.0§	—
Spain	—	8.7‡	—	—	—	20.5§	—

— Not available.
* Also includes forestry and fisheries.
† 'Uncertain'.
‡ 1976, 'proportion of national income arising in agriculture'.
§ 1976.
SOURCES EC '9': Eurostat (1973, Table A2). EC '10': Commission (1982, Table 01). Portugal and Spain: FAO (1980, p. 125).
Caution: This table has been compiled from a number of different sources and the statistical series are not necessarily compatible.

Table 9.3 Average size of holdings of 1 hectare and above.

	Average size of holding (ha)			Proportion of holdings in each size group (% 1978)				
	1960	1970	1978	1–5 ha	5–10 ha	10–20 ha	20–50 ha	>50 ha
Belgium	8.2	11.6	14.8	29	21	27	20	4
Denmark	15.7	20.7	23.9	11	19	27	34	9
France	17.0	21.0	25.9	20	15	21	31	13
Germany	9.3	11.7	14.6	33	19	23	21	3
Ireland†	17.1	17.7	20.5	17	18	31	26	8
Italy†	6.8	7.7	7.8	68	18	8	4	2
Luxembourg	13.4	19.4	25.9	20	10	16	40	14
Netherlands	9.9*	13.0	15.2	24	21	30	23	3
United Kingdom	32.0*	56.8	66.0	14	13	16	26	31
EC '9'†	12.1	15.5	17.2	42	17	18	17	6

* Not comparable with later years.
† 1975, and not 1978, data.
SOURCE MAFF (1980, p. 10) based on Eurostat data.

Table 9.4 Average annual increases in size of enterprise in
England and Wales, 1968–75. (per cent per annum).

Enterprise	1968–71	1972–75	1968–75
Dairy cows	6.6	5.9	6.4
Beef cows	4.9	8.7	6.6
Breeding ewes	2.4	3.6	3.4
Breeding pigs	10.1	10.4	10.4
Laying fowls	9.5	8.1	8.8
Broilers	25.8	12.6	15.4
Wheat	6.8	2.6	4.9
Barley	1.6	1.0	1.6
Maincrop potatoes	2.7	2.5	2.6

SOURCE   MAFF (1977, p. 40).

Ministries and trade associations which draw on Eurostat and other data:
examples in Britain are the Ministry of Agriculture, Fisheries and Food
(MAFF, 1980, the last in the series) and the Milk Marketing Board (MMB,
1981).

Of the present Member States France has by far the largest land area, and
consequently the largest area of land devoted to farming (see Table 9.1). It is
only with the accession of Spain that this dominance will be challenged.
Because of the variability in the quality of land, and the intensity of its use, these
simple acreage figures do not give a complete guide to the relative size of the
national agricultures, but they do emphasize the importance of France to the
EC's agricultural economy. A surprising feature of Table 9.1 is the diversity of
experience revealed in the bottom line. This shows that the loss of agricultural
land in most of the Member States and in Spain has been significant, but
modest, in the period since the early 1960s and this probably reflects the loss of
land to industry, housing, and roads common to all growing economies.
However, in Italy and Portugal the rate of loss has been much greater and
possibly reflects the abandonment of farm land at the extensive margin. In
Ireland and Greece quite the opposite trend has occurred, and the farmed area
appears to have expanded at the expense of waste lands.

Common to the Member States has been a marked reduction in agricultural
employment—both in absolute and relative terms. Table 9.2—showing the
percentage share of agriculture, forestry, and fishing in total employment—
illustrates the trend. By 1980 the percentage share in France had fallen to 8.8
per cent although it had been 23.7 per cent two decades earlier; and the same
sort of change can be observed in the other Member States. These data are too
aggregate to tell the full story as they do not differentiate between farmers,
family workers, and farm workers; or between full and part-time employment.
Nor do they illustrate any regional variations that may exist within countries, or
the change that these demographic factors might have had on the electoral

process. One can conclude that there has been an exodus from farming in the Community. Between 1960 and 1980 the number of people engaged in EC-9 agriculture dropped by nearly 10 million from 17.1 to 7.7 million. However, this has not been as rapid as that thought necessary in the Mansholt Plan which foresaw a halving of the agricultural population in the Six in the decade between 1970 and 1980 (Commission, 1968, p. 53). The situation in Greece and the two applicants is different: their agriculture is still a labour intensive activity and a significant shedding of labour is to be expected over the coming years. The latter figures should be treated with more caution than most and the reader should not be too surprised to find different figures in other texts.[1]

The rate of change of the average size of holding (Table 9.3) has shown a different trend. Although a number of caveats[2] must be applied to the data, and although significant changes have taken place, it does appear that European agriculture cannot adapt sufficiently quickly to modern farming conditions given present economic, social, and legal systems. In 15 years the average size of holding in Italy grew by only one hectare and in that country in 1975 no less than 68 per cent of all holdings were of less than five hectares.

Another distinctive feature of the changing ways in which farms are organized is the extent to which farmers have specialized in their business activities. Thus the average size of farm enterprise—particularly involving poultry and pigs—has grown at a much faster rate than the average size of holding. In Table 9.4 some recent data from England and Wales are displayed. In Table 9.3 it was seen that the average size of holding in the United Kingdom increased by 16.2 per cent in the period 1970–1978; in Table 9.4 it was seen that the average size of broiler enterprise in England and Wales increased on average by 15.4 per cent *per annum* in the period 1968–75.

COMMUNITY POLICY MEASURES

Modernization of production and marketing

Individual projects

Although the Community's attempts to construct a co-ordinated structural policy were thwarted until 1972, and have only been partly successful since, there has in fact been an *ad hoc* structural policy programme in being since 1964. Under Regulation 17/64 individuals and organizations (private companies, co-operatives, local authorities, etc.) could apply to the Commission for a FEOGA financed grant of up to 25 per cent of the cost of an approved investment pertaining to the production or marketing of agricultural (and fishery) products. Certain criteria had to be fulfilled and aid was not automatically granted as a right: the Commission approved only the more attractive projects and those which in its view contributed most directly to increasing farm incomes. Since 1978 Regulation 355/77 has replaced 17/64 with respect to the marketing and processing of agricultural products; and 1979 was the last year

220

Table 9.5   Types of project financed under Regulation 17/64; 1964–1979

	Percentage of total funds allocated
'Production structures'	53.2
of which:	
land reparcelling	14.4
hydraulic works and irrigation	10.8
forestry	2.7
'Marketing structures'	40.8
of which:	
milk products	10.3
meat	8.7
fruit and vegetables	5.9
wine	6.2
'Mixed' production/marketing structures	6.0

SOURCE   Commission (1980b, Annex Table 17).

in which applications for aids under 17/64 for investments in agricultural production were accepted.

Table 9.5 shows how the monies under 17/64 were allocated: roughly half the grants helped finance the infrastructure of farming and the remainder aided the off-farm activities of marketing and processing. The extent to which low income small farmers (for whom the CAP supposedly exists) directly benefited from this policy is debatable. It is unlikely that such an individual would have taken the initiative in drawing-up detailed costings of farm improvement programmes for submission to Brussels, or that he could have financed the remainder of the investment programmes; it is more likely that large estates with access to the necessary technical expertise, or government backed land reclamation programmes, would have benefited most. Equally the financing of new slaughterhouses, creameries, and distilleries can only be said to have provided an indirect gain to small farmers.

Industry programmes

As noted above finance is now available under Regulation 355/77 to meet part of the investment cost for buildings and equipment designed to rationalize and improve the processing and marketing of agricultural products. Projects 'must guarantee the producers of the basic agricultural product an adequate and lasting share in the resulting economic benefits'.[3] For a transitional period projects were considered on an *ad hoc* basis but, from the beginning of 1981 they have had to form part of a national or regional investment programme drawn up by the national authorities, but approved by the Commission. For example, in 1982, there were seven such programmes in the United Kingdom. These were for: horticulture, potatoes, fisheries, a red meat slaughterhouse improvement programme, milk, cereals storage, and pigmeat processing. The potatoes programme, for instance, encourages investment in three types of project: off-farm grading, off-farm storage, and in 'Those sectors of processing where an expansion of outlets is expected, for example crisps'.

As with 17/64 application must be made to Brussels; projects are judged on the basis of guidelines which lay down priorities as between different sectors and types of investment. Because of the need not to encourage further investment for products in surplus, the Commission applies a set of guidelines as to projects it is prepared to consider for investment aid. For 1982 the guidelines covered the following industries (European Report, 1982):

Dairy products: Priority investment areas were the use of liquid skimmed milk as feed on farms, investments which increased commercial outlets for milk, and the production of pasteurized drinking milk and fresh dairy products. Investments ineligible for assistance included any scheme aimed at increasing dairy product capacity and, in particular, those relating to the production of the traditional dairy products (e.g. butter, processed cheese, casein, powdered milk, etc.).

Meat products: Assistance was not available for any investment devoted to increasing capacity. Assistance was available for schemes bringing facilities up to EC hygiene standards. Priority was given to investments in meat cutting rooms.

Wine: Priority for investments leading to the closure of small wineries and marketing co-operation schemes. Assistance was not available for any wine project unless it was for wine of a type and quality which had reasonable marketing prospects.

Feedingstuffs: Assistance not available for production capacity increases unless there were offsetting capacity closures.

Fruit and vegetables: Assistance not available for tomato processing capacity except in regions where capacity was outdated or farm incomes particularly low.

Olives: Priority was given to projects for the processing and marketing of edible olives, and for the modernization of existing crushing plant. Investments in increased capacity had to be offset by capacity closures, so that there was not a net increase.

Cereals: Most investments were eligible for assistance, especially those concerned with storage facilities. The exceptions were investments for milling, malting, and starch manufacture.

Tobacco: Schemes to expand commercial outlets for quality tobacco were acceptable, but not those for oriental tobacco varieties.

Proteins: Priority given to schemes for peas, beans, and dried fodder where the measures reduced energy needs.

Regulation 355/7 is also noteworthy in being virtually the only Community investment aid which has an element of additionality. Unlike the regional fund, Community aid is not retained by the national exchequer. The rates of funding differ: in general FEOGA meets 25 per cent of the eligible costs, but this rises to 30 per cent in some regions, to 35 per cent for certain regions and products in the South of France, and to 50 per cent in the Mezzogiorno.

If one tried to judge the importance of structural measures by their importance in budgetary terms then 17/64 would rank as the most important measure to date. Between 1964 and 1978 nearly 80 per cent of monies granted (but not necessarily spent) from the Guidance Section of FEOGA were devoted to 17/64. Money will continue to be spent for many years into the future as the grants are often paid in parts on completion of a particular stage in the investment programme. In 1978 monies were still being paid for projects approved in 1965.[4] Similarly, Regulation 355/77 in 1978—its first year of operation—accounted for the largest proportion of monies committed (but again not necessarily spent) (Commission, 1979c, p. 2).

The structural directives of 1972

Between 1964 and 1972 a number of measures were enacted that fall within the broad heading 'structural policy' and which led to expenditure under the Guidance Section of FEOGA. Three measures in particular are important: these are the structural directives of 1972 and they mark the first real step to introduce an EC structural policy. These directives, sometimes known as the socio-structural directives, 'on the reform of agriculture' derive from the Mansholt plan and are indeed the only part of it ever adopted into legislation. They are judged to be important enough to warrant an annual report.

The three directives are respectively 72/159 on the modernization of farms: 72/160 concerning measures to encourage the cessation of farming and the reallocation of utilized agricultural area for the purposes of structural improvement; and 72/161 concerning the provision of socio-economic guidance for, and the acquisition of occupational skills by, persons engaged in agriculture.

These directives differ markedly in their *modus operandi* from the two regulations discussed above (17/64 and 355/77). A regulation has direct applicability and force of law whilst a directive must be implemented by supplementary national legislation. Thus the Member States are individually responsible for implementing these three structural directives and are allowed considerable flexibility in the mechanisms utilized.[5] Each directive specifies a list of objectives which are to be achieved; each national government is responsible for passing the implementing legislation which must in turn be approved by the Commission; and ultimately the Community reimburses the Member States a specified percentage of the costs incurred in implementing the legislation. The rate of reimbursement of national expenditure is typically 25 per cent though this is increased under specified circumstances particularly when a directive is operated in areas covered by the hill farming and less favoured areas Directive (see below).

In practice the performance of the Member States has been highly variable. Particular problems arose in Italy. At an early stage it was decided that the implementation of the directives in Italy would require not only national, but also regional, legislation. Thus in July 1979 there were still regions in Italy in which Directive 72/159 was not being implemented; Luxembourg had only just passed the necessary legislation to implement 72/159; and in Denmark 72/160 was still not being applied (Commission, 1979b, p. 1). Considering that 72/159 and 72/160 are seen by many as central elements in the Community's structural policy, it is difficult to discern a consensus view amongst the Member States that the directives should be enthusiastically supported. During the five-year period 1974 to 1979 four Member States (UK, 34.4 per cent; Germany, 23.7 per cent; France, 19.2 per cent; and Ireland 12.6 per cent) accounted for nearly 90 per cent of total FEOGA expenditure under these directives and Directive 75/268 (Commission 1980a, p. 19).

The main feature of Directive 72/159 is that it permits Member States to aid full time farmers to modernize and develop their farms; provided that the development plan indicates that on completion the farm will generate an income comparable to that in other non-farm activities in the locality. The aid, which could, for example, be in grant form or interest rate subsidies, can cover most of the necessary investments except land purchase.

Directive 72/160 allows Member States to grant an annuity or lump sum payment to full time farmers, farm workers, and family workers between the ages of 55 and 65 who leave agriculture. In Ireland and certain regions in Italy the Community meets 65 per cent (normally 25 per cent) of the eligible expenditure. A particular feature of the legislation was that land released under the Directive should be used, wherever possible, to enlarge the farms receiving aid under 72/159. This aim seems to have met with mixed success: between 1975 and 1979 14.6 per cent of the land released in the Community passed to farmers receiving aid under 72/159, but the national figures ranged from 1.5 per cent in France to 37.5 per cent in Germany (Commission, 1982, p. 274). In part this may reflect the different structures of agriculture in the Member States, but it must also reflect the differing legal traditions and systems.

Farmers are less directly involved with Directive 72/161. This provides for Community funds to help create 'socio-economic guidance services' in the Member States, and to help meet the costs of running retraining schemes for farmers. Under a parallel provision of the European Social Fund Member States can seek assistance covering up to 50 per cent of eligible expenditure for income aids to individuals leaving agriculture and undergoing retraining. Advisory work in agriculture has traditionally focused on an internal review of the farm's structure and potential profitability; the basic idea behind the 'socio-economic' thinking of this Directive is that a wide range of possibilities ought to be considered by the farmer and his adviser including the feasibility of leaving farming altogether.

The socio-structural Directives described drew their rationale from the economic circumstances of the 1960s and early 1970s. Capital was replacing labour in agriculture at a rapid rate and, with high growth rates, other sectors of the economy were eager to absorb the population so displaced. The Mansholt

Plan, and the Directives which resulted from it, aimed to increase further the pace at which existing developments were already taking place. In fact, however, it became evident quite soon after the Directives were adopted, that the underlying economic situation was changing. Overall economic growth in the EC slowed following the oil crisis of 1973, and the peripheral and largely rural regions of the Community suffered earliest and most severely. By 1975, Community policy makers in many sectors were becoming more aware of the need for a regional dimension to policy. The European Regional Development Fund was one result. Another, which was stimulated by existing policy in the United Kingdom,[6] was the adoption of a Directive dealing with the problem of specified regions and types of farming.

The ten-year period during which these three structural directives were applicable ended in April 1982. However, in the context of the 1982–83 price review, it was agreed that they be continued until December 1983, during which time the Commission would review their operation and suggest what changes, if any, were necessary.

Regional measures

The Directive on mountain and hill farming and farming in certain less favoured areas

Directive 75/268 defined certain areas as being of hill farming or as being less favoured areas by reason of natural physical handicap, and in particular, altitude, slope, infertility, or 'low productivity of the environment'. Subsequent Directives (75/276 for the United Kingdom) defined the areas in the different Member States. These Directives introduced a number of new concepts into the Community's structural policy. First, the concept of discrimination between regions and thus between producers, within the CAP. This concept has been substantially developed and extended since, and the Directives have provided the basis for a variety of exceptions and exemptions to CAP measures, notably the co-responsibility levy discussed in Chapter 5. Second, the concept of direct income payments on a Community basis was introduced and Article 1 of the Directive gave as the primary reasons, 'the continuation of farming, thereby maintaining a minimum population level or conserving the countryside'. A very different approach indeed to that of the socio-structural Directives so recently adopted.

The Hill Farming Directive has two main provisions. The first allows the Member States to grant annual subsidies (compensatory allowances) for hill cattle and sheep—thus continuing the pre-existing UK scheme—with FEOGA reimbursing 25 per cent of the cost except in Italy and Ireland (35 per cent). There is a great deal of variability in the aids actually granted. The second provision modified the requirements demanded of farms undergoing a modernization programme funded under Directive 72/159; and also permitted farmers in these areas to receive aid (again partly funded by FEOGA) even if not undergoing a modernization programme within the provisions of the Directive.

The Mediterranean package

In 1977 a further step was taken by the Commission in recognizing that the problems of rural regions went beyond those of the farm alone, and could not be solved by the previous policies of exodus and farm development plans. The 'Mediterranean Package' (Commission, 1977) as it was known, was put forward by the Commission in recognition of the fact that the benefits of the structural policy had largely passed the region by; and as a preventative measure against the problems expected from the future enlargement of the Community to include Greece, Spain, and Portugal, the effects of which would be most directly felt by the regions of Mediterranean type agriculture in Italy and southern France. The measures proposed for the region were in the form of special investment programmes for irrigation, for forestry, the development of rural infrastructure and a programme for the development of rural information services. In addition a programme for the restructuring of vineyards in Languedoc-Roussillon was put forward and eventually adopted, as well as one for flood protection in Hérault. In addition, a higher rate of FEOGA contribution for investments under Regulation 355/77, at 50 per cent, was proposed and adopted.

The 1979 package

In 1979 the Commission put forward a new series of proposals which further developed the regional approach to agricultural structures policy (Commission, 1979a). It proposed specific programmes for the development of cattle farming in Italy, for sheep farming in Greenland, and for the general development of agriculture in Western Ireland. In addition, however, a new concept was put forward, that of the integrated development programme. These were to cover the Western Isles of Scotland, the Department of Lozère in France, and the Province of Luxembourg in Belgium. Their aim was to integrate agricultural development measures with the development of other activities of importance to the rural economy; 'the food industry, the development of craft industries or activities directly connected with the hotel, holiday and leisure industries'. This was to be achieved by 'taking advantage of both the various development possibilities which exist and the available means (FEOGA, European Regional Development Fund, European Social Fund, and national funds)'. Since 1979, further programmes have been adopted for Northern Ireland, for the French Overseas Departments, and for certain less favoured areas in Germany.

The criteria for the choice of areas are not yet very clearly defined, but from the preambles to the different regulations, it would seem that they are related to particularly low levels of farm income, to high percentages of the active population in farming, and to deficient infrastructures including electricity, drinking water supplies, farm and local roads. It is also rather clearly the case that a political balance has had to be struck in the choice of regions; thus the programmes for Northern Ireland proposed in June 1980 and in March 1981 were put forward as a subsequent counterpart to the proposals for the Irish Republic. Similarly, certain less favoured areas in Germany were given special programmes as part of the 1981/82 prices package.

The major features of current Community structural policy may be listed as a strong regional specific approach; a programme basis rather than the project by project approach of earlier years; and finally an attempt to bring together the use of the different Community and national funds into a series of integrated programmes.

Other structural measures

Over the years a wide variety of other measures has been adopted by the Community, relating either to the encouragement of the formation of producer groups and cooperatives, or to the improvement of production in particular sectors.

Producer organizations

It has for long been an aim of the Common Agricultural Policy to encourage the formation and spread of producer groups and their associations. This has been in the belief that the bargaining power of producers in the market can be enhanced, and that a more collective approach to marketing leads to greater price stability and to a higher level of returns. In addition, producer organizations are used within the CAP as the means to make support payments. For example in the fruit and vegetable sector, the withdrawal price system is effectively administered through the producer organizations. There have also been proposals, although these were not adopted by the Council, to make mandatory upon all producers, whether members of the producer group or not, the decisions on prices and withdrawal of the producer group. The political connotations of this 'extension of disciplines', as it was known, proved too great.

The first legislation was passed in 1966 and concerned the olive oil sector. Subsequently the legislation was extended to other crop sectors, notably hops, fruit and vegetables, and silk worm producers. In 1978 after 12 years of negotiations in the Council, a general regulation was adopted, extending the range of products for which grants to establish producer organizations are payable. However, the geographical coverage of the measures is highly variable, being limited to Italy, certain French Departments, the French Overseas Departments and Corsica, and Belgium. The products covered are also limited and differentiated between the areas given. The legislation provides for subsidies of 3, 2, and 1 per cent of the value of the products supplied in the first, second, and third years of existence respectively, within a maximum amount. Associations of producer groups are also eligible for aid.

Improvement of production structures

Milk and meat sectors

Over the years a number of schemes have been introduced, and then phased out, whose objective has been to encourage milk producers to cease production (such as the non-marketing premium) or to convert to specialist beef production. At present all these schemes have been ended, largely as a result of doubts as to their effectiveness. It is often felt that producers leaving milk production would have done so without any payment of grant. It is worth recording the costs of the most recent scheme, which was ended in March 1981, and which although staged over eight years, are very substantial (Table 9.6).

Apart from such schemes, Community finance is available under Directive 77/391/EEC for the improvement of cattle and pig herds. Under this scheme, compensation is paid to farmers for animals slaughtered as a result of campaigns for the eradication of brucellosis, tuberculosis, leucosis, and swine fever.

Wine sector

The Community has given much attention in recent years to the improvement of viticulture. There has increasingly been concern at the development of structural surpluses of wine, particularly as a result of the increasing production of high yielding, but low quality, vineyards in the poorer Mediterranean regions. Action has been taken both on a regional basis in the context of the Mediterranean package described earlier in the chapter, and also in the adoption of a series of proposals aimed at limiting new plantings and at encouraging the grubbing of vineyards in areas of poor quality production. Regulations adopted in 1980 form a group of measures and provide for:

(a) The granting of aids to producers who leave vine growing. The amounts are differentiated as between those agreeing to cease production for at least eight years, and those who agree definitely not to replant,

(b) Specific annual grants to those producers in France and Italy aged

Table 9.6 Milk non-marketing and conversion premiums (Regulation 1078/77). Cost to FEOGA Guidance Section, million ecu.

1977	5.0	1982	66.0
1978	68.1	1983	61.3
1979	71.7	1984	32.9
1980	105.5	1985	24.8
1981	101.5	Total	536.8

SOURCE Commission (1981).

between 55 and 60 years who cease production. The programme is intended to supplement the premiums granted under Directive 72/160,

(c) Grants for restructuring and replanting programmes carried out on a collective basis by groups of producers.

Fruit and vegetables

The most important measure in this sector is one which provides for the improvement of production and marketing of Community citrus fruit. The objectives of these measures, for which FEOGA pays 50 per cent of the amount funded by national authorities, are the varietal conversion of orange and mandarin groves and the improvement of market preparation, storage, and processing facilities.

In passing, it may be mentioned that the Community has in the past funded schemes for the grubbing of apple and pear orchards, although these have now been ended. Under Regulation 794/76 some 12 000 hectares of apples (including those planted to the Golden Delicious variety) and pears were grubbed.

Other measures

For completeness mention may be made of a number of other programmes funded by the Guidance section of FEOGA. These include the cost of the Farm Accountancy Data Network, agricultural surveys, and the information system for agricultural research.

Funding of the structural policy

FEOGA participation rates

The general rate of FEOGA participation in expenditure on structural measures has been 25 per cent of eligible expenditure. However, higher rates have been accepted for areas of particular difficulty, and a range of different rates has been accepted through the bargaining process in the Council. The 'base' rate remains 25 per cent, but the highest rate has become 65 per cent for payments in Italy and in Ireland under the socio-structural Directive 72/160. A 50 per cent FEOGA contribution is payable on a wide variety of structural programmes in the poorer regions and has in practice become the normal rate for the Mediterranean regions, for Ireland, and for the integrated programme areas described earlier in the chapter. The only structural measure for which FEOGA has paid 100 per cent of eligible costs is in the case of the non-marketing premium for milk, where the Guidance section pays 40 per cent and the Guarantee section the remaining 60 per cent.

Expenditure on structural policy

Until 1979, expenditure on structural policy was limited to 325 million units of account per year, despite the fact that the first financial regulation of 1962 envisaged that up to one-third of total expenditure should have been on structural policy. In 1979, the Community moved to a system under which appropriations were agreed for the five-year period 1979–1984. These were put at 3600 million ecu, thus averaging some 750 million ecu per annum, over twice the previous amount.

In Table 9.7 the estimates for commitments entered into in 1981 and 1982 are shown to give some idea of the budgetary impact of the various measures discussed. The classification follows that adopted in this chapter: thus the first heading covers Regulations 17/64 and 355/77, the second the three structural directives of 1972, the third the hill farming subsidies and payments on a regional basis, the fourth, aid for producer groups and specific products and the final heading covers a whole series of items including research and the farm accountancy data network. Fisheries have been excluded. It should be noted that the figures indicate the budgetary costs of projects approved in the two years cited, not the expenditure incurred.

STATE AIDS

Many of the measures referred to in this chapter give rise to the direct involvement of national governments: to enact the necessary implementing legislation, to put into effect the schemes, and to meet some part of the financial burden. Often the degree of discretion available to the Member States is wide. Thus some countries operate Directive 72/159 on the modernization of farms by

Table 9.7 1982 Preliminary draft budgetary appropriations by measure, FEOGA Guidance Section (Commitment Appropriations), million ecu.

	1981	1982
1. Projects for the improvement of agricultural structures	151.000	153.000
2. General socio-structural measures	95.000	113.600
3. Measures to assist less favoured areas	280.870	356.950
4. Structural measures connected with the common organization of the markets	170.500	146.800
5. Other	14.644	16.472
Total	712.014	786.822

SOURCE Commission (1981, volume 7A, p. 127).

giving grant aid for eligible schemes (for example in the United Kingdom, under the Agriculture and Horticulture Development Scheme) whereas others give interest rate subsidies. This same Directive allows Member States to operate national schemes, for businesses which would not otherwise qualify under the EC scheme, but on a less favourable basis. In the United Kingdom this takes the form of the Agricultural and Horticultural Grant Scheme (AHGS as opposed to AHDS referred to above). Complete freedom of action is not, however, allowed: for example, Directive 72/159 prohibits the granting of aid for the purchase of pigs, poultry, or dairy cows under both the EC scheme and the national scheme.

In addition to the EC's structural policy measures referred to in this chapter, and the price support measures referred to elsewhere in the book, all the Member States operate an additional series of measures to aid the farm sector. These are state aids, and fall within the ambit of Article 92 of the EEC Treaty.

Article 92 (paragraph 1) states:

> Save as otherwise provided in this Treaty, any aid granted by a Member State or through State resources in any form whatsoever which distorts or threatens to distort competition by favouring certain goods shall, in so far as it affects trade between Member States, be incompatible with the common market.

The Commission has the main responsibility in ensuring that the state aid provisions are respected. It is the Commission that must monitor all existing aids (though the Member States are obliged to inform the Commission of their intention to introduce new aids), rule on the compatibility of the aids with the Treaty provisions and, if necessary, take action against the Member States in the European Court.

In practice, until the early 1980s, the Commission devoted too few resources to its task of implementing the state aid provisions.[7] There is much confusion over what is and is not permitted, over the extent and practical importance of the state aids which have been approved, and over the alleged illegal aids that all Member States are said to have paid at one time or another. The following paragraphs can only sketch the main features of a very complex, and still uncharted, subject area.[8]

Article 92 covers any governmental activity which, at a cost to the State, confers a financial advantage on a selected group of a country's citizens. A direct subsidy would fall into this category, as would any partial or complete exemption of a national or local government tax. It would also appear to cover the advantage gained by any enterprise because of the preferential pricing policies of a state owned public utility. Thus, when it was alleged that the Dutch were favouring their glasshouse industry, one of the important questions to be settled was whether or not the Dutch government had a controlling interest in the company supplying gas, and was thereby able to influence the pricing policies of the company.

Specific exemptions are provided for: consumer subsidies provided that all products of the same type, whatever the origin, are treated equally; and aid given to make good the damage caused by natural disasters. For other policies—for example aid to assist depressed regions—there is a strong presumption that they will be permitted.

In the farm sector the Member States have been allowed to maintain national aid schemes for those products not covered by a specific CAP support mechanism (at the time of writing the main products concerned are potatoes and agricultural alcohol), although other Treaty provisions and Court rulings have limited the ability of the Member States to control intra-Community trade in these products. For the CAP supported products any national price guarantee, or subsidy on production, would be illegal; though the Commission has, as yet, no clear view whether state aids for advertising these products are permissible. National aids on 'consumable' inputs (e.g. fertilizers, fuels) into the farming process are not permissible; though aids on some 'capital' inputs are and, as seen above, in some cases specifically provided for under Directive 72/159.

The Commission has compiled an inventory of state aids in agriculture. This is a vast document, stretching to nine volumes in its original version (House of Lords, 1982a) and not publicly available. This latter fact has generated much controversy, as without a publicly available document it is very difficult to gauge the importance of state aids to European agriculture and for the lobbyists to confirm or refute their suspicions on the extent of state involvement in the activities of competing industries in other Member States.

The inventory was made available to the House of Lords Select Committee on the European Communities, and they reported that:

> the document is defective on a number of counts: it is badly out of date; there is no guarantee that the document is complete; . . . the declarations of Member States are not necessarily comparable; and it is difficult, without detailed study, to differentiate between state aids of significance and those with little practical effect. (House of Lords, 1982a, p. xvi).

Despite these defects the Committee were of the opinion that the document should be made publicly available.

It is on the basis of the information provided for this inventory that the Commission has, in the past, published estimates showing the extent of national expenditure on agriculture. Such a table was published in their 1980 report 'The Agricultural Situation in the Community' (Commission, 1980c, Table 60), though no such table appeared in their 1981 report (Commission, 1982). This table seemed to show that national expenditure on agriculture is greater than total spending by the Community on price support and structural policy. The evidence collected by the House of Lords Select Committee, and published in their report, casts doubt upon the reliability of these figures particularly those purporting to show 'tax relief' and the 'state contribution to the financing of farmers social insurance' which accounted for 13 and 46 per cent of the total respectively.

NOTES

1. For example, Rollo quotes 24.6 and 34.5 per cent, from different sources, as the agricultural working population as a proportion of the total in Greece in 1976 (Rollo, 1979, p. 334).

2. A holding may be fragmented into a number of parcels of land thus hindering the operational efficiency of the holding; one individual may in fact control more than one holding in an integrated farming business; the quality of the land, the availability of irrigation, and the nature of the farming enterprise all help determine the viable size of a particular holding; and finally the availability of part-time employment away from the holding will affect its viability.

3. Article 9. The food industries have been critical of the fact that the schemes only apply to Annex II products (i.e. agricultural and first stage processed products to which the CAP applies, but not manufactured food products—the difference is outlined more carefully in Chapter 10). Thus the British Food and Drink Industries Council, in evidence to the House of Lords Select Committee on the European Communities, commented 'it is not clear why, for example, aid under the Regulation is available for natural yoghurt or cream but not for flavoured yoghurts, flavoured milks and chocolate crumb'. (House of Lords, 1982b, p. 78—see also the evidence of other food trade associations printed in this report.) The Regulation had in fact a five-year life, but its provisions were extended to December 1983. Whether it will then be retained, or its scope expanded, are as yet unanswered questions.

4. Commission (1979c, Table 0 VI). The intricacies of the FEOGA Guidance Section accounts are almost impossible to fathom. Care has to be taken to distinguish between commitments (decisions to spend money which does not necessarily appear in that year's budget) and appropriations (money in that year's budget which has to meet all the expenditure arising out of previous commitments). At the end of 1978, 755 million ecu's were outstanding on commitments under Regulation 17/64—some dating back to 1964. To complicate the issue even more those commitments entered into prior to 1971 are financed not by the own resources system (as outlined in Chapter 13) but by specified contributions from the six original Member States.

5. It is beyond the ambit of this text to describe the measures in force in each of the ten Member States. The annual reports, particularly the first (Commission, 1976), provide a mass of detail. In some instances existing national legislation could be adapted to suit the provisions of the directives.

6. A declaration on Hill Farming was attached to the Treaty of Accession. It stated that 'the special conditions obtaining in certain areas of the enlarged Community may indeed require action with a view to attempting to resolve the problems raised by these special conditions and, in particular, to preserve reasonable incomes for farmers in such areas'.

7. In fairness it should be noted that the Commission's ability to devote resources (particularly manpower) to particular activities is constrained by the willingness of the Council to vote funds for the establishment of new posts.

8. The discussion draws heavily upon a House of Lords report (House of Lords, 1982a) and evidence printed therein.

REFERENCES

Commission of the European Communities (1968) *Memorandum on the Reform of Agriculture in the European Economic Community*, COM (68) 1000 Part A, Brussels.

Commission of the European Communities (1976) *Report on the Application of the Council Directives on Agricultural Reform of 17th April 1972*, COM (76) 87, Brussels.

Commission of the European Communities (1977) *Guidelines Concerning the Development of the Mediterranean Regions of the Community, Together with Certain Measures Relating to Agriculture*, COM (77) 526, 2 volumes, Brussels.

Commission of the European Communities (1979a) *Proposals on Policy with Regard to Agricultural Structures*, COM (79) 122, Brussels.

Commission of the European Communities (1979b) *Third Report on the Implementation of the Council Directives on the Reform of Agriculture of 17th April 1972*, COM (79) 438, Brussels.

Commission of the European Communities (1979c) *Eighth Financial Report on the European Agricultural Guidance and Guarantee Fund 1978, Guidance Section*, COM (79) 579, Brussels.

Commission of the European Communities (1980a) *The Agricultural Structures Policy of the Community. Perspective and Evolution*, Commission Staff Paper SEC (80) 1471, Brussels.

Commission of the European Communities (1980b) *Ninth Financial Report on the European Agricultural Guidance and Guarantee Fund, 1979, Guidance Section*, COM (80) 639, Brussels.

Commission of the European Communities (1980c) *The Agricultural Situation in the Community 1980 Report*, Brussels.

Commission of the European Communities (1981) *Preliminary Draft General Budget of the European Communities for the Financial Year 1982*, 8 volumes, COM (81) 180, Brussels.

Commission of the European Communities (1982) *The Agricultural Situation in the Community, 1981 Report*, Brussels.

European Report (1982) Issue No. 851, Brussels.

Eurostat (1973) *Yearbook of Agricultural Statistics 1973*, Office for Official Publications of the European Communities, Luxembourg.

FAO (1979) *FAO Production Yearbook 1978*, Vol. 32 Food and Agriculture Organization of the United Nations, Rome.

FAO (1980) The Commodity Trade Implications of EEC Enlargement, in *FAO Commodity Review and Outlook: 1979–80* Food and Agriculture Organization of the United Nations, Rome.

House of Lords Select Committee on the European Communities (1982a) *State Aids to Agriculture*, Session 1981–82, 7th Report, HL 90, HMSO: London.

House of Lords Select Committee on the European Communities (1982b) *Socio-Structural Policy* Session 1982–83, 2nd Report, HL 30, HMSO: London.

MMB (1981) *EEC Dairy Facts and Figures 1981* Milk Marketing Board, Thames Ditton.

MAFF (1977) *The Changing Structure of Agriculture 1968–75* HMSO: London.

MAFF (1980) *EEC Agricultural and Food Statistics 1975–1978* Ministry of Agriculture, Fisheries and Food, London.

Rollo, J. M. C. (1979) 'The second enlargement of the European Economic Community: some economic implications with special reference to agriculture', *Journal of Agricultural Economics*, **30**.

Chapter 10

The Impact of Farm Policies on the Food Industry

INTRODUCTION

In all modern economies there is a good deal of mutual interdependence between individuals and sectors. Most manufacturing activities are dependent upon the supply of machinery, intermediate products, and fuel from other firms; and in turn rely on other businesses to purchase a major part, if not the whole, of their output for further transformation and distribution to consumers. This is certainly true of the farm sector with, on the one hand, its dependence upon the agricultural supply industries and, on the other, its links with food manufacturing and distribution. Any change in the economic circumstances affecting one part of the food chain—the farm sector say—will have consequences for the profitability and employment prospects of its linked industries. Thus, it has been noted that variations in the level of farm income are quickly reflected in the volume of machinery purchases by farmers. Similarly a change in the volume of milk output from farms will have implications for the capacity requirements of the dairy processing industry.

This chapter is concerned with CAP policy measures affecting activities beyond the farm gate involving agricultural raw materials, or products based thereon. It includes food processing and manufacture, animal feed preparation, the tobacco and drink industries, and the distribution of these products. For convenience these industries have all been subsumed, in the chapter's title, under the heading the 'food industry'. The data on the various industries is limited, and not necessarily comparable from one Member State to another. The figures presented below—on the food sector—are there to indicate orders of magnitude only. The paucity of data perhaps reflects the comparative lack of attention paid by economists and politicians to the whole food chain, compared to that devoted to the farm sector.

The Commission has published some data on the relative importance of the food industry to the European economy. The figures in Table 10.1 indicate the relative share of agriculture and the food industry in gross value added (at market prices) for certain of the EC Member States in 1979. There is a consider-

234

Table 10.1   Relative share of agriculture and the food industry in gross value added (at market prices) in 1979. (Percentages).

	Germany	France	Italy	Netherlands	Belgium	UK	Greece
Agriculture and food industry as a percentage of economy in general	6.4	9.8	10.7	7.5	6.3	6.4	20.7
Relative share of							
Agriculture	35.1	53.4	63.3	53.6	37.4	34.8	82.0
Food industry	64.9	46.6	36.7	46.4	62.6	65.2	18.0

Notes: The compilation of a table such as this, and similarly Table 10.2, is extremely difficult because, *inter alia*, of the different systems of classifying firms to industrial subheadings. It is not clear how the Commission has attempted to reconcile these difficulties, and construct these two tables. The figures for the United Kingdom, for example, are noticeably different from those of Mordue, of the British Ministry of Agriculture, Fisheries and Food, cited below. A careful research study would be required to produce comparable data for the EC Member States, but in the absence of that the Commission is to be commended for producing some figures, however doubtful they might be.
SOURCE   Commission (1982, p. 281).

able variation between the countries considered, with the structure in Germany, Belgium, and the United Kingdom being rather similar whilst the relative importance of the food industry in France, the Netherlands, Italy, and particularly Greece, is much less.

Mordue (1983), in a careful appraisal of the UK economy, concluded that 'each main stage of the food chain in the UK'—agriculture, food manufacturing and food distribution—contributed roughly a third 'to the whole sectors 7 to $7\frac{1}{2}$ per cent share in GDP'. Furthermore, when catering and the agricultural supply industries are included, 'the total contribution to national income would be approaching 10 per cent'.[1]

The range of activities engaged in by the food industry is indicated by Table 10.2. The classification into first and second stage processing is a useful one which mirrors the treatment in this chapter. First stage processing, amounting to some 48 per cent of the total turnover, involves the processing of agricultural products whereas second stage processing is concerned with the further manufacture of processed food products.

The economic importance of the food industries, and their important links with the farm sector, would be reason enough to include a discussion of the food industries in any text devoted to agricultural policy. However, in the context of the EC's common agricultural policy, and probably with most other agricultural policies around the world, the reasons go far beyond that. A major theme of this book, which is emphasized in this chapter, is that it is the food industries which are responsible for operating the major part of the CAP policy mechanisms. Few farmers are *directly* involved with the price support systems outlined in Chapters 3 to 8, rather they rely on receiving the price effects indirectly via the food industries.

Table 10.2 Relative importance of EC '9' food and drink industries by commodity handled. (Percentage of total turnover).

First stage processing	47.5	
Manufacture of dairy products		16.8
Slaughtering, preparing, and preserving of meat		13.3
Processing and preserving of fruit and vegetables		4.2
Sugar manufacturing and refining		3.9
Manufacture of vegetable and animal oils and fats		4.7
Grain milling		3.5
Processing and preserving of fish		1.0
Manufacture of cider and fruit wines		0.1
Second stage processing	52.3	
Brewing and malting		7.9
Bread and flour confectionery		4.5
Manufacture of cocoa, chocolate, and sugar confectionery		5.4
Manufacture of other food products		6.4
Distilling of ethyl alcohol from fermented materials		3.9
Manufacture of soft drinks, including the bottling of natural spa waters		2.5
Manufacture of starch and starch products		1.4
Manufacture of spaghetti, macaroni, etc.		0.8
Manufacture of tobacco products		9.9
Manufacture of animal feed		8.3
Manufacture of wine of fresh grapes and of beverages based thereon		1.3

Notes: Year not specified in original source. See also the comments under Table 10.1.
SOURCE Adapted from Commission (1980, p. 281).

The chapter falls into a number of parts: first, a discussion of CAP policy measures and their dependence on the food industries, emphasizing the differential impact on the various food processing and distributive activities; second an explanation of the need the policy-makers faced to create a parallel set of provisions for manufactured foods (known as non-Annex II products) and the details of that system; and finally a summary review of the response of the industry to the policies pursued. Chapter 9, dealing with structural policy, included a discussion of those structural policy measures which are of particular importance to the food industries (notably Regulation 355/77); and Chapter 12 will be devoted to the EC's food legislation programme.[2]

THE CAP AND THE FOOD INDUSTRIES

With the deficiency payments system that applied in the United Kingdom prior to EC entry, the government made most, but not all, the payments direct to farmers. Some payments were made via the marketing boards (notably the Milk Marketing Boards) so allowing in turn the payment of a 'pooled' price to producers which would reflect the return from the market and the deficiency

Table 10.3   CAP aids paid directly to farmers.

Sector	Aid
Cereals	Production aid on durum wheat
Milk	Subsidy on skim milk fed to animals on the farm
Olive oil	Production aid
Beef	Variable slaughter premium in the United Kingdom
	Calf premium
	Suckler cow premium
	Hill cattle premium in the areas covered by Directive 75/268
Sheepmeat	Variable slaughter premium in the United Kingdom
	Hill sheep premium in the areas covered by Directive 75/268
Flax and hemp	Production aid
Seeds for sowing	Production aid
Hops	Production aid
Silkworms	Rearing aid

payments. Within the CAP there are very few aids paid direct to farmers: those that are may be found listed in Table 10.3. These are generally flat rate aids paid per hectare sown or per tonne of product.

There may, from time to time, be some large producers of cereals and oilseeds that take advantage of the intervention buying facilities offered for these products; but most deliveries to intervention stores are probably made by merchants or other intermediaries who in turn will have obtained their supplies at a farm gate price which will have reflected a number of market factors including the merchant's confidence that any particular batch will meet the intervention agency's quality requirements. As a general rule, however, intervention buying is only available on products which have undergone some degree of transformation—butter, skim milk powder, white sugar, beef carcasses, for example—and hence offers a potential outlet for the first stage processers, not the farmer. All the other price support mechanisms of the CAP operate through the food industries.

Intervention products

In order to support the price of farm produce a number of intervention products have been designated. Although the detailed rules vary between the product sectors, the general arrangement is that the EC authorities maintain an open-ended commitment to purchase at the intervention price. The farmer is dependent upon the price guarantee being passed down the marketing chain and hence reflected in his sale price. In the case of sugar a processing margin is explicitly included in the intervention price calculation in that a minimum purchase price for sugar beet is laid down. For milk products a nominal processing margin is included in the intervention price, but dairies are free to negotiate with farmers their actual purchase price.

The result of this system, it is often claimed, is to put the first-stage agricultural processers into a privileged position. They have a guaranteed and unlimited outlet for their production, a known and stable price, and the benefit of a built-in 'cost plus' processing margin. The result, not unexpectedly, has been to encourage investment in these industries. For example, sugar beet processers have been encouraged, and have been able to afford, to modernize their factories by putting white 'ends' on many of those factories that previously only produced raw sugar. In the dairy sector there has been major investment in modernizing and expanding processing facilities, particularly to take advantage of the intervention mechanisms for skim milk powder.

Some firms have been criticized for producing for intervention. Thus van Dijk and Mackel comment:

> Where control mechanisms have intervention as the buyer in last resort we see that access to selling markets is no longer a necessity. There are clear examples in various EEC countries that groups of firms formulate agreements to the effect that one or more firms per group sell for intervention on behalf of the group. In the beef sector in the Netherlands we see a situation which is even worse: firms procuring carcasses which are just prepared for the intervention requirements. (van Dijk and Mackel, 1982, p. 7.)

This implicit criticism of the business activities of firms should, however, be redirected as a criticism of the policy. Given that the policy induces the farming community to produce in excess of market requirements the first stage processers actually perform two roles: the production of food products for the market and the transference of EC budget funds to farmers via the operation of the intervention system.

Despite the apparent advantages that the producers of intervention products seem to enjoy, their position is not without risk. For example, if the EC were successful in reducing the output of milk within Europe, or in encouraging farmers to use skim milk as a pig feed in liquid form, then there would be considerable over-capacity in skim milk powder manufacture. Similarly, were the Commission ever to succeed in its efforts to reduce the level of EC sugar production quotas (as it tried in 1974 and 1980) then a considerable degree of over capacity could result. The operation of the sugar policy has already caused over capacity among EC cane sugar refiners—because of its bias towards sugar beet processing—leading, as a result, to the closure of almost half of the UK's cane capacity during the 1970s.

Private storage aids

Private storage aids are paid for many products covered by the CAP—they are for example the main support mechanisms for pigmeat. In many cases it is the first stage processed product that is stored—pigmeat carcasses, wine, butter, cheese, sugar—and in almost all instances it will be the food industries rather than farmers that undertake the storage. Private storage has been favoured by the Commission in recent years because of its belief that privately stored products are better cared for than public stocks and hence that the overall costs of storage are less. For the firm undertaking private storage there is a certain return from its supply of storage (through the payment of the aid) plus the security of having its own products available, though it faces the risk that the resale value of the product at the end of the storage contract might not be that expected.

Aids paid directly to processers or packers in the food and feed industry

In addition to intervention buying, private storage aids, aids payable directly to farmers and the several import/export measures discussed below, various CAP payments are made to firms operating in the tobacco, drink, food, and animal-feed industries. These are outlined in Table 10.4. A somewhat arbitrary distinction has been made between those aids which are the principal means of price support for the product in question, and those that seek to enlarge the market for a product by means, in effect, of price discrimination between various sub-markets.

For the first group of products—with the exception of olive oil—the difficulty the Community faces is that relatively liberal import regimes apply. Consequently it is not possible to raise the return to farmers by manipulating the general level of market prices: any sign of a rise in price would attract Third Country imports and so keep the price down. However, rather than make subsidy payments directly to farmers, the Community has chosen to deal with a limited number of processers or first hand buyers as a means of avoiding the logistical problems inherent in contacting a much larger group of farmers. It is expected that these firms will pass on the benefits of the aid to the farmers—indeed, in the case of the premiums on processed fruits and vegetables, peas and beans, and soya the aid is conditional on a minimum price having been paid to growers. From time to time concern has been voiced that the small peasant farmers—particularly in Italy—have not received the full benefit of these schemes, and considerable controversy has centred on the processing premiums for fruit and vegetables.

In the case of olive oil the Community institutions have feared that if consumers had to pay the producer price for oil then consumption would slump. Thus in addition to the 'production aid' (listed in Table 10.3) a 'consumption aid' is paid to packers when they prepare retail packs of olive oil—there is, however, a curious discrepancy between the quantity of oil on which production aids are paid and the very much smaller quantity declared for consumption aids.

The main characteristic of the second group of products, in Part B of Table 10.4, is that the CAP price support mechanisms succeed in maintaining a market price corresponding to the producers' return, but at this price there is an excess of supply over demand. Whilst preserving the full price market, the Commission seeks to exploit other market opportunities where the product can only

Table 10.4   CAP price support aids to the processing industries.

Product	Aid
A. *Main mechanism of product price support*	
Oilseeds	Aids are paid when colza, rape, and sunflower seeds are processed
	Aids are paid to the purchasers of soya beans provided a minimum price has been paid to producers
Fruit and vegetables	Processing premiums are payable on certain processed fruit and vegetable products (including canned pineapple) provided a minimum price has been paid to producers
Dehydrated fodder ⎫ Peas and beans used ⎬ for animal feed ⎭	Production aids
Cotton, not carded or combed	Production aid
Tobacco	Premiums for the initial purchasers of tobacco
Potatoes	Production refunds for starch manufacture
Olive Oil	A 'consumption' aid is paid to packers of olive oil, and similarly a production refund is paid on olive oil used for canning
B. *Aids to enlarge the market*	
Cereals, and rice	Production refunds for the manufacture of a number of products including starch and beer but not isoglucose
	Formerly a denaturing premium on wheat used in animal feed
Milk and milk products	Subsidy on skim used for casein manufacture
	Subsidy on skim and skim milk powder used in animal feed
	Various schemes for butter: cheap butter for the pastry and ice cream industries; sales to the armed forces and non-profit making organizations; Christmas butter; general butter subsidy
	School milk subsidy
Sugar	Production refunds on sugar used in the chemical industry
Beef	Beef tokens distributed in 1974 and 1975
Citrus fruit	Marketing (or penetration) premium
Fruit and vegetables	Processing and distribution of products withdrawn
Wine	Various distillation measures
Grape must (concentrated grape juice)	Aids for must used to produce grape juice, 'British' wines, wine-making kits, and for enriching certain wines.

be sold at a lower price. Thus the rationale of the Christmas butter schemes was that if butter was made available at a price highly competitive with margarine for a limited period of time then the 'cheap' butter would displace margarine sales, but not 'full-priced' butter in the remainder of the year. In practice some leakage from low priced to high priced markets cannot be avoided. In order to limit the extent of the leakage, however, tight controls are applied to the activities of the industries making use of the cheap products.

Indeed, all the aids listed in Tables 10.3 and 10.4 can only be paid under some strict system of controls and checks to reduce the incidence of fraud. These controls will often hinder the freedom of the food industries to react to changing circumstances, and consequently reduce the value of the aids to the recipients. An example, from a report of the Special Committee of Inquiry set up by the Commission in 1973 'to examine the possibilities of fraud or irregularity in the administration of Community funds', may illustrate the need for control and the scope for fraud.

The case involved a business claiming a production refund for the processing of maize into groats. For this the producer has to use a specified form

> to state his intention of processing maize and the refund is made on the basis of this form. The producer receives visits from the customs inspectors who must approve his premises. . . . The producer must keep up to date accounts of stocks and production and a monthly summary of activity. The customs authority may inspect the premises during manufacture. (Commission, 1979, Annex II, p. 2.)

In this particular instance, although it was confirmed that the total quantities declared for the claim of the production refund were correct over the period as a whole, the monthly totals were not. The producer had been fraudulently claiming for a higher quantity during the periods when the production refund was greatest.

Many of the activities listed in Table 10.4 require the active participation of the food industries. Thus, for example, the general butter subsidy is paid to the packers of butter when retail packs are prepared; and the beef tokens for old age pensioners in 1974 and 1975 had to be redeemed through retail outlets.[3] Business activities will be adapted to take advantage of the aids, and firms may be adversely affected if the conditions under which the aids are granted are changed or terminated abruptly. The Community's starch industry, for example, has suffered from the many alterations in the levels of production refund granted on domestically produced cereals and potatoes used as raw materials for starch manufacture. (For further discussion see Chapter 4.)

Import and export arrangements for CAP products

As detailed in earlier chapters export refunds are granted for CAP products, and import levies (and sometimes import tariffs) are charged.[4] The Commission has a certain amount of discretion in setting export refunds, but much less in the fixing of import levies. In fixing the export refund for a particular product a number of factors will be considered: the supply—demand balance within the Community, the cost to the budget, political pressures from the Third Country to which the product is to be exported, and the state of the domestic processing industry. For example, the Commission might wish to encourage the export of the EC milk surplus in the form of whole milk powder and at other times in the form of cheese, or yet again as butter and skim milk powder. Clearly individual firms will not be indifferent to the pattern of milk product exports and they might be expected to lobby their governments, and the Commission, accordingly.[5]

The import arrangements, as well as affording protection to European farmers, give a measure of protection to the processing industry. An example from the farm sector can be taken to illustrate the situation.

Pigs and poultry can be regarded as processed cereals, as feed accounts for a major part of their production costs. Consequently any protection given these two industries would be ineffective unless due account were taken of the cereal regime's impact on the price of cereals. As explained in Chapter 4, import protection for the two industries is the sum of two components, although charged as a single unified rate of levy per product. The first, variable, component takes account of cereal costs in the EC and the rest of the world, while the second is a fixed component of processer protection which applies even if there is no difference between world and EC cereal prices. Indeed, this was the case in 1973/74 during the price boom for cereals on the world market. The fixed component, representing the specific element for processer protection, is set at 7 per cent of the calculated average world costs of pig and poultry production in the previous year.

For the intervention products—for example, sugar or butter—the intervention and threshold prices already include a processer margin. Thus, in fixing the import levy as the difference between the threshold price and the world market price, the first-stage processer as well as the farmer is afforded protection.[6] However, import levies are also charged on the other products covered by the commodity regimes—for example, the various cereal products listed on page 64 of Chapter 4. Typically the calculation of the import levy for all these other products will involve two parts: a variable component derived from the levy set on the basic product and a fixed component (a specific tariff rate) for processer protection.

For fruit and vegetables and oilseeds, *ad valorem* tariffs are applied rather than variable import levies. There is a progression in the level of tariff as the degree of processing increases. This is particularly marked for oilseeds which enter the Community duty free, but the *ad valorem* tariffs on vegetable oils go as high as 20 per cent. For fruit and vegetables, however, the degree of tariff escalation is less marked than for oilseeds.

The fixed component in the levy, and the tariff escalation on more highly processed products in other sectors, means that the CAP involves relatively high levels of *effective* protection of EC food processing activities. That is the level of protection given on the processed product is at such a level that it more than outweighs the cost disadvantage suffered because of the protection given farmers on their products.[7]

NON-ANNEX II PRODUCTS

Food manufacturers could not remain in business for long if they had to compete with imported products manufactured from cheaper raw materials. However the CAP, as defined in Article 38(1) of the EEC Treaty and listed by product in Annex II to the Treaty, was confined to agricultural products, defined as 'products of the soil, of stock farming and of fisheries and products of first stage processing directly related to these products'.[8] Manufactured food products were not mentioned, although it quickly became obvious that the competitive position of the food industry had to be taken into account. Hence, by October 1966, only four years after the transition period for the first CAP product regimes had started, a parallel trade system had been introduced for 'Non-Annex II products'—that is to say manufactured or second-stage food products not listed in Annex II to the Treaty. The rules are laid down in Regulation 3033/80.

Non-Annex II products are manufactured from one or more of the basic products listed in Table 10.5A. Processed products are also considered to be Non-Annex II products if they have been manufactured from other first-stage processed products which have been likened to one of the basic products listed. This second group are collected in Table 10.5B.

On imports a two-part charge is made, part of which is reviewed quarterly. The first part of the charge is the fixed component (actually an *ad valorem* import tariff) meant to protect EC processers and ranging between 6 and 13 per cent according to product. The second part of the charge is the so-called variable component which is reviewed quarterly and represents an average of the import levy charged in the preceding quarter for the various CAP basic products deemed to have been used for each processed product in accordance with a notional recipe. Thus each quarter the Commission publishes a list of import charges, which will be applied to Non-Annex II products for the following three months, arranged by CCT heading.

In some cases, where Third Countries have an Association agreement with the EEC (e.g. the ACP countries), only the variable charge, or a percentage of the variable and fixed charges, may be applied. For some products there is a maximum levy charge bound in GATT.

For many Non-Annex II products, however, food manufacturers are as worried about the competitive position of their products on world markets as they are about the threat of Third Country imports. For a short list of relatively simple products (e.g. puffed rice) an export refund is payable according to a notional recipe of ingredients used; whereas for more complicated products the refund is based on the actual ingredients used. In this latter case the exporter

Table 10.5 Products from which Non-Annex II goods are manufactured.

Part A

Basic product

Skim milk powder
Whole milk powder
Butter
Cereals
    common wheat
    durum wheat
    rye
    barley
    maize
    rice
Sugar
Molasses

Part B

First stage processed product	*Basic product*
Potato starch	Maize
Other starch (excluding rice and wheat starch) produced from starches of roots and tubers coming under CCT heading 07.06	Maize
Goods made from fresh milk, not concentrated or sweetened, with a milk fat content not exceeding 0.1 per cent	Skim milk powder
Goods made from fresh milk or cream, not concentrated or sweetened, with a milk fat content exceeding 0.1 per cent	Whole milk powder
Isoglucose	Sugar

can either lodge his recipe confidentially with his national Intervention Agency; or arrange for an analysis by a chemist approved by the national government or Intervention Agency to determine the quantities of basic products used in preparing the goods.

The refunds, which are set individually for each basic product, are normally fixed by the Management Committee procedure at the beginning of each month. A refund is also payable on egg products, even though eggs are not considered to be basic products. The refund rate for eggs is changed every three months. However, all the refund rates can be changed more or less frequently by the Commission to prevent trade distortions or to control export volumes of certain products.

Although the provisions governing the fixing of export refunds for Non-Annex II products would appear to be sufficiently widely drawn to allow the Commission to set whatever refund rates it felt necessary, the food industries have periodically complained that refunds are sometimes inadequate. A particular example concerned sugar in the spring of 1981.

Over the winter of 1980/81 the world white sugar price had exceeded the Community price, and as a result export levies were in force.[9] However, the world price fell and, on 1 April 1981, the Commission reinstated the export refund for bulk white sugar exported under tender (see Table 10.6). The export refund on bulk sugar granted at the weekly tenders increased markedly through the month and yet the sugar refund on Non-Annex II products was not reintroduced until 1 May 1981. The British Food Manufacturers' Federation (FMF) wrote,

> Furthermore, the refund level established for processed products on 1 May at £46.65/tonne and increased to £63.66/tonne on 9 May, was not sufficient to enable our exporters to compete in world markets. . . . The Commission then reacted swiftly to an increase in world prices in late May and early June and cut the already inadequate export refund levels. (FMF, 1981, pp. 93–94.)

This example—often quoted by the UK food industry lobby—does support the view that the Commission has paid more attention to the disposal, in bulk, of surpluses (its 'management of the markets') than meeting the needs of the food processors. How typical it is would only be revealed by a thorough review of export refund practice over the last few years.

The food industry lobby takes the question of export refunds on processed products very seriously, arguing that it is preferable (certainly from their point of view) to export the EC's farm surpluses in the form of 'value-added' products, rather than in bulk. Consequently they, like the Commission, are sensitive

Table 10.6   Export refunds on white sugar, 1981. (£/tonne).

	Export refund on bulk sugar exported under tender	Export refund on sugar in Non-Annex II goods	
1 April	24.85		
7 April	72.59		
15 April	87.47	April	0
22 April	98.87		
29 April	108.59		
6 May	119.39	1–8 May	46.65
13 May	121.19	9–25 May	63.66
20 May	114.64		
27 May	103.57	26–31 May	50.92
3 June	68.11	1 June	48.32
		2 June	30.93

SOURCE   FMF, 1981, p. 97.

about the term 'export refund'. The Confederation of the Food and Drink Industries of the EEC (the CIAA) have recently declared:

> Above all, CIAA wishes to stress the essential role played by refunds; they are not subsidies and serve only as compensation for the difference between the price levels of raw materials produced in the Community ... and those of the same raw materials used by the competitors of EEC industries in third countries. (CIAA, 1982, p. 14.)

A rather different view is taken by other exporters. The US Agricultural Attaché in London has asked: 'But why not broaden the principle? Why not allow for the higher cost of EC labor or fuel as well as the higher cost of the raw agricultural inputs?' (Oyloe, 1982, p. 35.)

Inward processing relief

The food industries have a number of complaints about the detailed application of the trade provisions for processed products, all of which reflect the complex rules that have had to be assembled because of the basic policy decision to support farmers' incomes by manipulating market prices. The Food and Drink Industries Council in the UK has claimed that the food and drink industries

> are subject to changes in the rules without notice, inconsistencies in their application and inadequacies in the basic rules themselves. Examples of how the implementation of the rules could be improved are such technical matters as prefixation of the refund levels, more liberal inward processing arrangements, easier prefinancing rules and better ways of dealing with the non-return of copy T5s required when goods cross the Community for ultimate export from it. (FDIC, 1982, p. 25.)

Inward processing relief allows a food manufacturer to import from Third Countries certain raw materials free of all duties, levies, and MCAs provided that the processed product into which they are incorporated is exported from the Community within six months. Of course export refunds are not available on products manufactured from raw materials imported levy and duty free under these arrangements. Usually inward processing relief is not available on raw materials which are in surplus in the EC (FMF, 1981, p. 94). When inward processing relief is available, then manufacturers using CAP raw materials in their export products can apply for prefinancing of export refunds on the CAP products. 'This facility was introduced to put processers using CAP raw materials produced in the EEC under competitive conditions equal to those enjoyed by processers using inward processing relief' (FMF, 1982, p. 94). And so the whole complex web gets more and more convoluted!

LEAST COST SOLUTIONS—THE INDUSTRY'S RESPONSE

The CAP policy mechanisms, and the parallel set of provisions for Non-Annex II products, generate a complex and sometimes conflicting set of price signals for the food and feed industries. All industrial sectors operate under particular legal and economic constraints, and consequently the food industries are not unique in their expression of concern about the impact of national and EC policies; but it is hoped that the earlier parts of this chapter have demonstrated that a discussion of the CAP without a consideration of its impact on the food industries would be just as unbalanced as a review of the food industries without a look at the CAP. However, as different firms operating within the industries seek the least cost solution to their business and trading problems, it would be surprising to find that they were all equally affected. They are not; the CAP has a differential impact on particular activities which sometimes vary on a regional basis and which are always subject to change—because of new directions in policy—through time. Consequently it is not to be expected that the industry will always speak with one voice.

Some conflicts of interest are widely recognized: for example, because of the relatively low import charges on oilseeds, margarine has a price advantage over butter. Any attempt to raise a tax on vegetable oils would change the relative position of the two industries; and would also have implications for the profitability of the Community's oilseed crushing industry.

In some cases the interest of the food industry is not readily apparent. Thus the school milk programme might simply be seen as a surplus disposal measure. However, if it is successful in expanding the market for liquid milk it has clear distributional implications for those firms operating in the dairy industry: for some the volume of business will expand (the heat treatment, bottling and handling of liquid milk) and for others it may well contract (butter and skim milk powder manufacture).

There will be occasions when the farm and food industry lobbies are at one, and seemingly similar situations when their interests diverge. Thus Scottish raspberry growers have complained about imports of cheap raspberry pulp for making jams from Eastern Europe. The FMF, however, objected to the import of cheap marmalades and jams but wished to have access to low priced fruit pulps.[10]

There is in fact a curious duality of interest that pervades the sector. On the one hand the industry in general shares the interest of the farm sector in having a large, protected, European market and even—as discussed above—aspires to the vocation of manufacturer of processed export products. On the other hand each firm, wishing to minimize its own costs, objects to the level of raw material prices within the EC. The lobbying against the imposition of high import levies and tariffs on imported goods—be it 'strong' breadmaking wheat, long grain rice, or dehydrated onions—is particularly marked.

It is in this respect that the difference in position between the first stage and second stage processers is most marked. Basically the former have a secure outlet for their production, in intervention, no matter what the volume, at a fixed and relatively risk free price. When intervention prices are raised, so are processing margins although processers have to pay a higher price to farmers. Thus, as a broad generalization, it can be said that it is in the joint interest of first-stage processers and farmers to seek higher intervention prices.

By contrast, second stage processers are in a very much less favoured position as a result of the CAP. Some of their purchase prices—those for supported CAP products—are firm and subject to little negotiation whereas their output, of manufactured food products, must be placed in an highly competitive retail market. Thus food manufacturers have found themselves caught between the rigidities of CAP supported raw material prices on the one hand, and the pressures from retailers on the other.

One sector, however, which has had noticeable success in avoiding some of the CAP's effects for raw material prices is that of the animal feed compounders. They have successfully diversified their sources of supply and obtained, perfectly legitimately, imported raw materials which are cheaper than CAP feedstuffs. There was a discussion, in Chapter 4, of the policy issues involved over the importation of manioc from Thailand and maize gluten from the USA. Internally, however, the conflict of interest is not simply that between the compounders and the livestock rearing industries on the one hand, and the cereal growers on the other. There is also a regional effect. French feed mills tend to be located inland away from deep water ports—reflecting the country's position as a major cereal producer—and hence cannot gain the same advantage from cheap imports as their competitors in the Netherlands. Consequently, French feed manufacturers are more likely to side with the cereal growers than with their fellow compounders in the Netherlands. Similarly there will be a knock-on effect right through the industry: pig producers, slaughter-houses, and the manufacturers of pigmeat products located in France will object to the 'unfair' competition from their Dutch counterparts.

Similar problems have befallen the pigmeat industry in Northern Ireland which had been based, prior to Britain's accession to the EEC, on cheap grains from North America. The Northern Ireland industry has also been troubled by the machinations of the green 'money'/MCA system: when the price level in the Republic was higher than that in Northern Ireland there was a thriving, if illegal, trade in pigs from North to South. This, not surprisingly, significantly reduced the throughput of the slaughter-houses located in the North.

Over the years the MCA system has caused many distortions in trade flows and generated endless problems for the food industries. One more example in Anglo-Irish trade might be cited—though this activity was quite legal. Prior to 1977 there were no MCAs applied on biscuit exports from the UK to Ireland although at the time, because of the overvaluation of the 'green pound', British biscuit manufacturers had access to raw materials at a much cheaper price than did their counterparts in Ireland. In the end MCAs had to be extended to biscuits to relieve the pressures upon the Irish biscuit industry.

It is not too fanciful to claim that there is a constant battle of wits between the politicians and civil servants seeking to preserve the integrity of the policy and minimize its cost; and the trade seeking—in the main legally—to spot the loopholes and maximize their profits. The CAP is rather like a tax system which grows more complicated as the years go by, as particular loopholes are plugged and more powerful brains are trained on the edifice. Undoubtedly the food manufacturer has to develop new skills: a European firm, particularly one engaged in trade, must have access to a wide range of specialist skills and knowledge in order to survive.

Sometimes, however, the policy makers cannot allow new endeavour to survive, particularly if it threatens to increase substantially the cost of the CAP. A major case in point is that of isoglucose. During the 1970s technology became available which allowed the production of sweeteners from cereals which, in the Community, had a price advantage in certain uses over sugar derived from beet or cane. The threat that this posed to the CAP was such that restrictive production quotas (outlined in Chapter 6) were imposed upon the fledgeling industry to thwart its further development.

The Commission's proposals for ethyl alcohol (discussed in Chapter 7) would have an equivalent effect in that they seek to reserve certain markets for alcohol of agricultural origin. If accepted, this measure would discriminate against manufacturers of ethyl alcohol from petrochemicals, as they would be denied access to markets they had formerly enjoyed.

Finally, an under-recognized consequence of the CAP which is important to note, is that it discriminates against small firms. Such are the complexities of the CAP that only large firms can afford the necessary resources to master the detail (for example by the creation of specialist departments: see Nicholls, 1979). Small firms are forced to rely on trade associations—which can vary in quality—and government departments. Inevitably information derived from such sources can never be as timely, or as specific, as that received from in-house specialists.

NOTES

1. Mordue's chapter (Mordue, 1983) is the most comprehensive source on the economic role of the food manufacturing and distribution industries in the UK economy. See also the chapter by Burns (Burns, 1983), in the same book, for a useful summary view of the economic importance of the food industries.
2. To keep the book to manageable size a number of topics have had to be ruled out. The book is limited to EC policies which are directed at the farm and food sectors; thus it excludes other EC policies which affect all industries but which might have been included—for example, competition policy or transport policy—and also the impact of the EC's farm and food policies on the agricultural supply industries.
3. In the United Kingdom 'approximately 8.5 million pensioners were issued with 18 tokens worth 20p each by the Social Security Departments . . . for fresh, frozen, or chilled beef or veal for the weeks between 2 December 1974 and 31 March 1975 provided that at least another 20p was spent on those meats with each token' (Intervention Board, 1975, p. 12).
4. The distinction between a variable import levy and an import duty or tariff was drawn in Chapter 3. The difference is important because the former can guarantee domestic producers a minimum price below which foreign imports cannot compete, whereas the latter cannot except when combined with a reference price system.
5. Of course there is a closeness of interest here between the Commission and the food lobby. The Commission relies on sectors of the food industry to export EC produce to Third Countries; and yet the food industry in turn is dependent upon the Commission ensuring that levels of refund are adequate to permit profitable exports.

6. For milk, basic import levies are fixed for 12 pilot products rather than just for the intervention products; but again the same principle applies—the levy also affords protection to the first stage processer.
7. The theory of effective protection is discussed by Corden (1971). Although grossly over-simplified the following example may help. Suppose the world market cost of the raw material to be £100, the cost of processing both home and abroad to be £20, the tariff on the raw material to be 10 per cent and that on the finished product to be 20 per cent. The cost to domestic manufacturers purchasing the raw material on the world market would be £110 (£100 plus 10 per cent tariff) and they could then afford to sell at £130 (£110 plus £20 processing cost). However, imports of the finished products could only be had for £144 (£120 basic cost plus 20 per cent tariff). Thus the cost advantage to domestic producers because of the tariff structure would be £14—giving an effective tariff rate on the domestic industry's 'value added' of 70 per cent (£14 cost advantage compared to £20 processing cost).

    Calculations of the degree of effective protection offered the food industries have been performed—see for example Yeats (1977) and the reproduction of the same computations in Snape (1981). For a number of reasons these figures are suspect, but the central idea—that the tariff structure of most countries escalates and hence makes the importation of *processed* products more difficult—remains valid. Snape's essay is a lucid exposition of the difficulties the less developed countries face in exporting processed food products to the developed markets.
8. As well as the products referred to in Chapters 4 to 7 of this book, Annex II to the Treaty covers fish, live trees and other plants, bulbs, cut flowers, coffee, tea, spices, cocoa, and cork.
9. The Food Manufacturers' Federation, upon whose evidence to the House of Lords Select Committee on the European Communities this paragraph is based, did concede that Non-Annex II products had been exempted from the export levy on sugar (Food Manufacturers' Federation, 1981).
10. See the evidence by the National Farmers' Union of Scotland, and the Food Manufacturers' Federation, submitted to the House of Lords Select Committee on the European Communities, and the Committee's discussion in paragraph 49 (House of Lords, 1981).

REFERENCES

Burns, J. A. (1983) 'A synoptic view of the food industries', in Burns, J. A. McInerney, J. P., and Swinbank, A. (eds.) *The Food Industry: Economics and Policies*, Heinemann: London.

Commission of the European Communities (1979) *Report Concerning the Guarantee Section of The EAGGF, Cereal Sector*, COM (79) 686, Brussels. (A report by the Special Committee of Inquiry set up to examine the possibilities of fraud or irregularity in the administration of Community funds.)

Commission of the European Communities (1980) *The Agricultural Situation in the Community, 1980 Report*, Brussels.

Commission of the European Communities (1982) *The Agricultural Situation in the Community, 1981 Report*, Brussels.

Confederation of the Food and Drink Industries of EEC (1982), edited by Stevens, M. 'A CIAA paper—The Improvement of Export Conditions', *FDIC Bulletin* 21, 14–20.

Corden, W. M. (1971) *The Theory of Protection*, Clarendon Press: Oxford.

Food and Drink Industries Council (1982) *The Food Industry and the Farmer*, occasional paper, FDIC: London.

Food Manufacturers' Federation (1981) 'The Impact of EEC Trade Policy upon UK Exports of Processed Food Products', in House of Lords Select Committee on the

European Communities, *Agricultural Trade Policy*, 2nd Report, Session 1981–82, HL 29, HMSO: London; pp. 92–97.

House of Lords Select Committee on the European Communities (1981) *Fruit and Vegetables*, Session 1980–81, 22nd Report, HL 147, HMSO: London.

Intervention Board for Agricultural Produce (1975) *Report for the Calendar Year 1974*, Cmnd. 6033, HMSO: London.

Mordue, R. E. (1983) 'The food sector in the context of the UK economy', in Burns, J. A., McInerney, J. P., and Swinbank, A. (eds.) *The Food Industry: Economics and Policies*, Heinemann: London.

Nicholls, J. R. (1979) *Case Studies on the Effects of the EEC on the UK Food and Drink Industry*, Bath University Press: Bath.

Oyloe, T. (1982) 'The Treadmill Theory—An American Point of View', *FDIC Bulletin* **21**, 34–36.

Snape, R. H. (1981) *Barriers to Processed Food Imports in Developed Countries*, UNIDO/PC.12, United Nations Industrial Development Organization: Vienna.

Van Dijk, G., and Mackel, C. (1982) *Future Constraints to the Food Industries Arising from Policy Developments in the Animal Production Sector in Europe*, paper presented to the OECD Symposium on 'The Adjustment and the Challenge Facing the Food Industries in the 1980s', Paris 11–14 January 1982.

Yeats, A. J. (1977) 'Effective Protection for Processed Agricultural Commodities: a Comparison of Industrial Countries', *Journal of Economics and Business* **29**, 31–39.

Chapter 11

The CAP and Third Countries

For Third Countries the operation of the CAP has proved to be probably the single most controversial aspect of the EC's existence. Not surprisingly many issues are involved. To set these in context, however, an appreciation is necessary of how CAP external frontier measures are applied. Accordingly this chapter is arranged to cover the economic and institutional aspects of the CAP's external effects before drawing them together in a discussion of the issues involved in the EC's agricultural trade relations with Third Countries. The chapter's arrangement is as follows:

EC external policies
   Industrial trade policy
   Agricultural trade policy
Economic aspects of the CAP for Third Countries
   Volume effects
   Price effects
Two hierarchies
   CAP import mechanisms
   Preferential trade concessions
   The Lomé Convention
   The Mediterranean arrangements
   The Generalized Preferences Scheme
   Ad hoc trade concessions
Other issues
   Food aid
   Long term supply contracts
   International commodity agreements
   The General Agreement on Tariffs and Trade
EC agricultural trade relations with Third Countries
   Temperate zone agricultural producers
   Mediterranean zone agricultural producers
   Tropical zone agricultural producers.

EC EXTERNAL POLICIES

Although it is not yet possible to speak of an EC foreign policy[1] as such, to some extent the Community has started moving down this road. Thus the EC's external policies as they have developed—because of their substantial political content—are more than the sum of the Common Commercial Policy (CCP) and the Association Arrangements for Overseas Countries and Territories, the only specific external policies mentioned in the Treaty of Rome.[2] Evidence of this may be seen in the EC's development of a wide-ranging series of institutional relationships with Third Countries with varying degrees of political content, and its acting as a single entity—for the most part with the European Commission as spokesman—in international economic negotiations.[3]

Nevertheless the core of the EC's institutional relations with Third Countries has tended so far to be in the area of the charges the Community applies to imports and the possibility of negotiating reductions in these charges. The EC has developed what is often referred to as a 'Hierarchy' in its trade relations, with countries at the top of the hierarchy being most favoured in terms of reductions in the level of import charge applied to their exports at EC frontiers. Thus the Common Customs Tariff (CCT), which covers *all* such import charges is of great importance, not only as the principal component of the Common Commercial Policy but also as a means of distinguishing the Community from the rest of the world and as a bargaining weapon in trade negotiations with Third Countries. The Commission (1977) has pointed-out that 'the duty instrument has been one of the main vehicles through which the Community has been able to express itself in its external relations'.

Industrial trade policy

For industrial products[4] the EC has consistently operated a liberal trade policy and supported an open world trading system.[5] The formation of the EC led over time to the adoption of a single type of import charge (the import duty), the abolition of import quotas on trade with most Third Countries and the harmonization of the six founding countries' January 1957 tariff tables and the duties contained therein to create the CCT. Since then the original CCT duty rates have been reduced substantially as part of the GATT rounds of trade negotiations during the 1960s and 1970s, in which the EC played a major role. In general, the EC applies a lower level of import protection for industrial products than its major trading partners. Using data for the year 1976, Olechowski and Sampson (1980, p. 225) estimated that average trade weighted duty rates then applied to imports of manufactured goods were 6.2 per cent (USA), 5.4 per cent (Japan), and 4.5 per cent (EEC). The industrial trade philosophy followed by the EC consistently has been one of relatively free competition between its industries and those in Third Countries with the minimum of trade distorting measures. At the beginning of the 1980s, however, the EC's liberalism had tended to be curtailed somewhat for those of its industries which had become particularly vulnerable. These pressures had led the EC to apply some of the measures of the 'new' protectionism.[6]

Agricultural trade policy

Despite the EC's importance as both an importer and exporter of agricultural and food commodities, it does not have an explicitly formulated agricultural trade policy. This represents a major philosophical difference from the EC's trade treatment of industrial products. Whereas for industrial products the Commission has an external constituency to take into account because of the need to maintain and improve access for EC industrial exports to Third Country markets, traditionally this has not been the case for agriculture and food. Community Ministers of Agriculture and the Commission have perceived themselves as responding to a domestic constituency with the result that effects for Third Countries and world markets have not been (and are not) generally part of the decision taking process or the political consensus. In so far as there are effects for Third Countries of the CAP's operations, these arise as external reflections of decisions taken for domestic reasons. A striking example of this comparative isolation of the EC's Ministers of Agriculture occurred in 1975 when the decision to suspend the import of beef—a decision particularly affecting Australia, Brazil, Argentina, and Yugoslavia—was taken without consulting EC Foreign Ministers, or the countries most closely affected.

At the institutional level the effects for Third Countries of the CAP's operation arise through the levels of import charge applied under the CCT to imports of agricultural and food products[7] and the availability of export refunds for many CAP products. At an economic level the effects for Third Countries of the CAP's operation arise because EC production is higher than it otherwise would have been and consumption is lower as support prices are generally above world market levels. Consequently the EC's imports are reduced, and its exports increased, as a result of the CAP's operations.

Taking the institutional aspects first, for trade in agricultural and food items the EC not only follows a different philosophy to that for industrial products, but also applies different types and levels of charge to imports from Third Countries, with a 'hierarchy' of their effectiveness in controlling the price at which imports enter the EC graduated according to the importance of the product. Thus for the most important CAP items import duties are not used, but variable import levies which have the effect of preventing Third Country exports undercutting EC threshold prices, no matter how competitive their offers—as discussed in Chapter 3. For import levies extremely high rates of import charge can be involved, many times higher than the average EC duty charged on industrial imports. Table 11.1 shows the levies charged over a period of years expressed as the equivalent percentage rates of import duty. It is difficult to generalize, however, about levy rates as they vary from year-to-year due to movements in world prices (the most extreme example of this is sugar). On occasions when world prices have risen above EC levels, export taxes have been applied for several CAP products rather than import levies. These occasions are represented by the negative figures shown. Even for those agricultural and food items where import duties are used (covering the minor agricultural products and most manufactured food items), the rates of charge tend to be

Table 11.1   For years shown, average annual rates of EC variable import levy expressed as equivalent per cent rates of import duty. (Per cent).

	1968/69	1973/74	1978/79	1979/80
Common wheat	95	−21	93	63
Durum wheat	114	16	116	59
Husked rice	38	−40	57	31
Barley	97	−4	125	61
Maize	78	−2	101	90
White sugar	255	−44	176	31
Beef	69	10	99	104
Pigmeat	34	31	55	52
Butter	404	220	303	311
Skimmed milk powder	265	56	358	279
Olive oil	73	−4	100	93

SOURCE   Adapted from Commission (1976 and 1980a).

Note: For a number of products (e.g. butter) offers to the EC are extremely limited and hence the representativeness of the import levies as a measure of the difference between world and EC domestic levels must be limited.

higher than for industrial products—the agricultural duty rates are generally over 10 per cent and frequently over 20 per cent (e.g. the duty on several canned food items is 26 per cent)—and, in several cases, are underpinned by the setting of minimum import prices supported by countervailing duties.

Another institutional feature of the CAP market support systems is that for the products covered, a 'safeguard clause' is included allowing imports to be restricted 'where the Community market . . . is threatened with serious disturbances which may endanger the objectives set out in Article 39 of the Treaty [of Rome]. . . .'[8] This provision, however, has been used very seldom—the most notorious example being the suspension of beef imports between 1974 and 1977 mentioned above.

The CAP is unique in its comprehensive coverage of product sectors and in the degree of insulation from world markets it affords the Community's agriculture and, to some extent, its food industry. In terms of coverage, CAP regulations apply to all agricultural and first-stage processed products virtually without exception;[9] a breadth of coverage which no other developed country matches. Of more significance for world markets, however, is the degree of insulation which the CAP provides for its domestic markets in the major

EC Trade Measures

	EC deficit	EC surplus
World prices above threshold	Import refunds Export levies	Export levies
World prices below threshold	Import levies	Export refunds Import levies

agricultural products. This comes about through the EC's variable import levy/export refund mechanisms.

For products which the Community imports, the variable levies ensure that imports cannot undercut threshold prices where world prices are below Community levels. When, however, world prices are above threshold levels for products in which it has a deficit, the Community is not as automatic in applying the opposite measure of import subsidies. (Indeed, import subsidies have only been applied once—for sugar in 1974/75.[10]) Conversely, when the EC is in surplus it grants export refunds in order to enable its exports to compete on world markets when world prices are below threshold levels, and charges export taxes when world prices are above threshold levels—as happened for cereals, sugar, and beef in 1974, and sugar in 1980 and 1981. The economic significance of this degree of insulation from world market influences is discussed below.

ECONOMIC ASPECTS OF CAP FOR THIRD COUNTRIES

(a) Volume effects

For Third Countries the economic aspects of the CAP's operations arise primarily from the levels at which domestic EC support prices are set and from the degree of insulation from world market influences afforded the EC's agricultural and food sectors. As support prices generally have been significantly above world levels it is not surprising that levels of EC production have grown in such a fashion that, despite a rise in domestic demand due to an increased population and greater affluence, EC levels of self-sufficiency in virtually all the major agricultural commodities covered by the CAP have risen (Table 11.2). The consequence has been that the size of the EC market for

Table 11.2 Comparison of EC '9' levels of self-sufficiency. (Per cent).

	1968	1979	Change
Butter	91	111*	22.0
Cheese	98	103*	5.1
Concentrated milk	142	156*	9.9
Skimmed milk powder	140	110*	−21.4
Beef	89	99	11.2
Poultrymeat	101	105	4.0
Pigmeat	100	100*	Nil
Wheat	94	108	14.9
Maize	45	60	33.3
Barley	103	112	8.7
Sugar	82	124	51.2
Wine	97	99	2.1

* Figures are for 1978.
SOURCE Commission (1980a and 1982a).

Table 11.3 EC '9' Share of world markets for food and agricultural products.

	Change in the value of Community trade with Third Countries (Index 1973 = 100)		Community trade with Third Countries as a proportion of total world trade (%)	
	Imports	Exports	Imports	Exports
1973	100.0	100.0	30.9	9.8
1975	107.7	123.4	25.5	9.3
1978	153.7	179.8	27.3	10.3
1980	196.1	289.4	24.5	11.5
Change 1973 to 1980	96.1%	189.4%	−20.7%	17.3%

SOURCE Calculated from Commission (1982a) using base figures given in US dollars.

imports has declined while its importance as an exporter has risen (Table 11.3). Thus from taking over 30 per cent of world imports of agricultural and food products in 1973, the EC '9' share had dropped to about a quarter by 1980, while conversely its share of world exports had risen from about a tenth to some 11.5 per cent over the same period.[11] These results form the basis for the earlier statement that the EC is important both as an importer and as an exporter to the world market, with its import share being some two and a half times its export share. Indeed, the EC is still the single largest agricultural and food importer in the world.

It is not surprising that the EC's experience has varied by commodity, both because of the Community's varying agricultural potential between products, and because of the varying levels of import charge applied. Thus in the EC the

Table 11.4 Net Trade Balance in agriculture and food—EC '9'— for 1979.

SITC code No.		£s million
07	Tropical products	3299
05	Fruit and vegetables	3104
08	Animal feedingstuffs	1527
03	Fish	800
01	Meat	449
00	Live animals	146
04	Cereals	85
06	Sugar	54
09	Miscellaneous	−284
02	Dairy and eggs	−1250
0	Total for Chapter 0	7861

Note: Minus sign shows net exports.
SOURCE House of Lords (1981, p. xi)..

cereal market is highly protected against imports, but various cereal substitutes (such as manioc) can enter the Community relatively freely. Oilseeds—from which protein-rich meals for animal feed, and vegetable oils, are extracted—also enter the EC with relatively little hindrance. The results for 1979 given in Table 11.4 show that the EC's principal food import categories (tropical products, fruit, and vegetables) cover items which the Community either cannot produce at all, or cannot produce in adequate volume to meet domestic demand. The next largest category covers non-cereal feeding-stuffs—imports which are encouraged by the EC's high internal price for cereals. In some of the major temperate agricultural products, however, the EC has very much smaller import balances while in the case of dairy and egg products the Community is a net exporter.

(b) Price effects

Essentially the effects of the CAP for prices on world markets, arising from the volume changes discussed above, are twofold affecting both price levels and their relative stability. The price-depressing effects, for world markets, of the CAP's operations are clear. The EC both imports less and exports more than it would had its domestic market prices not been set relatively high in relation to world prices. As a result the import demand from the world market is reduced for some commodities, while for others an increased export supply presses on the world market. Recognizing the EC's importance as a trading entity, it is likely that the CAP's operations are a significant element in affecting world prices.[12] Particular commodity examples of the EC's ability to influence world prices at the beginning of the 1980s were in the dairy sector (where the EC was co-operating with New Zealand to hold prices up) and sugar (where the EC had to withhold some of its potential export surplus to avoid depressing world prices further).

The impact of agricultural policies on the stability of world prices is not quite so obvious. The essential point, however, is that domestic price stability for a large entity such as the EC may be achieved only at the expense of increasing international price instability. According to the then Australian Special Trade Representative, the result has been 'that the stability created in the EC market has been achieved at the direct cost of increasing instability in the rest of the world' (Garland, 1978, p. 7). Although this view may be regarded as exaggerated, in that it neglects the role of other developed countries' domestic policies in destabilizing world markets, it does reflect the importance of the EC for at least some of the world's principal agricultural commodity markets.

The theoretical considerations leading to this conclusion, of aggravated world price instability, are outlined below. Three distinct policies which display this characteristic are:

(i) The activities of state trading countries—such as the USSR which might enter the world market to buy such quantities as is necessary to maintain a predetermined level of domestic consumption;

(ii) The deficiency payment system operated in the United Kingdom until 1973 which guaranteed minimum producer prices, although it allowed consumer prices to vary; and

(iii) Policies such as those operated by the EC involving variable import levies and export subsidies. Trading quantities are, in effect, manipulated to achieve domestic price stability.

The CAP does not have uniform characteristics for all farm products: in fact the policies for some commodities differ markedly. However, for many products—such as cereals—a variable import levy is operated such that the threshold (minimum import) price is respected. Any excess supply at the support price must either be added to stocks (intervention buying) or sold on world markets with the aid of a variable export refund. The effect of the import levy/export refund policy is that the EC's import demand (or export supply) of CAP products will *tend to be* perfectly inelastic with respect to *world* prices at prices lower than the EC's support price.[13] This is because EC production and consumption would remain constant whatever the level of the world market price, provided that EC price levels remain above world market prices.

However, even this latter supposition is not necessarily restrictive. In the mid-1970s world market prices rose above EC support levels and in an effort to provide price stability for consumers export levies and—in one instance—import refunds were enacted. Had this policy been perfectly successful then the EC's import demand and export supply schedules for CAP commodities would have been perfectly inelastic with respect to world prices over the entire range of world prices, whether above or below its own support levels. As a result any variation in the world supply situation would be reflected in EC levy revenue/subsidy expenditure, but not in traded quantities. The only shifts in traded quantities would come from season to season variations in the EC supply situation: but there would be little or no change in domestic prices. In both cases the fluctuation in the world market price is greater than would have been the case without such policies. This can be seen from Figure 11.1, which illustrates the impact of world supply variations. Let the world consist of two importing nations, plus a group of exporting nations, for the product under consideration. Each of the importing nations has identical supply and demand schedules (S and D) leading—under free trade—to two identical import demand schedules (D_d), which when summed give world demand D_w. One nation now maintains a given domestic price (P_d) with variable import levies/refunds such that its import demand schedule becomes $D_{d'}$ and hence world demand becomes $D_{w'}$.

It may be that the equilibrium world price is P_d and that—on average—no protection is afforded to domestic producers or consumers. However, unforeseen supply variations (S_1 and S_2) around the equilibrium now lead to a greater fluctuation in the world market price ($P_{1'} - P_{2'}$) than with free trade ($P_1 - P_2$). This is because world demand is less elastic than before, or than it would have been had a duty been the protective device. Similarly a variable export levy will tend to make world supply less elastic.[14]

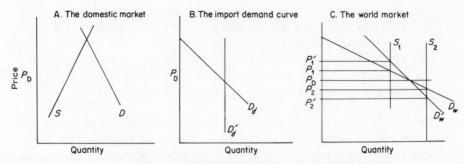

Figure 11.1   The CAP and international price stability.

(1) Part A of the figure shows the supply (S) and demand (D) schedules of the domestic market.

(2) The horizontal summation of S and D gives, in Part B, the import demand schedule (D_d).

(3) There is another, similar, country also with an import demand schedule D_d. The two, taken together, give the world import demand curve D_w (Part C).

(4) The equilibrium world market price is P_D, and this is fixed as the support price in the first country.

(5) Now, whatever happens to the world market price, production and consumption in the first country will be unaffected and the import demand curve, with respect to the world market price, becomes Dd'.

(6) Thus, taking the two importing countries together, the new world import demand curve is Dw' (Part C).

(7) World supply variations (S_1 and S_2) around the equilibrium now give rise to world market price fluctuations ($P_1' - P_2'$), rather than the narrower range ($P_1 - P_2$) in the absence of a domestic price stabilization scheme.

Such an analysis leads to the conclusion that those countries without the administrative capabilities or taxation base (to fund subsidies) will be the ones that bear the brunt of price and quantity variations; and that typically they will be low income less developed countries. In a very real sense—in this analysis—the world market is a residual. This is not because the traded quantities are small in proportion to total world output, but because the volume of production and consumption sensitive to world market prices is small in relation to world totals. In consequence world market price fluctuations are magnified. A major problem would be to establish how important in practice such policies really are. If all the major producing and consuming regions in the world adopt such policies then the impact would be great. If only one 'small country' were involved then no measurable impact would be felt.

An impressionistic view of the CAP in the 1970s would seem to indicate that the policy was less successful in maintaining domestic price stability when world market prices rose above CAP support levels than in periods of low world market prices. Equally the achievement for the various product groups is uneven and hence the impact on world markets. Thus surplus sugar tends to be exported whereas surplus EC dairy products tend to be added to intervention stocks or disposed of domestically in various sub-markets at lower prices.

Indeed, it would be wrong to view the farm sector as an indivisible whole in such analyses: not only does the CAP lead to distortions between the use of CAP and non-CAP products in EC agriculture (e.g. soya and manioc *vis-à-vis* cereals, as discussed in Chapter 4) but also in the use of CAP products themselves. Thus the insulating effect of the policy means that animal feed compounders may not experience a relative change in world market prices for feed grains and consequently not be induced to modify their feed mixes to minimize the Community's import bill (or maximize export receipts) for cereals while maintaining a given nutritional mix.

The ramifications of the policy are bizarre in that perverse price signals can be received by Community producers. Suppose there was a harvest failure for cereals somewhere in the world. Then the world price of cereals would rise and animal feed manufacturers would economize on their use of cereals by purchasing more cereal substitutes, thus forcing up the price of cereal substitutes. In the EC, however, the reaction would be the opposite of this if the EC did succeed in maintaining domestic price stability for cereals. This is because the rise in the price of cereal substitutes would be transmitted to the European market and EC millers would face a relative price change opposite to that on the world market. Thus they would increase their use of cereals and economize on the use of cereal substitutes.

TWO HIERARCHIES

In the Community's treatment of agricultural and food imports from Third Countries, two hierarchies can be discerned. The first relates to import mechanisms: both the type and level of frontier protection change according to the importance a product is felt to have for the EC's domestic producers. The second hierarchy relates to the trade concessions the EC is prepared to grant Third Countries. Those countries having association agreements with the EC receive more significant trade concessions (in both product coverage and degree of import charge reduction) than those not associated.

CAP import mechanisms

For the hierarchy of import measures (Table 11.5), the most complete degree of insulation from world markets, associated normally with the highest level of protection from Third Country supplies, is provided for the temperate zone agricultural products which traditionally have formed the core of the CAP—cereals, dairy products, sugar—plus certain important Mediterranean products (rice and olive oil). These products have variable import levies applied, in defence of the threshold prices, to Third Country supplies. The level of frontier protection, however, is variable depending on movements in world prices relative to EC prices. To prevent the undermining of the import levy regimes for these basic products, import levies are applied also to their processed derivatives in order for example to prevent lightly 'worked' cereals[15]

Table 11.5   A hierarchy of CAP import measures.

Products	General
1. Cereals, rice, sugar	Variable levies.
Dairy products	Variable levies.
Pigmeat, poultrymeat, eggs	Variable levies, plus additional levies if necessary.
First stage processed derivatives of these products	Variable levies, including a fixed element for processor protection.
Olive oil	Variable levies.
2. Beef	*Ad valorem* duties plus variable levies (related to domestic market prices as a proportion of guide prices).
Sheepmeat	Variable levies, subject to a GATT binding, and supported by 'voluntary' export restraint agreements.
3. Wine Fresh and preserved fruit and vegetables	*Ad valorem* duties, but with provision for use of countervailing duties to ensure minimum import prices are not undercut. For some fresh products duties are raised or lowered according to a seasonal calendar. Voluntary export restraints on apples from some Third Countries.
4. Second-stage processed agricultural products (not in Annex II to the Treaty of Rome) derived from basic products in Group I above	Fixed levies based on (normally) quarterly averages of variable levies applied to the basic products in a previous period, plus a fixed element for processer protection.
5. Oilseeds, forage, herbage seeds, tobacco, miscellaneous products in Annex II to Treaty of Rome	*Ad valorem* duties, with provision for use of safeguard clause if necessary.
Manioc	Voluntary export restraint.
6. Potatoes, ethyl alcohol, cork	Products not yet subject to a CAP market system. Member States may use national measures additional to the CCT.
7. Agricultural raw materials such as cotton, rubber, timber, and wool	Treated as industrial products with low rates of *ad valorem* duties.

being imported at lower prices. In trade terms, the use of variable import levies means that no matter how competitive Third Country supplies, the EC's threshold prices normally cannot be undercut. Consequently the EC's domestic producers of these products are protected from all Third Country competition except when market prices rise above threshold prices. The result is that Third Countries are pushed into the role of residual suppliers and denied the possibility of expanding their trade opportunities despite any improvements they may achieve in competitiveness.

For beef, when its support system was being created, a classic variable import levy mechanism was applied. However, due to the difficulty of establishing world beef prices and, hence the difficulty in setting import levies, the system was revised in the mid-1970s so that now import levies are linked also to the relationship of domestic market prices to EC support prices.

Another set of commodities includes wine and fruit and vegetables where, although a full variable import levy system is not applied, neither is the EC content just to rely on the charging of *ad valorem* import duties. Consequently for these 'intermediate' products (in terms of their import treatment) minimum import prices are set which underpin the import duties charged. In so far as Third Countries ship at below these prices, countervailing duties may be charged to bring their prices up to the minimum import price levels. The difference in the operation of the Threshold price/variable import levy and minimum import price/countervailing duty mechanisms was discussed in Chapter 3. In principle, however, minimum import prices are set at levels which, relative to world prices, are generally lower than threshold prices. Minimum import prices seem better thought of as floor prices above which the import duties provide the visible protection. One explanation for this difference may be that, particularly for fruit and vegetables and to a lesser extent wine, prices from Third Countries are subject to sudden, large price movements because of the instability of supply. The minimum import prices provide protection against such swings without setting very high domestic support prices relative to normal world levels.

For the rest of the products covered by the CAP, the EC is content to rely on the charging of *ad valorem* import duties; although, for particular items, these may be set at high levels compared with the EC's industrial duties. As compared with variable import levies, import duties provide a limited, rather than an absolute level of protection, and do not lead to distortions between Third Country suppliers. In so far as Third Countries alter their relative competitiveness this is apparent to the EC consumer as duties do not mask such changes.

A modification of this hierarchy, towards the end of the 1970s, came through the introduction of 'voluntary' restraint arrangements (v.r.a.'s) with some Third Countries for particular commodities. The use of v.r.a.'s by the EC seems to have been a means of avoiding having to go to the GATT to negotiate changes which might otherwise have been felt to be necessary in duty levels. Although v.r.a.'s are not quotas as such, they have much the same effect in so far as quantitative controls are being applied to imports, rather than any attempt to control the volume of imports through the rate of import charge applied.

As a rule, however, the EC does not apply import quotas, as one feature of the creation of the CAP was the elimination of any quotas Member States might have had. The only exceptions to this are first, the treatment of imports from the state trading countries, where the import of many products has not been liberalized and quotas are still applied and second, for certain fresh vegetables—principally tomatoes—where national import restrictions in force before 1970 are permitted still to operate.

Preferential trade concessions

So far the discussion has assumed that the Community applies the same treatment to its imports from all Third Countries. This is not the case in practice as the EC has developed a network of preferential trading relationships, (described in Parry and Hardies, 1981). On prima-facie grounds, such developments are against GATT rules whereby the same import treatment (the 'most-favoured-nation' duty rates) has to be applied to all GATT signatories. Only as part of regional free trade areas, and customs unions, are GATT signatories allowed to grant lower than m.f.n. duty rates to selected countries. Hence at the beginning of the 1970s the EC tried to dress up some of its then preferential arrangements as free trade areas, although manifestly they were not. For example, the agreement to grant preferences to 18 ex-French, Belgian, and Dutch colonies under the Yaounde Convention was justified as 18 separate free trade agreements (Evans, 1971, p. 324).

When the first Community attempt to introduce preferences on citrus fruit from Spain and Israel in 1969 was rejected by the GATT, the EC came back a year later with preferential agreements with Spain and Israel which were claimed to lead to the formation of free-trade areas in due course. That GATT members should be concerned by the EC's network of preferential arrangements is not surprising. There are fears of loss of markets within the EC due to preferential suppliers benefiting from lower, or nil, duty rates.

The EC's preferential trade relations form a definite hierarchy (Table 11.6), with five distinct groupings. The effect of the trade concessions given is to lower very significantly the EC rates of import charge where *ad valorem* duties are applied. For 1976, it has been calculated that on only some 72 per cent of EC imports of agricultural products, where *ad valorem* duties were due, was the full m.f.n. rate of duty paid (Olechowski and Sampson, 1980).

The relative size of the trade magnitudes is consonant with the Community's general policy of applying preferences to developing countries. Only some 5 per cent of the EC's dutiable agricultural imports come from developed countries at preferential rates, although just over half of the EC's total dutiable agricultural imports came from developed countries. Even though most of the preferences were concentrated on developing countries it is noticeable that, even for them, more than half their total exports to the EC of dutiable agricultural items paid full m.f.n. rates. Table 11.7 also confirms the value of the Special Preferences to their recipients (ACP and Mediterranean countries) with an average preferential duty rate of 1.1 per cent, as against the average GSP preferential rate of 8.1 per cent paid by those developing countries not associated with the EC.

The Community is consistent in its treatment of agricultural products on which import concessions are demanded by its Associates. Core commodities (generally protected by variable levies) have the fewest concessions, both

Table 11.6   A hierarchy of EC agricultural trade relations.

Countries	Extent of Trade Concessions
1. The Lomé Convention covering mainly ex-colonies of Community Member States – 63 countries in Africa, the Caribbean and the Pacific (hence the acronym 'ACP states'). Lomé I signed 1975, Lomé II signed 1980. The remaining European dependencies (16 in all) receive equivalent preferential trade arrangements.	Exemption from import duties for *all* industrial and virtually all agricultural products. Some concessions on leviable agricultural products so that levies charged are reduced for cereals, rice, and manufactured foodstuffs. Special import arrangements for sugar, rum, and beef where the concessions are limited in volume by quotas.
2. The Mediterranean Agreements. All the countries of the Mediterranean littoral (except Albania and Libya) are covered, although the agreement with the Lebanon is moribund. Greece and Turkey agreements provide for eventual EC membership – achieved for Greece in 1981. Cyprus and Malta have Association Agreements. The other agreements provide for looser degrees of relationship.	Reduction in import duties on most industrial and agricultural products. Very few concessions on leviable agricultural products. Many of the duty concessions on agricultural products limited by seasonal calendars, quotas and/or minimum import prices.
3. The Generalized Preferences Scheme applies to all developing countries. Introduced in 1971 at the request of UNCTAD.	Exemptions or reduced rates of duty for many industrial and some agricultural products. Very few products sensitive for domestic EC interests covered.
4. *Ad hoc* arrangements. Range of Co-operation Agreements with most important countries or groups of countries in the world, apart from the members of COMECON. Some trade concessions applied for individual countries (New Zealand, Australia, USA): such concessions generally result from bilateral agreements under GATT.	Agreements here may give no trade preferences at all, or only apply them for a few key products for the country(ies) concerned. (Examples include concessions on dairy products and sheepmeat from New Zealand, and 'Hilton' beef from the USA.)
5. The EFTA countries – Iceland, Sweden, Norway, Finland, Austria, Switzerland, and Portugal – which did not join the EC when it was first enlarged in 1973. (Norway negotiated for membership but the entry terms were unacceptable domestically. Portugal has applied for EC membership.)	Virtually complete industrial free trade through North-Western Europe. No agricultural trade concessions, apart from a few minor ones on live cattle from Austria and Switzerland.

Table 11.7   Average *ad valorem* duties paid on those EC agricultural imports in 1976 where duties were applicable.

	Value of imports (US $ bn)	Average duty rate paid (%)
Developed countries not receiving preferences		
Imports at m.f.n. rates	9.0	8.9
Average Import Rate applied		8.9
Developed countries receiving preferences		
Imports at m.f.n. rates	1.6	8.8
Imports at Special Preference rates	1.1	4.4
Average Import Rate applied		7.1
Developing countries receiving preferences		
Imports at m.f.n. rates	5.8	7.3
Imports at Special Preference rates	3.9	1.1
Imports at GSP rates	1.4	8.1
Average Import Rate applied		5.2
Overall total	22.8	6.9

SOURCE   Derived from Olechowski and Sampson (1980, Table 1).

because of their significance for the CAP and because the developing countries associated with the EC are not exporters of most of the products in question. The Community shows an increased willingness to grant concessions as the products become less 'sensitive'—i.e. they are further from the farm-gate because they have been through various processing stages, or the products are not ones of great CAP significance. The result is that the further the products are down the hierarchy of import measures the more likely the EC is to grant import concessions. Again, countries which are at the top of the hierarchy of trading relationships with the EC are more likely to get the trade concessions they want than those lower down. Consequently one would expect to find that the ACP states secure the most concessions including a few variable levy products. By contrast, developing countries with whom the EC has no particular relationship are likely only to get reductions in duty rates on the least important food products entering international trade.

(a) The Lomé Convention

The motives behind the EC's arrangements with its ex-colonies are complex. When the Community was formed Belgium, the Netherlands, and France gave various preferences to imports from their colonies. As these territories became independent, these preferences were maintained on a Community-wide basis under the two consecutive Yaounde Conventions—Yaounde I effective from 1964 and Yaounde II effective from 1971.[16] On the Community's first enlargement it was agreed that equivalent arrangements would be applied to most of the UK's ex-colonies. This was done under the first Lomé Convention, signed in 1975, where because so much of the African Continent was going to be covered, it was decided that any other African countries at an equivalent stage of development also would be allowed to join. Non-African members of the Lomé Convention are mainly islands in the Caribbean and Pacific. The major ex-colonies in Asia—India, Pakistan, Bangladesh, Sri Lanka, Malaysia, Singapore, and Hong Kong which is still a colony—were not allowed to join, however, because it was felt their development needs would be too expensive for the funds the EC was prepared to make available.

The EC's concessions on agricultural products to the ACP states—which were extended slightly in the second Lomé Convention[17] signed in 1979[18]—are far-ranging and in some instances, highly significant for the countries able to take advantage of them. For virtually all agricultural imports where the EC applies *ad valorem* import duties, complete exemption is granted. However, for a few products which are particularly 'sensitive' to domestic EC producers—principally fresh temperate horticultural products and also oranges—concessions are not granted. For items to which CAP import levies apply, limited concessions are made, principally through the removal of the fixed component for processer protection included in the levy applied to processed product imports. This is in fulfilment of the EC's commitment for leviable products to apply to them 'more favourable treatment than the general treatment applicable to the same products originating in Third Countries to which the most-favoured-nation clause applies'. Thus, there are reductions in the levies applied to imports of cereals, rice, and processed cereals and manufactured foodstuffs.

For sugar, beef, bananas, rum, and certain fresh vegetables there are special arrangements for imports from the ACP states. These arrangements cover either leviable products (beef, sugar) or especially sensitive products because of the position of particular sets of producers—either ACP (bananas and rum), or Metropolitan EC (vegetables). In brief these concessions are below. The concessions for beef and sugar are discussed also in the appropriate commodity chapters.

> *Sugar.* A commitment of indefinite duration (i.e. which continues should the Lomé Convention not be renewed at some future date) by the EC to import up to 1.3 million tonnes white sugar equivalent from specified ACP states annually. This cane sugar is imported mainly in the raw state and refined in the EC—principally in the UK. The Community pays a guaranteed price for this sugar within the support price band applicable to its domestic sugar producers. No import levy is applied to this 'preferential' sugar.

Beef. Imports of up to 38 100 tonnes (it was 27 532 tonnes under Lomé I) of fresh, chilled, and frozen beef from Botswana, Kenya, Madagascar, Swaziland, and Zimbabwe are allowed duty free entry and with an abated levy. The EC charges only 10 per cent of its normal levy provided the ACP exporters charge the rest of the EC levy as an export tax.

Bananas. Duty free import into the EC. The position of traditional ACP suppliers has been safeguarded by an EC Declaration that no ACP state will be worse placed in Community markets through the operation of Lomé than prior to its adoption. This is implemented through the EC's Member States applying national licensing systems to their banana imports.

Rum. Duty free entry for a specified annual quantity of ACP rum. The annual quotas are based on the largest annual quantities imported into the EC in the preceding three years increased by a factor of 40 per cent for the UK market and 18 per cent for the rest of the Community.

Fresh vegetables. Reduced rate duty quotas for tomatoes, onions, carrots, and asparagus for limited time periods each year, and reduced duty rates for many other fruit and vegetable items not limited by quotas.

Of the other provisions of the Lomé Convention affecting agriculture/food, by far the most significant are the Stabex arrangements which apply, under Lomé II, to 44 primary commodities. These arrangements provide compensation or soft loans to the ACP States when they suffer a fall in export revenues from these products in EC markets. Certain criteria apply relating to the significance of the product in the exports of the ACP State concerned and the extent of the fall in revenue which is regarded as significant.

(b) The Mediterranean arrangements

The Community's arrangements with the Mediterranean countries present a more complex picture.[19] A set of varied arrangements evolved during the 1960s, but the EC lacked any consistent policy. Thus Greece (1961) and Turkey (1963) secured Association Agreements designed to lead ultimately to full Community membership. The EC was willing to enter into these arrangements as a means of securing the political situation in these countries as well as seeing them as evidence of the Community's international acceptability. Eight more Mediterranean countries signed agreements with the EC in the period 1968–1972. The motives for these agreements were more economic in character, with the Maghreb countries seeking compensation in the wider Community market for the loss of their bilateral concessions in the French market. Other Mediterranean countries were concerned to secure their traditional share of the Community's market in the light of the trade preferences given to their competitors in Greece and Turkey, and their potential competitors in the Yaounde Associates.

The Community, when faced with its first enlargement and the need to extend these agreements to the three new Member States, felt this was the moment to adopt an overall approach to the countries of the Mediterranean Basin by which they would all be eligible for Community aid and receive trade concessions of approximately the same structure and scope. This was the basis of the EC's Global Mediterranean Policy launched in 1972 which took account of the mutual interests of Mediterranean and Community countries in the fields of trade, energy provision and labour movement. However, these agreements—mainly titled Co-operation Agreements—do not envisage eventual Community membership. This is an option only open to the countries of the Northern Mediterranean littoral (i.e. the 'European' Mediterranean).

The Community was faced with difficulties over imported Mediterranean agricultural products competing with its domestic production. For fresh fruit and vegetables, duty reductions are granted as far as possible in the off-season for Community production—as for example, with tomatoes and fresh grapes. Luckily agricultural production on the Northern and Southern shores of the Mediterranean Basin is to some extent complementary because of differences in the timing of production seasons. For processed food items, the duty reductions for 'sensitive' products—e.g. tomato concentrate, fruit salads—are limited by quotas, or 'within a system of self-restraint on quantities exported' (Commission, 1980b, p. 34). For those few CAP leviable products where concessions were granted, mainly the continuance of historic concessions rather than new ones, the concessions 'were adjusted to give them an economic, rather than a commercial value' (Commission, 1980b, p. 34). Thus the levy on olive oil imported into the EC was reduced on condition exports to the EC were subjected to a tax, equivalent to the reduction, in the exporting country. Similarly for wine, the duty reduction was made subject to preferential exports not entering the Community at less than reference prices (i.e. minimum import prices).

The main concessions by country are summarized below.

The Maghreb (Algeria, Morocco, Tunisia). Non-Reciprocal Agreements. Concessions of from 20 to 100 per cent of the duties on fresh and dried vegetables, dates, citrus fruit, apricot pulp, canned fruit, and vegetables. Also reductions in duties on wines (subject to observance of minimum import prices) and in the levies on olive oil.

The Mashraq (Egypt, Lebanon, Jordan, Syria). Non-Reciprocal Agreements. Concessions of from 40 to 80 per cent of the duties on certain products—mainly fresh and dried fruit and vegetables.

Israel. Reciprocal Agreement leading to free trade in due course. Already about 85 per cent of Israel's agricultural exports to the EC are covered. Concessions of from 20 to 80 per cent of the duties on certain products—mainly fresh and preserved fruit and vegetables and fruit juices. Some of the concessions are subject to seasonal calendars, while there is a duty quota for apricot pulp and voluntary restraint ('autolimitation' in EC jargon) for tomato concentrate.

Spain/Portugal. Reciprocal Agreements leading to free trade in due course, although both countries have short-circuited this procedure by applying for full membership of the Community. Concessions of from 25 to 100 per cent on fresh and preserved fruit and vegetables including grapes, tomatoes, and figs. Also a reduction in the levy on olive oil. Several concessions limited by seasonal calendars or duty quotas. At the time of writing the agreement with Spain had expired and was being maintained under a 'standstill' provision.

Turkey. Association Agreement under which all import duties between Turkey and the EC should be removed by 1995. Only a limited number of fruit and vegetable items were covered originally, but the concessions were extended as a result of the Community's decision to revitalize this agreement in 1980. Under the revised agreement the EC is to remove all duties on Turkish agricultural exports by 1987, although for some products quota limitation and/or seasonal calendars will apply.

Cyprus/Malta. Both agreements are meant eventually to lead to customs unions. In their first stages, however, the agreements deal mainly with a limited set of duty reductions, and are overdue for revision.

(c) The Generalized Preferences Scheme

As would be expected the Community has granted the fewest concessions and those of least importance to the developing world at large under its Generalized Preferences Scheme (GSP).[20] There are several reasons for the paucity of agricultural concessions under the GSP. First, that developed country generalized preferences schemes were originally meant by UNCTAD to encourage the industrialization of developing countries. Second, and of particular significance, that the Community's existing associates did not want their preferences in the EC market to be eroded. Third, the perceived need to limit the scope of further agricultural concessions because of domestic producers' complaints about the extent of the existing concessions to the Lomé and Mediterranean associates.

In its review of the GSP, which it suggested should be maintained to the year 2000, the Commission (1980c) made clear there was little scope for expanding its coverage of agricultural products: 'Given the constraints of the common agricultural policy and the need to safeguard opportunities for access for the ACP countries—or, in the case of certain products, opportunities for the Mediterranean countries—and the possibility of the accession of new countries, it would be inappropriate to widen the present product coverage.' The Commission has a commitment to consult countries with Association Agreements before granting any trade concessions to other countries which would adversely affect their interest. This commitment to consult is taken seriously by the Commission, which appears to go to great lengths to avoid upsetting Associates where they have an existing Community trade concession. Greece even had a formal veto included in its Association Agreement over Community changes in CCT rates for raisins, olives, tobacco, and turpentine.[21]

Hence it seems unlikely that the scope of the GSP will be widened significantly for agricultural products from the 322 duty headings included in the 1980 GSP. For these products the preferences consist of duty reductions and/or complete duty suspensions. For the six most sensitive products—soluble coffee, cocoa butter, canned pineapples in slices, canned pineapples other than in slices, raw Virginia type tobacco, raw tobacco other than Virginia—the concessions are limited by quotas. Overall the agricultural concessions under the GSP seem designed to give the maximum appearance of liberality without giving away anything of significance. Thus Community GSP duty reductions tend to be either:

(a) For products which are insignificant in international trade (e.g. frogs' legs), or
(b) Where the product is of more importance, the duty reduction tends to be extremely small (e.g. a reduction of two percentage points in the CCT duty rate of 27 per cent *ad valorem* for natural honey).

(d) Ad Hoc trade concessions

The only other Community trade concessions for agricultural products arise for particular countries as a result of bilateral negotiations. Such concessions, may, or may not, be included in overall trade co-operation agreements with the countries in question. The main items and countries for which such individual arrangements exist are listed below. It is difficult to see any general pattern: the products covered are leviable ones where either the countries in question have persuaded the Community that their dependence on the EC market is such that some form of *ad hoc* arrangement was necessary, or a concession has been granted as a result of negotiations in the GATT.

Products covered	*Country*
(a) *Agreements in GATT*	
1. Beef—frozen: levy-free quota	Argentina, Australia, Brazil, Uruguay
2. Beef—high quality chilled: levy-free quota	Argentina, Australia, Uruguay, USA, Canada
3. Cheeses: reduced levy quota	Australia, Canada, and New Zealand
4. Buffalomeat: levy-free quota	Australia
(b) *Agreements negotiated outside GATT*	
5. Live cattle—specific breeds: reduced duty quota	Austria, Switzerland
6. Calves for fattening: reduced levy quota	Yugoslavia
7. Butter: reduced levy quota	New Zealand
8. Beef—manufacturing quality: reduced levy quotas	Open to approved Third Countries
9. Lamb and mutton: reduced levy quotas with 'voluntary' restraint agreements	All major Third Country suppliers

OTHER ISSUES

So far the CAP's effects for the rest of the world have been discussed in terms of the EC's import arrangements and the share of world markets taken by EC exports. Other issues, however, relate to the EC's use of food aid, the proposals for long term contracts, its position in GATT, and its attitudes towards International Commodity Agreements.

(a) Food aid

The EC has developed a major food aid programme which accounts for a significant proportion of the world's total food aid flows. Pronk (1979) estimated the share by value of the world's three largest food aid donors as being about 58 per cent (the USA), 19 per cent (the EEC), and 10 per cent (Canada) in total world food aid operations during the 1970s.

It is not surprising that other countries with substantial food surpluses of their own, for which sufficient commercial markets could not be found, should have followed the American example and developed food aid programmes. During the 1960s these programmes ostensibly became geared more towards the needs of developing countries and away from the original concept of surplus disposal. Thus the US programme changed its title to 'Food for Peace', while the 1967 Food Aid Convention was created as part of the Kennedy Round of GATT negotiations. (The Convention was novel in that not only was it signed by traditional exporters such as the US, Canada, Australia, and France which had all developed food aid programmes, but also by developed country food importers such as the UK.)

The commitment of donor countries to food aid as a separate and additional source of development assistance having distinctive characteristics, rather than as a means of maximizing grain disposals by operating a multi-tier international grain market with each succeeding rung down involving less commercial content, was strained during the early 1970s. Whereas in 1970/71 total food aid flows of cereals were 12.8 millon tonnes, by 1973/74 they had dropped to 5.7 million tonnes reflecting the rise in world market prices for grain due to the shortages of the 1972 to 1974 period (FAO, 1979a, p. 1–19) and the fact that most countries made Budget provisions for their food aid commitments in financial terms. As world prices rose these provisions were not revised and hence they bought smaller quantities of foodstuffs, just at the time when developing countries were particularly in need of concessionary supplies. World food aid flows of cereals gradually recovered to some 9.5 million tonnes in 1979/80, but the target set at the 1974 World Food Conference of 10 million tonnes of cereals was not achieved by the end of the decade. In 1980 a new Food Aid Convention was signed which involved total pledges of 7.6 million tonnes of cereals, as against 4.2 million tonnes under the 1967 Convention; the presumption being that the increase in pledges should allow the achievement of the 1974 WFC target.

The Community's food aid effort, as distinct from that of individual Member States, started in 1969 with an allocation of 310 000 tonnes of cereals. In 1971 the Food Aid Convention was renewed and the Community and Member States combined undertook a commitment of 1.035 million tonnes of cereals which was raised to 1.287 million tonnes in 1973/74 when the Community first was enlarged. As part of the 1980 Food Aid Convention the share for the Community and the Member States combined was raised to 1.650 million tonnes.

Although the total of Community food aid flows has risen there have been serious disagreements both as to the purposes it was meant to fulfil and the appropriate balance between food aid given directly by the individual EC States and food aid given by the EC acting as a single entity. In particular France has argued that food aid given directly by the individual EC States should not be allowed to drop below the level which prevailed during the 1970s of about 44 per cent of total Community food aid. (In other words, some 56 per cent of EC food aid was given by the Community acting as a whole with the Commission making the arrangements.) The French argument was in part philosophical, concerned with preventing the Commission increasing its role, and in part practical in that French national food aid was a significant part of its total aid disbursements which it did not want to see submerged within the Community total.

In several reports the Commission (1974, 1980d, 1980e, 1981a) has pressed for changes in the EC's food aid programmes so that any link with the concept of surplus disposal was broken. The Commission has attempted to make food aid provision a part of the EC's overall development policy, rather than it being an adjunct to its agricultural policies. In particular it has urged that the legal basis for food aid actions be changed from Article 43 of the Treaty of Rome (concerned with CAP development) to Article 235 (concerned with developing new policies in accord with the Treaty's objectives). In order to make EC food aid of greater value to its recipients the Commission proposed that EC food aid programmes should offer products which are important in developing country diets (e.g. rice, vegetable oils, and sugar) rather than those which it was convenient for the Community to get rid of, i.e. wheat, skimmed milk powder, and butter oil. The Commission also wanted larger volumes of EC food aid: thus during the five years 1976 to 1980 EC food aid flows were fixed at 1.287 million tonnes of cereals, 150 000 tonnes of SMP and 45 000 tonnes of butter oil as compared with requests in 1979 alone for 2.337 million tonnes of cereals, 295 287 tonnes SMP, and 135 895 tonnes butter oil. The Commission has urged also that the EC should make food aid commitments to particular developing countries for a period of years so that the recipients could rely on these levels. This proposal, however, encountered considerable difficulty in the Council of Ministers because it would involve reducing the Council's level of political control over food aid disbursements, as they would not all have to be agreed annually by the Council: however, in 1980, agreement in principle was reached to longer-term food aid commitments. At the beginning of the 1980s the Commission (1981a) was urging a broad policy 'to combat world hunger' involving increased food aid levels, action to help developing countries create coherent food supply strategies, help for regional programmes to improve tropical agricultural production and measures to improve external food security (e.g. through the creation of an international food security reserve), and being prepared to make food supplies available on a long term contractual basis to those developing countries requesting them.

(b) Long term supply contracts

The issue of long term supply contracts has been one supported by the major agricultural exporting countries of the EC, and resisted by those countries which are not large exporters and hence would get little benefit from such a policy but would have to contribute towards the Budget costs involved. The Community attempted to introduce multiannual agricultural supply contracts in 1974. Three importing countries—Egypt, Iran, and Morocco—were particularly interested (Iran and Morocco only for sugar), but lost interest when it turned out that the EC was unable to guarantee a fixed price, and that its sale prices would not be significantly under world levels.

In 1981 the Commission revived the idea as a means of increasing EC agricultural exports against the competition from other exporters to world markets. The Commission claimed (1981b) that other exporters had available facilities—such as buffer stocks, credit facilities, long term agreements, export promotion funds—which the EC lacked and hence Community exports were hampered. Although keen interest in the proposal was expressed by Morocco, Tunisia, Algeria, and Egypt, it became clear according to the Commission (1982) that these countries wanted their supplies at preferential prices. As the Commission had promised the Council of Ministers that there would not be any extra Budget expenditure as a result of the introduction of such long term contracts, the scope for them seemed limited.

(c) International commodity agreements

The EC has a clear philosophical position towards the negotiation of international commodity agreements (ICAs) which is generally supportive. Thus the Commission (1981c, p. 29) said that ICAs should be supported where this was appropriate as a means of 'aiming at stable prices which are remunerative over a longer period for producers and equitable for consumers'. In practice, EC attitudes are more complex and related to the circumstances of each ICA.

In the agriculture and food area, up to 1982 there had been four major ICAs which had operated for varying lengths of time covering sugar, coffee, cocoa, and wheat, although agreements for olive oil and rubber were signed in 1979. The EC was a member of the coffee and cocoa agreements as an importer whose interests roughly paralleled those of other importers. For wheat, the EC as a major exporter was interested in a successful agreement as a means of stabilizing (and raising?) world prices with, hopefully, consequent savings for the EC

Budget on the cost of export refunds. Problems arose with the other main exporters of wheat as to the appropriate price bands within which they should try to stabilize world prices, and shares of world stocks which each exporter should be prepared to hold. For the International Sugar Agreement the EC has appeared at its most cynical. It was not willing to join either the 1968 or the 1977 ISAs primarily because it was not given a large enough export quota. Yet, when ISA member countries were restricting their exports to the world market in 1978 and 1979, in an effort to raise world prices from the very depressed levels to which they had sunk, the EC expanded its exports to the world market so in effect increasing its share at the expense of the other major exporters.[22] It should be recognized, however, that the EC did co-operate with members of the ISA in 1981/82 in attempting to control supplies to the world market.

The general feature of the EC's attitude to ICAs for agricultural products is that, while in principle it supports them, it has difficulties when its own interests are heavily involved as an exporter of CAP products. For products where the EC is an importer it has fewer problems, except the traditional one of developed country importers relating to the price level at which imports can be obtained.

(d) The General Agreement on Tariffs and Trade (GATT)

The GATT[23] has been a significant factor in the CAP's development because, at least for the developed world, trade disagreements are generally pursued through GATT channels if bilateral discussions have failed.

Ironically the Community's creation of the CAP in its current form, with its use of variable import levies and export refunds as its principal agricultural trade measures, was only possible as a result of earlier actions by, principally, the USA. Thus, in 1955 the US achieved a formal waiver from GATT provisions so that it could continue to use import quotas and fees to the extent necessary to prevent material interference with its domestic agricultural support programmes, so legitimizing the primacy of such programmes over international trade obligations. Then, in 1958, the USA was foremost among those countries which refused to endorse an absolute prohibition on the use of export subsidies. As a result, GATT allowed export subsidies to continue to be used for primary products, subject to the condition that they did not allow a country 'more than an equitable share of world trade' (Article XVI of the GATT). Hence the EC has been able to use export refunds as a principal CAP policy instrument.

Since the CAP support mechanisms were first devised at the beginning of the 1960s there have been endless rounds of bilateral discussions as to their effect. These discussions in turn have been caught up in three rounds of multilateral negotiations in the GATT—the Dillon Round (1960/61), the Kennedy Round (1964/67), and the Tokyo Round (1973/79).

The discussions in the Dillon Round, as far as the CAP was concerned, were concentrated on negotiating compensation for traditional agricultural exporters to the EC for the CAP's creation. The compensation, under GATT's Article XXIV(6), was necessary because duty rates for agricultural items bound under

GATT by individual Member States were altered by the move to a single Community duty and the switch from duties to variable import levies—a switch which was expected to lead to a reduction in agricultural exports to the EC. The US tried to obtain compensation by securing guaranteed access for its existing export level, but this was refused. In the event 'completing the Dillon Round and thereby not impeding the progress of the Community was judged to be more important than resolving the agricultural issue, so the United States and the EEC formally agreed that America had unsatisfied negotiating rights.' (Warley, 1976, p. 379). These were embodied in standstill agreements relating to the position as at 1 September 1960 for wheat, maize, rice, sorghum, and poultry.

The US and other agricultural exporters, however, did achieve what have turned out to be extremely important concessions—even if not full compensation—in the binding of EC duty rates at low or zero levels for manioc, oilseeds, and oilseed products, and at 20 per cent *ad valorem* for sheepmeat. It is the fact that these duties have been bound in GATT which has prevented the Community from raising them, despite domestic political pressures to do so.

It was the value of the bilateral standstill agreements which was tested by the US in the so-called 'chicken war'. The US had built up a thriving trade in the export of chickens to West Germany. Prior to the introduction of the Community's levy and sluice-gate price system in July 1962, West Germany applied a bound rate of duty of 15 per cent to US poultry exports. The introduction of the levy at a much higher level threatened US exports. Following the arbitration of an independent GATT panel the US withdrew concessions on an equivalent volume of EC exports—potato starch, light trucks valued at over $1,000, high priced brandy (i.e. cognac), and dextrine. The products were chosen to hurt the EC countries, and leave relatively unscathed other trading partners. As the Curzons have commented 'this compensation was intended to be symbolic only, because the US poultry producers could in no way gain from the fact that Volkswagen buses and French cognac had become more expensive on the US market' (Curzon and Curzon, 1976, p. 212).

'In terms of pre-Kennedy Round negotiating tactics, the United States had made its point that it still expected to receive compensation for the loss of its agricultural "rights" due to the erection of the CAP' (Curzon and Curzon, 1976, p. 213). Indeed, agriculture was at the centre of the Kennedy Round with the US and the other principal temperate agricultural exporters attempting to apply an equivalent liberalization of world agricultural trade as had been achieved for industrial trade. Although this concept was seen principally in terms of negotiating access to the EC for grains, progress was limited—in part because of the Community's difficulty in agreeing a negotiating mandate as for many important agricultural products (dairy products, beef, sugar, fruit, and vegetables) CAP support regimes were not agreed until July 1966. Progress was limited also by misunderstandings of each others' positions by the US and EC (Evans, 1971, p. 270). Principally, however, progress was limited by the traditional and widespread use throughout the world of non-duty measures for import protection in the agricultural sector (which are always more difficult to negotiate than duties) plus the fact that many of these measures were an essential part of domestic support programmes and hence could not be negotiated meaningfully unless countries were prepared to negotiate their domestic support policies, which they were not. Thus the EC proposal to reduce to a common denominator all governmental support measures and to bind this 'margin of support' (known as the *montant de soutien*) was rejected by the temperate agricultural exporters, ostensibly because it would not mean a reduction in agricultural protection and hence no increase in access, but principally because they were not prepared to 'negotiate major elements of their domestic support policies, an inherent consequence of their acceptance of the applicability to themselves of the "montant de soutien' and the self-sufficiency ratio proposals' (Warley, 1976, p. 385). The self-sufficiency proposal was put forward by the grain exporters as a means of securing access guarantees, but one which foundered because of the high levels demanded by the EEC and the UK, at 90 per cent and 75 per cent respectively.

The most important agricultural achievement, at least potentially, of the Kennedy Round was the negotiation of the 1967 International Grains Agreement (IGA) which raised floor prices for wheat, as a successor to the then eighteen-year-old International Wheat Agreement. Linked to the IGA was the signing of a Food Aid Convention concerned with making available 4.2 million tonnes of grain annually for the developing world. The Community was interested in the IGA both as a means of spreading the cost of food aid among as many donors as possible, and as a means of raising world grain prices, so reducing the cost of export subsidies—reasons shared also by the world's other major grain exporters. Additionally, as Preeg (1970, p. 155) points out, 'the Community hoped to gain its trading partners' acceptance of its farm policy'. In the event, the IGA was stillborn as world market prices fell below the agreed minimum levels in 1968. But the IGA's successful negotiation, plus various agricultural duty concessions, allowed the appearance of success to be claimed for the agricultural part of the Kennedy Round and thus allowed the important results of the industrial negotiations to be implemented. The EC had defended successfully the CAP, the development of which had been continuing throughout the Kennedy Round, while the US had avoided legitimizing the CAP and its variable levy provisions and had secured higher floor prices for wheat in the IGA. But it had failed in its primary objective of increasing its share of the Community's market for agricultural products.

During the 1970s, the emphasis in GATT discussions turned towards the growing impact of the 'new protectionism', characterized by the expanded use of non-duty restrictions on trade, the granting of government aids to domestic industries and attempts to 'organize' world trade for products where imports were causing particular problems, all features which were already to be found in world agricultural trade. By 1977, GATT was warning that the spread of protectionist measures 'had reached a point at which the continued existence of an international order based on agreed and observed rules may be said to be open to question' (GATT, 1977, p. 22). Not surprisingly, the focus of the Tokyo Round was concerned with attempting to control the spread of non-duty import measures and to strengthen the GATT with codes of conduct which are meant to guide world trade.

Agriculture was again a key sector in the Tokyo Round as it had been in the preceding Kennedy Round, with the agricultural exporters trying to increase their access to the EC's market and attempting to bring international agricultural trade under the same disciplines as industrial trade: in other words, a continuation of their Kennedy Round objectives. By the same token, the EC was concerned to defend the CAP and to prevent the efficacy of its import control measures being weakened. The Community's negotiating mandate said that the CAP's 'principles and mechanisms shall not be called into question and therefore do not constitute a matter for negotiation' (discussed in Harris, 1977, p. 7). The EC, however, maintained its support for international commodity agreements as mechanisms for managing international agricultural trade—both as a means of stabilizing and raising world prices, so reducing the CAP's political exposure and the cost of export subsidies. Developments during the 1970s, however, meant that the general GATT preoccupation with non-duty barriers and the conduct of international trade were also important in the agricultural negotiations.

Thus, on the one hand, traditional agricultural exporters saw the Tokyo Round negotiating group on non-duty barriers as the arena to control the EC's use of export subsidies in order to protect their own traditional export markets. For example, the US claimed to have lost its traditional export market for malt in Japan to EC exports, as did Australia with its traditional export market for wheat flour in Sri Lanka. The Community, on the other hand, was concerned to clarify when countries could use countervailing duties, claiming that the US, in particular, was short-circuiting GATT procedures in not proving material injury to its domestic producers before applying countervailing duties. The EC had seen the US apply countervailing duties to its exports of beef (1976), and had only averted their application to its cheese exports (1976) and canned ham exports (1975) by reducing the levels of export subsidy it granted on sales to the US market.

Other EC non-duty actions which the temperate agricultural exporters were able to cite during the Tokyo Round were two important *ad hoc* decisions which appeared to have been taken solely in response to domestic considerations. These were the three-year beef import ban (1974 to 1977) and the 1976 scheme for soya imports whereby special deposits had to be lodged which were released only when a set amount of Community milk powder had been bought from intervention stocks.

The results of the Tokyo Round for international agricultural trade were as limited as they had been in the Kennedy Round. No changes were made in countries' domestic support policies, while the attempts to introduce international commodity agreements were only partially successful. (The negotiations for three linked agreements on coarse grains, wheat and food aid failed—although that for food aid was signed separately subsequently—while agreements on dairy products and beef were successfully concluded essentially because these were little more than discussion groups.) Various bilateral trade concessions were reached between the EC and the major temperate agricultural exporters which, although not of major importance, enabled a limited degree of success to be claimed for the agricultural negotiations including a final settlement of the 'chicken war'.[24] Enough was achieved however, for the then Agricultural Commissioner to claim that the CAP and its international ramifications were accepted by the other major trading nations as they realized the CAP was 'a necessary pre-requisite' of the Community's 'free market for industrial goods' (Gundelach, 1979). More important, potentially, were the agreements reached in the non-duty measures negotiating group which tightened up the GATT codes on dumping and the use of countervailing duties.

EC AGRICULTURAL RELATIONS WITH THIRD COUNTRIES

A convenient method for examining the trade issues raised by the CAP is to look at EC relations with groups of countries classified by their main type of agricultural production. Three broad categories are used according to whether countries are predominantly temperate, Mediterranean, or tropical zone agricultural producers.

(a) Temperate zone agricultural producers

This grouping covers mainly developed countries in Europe,[25] North America, and Oceania. Included are such major agricultural exporters as Australia, Canada, New Zealand, South Africa, and the USA. It is convenient also to include two developing countries—Argentina and Brazil—on the grounds that the majority of their farm exports would be classed as temperate zone agricultural products.

The commodities in question—cereals, dairy products, and meats—are among the CAP's core products. As a consequence import mechanisms at the frontier are variable import levies, levels of protection are relatively high and trade concessions extremely few. It is not surprising therefore that the majority of the complaints about the CAP's trade effects have come from the countries listed above.

As all the countries in question are GATT members, problems with the EC's agricultural trade policies tend to be voiced in the GATT, and its mechanisms to be used for discussions and dispute settlement. The history of EC discussions in the GATT over the CAP's effects has been outlined above. In summary the traditional complaint about the CAP has been that its variable import levy mechanism created a trade barrier which was impossible to surmount, and that as a result access to the EC's domestic market was unduly restricted.

It is pertinent to point out, however, that Third Country experience with the CAP has varied according to the mix of commodities exported. Although the

Table 11.8   Australian exports to the EC ('9') of certain agricultural products.
(1000 tonnes).

	1965/66	1975/76	1977/78
Sugar	461	64	29*
Wheat	693	73	0
Beef	92	14	19
Butter	64	24	0
Cheese	11	0.4	0
Canned fruits	113	42	31
Fresh apples and pears	164	54	28

* Re-exported to the world market.
SOURCE   Department of the Special Trade Representative (1979).

CAP has raised levels of EC self-sufficiency for many products, the increased livestock numbers in the EC have created an enlarged market for maize and soya beans which could not be fully supplied domestically because of climatic limitations. The USA, as the world's principal exporter of both maize and soya, has gained from this. Australia, however, suffered badly as many of its traditional exports to the UK were displaced (Table 11.8) as the effects of EC-accession led the UK to re-orientate its import sources and to grow more domestically.

Over time some of the heat seems to have been taken out of the access issue, not necessarily because Third Countries have so much accepted these results as because they have had little success in attempting to persuade the EC to alter its CAP mechanisms. It is one thing, however, when the EC raises its own domestic self-sufficiency and quite another where the EC has gone beyond this to emerge as a major exporter for temperate zone agricultural products. In the former case, while Third Countries may not like the results, there seems to be a general acceptance of a country's right to follow its own domestic support policies for agriculture. In the latter case, however, with the EC emerging as a major exporter (Table 11.9) Third Countries have complained that the EC's systematic use of export refunds has enabled it to increase its share of world markets at the expense of more traditional exporters—countries which in most cases provide a far lower level of protection to their producers than does the EC. At the time of writing the issue of the use of export subsidies, and what constitutes an equitable share of world markets, seems likely to be the most important issue in Third Country agricultural trade relations with the EC in the 1980s and one that is likely to provide a major test of the code on dumping and countervailing duties agreed as part of the Tokyo Round of GATT negotiations.

The sensitivity of agricultural exporters to the Community's use of export refunds was illustrated in 1980 when the Community was finalizing its sheep-meat regime. One of the principal concerns of Australia and New Zealand was that the Community might use its export refund mechanisms to dump on the

Table 11.9   EC '9' significance as a world exporter for particular commodities.

	EC exports‡	World exports	EC as % of world
Sugar* (million tonnes raw value)			
1976	1.174§	15.553	7.5
1978	3.321	17.443	19.0
1980	4.233	19.473	21.7
Beef (million tonnes carcass weight equivalent)			
1978	0.178	2.778†	6.4
1980	0.650	2.659†	24.4
Wheat and wheat flour (million tonnes)			
1976/77	3.900§	61.800	6.3
1978/79	7.800	71.200	11.0
1980/81	13.000	93.000	14.0
Butter			
1975			16.0
1979			62.0
Skimmed milk powder			
1975			32.0
1979			61.0
Cheese			
1975			34.0
1979			41.0

* Net exports to the 'free' market.
† Total of exports from the world's seven principal exporters.
‡ Excluding intra-Community trade.
§ Community crop production in 1976 was depressed.
SOURCE   House of Lords (1981, p. xx).

world market any increase in production caused by the regime. At one stage Australia threatened to withdraw substantial volumes of industrial trade from the Community unless it was given satisfactory assurances about EC export policy.[26] The issue was settled only by the EC pledging that any subsidized EC sheepmeat exports 'shall take place only at prices and under conditions which comply with existing international obligations and in respect of traditional shares of the Community in world export trade'.[27]

The EC's emergence as a major sugar exporter—shown in Table 11.9—has caused particular difficulties with other sugar exporters. In 1978 Australia and Brazil made separate complaints about the EC's use of export subsidies[28] to take an inequitable share of world markets. After four years, during which a GATT ruling had been secured that EC exports depressed world prices, but not that Australian and Brazilian exports had been displaced, the original complaints were replaced in 1982 by one composite complaint from ten of the world's sugar exporters about the EC's use of export subsidies for sugar. At the same time the USA lodged its own complaint in GATT not only about the EC's use of export subsidies on sugar, but on five other products as well.

(b) Mediterranean zone agricultural producers

The products principally covered in this categorization are fruit and vegetables, olive oil, durum wheat, tobacco, and wine. In CAP terms these are products where, apart from wine and olive oil, EC self-sufficiency is lower than for the temperate zone agricultural products. CAP import mechanisms for these products tend to be 'intermediate', based on *ad valorem* import duties underpinned by minimum import prices.

On imports, the Community has found it easier to be generous in its trade concessions because of the complementarity between agricultural production in the Mediterranean Basin and within the EC. Thus, through the use of seasonal calendars for duty concessions (so that duty rates rise at times when EC domestic production is important), and duty concessions bounded by quotas, some of the aspirations of the Mediterranean countries have been met. Hence the EC's problems in this area are the potential ones arising from the EC's second enlargement to include Greece, Spain, and Portugal. The result of enlargement is likely to be an increase in the Community of Twelve's self-sufficiency rates for many Mediterranean products, through the expansion in production which can be expected in the three new Member States as they adjust to the CAP. The FAO (1979b, p. 129) concluded that 'Third Country suppliers including those with preferential agreements will almost inevitably see their market shares decline. This will particularly affect suppliers in the Mediterranean Basin and developing countries in various regions, including both present suppliers to the EEC and those countries that could have hoped to develop a share of the market over the years ahead'. The problem, probably, will be most acute in relation to olive oil. Estimates within the EC suggest it will have an annual surplus of around 200 000 tonnes and be responsible for most of the world's production.

In this context, the Mediterranean countries have fears not only about the potential increase in EC self-sufficiency, but also of quite how much value their trade concessions may turn out to be in the future. Whether the EC can maintain its existing trade concessions, or whether its new members will press for them to be reduced, will obviously be a key feature in trade relations with Mediterranean countries.

Of course, the countries of the Mediterranean Basin are not the only producers of Mediterranean zone agricultural products. Thus the US is a major exporter of citrus fruit, dried fruit, and nuts. However, it is extremely unlikely that the EC will grant any trade concessions on these products to the US. While this may not be all that serious for the USA, it may be of significance for other countries which have the resources necessary to emerge as exporters of Mediterranean zone agricultural products (e.g. Kenya) but whose potential is reduced because of the comprehensive nature of the EC's import protection.

(c) Tropical zone agricultural producers

Exporters of tropical zone agricultural products are almost entirely developing countries. As the EC is not itself a significant producer of such items it has been able to take a relatively relaxed attitude in its treatment of their products. Consequently the standard import measure is an *ad valorem* duty which is waived for the ACP States. The effect is to discriminate between developing countries as non-ACP States are given very few concessions under the GSP, because the EC does not want to dilute the preferential position of the ACP states within its market.

The CAP has created trade opportunities for some non-ACP developing countries, because of the trade distorting effects of the cereals regime. The result has been to encourage the production of manioc in Thailand, China, and Indonesia for export to the EC. Indeed so successful have these countries been in developing this export trade that the EC has felt compelled to negotiate voluntary restraint agreements with them to prevent EC produced cereals being displaced from compound animal feeds.

On the export side the effects of the CAP for the countries under consideration are mixed. The EC is a significant provider of food aid, while its export surpluses and use of export refunds hold down world prices for staple foodstuffs—in particular cereals. The effects for developing countries, however, are not unambiguous.

World prices cheaper than they otherwise would be help food importers in the short run. At the same time the incentive is reduced for them to develop their own production of basic foodstuffs necessary to improve food security. It was a key recommendation of the Brandt Commission (1980, p. 103) that developing countries must expand their ability to feed themselves from their own resources—a theme familiar from the World Food Council. Hence although the EC can claim it is helping to feed people in developing countries, it would appear the EC is reducing the incentive for them to improve their own self-sufficiency in basic foodstuffs.

NOTES

1. The distinction between a full foreign policy, which would include defence and political relations, and the EC's external policies is discussed in Henig (1971).
2. Articles 3(b), 111 to 116 and 238 on the Common Commercial Policy, and Articles 3(k), and 131 to 136 on the Association of non-European countries and territories having special relations with the EC Member States.
3. The Treaty of Rome (Article 116) specifies that the EC should act as a single entity within 'the framework of international organisations of an economic character'.
4. Generally goods classified under Chapters 25 to 99 of the CCT.
5. Article 110 of the Treaty of Rome specifies '... the harmonious development of world trade' as its objective.
6. A phrase used by GATT to describe the spread of special support measures for industries under pressure and the use of non-duty barriers to trade. As a result of the reduction in levels of protection available from import duties, because of the cuts in their levels due to the successive rounds of GATT duty negotiations, countries have turned to such devices as special assistance schemes of national subsidies for industries in trouble and the application of 'voluntary' export restraints (v.e.r.'s) to imports from Third Countries. The 'new protectionism' is discussed by, among others, Blackhurst *et al.* (1977), Nowzad (1978), and Balassa (1978), while the use of non-duty measures in international agricultural trade is surveyed by Hillman (1978).

7. Goods classified under Chapters 1 to 24 of the CCT.

8. Article 20—governing the use of the 'Safeguard Clause'—from the basic cereals regulation (Regulation (EEC) No. 2727/75).

9. The only significant exceptions are potatoes, ethyl alcohol, and cork for which CAP market regimes had not been introduced at the time of writing.

10. There is the suspicion that the EC applied these import subsidies not so much because the Community had a deficit of sugar in that year, but because the UK referendum on continuing Community membership was to be held in June 1975 and there was a need to present the CAP in the best possible light.

11. Although presented in index form, the figures in Table 11.3 are derived from trade data valued in current United States dollars; thus the doubling of the figures partly represents the inflation of the period. Another consequence is that relative price movements distort the picture: if the price of EC agricultural exports has been rising at a faster rate than the price of EC agricultural imports then this will be reflected in the indices. Despite these problems the general conclusions are clear enough that EC agricultural imports have declined in terms of total world trade in agricultural products, while the importance of EC agricultural exports has tended to increase.

12. The 'small country' assumption used in Chapter 3 is unlikely to hold for most commodities. As a result the EC's activities will tend to reduce world prices and hence to improve the terms of trade which the EC might face as an importer, but to worsen them where the EC is an exporter. How significant these effects are leads to a wide diversity of opinion among economists, especially as with other developed (and developing) countries following protectionist policies, it would involve the need to disentangle the effects of the CAP from the support policies followed by Japan or the USA. Both Johnson (1973, p. 142) and Josling (1980, p. 26) concluded that the effects of developed country agricultural support policies for world cereal prices were not all that significant. But for dairy products, sugar and perhaps rice, Johnson (1973, p. 159) felt that world prices had been seriously distorted by such policies. GATT (1979, p. 32) concluded that 'the Community system for granting refunds on sugar exports and its application had contributed to depress world sugar prices in recent years. . .'.

13. See Johnson (1975) and Josling (1977b).

14. Josling (1977b) was concerned with a world in which all countries pursued such policies, and concluded that—in the context of the model—there was no reason to suppose that there would be a determinate world market price or traded quantity unless, for example, somebody sensitive to price were to perform a stockholding role.

15. 'Worked' cereals are the products of what is termed first-stage processing where their essential nature has not been changed, e.g. flaked maize, rolled barley, crushed oats.

16. At their inception there was the need to compensate the countries involved for the loss of bilateral preferences on individual Member States' markets due to the creation of the Common External Tariff. Other motives have become of greater importance during the 1960s and 1970s. These can best be summed up in the phrase 'enlightened self-interest'. The EC needs good relations with these countries as significant markets for its exports of manufactures and as reliable sources of supply for many of the raw materials needed by the EC's processing industries. The need for security of supply has become an important influence in EC behaviour since the world commodity boom of 1973 and the success of OPEC as an exporters' cartel in the 1970s.

17. For a review of the agricultural issues involved when Lomé II was renegotiated, see Harris et al. (1978). The most comprehensive texts of the Lomé Conventions I and II are those published by the UK Government as they include certain Declarations and Statements not given in the Community versions, see Foreign and Commonwealth Office (1975 and 1980). A wide literature has grown up on the Community's

Association Agreements and the Lomé Convention, including Matthews (1977), Twitchett (1976), and Frey-Wouters (1980).

18. The chronology of these arrangements is confusing:

	Date of signature	Date of entry into force
Yaounde I	20.7.63	1.6.64
Yaounde II	29.7.69	1.1.71
Lomé I	28.2.75	1.4.76
Lomé II	31.10.79	1.1.81

Despite the apparent gap between the successive five-year agreements, the trade provisions have been maintained on a continuous basis using interim trade decisions when necessary.

19. The best study of the Community's Mediterranean arrangements is to be found in Tovias (1977).
20. Tulloch (1975) analyses the political and economic forces leading to the particular shape of the Community's GSP.
21. For more on this, see Harris *et al.* (1978, p. 20).
22. The issue of the EC's attitude to the 1977 International Sugar Agreement is discussed in Harris (1980).
23. For the most comprehensive and invaluable analysis of GATT's involvement in the development of agricultural trade issues up to the end of the Kennedy Round, see Warley (1976). For a detailed comparison of US and EEC negotiating stances on agricultural trade issues in the Tokyo Round, see Harris (1977); while for a discussion of the wider setting of world agricultural trade and the Tokyo Round, see Josling (1977a).
24. The EC agreed to alter the coefficients used for calculating import levies for turkeys so that, in effect, entry prices were cut by 17 per cent for drumsticks, 13 per cent for thighs, and 3 per cent for breasts.
25. The countries of the Soviet block would also be included.
26. Action threatened included the diversion away from the Community of up to A$1 billion (about £500 million) of Australian purchases of EC industrial products. Prominent among the contracts threatened with cancellation was one for the purchase of four European Airbus aeroplanes valued at A$200 million (about £100 million)—an action seen particularly as hurtful to France, which Australia appeared to have identified as its key opponent over the CAP. See *The Financial Times* (1980).
27. It is significant that Australia insisted that a further paragraph be added to the EC's export policy undertaking for sheepmeat to ensure that no breach of the GATT subsidy code occurred, by referring to the interpretation of the undertaking 'in a manner consistent with Article 16 of the GATT. . .' *Agra Europe* (1980).
28. The EC views its use of export refunds as a mechanism to place its exporters in the position they would have been in had they not had to pay the EC's high domestic prices. Third Countries, however, tend to view the EC's use of export refunds as export subsidies which allow it to dispose of artificially produced surpluses on world markets at their expense. For further discussion see House of Lords (1981, p. xiii).

REFERENCES

Agra Europe (1980) Issue dated 3 October, Tunbridge Wells.

Balassa, B. (1978) 'The "new protectionism" and the international economy', *Journal of World Trade Law*, **12**.

Blackhurst, R., Marian, N., and Tumlir, J. (1977) *Trade Liberalisation, Protectionism and Interdependence*, Studies in International Trade No. 5, GATT: Geneva.

The Brandt Commission (1980) *North-South: a Programme for Survival*, Pan Books: London.

Commission of the European Communities (1974) *Memorandum on Food Aid Policy of the European Economic Community*, COM (74) 3000, Brussels.

Commission of the European Communities (1976) *The Agricultural Situation in the Community: 1975 Report*, Brussels.

Commission of the European Communities (1977) *Practical Guide to the Use of the European Communities' Scheme of Generalised Tariff Preferences*, Brussels.

Commission of the European Communities (1980a) *The Agricultural Situation in the Community: 1980 Report*, Brussels.

Commission of the European Communities (1980b) *EEC Agriculture: The World Dimension*, Newsletter on the Common Agricultural Policy, No. 167, Brussels.

Commission of the European Communities (1980c) *Guidelines for the European Community's Scheme for Generalised Tariff Preferences for the post-1980 period*, COM (80) 104, Brussels.

Commission of the European Communities (1980d) *Communication from the Commission to the Council concerning Participation by the Community in the Food Aid Convention*, COM (80) 167, Brussels.

Commission of the European Communities (1980e) *Food Aid: Communication from the Commission to the Council*, COM (80) 478, Brussels.

Commission of the European Communities (1981a) *Commission Communication to the Council concerning a Plan of Action against World Hunger*, COM (81) 560, Brussels.

Commission of the European Communities (1981b) *Negotiation of Framework Agreements relating to the Multiannual Supply of Agricultural Products*, COM (81) 429, Brussels.

Commission of the European Communities (1981c) *Community Policy for the North-South Dialogue*, COM (81) 68, Brussels.

Commission of the European Communities (1982a) *The Agricultural Situation in the Community: 1981 Report*, Brussels.

Commission of the European Communities (1982b) *Recommendation for a Council Decision on the Directives to be followed in Negotiations with certain Third Countries on the Framework Agreements relating to Multiannual Supply of Agricultural Products*, COM (82) 73, Brussels.

Curzon, G., and Curzon, V. (1976) 'The Management of Trade Relations in GATT', in A. Shonfield (ed.), *International Economic Relations in the Western World 1959–1971*, Vol. 1, Royal Institute of International Affairs/Oxford University Press: London.

Department of the Special Trade Representative (1979) *Annual Report 1978/79*, Canberra.

Evans, J. (1971) *The Kennedy Round in American Trade Policy*, Harvard University Press: Massachusetts.

The Financial Times (1980) Issues dated 21 July and 13 August, London.

Food and Agriculture Organization (1979a) *The State of Food and Agriculture 1978*, Rome.

Food and Agriculture Organization (1979b) *Commodity Review and Outlook: 1979–80*, Rome.

Foreign and Commonwealth Office (1975) *ACP–EEC Convention of Lomé*, Cmnd. 6220, HMSO: London.

Foreign and Commonwealth Office (1980) *The Second ACP/EEC Convention*, Cmnd. 7895, HMSO: London.

Frey-Wouters, E. (1980) *The European Community and the Third World*, Praeger Publishers: New York.

Garland, R. V. (1978) *Some Thoughts on Developments in the International Trading System: an Australian Perspective*, Address to the Trade Policy Research Centre: London.

General Agreement on Tariffs and Trade (1977) *International Trade 1976/77*, Geneva.

General Agreement on Tariffs and Trade (1979) *European Communities—Refunds on Exports of Sugar: Complaint by Australia*, Report of the Panel, L/4833, Geneva.

Gundelach, F. (1979) Speech at 1979 Cologne Food Fair, reported in *Agra Europe*, issue dated 14 September, Tunbridge Wells.

Harris, S. (1975) *The CAP and the World Commodity Scene*, Occasional Paper No. 1, CEAS: Wye College.

Harris, S. (1977) *EEC Trade Relations with the USA in Agricultural Products: Multilateral Tariff Negotiations*, Occasional Paper No. 3, CEAS: Wye College.

Harris, S. (1980) 'US and EEC policy attitudes compared towards the 1977 International Sugar Agreement', *Journal of Agricultural Economics*, **31**.

Harris, S., Parris, K., Ritson, C., and Tollens, E. (1978) *The Renegotiation of the ACP–EEC Convention of Lomé with special reference to agricultural products*, Commonwealth Economic Papers No. 12, The Commonwealth Secretariat: London.

Henig, S. (1971) *External Relations of the European Community—Association and Trade Agreements*, European Series No. 19, Chatham House/PEP: London.

Hillman, J. (1978) *Non-Tariff Agricultural Trade Barriers*, University of Nebraska Press: Lincoln.

House of Lords Select Committee on the European Communities (1981) *Agricultural Trade Policy*, Session 1981–82, 2nd Report, HL 29, HMSO: London.

Johnson, D. G. (1973) *World Agriculture in Disarray*, Fontana/Collins: London.

Johnson, D. G. (1975) 'World Agriculture, Commodity Policy, and Price Variability', *American Journal of Agricultural Economics*, **57**, 823–828.

Josling, T. E. (1977a) *Agriculture in the Tokyo Round Negotiations*, TPRC: London.

Josling, T. E. (1977b) 'Government Price Policies and the Structure of International Agricultural Trade', *Journal of Agricultural Economics*, **28**, 261–276.

Josling, T. E. (1980) *Developed Country Agricultural Policies and Developing Country Supplies: The Case of Wheat*, Research Report No. 14, IFPRI: Washington.

Matthews, J. (1977) *Association System of the European Community*, Praeger Publishers: New York.

Nowzad, B. (1978) *The Rise in Protectionism*, IMF: Washington.

Olechowski, A., and Sampson, G. (1980) 'Current Trade Restrictions in the EEC, the United States and Japan', *Journal of World Trade Law*, **14**, No. 3.

Parry, A., and Hardies, E. (1981) *EEC Law*, Sweet & Maxwell: London.

Preeg, Ernest (1970) *Traders and Diplomats*, Brookings Institution: Washington.

Pronk, F. (1979) 'Food Aid', in Tracy, M. and Hodac, I. (eds.), *Prospects for Agriculture in the EEC*, College of Europe: Bruges.

Tovias, A. (1977) *Tariff Preferences in Mediterranean Diplomacy*, Macmillan: London.

Tulloch, P. (1975) *The Politics of Preferences*, Overseas Development Institute/Croom Helm: London.

Twitchett, K. (1976) *Europe and the World—the external relations of the Common Market*, Europa Publications: London.

Warley, T. K. (1976) 'Western Trade in Agricultural Products', in A. Shonfield (ed.), *International Economic Relations in the Western World 1959–1971*, Vol. 1, Royal Institute of International Affairs/Oxford University Press: London.

Chapter 12

Food Legislation

In 1824 in Pennsylvania, George Rapp, a native of Württemberg, founded one town called Harmony and another called Economy. The subsequent history of economists is well enough known. The Harmonists appear to have lived in almost total obscurity until life was breathed into them by the Treaty of Rome.[1]

Few activities of the European Community have led to more controversy than has its activity in the realm of food legislation. 'Harmonization' or the 'approximation of laws' has, particularly since Britain's entry to the Community, provoked much wrath and indignation, largely on the basis of an almost complete lack of understanding of the aims, methods, and scope of the harmonization programme.

This chapter aims to provide an overview, albeit necessarily a cursory one, of European Community food legislation. 'Food legislation' is taken to include legislation dealing with food as a raw material, as a processed foodstuff, and as a packaged consumer good. The scope is thus considerably wider than the series of Directives on processed foodstuffs which form the basis of the Commission's most widely known programme of harmonization. Thus the chapter begins with a description of some of the more common terminology and methods used in this field; and describes the Commission's legislative programmes and processes. It then considers the legislation along the whole length of the food chain, beginning with the raw materials, through the processed foodstuffs to matters of direct concern to the consumer.

The origins of modern food legislation in the United Kingdom go back to the Sale of Food and Drugs Act of 1875, which required that food must be of the nature, substance and quality demanded by the purchaser although earlier legislation dates back to 1266. In Italy the modern laws go back to 1888, in France to 1905, and in Germany to 1916; in Bavaria there were already in mediaeval times absolute requirements on the composition and quality of beer under the *Rheinheitsgebot* which to this day permits only hops, water, barley, and malt in the brewing of beer. No doubt at the time this was considered a monstrous interference with the time honoured methods of making beer in the area.

The fundamental preoccupation of nineteenth century and subsequent national food legislation was with the introduction and maintenance of high standards of health and hygiene in the preparation and processing of foodstuffs and with the prevention of adulteration. Since then legislators' interest has been greatly extended to reflect developments in modern food technology and to ensure that substances added to foods for flavouring, colouring or other purposes, meet adequate safety standards. More recently the national legislators have turned their attention downstream to the consumer to encompass labelling, packaging, and advertising, and upstream to the farm to regulate the quality of the raw material entering the food chain either domestically or imported.

This range of activity by national authorities gave rise, of course, to potential obstacles to trade in food between the Member States of the Community which national authorities have not been slow to exploit. When the Treaty of Rome, and the CAP in particular, was drawn up it became clear at once that merely to put farm prices and support systems on to a common basis and to remove tariff barriers was quite insufficient; action had to be taken to ensure that national food legislation did not undermine the objectives of free trade. At the same time, it was recognized that no national authority would be able to accept any significant dilution of the standards set for their own consumers where the basic conditions of health and hygiene in food processing were concerned.

The material in this chapter is arranged in three sections. First, an outline of the form and scope of food legislation in the EC, second a more detailed look at the measures in force, and third a consideration of the Cassis de Dijon case.

THE FORM AND SCOPE OF FOOD LEGISLATION IN THE EC

Legal

The twin concerns—the establishment of free trade and the maintenance of basic national health standards—are reflected in Articles 2 and 36 of the EEC Treaty. Article 2 states that 'The Community shall have as its task, by establishing a common market and progressively approximating the economic policies of Member States, to promote throughout the Community a harmonious development of economic activities, a continuous and balanced expansion, an increase in stability, an accelerated raising of the standard of living, and closer relations between the States belonging to it'.

Article 36 indicates the importance attached to public health requirements in the exemptions it provides. Thus restrictions on imports *may* be justified 'on grounds of public morality, public policy or public security; the protection of health and life of humans, animals or plants; the protection of national treasures possessing artistic, historic or archaeological value; or the protection of industrial and commercial property'. This Article finds its reflection in much of the Community's food legislation in providing for safeguard arrangements.

A number of other Treaty Articles are central to the Community's food legislation, and form the legal basis for 'all subsequent actions. Article 100, which provides that 'the Council shall, acting unanimously on a proposal from the Commission, issue directives for the approximation of such provisions laid down by law, regulation or administrative action in Member States as directly affect the establishment or functioning of the common market'; and Article 43, which provides the basis of action, in the form of regulations as well as directives, as part of the Common Agricultural Policy. The separating lines have never been very clearly drawn and whilst much of the legislation dealing with processed food products is based on Article 100, nevertheless in certain sectors, for example, wine, the levels of permitted additives such as sulphur dioxide, form part of the market regime legislation and are therefore based on Article 43. In addition, a number of market regimes within the CAP, notably that for fruit and vegetables, lay down quality standards, together with provisions enabling one or other category to be withdrawn from the market as a means of price support. In these cases therefore, legislation has a twin purpose, one of which would normally be considered a part of food legislation, the other of market management. In some instances the legislation is justified on the basis of both Articles 43 and 100 as for example with most of the directives dealing with health and veterinary matters in meat.

Article 235 of the Treaty of Rome provides a catch-all in that if other provisions do not expressly provide for measures to achieve the objectives of the Community, then the 'Council shall acting unanimously . . ., take the appropriate measures'. This has been of particular importance to the food and drink industries on environmental issues: for example, the Commission's environmentally motivated proposal for a directive on beverage packaging cites Article 235 (Commission, 1981).

Finally mention should be made of Article 30. This states that 'Quantitative restrictions on imports and all measures having equivalent effect shall . . . be prohibited between Member States'.

At the risk of oversimplifying a very complex legal framework it can be stated that Article 2 sets out the objectives of the Community, Article 30 establishes a presumption in favour of free trade whilst Article 36 provides the necessary checks on, for example, public health grounds. The Cassis de Dijon case —discussed below—was important because it seemed to shift the boundary between Articles 30 and 36. To the extent that national measures are justified then Articles 43, 100, and 235 are used to establish harmonized provisions.

It can be seen, therefore, that if, at the national level, food legislation is dictated by a variety of considerations, these are overlaid at the Community level by the need to ensure the highest degree of freedom for intra-Community trade; but also in certain sectors to make a contribution to the market management needs of the CAP. It is not surprising therefore that the development of Community food legislation has been a long and arduous process.

Form of the legislation

As with national foods legislation, Community legislation in this field is complex, and it is necessary at the outset to consider the different legislative techniques used and the basic terminology which has been developed. Most of the Community's law in the field of harmonization takes the form of directives.

1. Horizontal and vertical directives

The first food legislation directive was adopted by the Council on 23rd October 1962, and laid down a list of colourants that could be used as additives to any foodstuff to be sold in the Community. It thus concerned a product which cuts across the whole food processing industry, and is known as a *horizontal directive*. There are now a number of basic horizontal directives relating directly to foodstuffs, ranging from that on permitted preservatives, to the labelling and advertising of foodstuffs. In 1973 the Community adopted a directive on cocoa and chocolate products, the first of what are now eight *vertical directives* which deal with specific foodstuffs. These vertical directives lay down for a particular product or group of products their definition and compositional characteristics. A vertical directive may also provide for certain compulsory information to be provided on the package and for the analytical methods to be used in assessing its conformity with the specified composition.

The horizontal directive, with which the Community's original legislative programme began, has a number of advantages: it covers wide sectors of industry, and enables a consistent and uniform approach across all product groups to be adopted, particularly in the case of food additives for which all Member States already had their own legislation. The major disadvantage has been the complexity of the horizontal approach and the difficulty in achieving agreement by negotiation where so broad a field is in question. The vertical directive is by contrast more restricted, and has often been preferred by industry on the grounds that its narrower scope makes for quicker progress.

The interrelationship between horizontal and vertical directives—the point where they intersect—gives rise to difficulties and exceptions. It is difficult to find a general rule since in some cases the provisions of a vertical directive override the provisions of a horizontal directive; thus the labelling requirements for the vertical cocoa and chocolate Directive differ from those of the horizontal labelling Directive. On the other hand, where there are no vertical rules, the horizontal rules on labelling should apply. In the case of such directives as 76/893/EEC on packaging materials coming into contact with food, these are specifically drafted in such a way that subsequent vertical legislation (for example 78/142/EEC on vinyl chloride monomer, a carcinogen) interlocks with the original horizontal (or framework) directive.

2. Optional and total legislation

Community food legislation is often referred to as being either 'optional' or 'total' although the optional approach is not much used in foodstuffs legislation. Each of these terms may also be qualified by the word partial. Thus the Directive on colourants is a total directive, that on prepacked solid and liquid quantities is optional and that on sugar is total and partial. The essential difference lies in the effect on the relevant national legislation. A *total* directive requires that national legislation be drafted so as to apply the provisions of the directive to goods produced and consumed within the Member State as well as to goods entering into trade in the Community. In this sense, a total directive is the next thing to a regulation in effect. Directives, even total directives however, tend to contain more derogations and exceptions than do the normal regulations. The directive is designed to provide a Community norm in place of a national standard, and it is for this reason that it has given rise to considerable emotional opposition. It is from the total approach that the popular but quite inaccurate notions of Eurobeer, Euroloaf, and other such non-existent commodities have arisen.

The *optional* directive is designed to remove barriers to intra-Community trade through the amendment of national legislation. The Member States' own pre-existing legislation may remain in force on its own market, and is amended only to the extent of providing for a Community norm which must be accepted by all Member States. Where an imported product conforms to the norms laid down in the directive then it may not be refused entry, even though different standards may apply to domestically manufactured products. It thus leads to a more complex situation where there may apparently be several norms governing similar products within a given market. By the same token, however, it is a more flexible approach than the total method and has proved politically more acceptable in certain Member States. Where public health is at stake, however, the total directive has to be used since Member States will not be willing to accept on their market products with lower standards, or giving rise to a health risk greater than their own national requirements. The total approach was much used in the early years of Community legislation, but has now tended to give way to the optional approach at least outside the food sector.

There is finally for completeness, the *partial* approach under which one sector only of a market is covered either by total or optional methods, leaving the remainder to be dealt with by national legislation. Thus the Directive on jams and marmalades provides a specific description for various jam products, and reserves particular names for them. These products must then conform to the other provisions of the Directive. For example, the name 'marmalade' is reserved within the European Community to British type marmalade. All products not conforming to the description continue to be covered by each Member State's domestic legislation, but may not be called marmalade.

3. Positive and negative lists

The horizontal directives provide for the extent to which additives—for example, preservatives or colourants—may be included in the production of foodstuffs. These directives provide for a positive list of permitted substances. In general, it may be said that everything not authorized on a positive list is prohibited and on a negative list everything not forbidden is authorized. The positive list principle is generally used in Community legislation on additives, there being for example thirty products on the positive list of permitted antioxidants. The positive list approach can still cause problems since, although Member States commit themselves to permit the use of the additive in question, there are no general Community provisions on conditions of use. The list of permitted substances is applied in each Member State quite differently, and may have very little effect in liberating trade where a Member State authorizes use in a limited number of products. Thus in any particular processed foodstuff, the Member States may have authorized different additives even though all are drawn from the same positive list. The proposal for a Directive on flavourings[2] which follows the positive (or permitted) list system, is the outcome of a protracted discussion on the values of positive, negative, and mixed list systems. In general, flavouring and essence manufacturers wished to continue the system operating in Germany, Italy, and the Netherlands; this provided for a positive list of permitted 'artificial' flavourings and a negative list of 'nature identical' flavourings which restricts or prohibits the use of any which have been shown to be dangerous to health. Thus 'artificial' flavourings would be permitted only if they were on the positive list; 'nature identical' flavourings would be permitted unless they were prohibited by the negative list.

The legislative process

Chapter 2 deals with the general legislative and decision-making process on which the CAP is built. Nevertheless, some aspects in food legislation merit particular note. In outline a draft directive follows the normal patterns described in Chapter 2: preparatory work within the Commission, leading to a draft directive discussed within COREPER and its expert working groups, and finally decision by the Council of Ministers. First, however, the process takes substantially longer than most other areas of Community activity. The cocoa and chocolate Directive took ten years from the date of the Commission's proposal to that of the Council's adoption in July 1973; the draft legislation on health and hygiene rules for milk intended for heat treatment has still not been adopted more than ten years on from the original proposal by the Commission in February 1971. The reasons are not hard to find given the sensitive nature of legislation affecting public health, and the way in which national food industries have sometimes been built up behind barriers based on compositional rules. The second factor is the much greater need to consult and use outside experts. The subject matter is highly technical and legislation is widely different between the Member States, and the Commission clearly does not possess the staff to deal with the legislation on its own. Third, there is a greater need than in many areas of the Community's legislative activity, to be aware of food standards legislation adopted within other international bodies, notably the Joint FAO/WHO Codex Alimentarius Commission and the GATT. Finally, directives based on Article 100 must be adopted unanimously in the Council.

There are three types of Committees within the Community set up specifically to deal with different aspects of food legislation.

1. The standing committees

Five of these committees have been set up by the Council, and are in concept equivalent to the Management Committees existing for each product sector within the CAP. Each is composed of experts from the Member State's administrations, and is chaired by the Commission. Each Committee has somewhat different powers although their basic *modus operandi* is the same. The basic agreement for the Standing Committee on Foodstuffs was laid out in the Council Decision of 1969.[3] In a resolution of the same date the Council also provided for the detailed operating procedures of the Committee. Its function is to 'ensure close co-operation between the Member States and the Commission, and to enable the latter to consult experts'; 'The Committee shall . . . carry out the duties devolving upon it under the instruments relating to foodstuffs adopted by the Council. It may moreover consider any other question arising under such instruments and referred to it by its Chairman either on his own initiative or at the request of a Member State'.

The five standing committees are: for seeds and plants, for foodstuffs, for feedingstuffs, the Phytosanitary Committee, and the Standing Veterinary Committee.

Like the others the Standing Committee for Foodstuffs votes on the weighted majority basis laid down in Article 148 of the Rome Treaty, on a proposal from the Commission. In the event of the Committee voting against the Commission proposal, the latter must put a proposal to the Council which will decide by qualified majority. Without a decision by the Council within three months, the proposal is deemed adopted. In adopting any new directive, the Council will decide which aspects of the legislation will be subject to the Foodstuffs Committee procedures.

It was originally envisaged that these Committees would enable the process of food and feed legislation to move ahead rapidly, and would relieve the Council of the need to deal with highly technical questions of detail. Moreover, with the constant development of food processing technology and methods of control, there is a constant need for amendment of the basic legislation and an effective means of dealing with this was necessary. In the event the process of modification and amendment has worked rather well; it is the adoption of the basic legislation in Council which has proved so difficult.

2. Scientific Committee for Food

The Scientific Committee for Food was instituted in April 1974 by Commission, not Council, Decision.[4] Its role is to provide the Commission with a pool of the best technical expertise on which it can draw 'on a problem relating to the protection of the health and safety of persons arising from the consumption of food, and in particular on the composition of food, processes which are liable to modify food, the use of food additives and other processing aids as well as the presence of contaminants'. There are 15 members nominated by the Commission from highly qualified scientific persons (mainly toxicologists). It makes very considerable use of this Committee, whose members are frequently advisers to national food standards committees. It has the advantage therefore of knowing that a recommendation from the Scientific Committee is likely to be in line with national policy.

3. Advisory committees

The Advisory Committee on Foodstuffs[5] was the last of these committees to be brought into existence, in July 1975. Its workings are in line with the arrangements for advisory committees in each CAP product sector, and it is intended to provide the Commission with advice from farmers, manufacturers, labour unions, distributors, and consumers on proposals concerning the harmonization of legislation relating to foodstuffs. Like the other advisory committees, it does not vote and has only advisory powers. Two permanent members are appointed by the Commission from each of the European organizations representing the different interest groups. Four further members may be appointed by each group depending on the subject matter in question. In addition to the Advisory Committee on Foodstuffs, there are also similar bodies for veterinary matters and feedingstuffs.

The programme of work

The first Directive, that on colouring matters authorized for use in foodstuffs for human consumption, was adopted on 23 October 1962, and was followed in 1963 by the Directive on Preservatives and in 1967 by the Directive on the surface treatment of citrus fruit. Increasingly, however, the need was felt to bring some order and direction into the Community's legislative efforts in view of the wide scope of existing national legislation and the increasing tendency for the Member States to introduce new and more comprehensive legislation under pressure from consumer groups, and an expanding awareness of the possibilities of intra-Community trade.

In 1969 therefore, the Council adopted its first comprehensive programme of activity.[6] This programme is concerned with a wide range of industrial and other products as well as foodstuffs. Part II of the programme related to barriers to trade in food arising out of Member States' legislative or administrative arrangements, and set out five phases within each of which certain work was to be undertaken. The whole programme was to be completed before 1 January 1971. In the event the programme was hopelessly optimistic, and of the forty-two decisions to be taken during the five phases, only thirteen have actually been adopted to date. Part III of the programme provided for mutual recognition of existing methods of control and analysis. Part V was of particular importance because it provided that where a Commission proposal had already been put forward, Member States would abstain from introducing new national arrangements pending adoption by the Council. Furthermore, it was agreed that Member States would inform the Commission well in advance of their intention to introduce national food legislation in other areas, giving the Commission the right to make its own proposals first.

The 1973 programme

In May 1973, a further attempt was made to lay out a comprehensive programme of legislative activity for the Community's technological and industrial policy. Following the first enlargement of the Community, considerable new work was necessary in the field of harmonization of legislation. The Commission therefore put forward a Memorandum on Technological and Industrial policy (Commission, 1973) which was based on the traditional concept of the 'existence of a single market operating like a national market in which people, goods, services, capital and companies circulate freely'. The programme included food legislation, and resulted in a Council resolution,[7] which again provided for a timetable in five phases between 1 July 1974 and 1 January 1978 for the removal of technical barriers to trade in the food sector. The record has been no better than previously and only ten proposals have yet come to decision out of forty-one suggested. All but half a dozen of these were 'vertical' directives, and for the most part covered the same food products as suggested in the 1969 programme.

Since the 1973 programme, there has been a rather changed approach, which dated largely from a speech made in December by Finn Gundelach, then Commissioner for the Internal Market. He announced the withdrawal of several 'vertical' proposals, including those on beer and bread which had become politically sensitive in the United Kingdom,[8] indicated that a more pragmatic approach to harmonization of legislation would henceforward be adopted, and proposed a much greater use of the optional approach and of horizontal directives. The most recent attempt by the Commission to describe its programme for foodstuffs legislation is in its Draft for a Council resolution concerning the second programme for a consumer protection and information policy submitted in 1979 (Commission, 1979b). However, this is in far more general terms than the previous programmes and lays down no dates or deadlines for achievement.

EC FOOD LAW

This chapter has been concerned to set out the initial reasons for the Community's activity in foodstuffs legislation, the way in which this has developed, and the form which it has taken. As has been indicated, the areas of most direct importance to the food industries have been the vertical and horizontal directives concerned with processed foods, and these will be analysed in more detail below. In addition, however, there is a broad body of other Community legislation relating to each part of the food chain, aimed at activities both downstream and upstream of food manufacturing. The former relates mainly to 'consumer' type legislation on food labelling, unit pricing, and product liability for example. The latter relates to legislation on the quality of the raw material inputs entering the food chain and concerns the additives permitted in animal feedingstuffs, animal disease control and eradication schemes and more recently legislation to control the type and extent of growth promoting hormones used in animal husbandry.

This legislation is of importance not only to those parts of the food industry, such as the dairy sector, which have traditionally had a very close relationship with raw material quality, but increasingly to other sectors. Food manufacturing is now a highly integrated industry, and legislation acting on one part of the food chain will influence all other parts. This section of the chapter will therefore outline the major areas of legislation relating to the food chain as a whole.

This survey examines first the legislation on raw material inputs, and considers CAP quality standards, plant protection and pesticide residues and the legislation governing trade in meat and meat products. It goes on to consider the major processed foodstuffs regulated by vertical and horizontal directives and other legislation; and then consumer legislation (including quality standards). No classification of such a broad spectrum can be totally comprehensive, or completely satisfactory; the intention is to provide an overall picture of the scope of the legislation. The practitioner will need to delve into far greater detail than is possible in this chapter.

1. CAP quality standards

Each of the CAP product regimes includes legislation providing for the minimum quality standards which the product must reach to be eligible for intervention or for private storage aids. These standards often take on a wider importance and become a reference point for trade in the products across the Community as a whole. This is particularly the case for fruit and vegetables and eggs where the legislation on quality and marketing standards is of particular importance and is used to regulate supply and demand of these products for which the full intervention mechanisms are weaker than in most other regimes. The major fruit and vegetables are covered by standardized quality standards which describe for each product the characteristics which determine whether it shall be classified as Category Extra, I, II, or III. In times of over-supply, a prohibition may be placed upon the marketing of Category III produce.

In this sector, therefore, the quality standards act in part as a price support mechanism and in part as a consumer quality mechanism. With regard to eggs, marketing standards have been provided for within a CAP regulation in scope and detail which would more normally be found within consumer legislation, since in addition to describing basic quality categories, provision is included for date stamping and for information on weight and on packing stations. Similar regulations exist within the CAP for the content of water in poultry carcasses, for the level of fat in milk, for the quality characteristics of wine[9] and for the erucic acid content of rapeseed. In many ways this legislation is analogous to that contained within the vertical directives for processed foodstuffs described later.

2. Plant protection and pesticide residues

This legislation is concerned with three main areas; standards for seed quality, protective measures against the introduction into Member States of organisms harmful to plant health, and maximum levels for pesticide residues in and on fresh fruit and vegetables. The first of these is intended to ensure high levels of seed quality across the Community and provides for control and inspection methods necessary to ensure that the legislation is implemented effectively.

The second, the phytosanitary legislation, provides for a system of mutually recognized controls at the common Community frontier as well as on trade in plant material within the Community. In addition there are four specific directives on particular plant diseases originally adopted by the Council in 1969.

The provisions for pesticide residues adopted in 1976 are based jointly on Articles 43 and 100 of the Treaty of Rome, recognizing the overlap between the agricultural and industrial nature of the problem. The legislation provides for the 29 product groups deemed capable of containing pesticide residues and for 40 or so pesticide chemicals together with the maximum levels permitted, to ensure intra-Community trade in the products in question.

3. Meat and veterinary legislation

The legislation in this group is comprehensive and complex. It deals with a number of different aspects.

Feedingstuffs

This deals with the type and level of additives permitted in animal feedingstuffs. This group of directives is now complete, with the exception of proposals on single cell proteins, and is monitored by the Standing Committee for Feeding-stuffs. There are four basic directives, which provide *inter alia* for the additives which Member States must under certain circumstances accept; for a list of undesirable substances in feedingstuffs; and for the information to be provided in marketing simple and compound animal feeds.

Control of animal diseases

This group of Community provisions aims to counter and, if possible to eradicate, some of the most serious of animal diseases, notably brucellosis, tuberculosis, and leucosis and swine fever in the case of pigs. In addition, Community funds are available to counter outbreaks of certain animal diseases if the measures taken conform to the provisions of the directive. These are laid down in considerable detail and provide for conditions of inspection where infection is suspected, operation of veterinary laboratories, the level of compensation for slaughtered animals and for cleansing and disinfecting methods. It is interesting to note that the Community has provided financial support for the eradication of animal disease in certain Third Countries supplying the Community with meat.

Health and hygiene legislation for meat and live animals

The basic legislation is laid down in four directives[10] dealing with trade between Member States in live animals; fresh meat other than poultrymeat; poultrymeat; and other meat products. Of these only the Directive on poultrymeat is directly applicable to conditions within national territory in addition to trade between Member States, although the existence of Community standards for intra-Community trade does in practice bring about pressure to conform for national production as well. This is, however, a long term pressure given the size of the existing investment in plant built to national standards; as a result the current pattern of national standards and those for intra-Community trade at the same time, may be slow to change.

Veterinary legislation has always been the subject of considerable difficulty for the Community in finding common ground. The technical aspects are complex, and the risks to whole livestock sectors are so great that Member States have always been most reluctant to take any risks at all.

The first of the Directives on trade in live animals provides for comprehensive definitions of the relevant animal diseases, the conditions of the animal at the time of export, vaccination arrangements, and certification to cover animals in transit. The second Directive deals with fresh meat entering into intra-Community trade and provides for standardized 'health requirements for meat in slaughter-houses and cutting rooms and during storage and transportation' and for the issue of health certificates prepared by official veterinaries. The legislation lays down rather precise standards for the design and operation of slaughter-houses, cutting and preparation plant aimed at avoiding, for example, cross contamination and at ensuring satisfactory waste disposal systems; inspection of plant at regular intervals is provided for and conforming plant receive a number which is stamped on to the products produced by the plant; these are also accompanied by a health certificate. The Directive on poultrymeat makes similar, if more extensive provision and is applicable, subject to transitional arrangements, to internal production within each Member State. Finally, the more recent Directive on meat products provides for the conditions which manufacturers must satisfy if their products are to be eligible for export to another Member State.

Even this brief summary of the veterinary legislation provides some indication of the comprehensiveness and complexity of the provisions in this difficult field.

Their impact on the costs of the meat industry, and particularly on slaughter-house operators, has been considerable, and major investment has been necessary to achieve even the present modest number of slaughter-houses which fulfil the provisions of the legislation necessary to permit export.[11]

4. Foodstuffs legislation

The horizontal directives

The list at Table 12.1 gives the most important of the horizontal directives on foodstuffs. The 'consumer' directives on, for example, labèlling and advertising, are dealt with in a subsequent section.

The first four directives make provision for different additives in foodstuffs and are all rather similar. The basic[12] colourants Directive is typical and is in its principles relatively straightforward. It provides in Article 1 that with certain exceptions 'Member States shall not authorise the use for colouring foodstuffs intended for human consumption of any colouring matter other than those listed in Annex I'. In subsequent articles, provision is made for permitted products to dissolve or dilute colourants (Article 6), and for the labelling and description of permitted colourants (Article 9). The Annexes provide the positive list of permitted colourants and the criteria for their purity. In principle, the authorities of Member States may not refuse entry to products on the list. The proposals put forward by the Commission in 1980 for a Directive on flavourings for use in foodstuffs (Commission, 1980a) would bring within the scope of Community legislation an additive of major importance to the food industry. Here again, a positive list system is proposed of permitted flavourings. In the United

Table 12.1   Horizontal directives on foodstuffs.

Name	Directive	Official Journal
Colouring matters	*	OJ L115, 11.11.62
Preservatives	64/54/EEC	OJ L12, 27.1.64
Preservatives for the surface treatment of citrus fruit	67/427/EEC	OJ L148, 11.7.67
Antioxidants	70/357/EEC	OJ L157, 18.7.70
Emulsifiers, stabilizers, thickeners, and gelling agents	74/329/EEC	OJ L189, 12.7.74
Materials entering into contact with foodstuffs	76/893/EEC	OJ L340, 9.12.76
Pesticide residues	76/899/EEC	OJ L340, 9.12.76
Dietary foodstuffs	77/94/EEC	OJ L26, 31.1.77
Materials containing vinyl chloride monomer	78/142/EEC	OJ L44, 15.2.78
Synthetic sweeteners	Recommendation 78/358/EEC	OJ L103, 15.4.78

* not numbered.

Kingdom, this was opposed by the industry on grounds of cost, since there are claimed to be some 7000 different flavouring components already used within the flavour producing industry, which would all have to be tested[13], far more than is the case with other additives. Furthermore, it is suggested that research into new flavourings will be inhibited if all results will in practice have to be published through the positive list system. A mixed list system was proposed by the flavour industry as an alternative, in which listing would be limited to non-naturally occurring flavourings and to certain natural flavourings.

The Directive on Materials and Articles in contact with foodstuffs is of a rather different structure, and provides a framework of general provisions with which later, specific, directives dealing with particular materials must conform. Apart from the basic Directive, the Council has adopted a specific Directive on vinyl chloride monomer and the Commission has put forward proposals on ceramic articles in contact with food, and on the migration limits for the constituents of plastic materials in contact with foods. The framework Directive is intended to ensure that packaging materials for foodstuffs do not endanger human health or bring about an unacceptable change in their composition (Article 2). Article 3 provides for the measures which the specific directives may include to ensure these basic aims; these include the use of positive lists, migration limits, purity criteria, and other measures. Article 7 provides for basic labelling requirements. Commission Directive 80/590/EEC provides for a symbol which may accompany materials and articles in contact with foodstuffs, on similar lines to the 'E mark' which certifies the conformity of industrial goods with Community legislation.

The vertical directives

The list at Table 12.2 gives the vertical directives on foodstuffs adopted by the Council.

The vertical directives follow a common structural pattern of greater or lesser complexity according to the product. All of the vertical directives are total in character but are not necessarily entirely comprehensive for the class of foodstuff in question; thus for example those concerning coffee extracts and chicory extracts and sugar are of a partial nature and deal with only a limited product range. Each directive follows a similar pattern.

(a) *Definition*
The directives define the products subject to the legislation in some detail; thus the preserved milks Directive lists eleven products from 'unsweetened condensed milk' through 'sweetened condensed partly skimmed milk' to 'dried high fat milk or high fat milk powder'. The definitions are usually given in terms of the contents of the product and of the processing methods used to produce them. The Directive on fruit juices is particularly strict in this respect; it defines only four categories of fruit juices: fruit juice, concentrated fruit juice, fruit nectar, and dried fruit juice (Article 1) and states that 'the products referred to

Table 12.2   Vertical directives on foodstuffs.

Name	Directive	Official Journal
1. Cocoa and chocolate products	73/241/EEC	OJ L228, 16.8.73
2. Sugar	73/437/EEC	OJ L356, 27.12.73
3. Honey	74/409/EEC	OJ L221, 12.8.74
4. Fruit juices	75/726/EEC	OJ L311, 1.12.75
5. Partly or wholly dehydrated preserved milk	76/118/EEC	OJ L24, 30.1.76
6. Coffee extract and chicory extracts	77/436/EEC	OJ L172, 12.7.77
7. Fruit jams, jellies and marmalade, and chestnut puree	79/693/EEC	OJ L205, 13.8.79
8. Natural mineral water	80/777/EEC	OJ L229, 30.8.80

in Article 1 may be marketed only if they conform to the definitions and rules laid down in this Directive'. In practice this Directive permits only physical production processes such as heat treatment, centrifuging, and filtering, and does not yet provide for chemical processes. Article 4 therefore begins with the words 'Only the following (processes) shall be authorised for the production of fruit juices', and similar terms are used for the processes used in the other categories of fruit juice defined in the Directive.

The very process of defining the products can introduce considerable barriers to innovation in raw material content and production process. Any such innovation must pass through the whole consultative and legislative process before it can be authorized, and the confidentiality necessary to commercial success is unlikely to be maintained.

(b) *Additives*

The vertical directives also provide for the additives permitted in the product in question: thus the Cocoa and Chocolate Directive provides for the addition of sugars in the place of saccharose, certain foodstuffs with a flavouring or aromatic effect, pure plant lecithin and certain edible matters.

(c) *Labelling*

Detailed provisions are included for the information 'which is compulsory on the packages, containers or labels of the products . . . and which must be conspicuous, clearly legible and indelible'.[14] The provisions cover, for example, in the case of the Cocoa and Chocolate Directive, the name reserved for them, the total dry cocoa content, the types of chocolate used, the net weight and the name and address of the manufacturer or packer. In some cases provision is made for the maintenance of national provisions.

(d) *Purity criteria and analytical methods*

Finally, the basic Directives provide for the adoption of identification and purity criteria for additives and processes, and for 'the methods of analysis necessary for checking the above mentioned purity criteria'.[15] The Council is directly responsible for the purity criteria but acts through the Standing Committee on Foodstuffs in the case of the methods of analysis.

Even from this brief description of the vertical directives on foodstuffs, some appreciation of the complexity of the subject can be gained. Undoubtedly, the process of adopting Community legislation has brought some advantages especially in the encouragement it has given to trade, but many in the food industries are sceptical about the success of the programme. One quotation will illustrate this optimistic view well in relation to the Cocoa and Chocolate Directive. Some 'British chocolate did not qualify for description as chocolate in five of the six original Member States but had to be sold under names as barbaric as 'vegecoa' or 'fantaisie au cocoa'. In the sixth Member State, sales of some British chocolate was totally prohibited. The Directive eased this anomalous situation' (Barthelemy, 1976). However, British chocolate must now be described as 'Household chocolate', which still presents a significant marketing barrier. It may also be argued that the very complexity of the legislation, and the time consuming nature of its introduction or modification, has inhibited innovation and change.

5. The consumer legislation

It may be said that all food legislation is ultimately intended for the protection of the consumer; however, there is a range of Community legislation which governs the conditions in which food products are finally presented to the consumer and aims to ensure honesty in trade, and which may in that sense be regarded as specific consumer legislation. This includes provisions on labelling and advertising, unit pricing, types of containers, date marking, and other related matters. The provisions governing these matters are scattered throughout the whole body of Community agricultural and food legislation, and reference has already been made to the way in which certain CAP regulations contain such provisions. Similarly, the vertical directives on foodstuffs contain provisions for packaging and labelling although these are being incorporated into the general labelling provisions where possible. In addition to these, however, there are two important directives specifically concerned with consumer protection. They are:

1. Labelling, Presentation and Advertising of Foodstuffs for Sale to the Ultimate Consumer. (79/112/EEC, OJ L33).
2. Unit Pricing and Prescribed Quantities. (79/581/EEC, OJ L158).

Directive 79/112/EEC on labelling was adopted by the Council two years after the Commission's initial proposal. It is intended to provide a 'horizontal' framework for the specific labelling provisions found in the 'vertical' product directives. The Directive applies to foodstuffs in their final packaged form, including foods supplied to catering outlets such as schools, hospitals, or canteens, and covers in particular, the provisions applying to the permitted ingredients. Articles 1 to 4 provide definitions of 'labelling', 'ingredients', and 'prepackaged foodstuffs'; certain general prohibitions such that labelling must not be misleading 'to a material degree' and must not attribute properties to the foodstuff which it does not possess; finally (Article 3) lists the references which are compulsory, notably: the product name, list of ingredients, net quantities for prepackaged foodstuffs, date of minimum durability, special storage conditions, and instructions for use. The subsequent Articles specify detailed arrangements for these compulsory items and make provision for certain exceptions.

The second Directive (79/851/EEC) in this consumer category is more specific and deals with the way in which the selling price, and the price per unit, are to be indicated on foodstuffs sold to the final consumer; it does not apply to foods sold through catering outlets.

Recent developments

The range and extent of Community legislation on foodstuffs is considerable, and is very complex in its detailed interpretation. However, in many cases the legislation replaces rather than adds to national legislation. The major problem for the food industry has been in ensuring that new Community legislation takes account of the particularities of the multitude of special products and practices; and in adapting to the changes that Community legislation inevitably requires over a time scale which avoids the need for abrupt changes in production or marketing policy.

CASSIS DE DIJON

On 20 February 1979 and 20 June 1980 the European Court of Justice gave judgements[16] which have far reaching implications both for the Commission's programme of food law harmonization, and for the continued ability of Member States to protect their own industries by the use of non-tariff barriers.

The Cassis de Dijon case (120/78) related to exports of this liqueur from France to Germany. Under German law only liqueur containing at least 25 per cent alcohol could be marketed in Germany as liqueur. Cassis de Dijon contains only about some 16–18 per cent by volume and was thus refused an import licence. The would-be importer claimed that the German provisions infringed the prohibition in Article 30 of the Treaty of Rome on measures having an effect equivalent to a quantitative restriction on trade. The Court upheld the complaint and stated that any product legally made or sold in one Member State must in principle be admitted to the market in any other Member State; furthermore, even where national rules apply equally to domestic and imported goods, import barriers may only exist where these are necessary to satisfy 'mandatory requirements' such as public health, protection of consumers or the environment and fiscal law requirements. Subsequent cases have confirmed and clarified this judgement, particularly the Eyssen case and the Kelderman case.[17] The former concerned the use of the antibiotic nisin used in cheese manufacture, which is permitted in France and the United Kingdom, but not in the Netherlands. The Court held that the Dutch authorities were able to prevent the use of added nisin in domestic cheeses, even though Directive 64/54/EEC on preservatives expressly excludes nisin from its provisions; it is an added complication that cheeses containing added nisin may nevertheless be imported. The Court justified its view by reference to rules which are necessary in order to satisfy public health requirements. In the latter case, however, the Court held that a Dutch requirement that bread be sold under a standard format relating to dry weight was not justified; public health requirements could not be adduced, and consumer interests could be protected by measures other than a ban on imports.

Following these cases, the Commission set out in a letter to Member States the guidelines which it drew for policy (Commission, 1980b). With the exception of additives, the ruling has in practice moved the boundary between Article 100 which is the basis for the Commission's programme of harmonization, and Article 30, in favour of the latter. Thus the Commission will in future direct its work of harmonization 'mainly at national laws having an impact on the functioning of the common market where barriers to trade arise from national provisions which are admissible under the criteria set by the Court'.

Secondly, it is now clear that Member States cannot take an exclusively national viewpoint when drawing up legislation on technical or commercial practices; consideration must be given to the legal requirements for the product in other Member States since there is no longer any guarantee that national legislation alone can regulate imported products.

It will be some years yet before the full implications of the Cassis de Dijon case are felt, and a lot will depend upon the willingness of the Member States to accept the implications of the ruling. If the Member States wish to see a further liberalization of trade then the ruling does mean that the harmonization process, although still necessary, takes on a lesser importance. If the Member States are more convinced of the disadvantages of free trade in food and processed foodstuffs—either because of a concern to protect human, plant, and animal health, and to protect domestic industry—then progress will be slow. Under this alternative scenario trade will only be liberalized on a product by product basis as further case law is established in the European Court, or as the Commission's harmonization programme makes headway (see Swinbank, (1982) for an expansion of this theme).

NOTES

1. We are indebted to A. Kinch for this historical information.
2. Commission (1980a).
3. Council Decision 69/414/EEC of 13 November 1969 setting up a Standing Committee for Foodstuffs, OJ L148.
4. OJ L136.
5. OJ L182.
6. General Programme of 28 May 1969 for the elimination of technical barriers to trade resulting from differences in Member States' legislative, regulatory, and administrative arrangements, OJ C76.
7. Council Resolution of 17 December 1973 on Industrial Policy, OJ C117.

8. A further seven were withdrawn formally in 1979 (Commission, 1979a).
9. There are some 33 regulations in the wine sector covering a very wide variety of quality characteristics.
10. Although there were 43 amending and secondary directives by 1980.
11. Harris and Pickard (1979) point out that only 3 per cent of slaughter-houses in England and Wales conformed to the EEC standard in 1975.
12. It has been amended on eight occasions.
13. Evidence of the Cocoa, Chocolate and Confectionary Alliance to the House of Lords Select Committee on the European Communities (House of Lords, 1980).
14. Article 11.1, Directive 75/726/EEC, OJ L311.
15. Article 13(a), Directive 75/726/EEC, OJ L311.
16. Case 120/78 and Case 788/79.
17. Case 53/80 of 5 February 1981, and Case 130/80 of 19 February 1981.

REFERENCES

(a) *References cited in the text*

Barthelemy, M. (1976) Harmonisation in the EEC of National Legislation of Foodstuffs, in Ministry of Agriculture, Fisheries and Food, *Food Quality and Safety: a Century of Progress*, HMSO: London.

Commission of the European Communities, (1973) *Memorandum on Technological and Industrial Policy*, COM (73) 1090, Brussels.

Commission of the European Communities (1979a) *Withdrawal of Certain Proposals for Directives on the Approximation of the Laws of the Member States Relating to Foodstuffs*, COM (79) 128, Brussels.

Commission of the European Communities (1979b) *Draft Action Programme of the European Communities with Regard to Consumers*, COM (79) 336, Brussels.

Commission of the European Communities (1980a) *Proposal for a Council Directive on the Approximation of the Laws of the Member States Relating to Flavourings for use in Foodstuffs and to Source Materials for Their Production*, COM (80) 268, Brussels.

Commission of the European Communities (1980b) Communication from the Commission Concerning the Consequences of the Judgement given by the Court of Justice on 20th February 1979 in case 120/78 ('Cassis de Dijon'), *Official Journal of the European Communities*, C256.

Commission of the European Communities (1981) *Draft Directive on Containers of Liquids for Human Consumption*, COM (81) 187, Brussels.

Harris, S. A., and Pickard, D. H. (1979) *Livestock Slaughtering in Britain: A Changing Industry*, Centre for European Agricultural Studies, Wye College.

House of Lords Select Committee on the European Communities (1980) *Flavourings*, Session 1980–81 3rd Report, HL38, HMSO: London.

Swinbank, A. (1982) 'EEC food law and trade in food products', *Journal of Agricultural Economics*, **33**.

(b) *Other sources drawn upon*

Haigh, R. (1978), 'Harmonisation of legislation on foodstuffs, food additives and contaminants in the EEC', *Journal of Food Technology*, **13**, 255–264; 491–509.

House of Lords Select Committee on the European Communities (1978) *Approximation of Laws Under Article 100 of the EEC Treaty*, Session 1977–78, 22nd Report, HL131, HMSO: London.

Institute of Trading Standards Administration (1980) *A Comparative Directory of European Community Legislation*.

McGowan, G. (1981) *The Formulation of Foodstuffs Legislation*, European News Agency, Brussels.

Chapter 13

The Community Budget

THE BUDGET: AN HISTORICAL PERSPECTIVE

Article 40(4) of the EEC Treaty specifies that 'one or more agricultural guidance and guarantee funds may be set up' so as to enable the objectives of the common agricultural policy to be achieved. It was not, however, until 1962—following the first marathon session of the Council of farm ministers—that the necessary regulation was passed establishing the European Agricultural Guidance and Guarantee Fund.[1]

This regulation laid down the central criteria for financing agricultural policy (and indeed all Community policies). It stated that as agricultural policy would be organized on a Community basis 'the financial consequences thereof shall devolve upon the Community'. This would involve expenditure on export refunds to Third Countries, intervention in the domestic market, and 'common measures adopted in order to attain the objectives set out in Article 39(1)(a) of the Treaty'.

The term 'intervention' is not limited to intervention purchases, but covers many other activities including aids to private storage, denaturing premia, production aids, etc.; as discussed in previous chapters. The 'common measures' are the items of structural policy discussed in Chapter 9. Community financing for all these activities was to be introduced progressively during the transitional period extending to 1 January 1970.

With respect to revenue, the regulation extended the provisions of the EEC Treaty. Article 200 of the Treaty had specified the scale of contributions which would be made by the Member States; however, Article 201 went on to charge the Commission with the task of preparing proposals to replace the system of financial contributions from Member States with one involving the 'Community's own resources' including in particular 'revenue accruing from the common customs tariff'. Regulation No. 25 established as a point of principle that 'levies on imports (of agricultural produce) from third countries' would, at the appropriate time, be included in the own resources system. In the interval the financing of expenditure from FEOGA would be partly based on the net agricultural import requirements of the Member States. In 1963/64 10 per cent, and in 1964/65 20 per cent, of FEOGA expenditure was to be covered by contributions from Member States in proportion to their net agricultural imports, and the remainder in accordance with the scale laid down in the EEC Treaty.

The provisions of Regulation No. 25, though setting the scene for a longer period, only extended until mid-1965. In March 1965 the Commission put forward its proposals. It had already been agreed that common support prices in the farm sector would be established in July 1967, two and a half years ahead of schedule, and it was now proposed that the customs union should be established at the same time. Second, that all agricultural levies and customs duties should accrue to the Community budget, as foreshadowed in Regulation No. 25 and in the EEC Treaty. And third, that the European Parliament should be given wider budgetary powers. President de Gaulle objected to these proposals and withdrew the French delegation from the Council of Ministers. The ensuing 'empty chair crisis' extended until 28 January 1966 when, in the context of the Luxembourg compromise, agreement was reached not only on the financing of the agricultural policy but also on the vexed question of majority voting in the Council of Ministers.[2]

Regulation No. 25 was subsequently supplemented by Regulation 130/66/EEC for the period 1 July 1965 to 1 January 1970. This laid down that from 1 July 1967 *all* expenditure on market support (the Guarantee Section of FEOGA) would be reimbursed from Community funds. Expediture on structural policy (the Guidance Section of FEOGA) would, however, only partially fund eligible projects, and the total sums available would be subject to an upper limit in any one year.[3] The financing of FEOGA expenditure for the two-year period 1965/66–1966/67 was covered by a scale of financial contributions from Member States, which differed in the two years. From 1 July 1967 the idea of linking contributions to levy proceeds was reintroduced such that the contribution was equal to 90 per cent of the total amount of agricultural levy collected on Third Country trade; with the balance made up according to a fixed scale of contributions.

Although the 'definitive' system of Community financing should have begun at the end of the EEC Treaty's transitional period (31 December 1969) it was not in fact until the Hague summit conference of 1–2 December 1969 that a way forward was found,[4] and April 1970 that the necessary legislation was passed. Consequently special arrangements had to be made for 1970, with the definitive financial arrangements entering into force on 1 January 1971.[5] With the implementation in 1971 of the definitive system of financing, the bulk of the financial activities of the three European Communities was funded from a common revenue pool. This is the General Budget of the European Communities, and is the subject of this chapter. Certain other Community financial activities, including operational expenditure under the ECSC Treaty, the European Development Fund, and others, are not covered by the General Budget and are not discussed in this text. (See also Wallace, 1980.)

OWN RESOURCES

The central feature of the definitive system of financing the Community budget was the financial decision of 21 April 1970. Its authority rested on the fact that

Article 201 of the EEC Treaty had, as has been seen above, provided for a system of own resources. The implementation of such a system was dependent upon a decision of the Council, after consultation of the European Parliament, and its adoption by the Member States 'in accordance with their respective constitutional requirements'. Similarly any amendment, or extension, of the own resources system would necessitate the approval of the national parliaments. This requirement later gained considerable importance because, by the 1980s, as will be discussed below, expenditure was rapidly approaching a ceiling set by the availability of own resources.

The financial decision of 21 April 1970 created three forms of own resources. First, from 1 January 1971, all levies charged on agricultural imports from Third Countries, as well as the levies charged to sugar producers, were to be credited to the Budget of the Community, and second—in a steadily increasing proportion reaching 100 per cent on 1 January 1975—all customs duties charged on imports from Third Countries. Customs duties are mainly applied to industrial products, but some agricultural and food products are also covered—in particular those that are not subject to import levies. The Member States receive a 10 per cent refund to cover collection costs on these two elements.

The third element was to come from the value added taxation applied by the Member States in a uniform manner, of which the Community's share would be a 'rate not exceeding one per cent'. Provided at least three Member States had inaugurated the necessary provisions, this third element was to have been introduced on 1 January 1975 and would have replaced the remaining element of financial contributions. In the event, it was not until 1 January 1979 that the VAT element began to operate,[6] and in the interval this VAT element was replaced by national contributions based on total national GNP in relation to total Community GNP. In 1980 the Budget was entirely funded from own resources; but, on accession, Greece paid a contribution based on GNP in lieu of the VAT element, having been permitted a delay in the introduction of VAT.

The Community now takes the view that the own resources system is established and unchallengeable: it is *acquis communautaire* and thus not negotiable either by existing Member States or newcomers. Thus the Act of Accession for the Hellenic Republic provides that Greece should pay over the own resources arising in that country in full; however, recognizing that this would prove a burden to the Greek economy, Article 127 of this Act goes on to specify that refunds shall be made. The refund was 70 per cent in 1981 and will fall to 10 per cent at the end of the transition period in 1985. These arrangements should lead to fewer difficulties in the years to come than did those enacted for the first Enlargement.

As justification of the own resources system it is argued that, as the EC is a customs union with a common external tariff and no duties on internal trade, it is only logical that the duties collected on trade with Third Countries should be treated as own resources. The port of Rotterdam is often cited as an example; many of the products imported into the Community through this port will not be consumed in the Netherlands but elsewhere within the EC and it would be inequitable if the Dutch exchequer were to benefit from that fact. Similar arguments apply to agricultural levies.

From year to year the percentage share coming from agricultural levies, customs duties and VAT does vary; and so does the geographical origin. Table 13.1 dealing with the 1983 Budget *estimates*, illustrates the situation in a recent year. Of note is the relatively small proportion of own resources arising from agricultural levies and sugar levies. The VAT rate of 0.7945 per cent is misleadingly low as the refund measures for the UK had not been agreed by the Council of Ministers when the Commission was making its estimates (In 1982, the VAT rate was 0.9248 per cent.) The table deals only with the own resources of the Community: strangely some sources of revenue, notably monetary compensatory amounts collected on intra-Community trade and the co-responsibility levy in the milk sector, are treated as 'negative expenditure' and so are not entered on the income side of the Budget. In addition to own resources there are some miscellaneous revenues, including revenue from the sale of publications and the Community income tax on officials' salaries, that are not included in the table.

Unfortunately, the amount of detail available concerning the agricultural

Table 13.1 The Community's 'Own Resources'—estimated from the Preliminary Draft Budget 1983. (Million ecu).

	Agricultural levies	Sugar and isoglucose levies	Customs duties	VAT at a rate of 0.7945%	Total
Belgium	175.6	68.2	415.0	393.29	1 052.09
Denmark	6.2	39.6	150.0	234.39	430.19
Germany	209.8	264.8	2 200.0	3 150.32	5 824.92
Greece	39.8	21.3	120.0	180.40*	361.50
France	97.7	328.6	1 250.0	2 848.40	4 524.70
Ireland	2.8	9.1	105.0	95.34	212.24
Italy	307.9	123.0	770.0	1 692.35	2 893.25
Luxembourg	0.1	—	4.5	22.64	27.24
Netherlands	222.8	81.2	660.0	564.12	1 528.12
UK	495.8	77.4	1 900.0	2 383.60	4 856.80
Total	1 558.5	1 013.2	7 574.5	11 564.85	21 711.07
Per cent	7.2	4.7	34.9	53.3	100

* Financial contribution.

Notes: These are gross figures. Member States are entitled to a 10 per cent reimbursement of collection costs on levies and duties. Refunds are payable also to Greece and the United Kingdom as discussed in the text.

The Preliminary Draft Budget is that presented by the Commission; it is subject to amendment by Council and Parliament.

Miscellaneous revenue is excluded.

Individual items may not add to totals shown due to roundings.

SOURCE Commission (1982, Vol. 1, p. 61).

Table 13.2 Estimates of agricultural import levies, by product, for 1983.

	(%)
Cereals	73.6
of which:	
common wheat	20.9
maize	40.0
Beef and veal	4.7
Pigmeat	3.8
Rice	6.3
Sugar	3.8
Dairy products	5.4
Other	2.4
	100

SOURCE Commission (1982, Vol. 7, p. B/865).

import levies is small; in the Budget documents actual expenditure for preceding periods, and estimated expenditure for the period under review, are presented by product and policy (for example: export refunds on cereals) but not by Member State. For own resources actual receipts in earlier periods from agricultural levies are detailed by country but not by product. The Commission, however, does publish an estimate of the breakdown of agricultural levies for the period under review, and this is presented in Table 13.2 for the 1983 estimates. The cereals sector emerges as the major contributor to Community coffers, reflecting in particular the substantial imports of maize and breadmaking wheat.

There is, however, a serious underestimate of the extent to which import taxes on agricultural products contribute to the income of the Community. This is because on many products a tariff is applied at the time of import rather than an agricultural levy. Thus in Table 13.1 under the heading customs duties will be included tariff revenues on oilseeds, fruits and vegetables, tobacco, and other products. There is no estimate of the total revenue generated in this way; but, by way of example, it can be noted that the total duty paid on agricultural and processed products imported into the United Kingdom in 1980 was £188 million,[7] compared to £210 million collected by the UK as agricultural import levies (Customs and Excise, 1982, pp. 100, 102).

EXPENDITURE[8]

Article 199 of the EEC Treaty states quite clearly that 'the revenue and expenditure shown in the Budget shall be in balance': there is consequently no scope for using the budget as a tool of economic policy in the Keynesian sense.

Table 13.3   FEOGA Guarantee Section
spending (1973–1983) as a proportion of
the General Budget of the community.

	(%)
1973	77.4
1974	67.3
1975	69.6
1976	71.4
1977	76.8
1978	70.8
1979	71.0
1980	70.2
1981	61.6
1982	62.2*
1983	64.2*

* As these figures do not relate to actual spending, but represent appropriations for payment (1982) and provisional levels before the Budget had been established (1983), they are not directly comparable with the figures for earlier years.
SOURCE Commission (1982, Vol. 7, p. A/83).

Much expenditure is a direct consequence of the application of the EEC Treaty, or acts adopted on the basis of the Treaty, and is known as 'compulsory expenditure'. The distinction is important because the powers of the European Parliament to amend the Budget differ according to whether the expenditure is classified as compulsory or non-compulsory.[9] Essentially the view is taken that no discretion can be allowed on compulsory expenditure: decisions taken elsewhere have committed the Community to expenditure and the Budget merely implements those decisions. Thus the Budget as presented at the beginning of the financial year is an authorization to incur expected expenditure; the actual out-turn may differ and if the difference is significant a supplementary or rectifying Budget will be required.

The most important item of compulsory expenditure is that channelled through the guarantee section of FEOGA for price support. Until the 1980s—as can be seen from Table 13.3—this was rarely less than 70 per cent of the total budget, and in 1973 and 1977 reached 77 per cent of the total. The total appropriations for payments in 1983 are given in Table 13.4 by way of illustration.

According to the Commission's draft budget for 1983, expenditure on the guarantee section of FEOGA was estimated to account for 64 per cent of total expenditure. One reason for this percentage being lower than the actual out-turn in the 1970s is that the 1981 and 1982 budgets included considerable sums for payments to Greece—as provided for in the Treaty of Accession—and to the United Kingdom (discussed below on pages 319 to 320). From Table 13.4 the

Table 13.4   Total appropriations for payment, Preliminary Draft Budget for 1983.

	million ecu	per cent
Agriculture	14 717	67.2
of which:		
FEOGA Guarantee	14 050	64.2
FEOGA Guidance	667	3.0
Fisheries	85	0.4
Regional policy	1 460	6.7
Social policy	1 414	6.5
Additional spending in the UK	—*	—
EMS subsidies	200	0.9
Energy, research, etc.,	678	3.1
Development aid	1 023	4.7
Reserve	5	0.0
Administration	1 195	5.5
Reimbursement of 10% collection costs	1 015	4.6
Repayment to UK	53	0.2
Repayment to Greece	57	0.3
Total	21 902	100
Less miscellaneous revenue	−191	
Sum to be funded from 'own resources'	21 711†	

Notes: Individual items may not add to totals shown because of roundings.
* When the Commission prepared the Preliminary Draft Budget, the Council had not reached a decision on the 'Supplementary Measures to be taken in favour of the UK'. (For 1982, these measures amounted to 1654 million ecu, equal to 7.5 per cent of the total budget.)
† Table 13.1 gives the make-up of the 'own resources' to fund this total.
SOURCES   Commission (1982, Vol. 7, pp. A/17–A/18, Vol. 1, p. 59).

relatively minor role of social and regional policy—both 'non-compulsory expenditures'—is readily apparent. It should none the less be noted that many commentators would contend that expenditure on agriculture has a major social and regional justification.

Two products account for a substantial proportion of FEOGA guarantee expenditure: milk and cereals (see Table 13.5). The preliminary draft budget of 1983 is not dissimilar to the situation in other years in allocating nearly 30 per cent of the total to milk and milk products, and 16 per cent to cereals. In the case of sugar it should be noted that the sugar levies are credited as own resources on the income side of the Budget and are supposed—one year with another—to match expenditure. On the other hand, the milk co-responsibility levies and monetary compensatory amounts collected on intra-community trade are treated as negative expenditure and thus the percentages shown are net figures.

The term 'fund', as applied to FEOGA, is rather a misnomer for—other than as explained above—the monies devoted to agricultural expenditure neither come from identifiable sources nor are treated in any distinguishable fashion. All own resources—whether agricultural and sugar levies or not—are treated as

Table 13.5   Community expenditure on farm price support—estimates from the Preliminary Draft Budget 1983.

Products	million ecu	per cent
Cereals and rice	2 255*	16.0
Sugar and isoglucose†	1 536‡	10.9
Olive oil	742	5.3
Oilseeds and protein plants	768	5.5
Textile plants and silkworms	145	1.0
Fruit and vegetables	932	6.6
Wine	469	3.3
Tobacco	668	4.8
Milk§	4 113**	29.3
Beef and veal	1 283	9.1
Sheepmeat	237	1.7
Pigmeat	180	1.3
Eggs and poultrymeat	125	0.9
Non-Annex II products	300	2.1
Other products	56	0.4
Accession compensatory amounts	1	—
Monetary compensatory amounts	240	1.7
Total	14 050	100

* Includes 90 million ecu for food aid.
† Gross expenditure with no offset for sugar and isoglucose levies.
‡ Includes 5 million ecu for food aid.
§ Net of co-responsibility levies.
** Includes 163 million ecu for food aid.
SOURCE   Commission (1982, Vol. 7, pp. A/91 and B/761).

the general revenue of the Community which is then expended on various activities, and that part which goes to agriculture passes via FEOGA.[10]

For much of the structural policy, and all price support policy, the Member States are responsible for implementing Community legislation. The Intervention Board for Agricultural Produce is the United Kingdom body which implements most of the legislation dealing with price support (intervention buying, private storage aids, consumer subsidies, etc.). The Home-Grown Cereals Authority and the Meat and Livestock Commission act as the Board's agents in some countries of the Kingdom; the Ministry of Agriculture, Fisheries and Food and the other Agriculture Departments provide a range of services. Customs and Excise monitor and control imports and exports and collect import levies and MCAs charged on imports from other Member States. However, it is the Board that pays import and export refunds and MCAs on intra-Community trade, and collects MCAs payable on exports to other Member States when the British MCA is negative (Intervention Board, 1981, paragraph 5).

Thus the Intervention Board is responsible for most FEOGA guarantee monies in the United Kingdom. Its *modus operandi* are described in its first annual report (Intervention Board, 1974). Each of the Member States has implemented a slightly different system, though each has its 'intervention agencies' (even if simply the Ministry of Agriculture) which act in a similar fashion to the UK's Intervention Board.

In implementing Community legislation the intervention agencies incur operational expenditure which is reimbursed by FEOGA: in practice a monthly advance is made based on estimated expenditure. Most of the expenditure incurred by the Member States is reimbursed directly, but that relating to intervention purchases only indirectly. When a Member State, on behalf of the Community, purchases products into intervention the cash outlay is provided by the Member State in question. Only on the subsequent sale will any loss incurred be reimbursed (or gain accrued credited) by FEOGA. In the interval—which could extend to several years—the incidental expenses of storage, including interest payments on the capital outlay, are met by FEOGA on a flat rate basis.

The net result of the revenue raising and expenditure generating aspects of the CAP is a budgetary cost to the Community: the 1983 preliminary draft Budget forecasts that the CAP will generate 2572 million ecu in levy revenue, but tariff revenue on agricultural products is lost in the estimates of customs duties. On the other hand 14 050 million ecu will be spent on price support (see Tables 13.1 and 13.4). The CAP is thus a major net spender of Community funds and, as will be noted later, has been the major contributory factor in causing budgetary transfers between the Member States.

THE BUDGETARY PROCEDURE[11]

No attempt can be made in the present text to outline the respective roles of Council and Parliament, for this is a complex constitutional issue, nor to document the conflicts which, in recent years, have developed between the two. (But see House of Lords, 1979 and 1980.) Council and Parliament together should adopt the budget for any given calendar year by the beginning of that year, and so their discussions take up much of the final months of the preceding year. For this to happen the Commission's proposals (the 'preliminary draft') must be ready by the early summer—based on studies undertaken in the spring. Although revised estimates are usually submitted (in the form of a 'letter of amendment') it will be apparent that estimates undertaken so far in advance will be subject to great uncertainty. This is particularly so for agriculture where expenditure will depend on the margin between production and consumption, and not just on the total production levels achieved. If, for instance, the self-sufficiency ratio for a particular crop turned out to be 102 per cent, instead of the forecast 101 per cent, then the budget estimate for that item could be 100 per cent inaccurate.

If the estimates prove to be inaccurate a mechanism does exist for the adoption of a Supplementary Budget during the course of the financial year. There is, however, some embarrassment, and considerable labour, involved in cajoling the Council and Parliament to pass a Supplementary Budget. Hence the Commission may well attempt to match actual expenditure to the Budget provisions.

This could involve either speeding up, or slowing down, payments at the end of the financial year depending upon the state of the finances; or even modifying the management of the market. Thus the export of a Community surplus involves an almost immediate call on the Community's Budget, whereas an addition to intervention stocks tends to defer Community—as opposed to national—expenditure to a later time period.

THE BUDGET AND THE MANAGED MARKET

The policies pursued by the Community in striving to achieve the objectives of the CAP can often be influenced by budgetary criteria. This applies to short-run budgetary constraints, as outlined in the previous paragraph, as well as to longer run considerations of the total budgetary cost of the CAP. This is because the different policy mechanisms, as outlined in previous chapters, involve different budgetary costs.

The problems that emerge can neatly be illustrated by the example of butter. The public often has difficulty understanding why surplus butter is sold abroad at subsidized prices and not on the domestic market. In Figure 13.1 the support price of butter (P_0) is taken to be 100 monetary units. The quantity demanded at that price (Q_D) is taken to be 100 units, and the quantity supplied (Q_S) as 110 units: a surplus volume of 10 per cent which must be disposed of if the price guarantee is to be maintained. One method would be to purchase the excess (10 units) at the guarantee price (100) and destroy it. The costs, abstracting from administrative expenses and the cost of matches, would be $10 \times 100 = 1000$. An even cheaper policy would be to sell the excess on the world market at a price greater than zero.

An alternative is to subsidize the sale of the produce on the domestic market. To stimulate demand from Q_D to Q_S the price to consumers must be reduced (to P_1). To ascertain the extent to which P_1 must be reduced below P_0 the policy maker must have some factual, or intuitive, knowledge about the nature of the demand for butter. In fact it is quite probable that to stimulate demand by 10 per cent the price will have to fall by 30 per cent (that is to 70 monetary units). Thus the subsidy $(P_0 - P_1)$ will be 30 per unit and will be paid on the entire quantity marketed (110 units). The cost will thus be 3300, over three times more expensive than the policy of destruction or subsidized export.

It is this calculation that EC Finance Ministers are forced to consider when they are faced with difficulties of funding agricultural and other policies from a limited Community Budget, and when the governments of the Member States are pursuing national policies of financial stringency. However, the simple comparison of budgetary costs fails to account for the fact that the position of consumers is transformed in the two cases cited. In the first instance the consumer and taxpayer are jointly called upon to support the price at P_0: though the taxpayers' share will depend upon the extent to which supply exceeds demand at the support price, and will even result in tax revenue should the volume supplied fall short of demand. In the second instance the cost to the consumer is

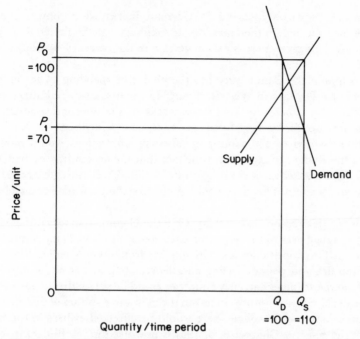

Figure 13.1   The budgetary costs of price support. Budgetary cost of surplus buying and destruction = $(Q_S - Q_D) = P_0 = 10 \times 100 = 1000$. Budgetary cost of domestic consumer subsidy = $Q_S \times (P_0 - P_1) = 110 \times 30 = 3300$.

reduced and the burden of the policy shifts to the taxpayer. The policy is essentially one of price discrimination with the objective of minimizing budget cost whilst stabilizing the support price. It can quickly be shown that whatever the world price (provided it is less than P_0) the cheapest policy of surplus disposal is by export subsidy.

COSMETIC ATTEMPTS TO 'MINIMIZE' FEOGA EXPENDITURE

The percentage share attributed to FEOGA in the Budget has, from time to time, attracted adverse comment. Consequently there have been several attempts to minimize the sums debited to FEOGA by shifting expenditure to other budget headings. The confusing array of units of account and conversion rates into national currencies, discussed briefly in Chapter 8, provided the Commission in the past with the opportunity to reduce apparent expenditure on monetary compensatory amounts at a stroke.

Until the end of 1977 the gold parity unit of account was used in the Community Budget. Thus, although the dollar had depreciated against the unit of account, and the sterling/dollar exchange rate had dropped from £1 = $2.40 to, say, £1 = $2, all receipts and expenses incurred in sterling were still converted into units of account for budgetary purposes at £1 = 2.40 ua. Similarly all receipts and expenses incurred in German marks were converted at 3.66 DM = 1 ua even though the mark/dollar exchange rate had risen to, say, 2 D-Mark = $1. This gives a cross exchange rate in the currency markets of £1 = 4 D-Mark.

Now suppose the Community has the choice of spending £1 in the United Kingdom or 4 D-Mark in West Germany. In the first case the budget heading would show an expense of 2.40 ua whereas in the alternative situation the expenditure would be registered at 1.09 ua (4 divided by 3.66). Real expenditure would be the same and offsetting corrections would have to be made to the Budget to account for the fact that the accounting exchange rates differed from market rates (as in any international accounting exercise). None the less, an apparent difference would appear for the particular budget heading shown.[12]

It was for this reason that in May 1976 the Commission asked the Member States to change over to the 'exporter pays' system for monetary compensatory amounts (MCAs) on Italian and UK imports from other Member States. Both the Italian lira and pound sterling had depreciated, and so if the intervention agencies in the stronger currency countries could be persuaded to pay the MCA then the declared expenditure (in ua) in the guarantee section of FEOGA would be reduced, although of course there would be offsets elsewhere in the Budget. Because the ecu (see Chapter 8, p. 196) is now used in the Budget there is no longer a budgetary advantage in retaining the 'exporter pays' system, and yet it is still in operation.

A similar 'benefit' was a by-product of the scheme to transfer intervention stocks from other Member States to Italy to supply the Italian Market. If the transfer price between the intervention agencies were fixed at zero then a loss would be recorded in a hard currency country and a gain in a weak currency country (Italy) which would be reflected in a net benefit in the FEOGA accounts (Commission, 1978c, p. 18). There would of course be the real costs of the operation—the transport costs—but if these could be paid in hard currencies the operation could still look quite attractive on paper.

Attempts to shift FEOGA expenditure to some other budget heading also arise in other contexts. Thus at one time all the raw material costs of food aid bought at CAP prices appeared in the FEOGA budget, but gradually the FEOGA involvement was reduced to a sum equivalent to the export subsidies payable, with the Food Aid heading in the Budget under Development Aid bearing the equivalent of the world market price and any transport costs. From time to time there have been attempts to shift all the costs of acquiring food at CAP prices to the Food Aid budget heading; and the export subsidies paid on a quantity of sugar equivalent to the ACP imports were moved from FEOGA to the Development Aid heading in 1981.

CRITICAL ISSUES FOR THE 1980s

There are two interrelated budgetary problems facing the Community in the 1980s and both have a common element: the level of FEOGA guarantee expenditure. Agriculture accounts for the major part of Community expenditure and consequently it is not surprising to find that a disproportionately low flow of budgetary funds is received by those countries, such as the United Kingdom, which have relatively less important agricultural sectors than have other Member States. This budgetary imbalance has been a major source of friction between Britain and her partners. The second problem arises from the fact that EC spending, and spending on agriculture in particular, has been rising at a faster rate then has the total availability of income from own resources. Although estimates differ it is expected that at some stage in the early 1980s the own resources budget ceiling will inevitability limit Community spending unless other sources of revenue are found.[13] In practice it would be extremely difficult politically to pass the necessary legislation expanding the own resources system through the ten national parliaments; and so it does appear likely that expenditure will have to be curbed.

The first of these issues must also be discussed in the next chapter, because the budgetary flows form only part of the transfers between Member States generated by the CAP. The purely budgetary aspects, however, are outlined below.

It was always recognized that the common agricultural policy favoured food exporters, at the expense of food importers, but in Britain's case, at the time of the entry negotiations, it was believed that the political and the dynamic economic benefits partly outweighed those costs. And it was hoped that 'As the Community develops there will be other purposes for which Community funds will be spent, such as technological, industrial and regional policies, from which, unlike agriculture, Britain could expect to receive back money commensurate with her contribution to the Community's budget.' (The United Kingdom and the European Communities, 1971.)

These other policies did not develop as the British government had hoped. However, soon after accession, world market prices for many foodstuffs rose to very high levels ensuring that, contrary to expectations, Britain initially gained from membership of the Community (Harris and Josling, 1977). It was against this background that the incoming British Labour government of 1974 'renegotiated' the terms of British entry. One of the results of this renegotiation—as agreed at the Dublin meeting of the European Council in March 1975—was the financial mechanism.

The financial mechanism was the Community's response to the British plea for more equitable sharing of the Budget costs. It dealt, however, only with gross contributions. The various criteria laid down were complex and, in the event, resulted in the fact that by 1980 the United Kingdom had not received any repayment.[14] However, by then Britain had re-negotiated the renegotiations.

In a series of meetings in the winter of 1979/80 the British Government argued its case that Britain's net contribution to the Community Budget was excessive. The agreement that finally emerged is complicated but the outlines are as follows: additional spending programmes to benefit Britain would be devised, the financial mechanism would be revamped to benefit Britain (both measures are reflected in Table 13.4) and a ceiling would be placed on Britain's net contribution to the Budget in 1980 and 1981. This ceiling was not an absolute limit but an agreement that Britain would only pay a proportion of any excess above the agreed ceiling. For 1982 the Council of Ministers agreed that the Community was 'pledged to resolve the problem by means of structural changes' (Commission, 1981, p. 1).

Accordingly the Council gave the Commission the following mandate, to be completed by June 1981:

> The examination will concern the development of Community policies, without calling into question the common financial responsibility for those policies which are financed from the Community's own resources, or the basic principles of the common agricultural policy. Taking into account the situations and interests of all Member States, this examination will aim to prevent the recurrence of unacceptable situations for any of them. (Commission, 1981, p. 1)

The Commission's response to this instruction, which over a year later were being considered by the Community's institutions as this book went to press,[15] envisaged a budget rebate to Britain (of unspecified proportions) based on the difference between 'the United Kingdom's share of the Community's gross national product with the proportion it obtains of FEOGA Guarantee section expenditure'. (Commission, 1981, p. 23.) If this could not be financed out of own resources given the current pattern of expenditure then the Commission envisages that consideration would be given to

> a subsidiary measure by which the Member States which benefit more from the CAP than their British partner would demonstrate their solidarity. In practice, the compensation could be financed by Member States other than the United Kingdom via abatements on their receipts from the Community, based on the payments they receive under the FEOGA Guarantee Section. (Commission, 1981, p. 23.)

The proposal thus envisages that some degree of national financing of the CAP may be necessary; a topic which is taken up again in Chapter 14.

The Commission's Mandate document also discussed the need for some element of 'reform' of the CAP, involving in particular a narrowing of the gap between EC prices and world prices; and a shift in emphasis to benefit the Mediterranean regions. The Commission believed that:

> if the guidelines are agreed, their application will mean that agricultural spending in the years ahead will grow less rapidly than the Community's own resources, making it possible to release additional resources to reinforce Community solidarity in other sectors (Commission, 1981, p. 17).

If this is to be the case then either world market prices need to remain at high levels or spending on agriculture really will have to be curtailed.

NOTES

1. Known by its French acronym: FEOGA. Regulation No. 25 on the financing of the common agricultural policy.
2. See also the discussion in Chapter 2, p. 32.
3. Regulation No. 25 had specified that expenditure under the guidance section, should amount 'as far as possible' to one-third of the expenditure under the guarantee section. Although the change was viewed as a limitation to guidance expenditure it was not, in fact, until 1979 that the expenditure ceiling proved restrictive. Until recent years guidance spending represented less than 5 per cent of spending on price support: see also Table 13.4.
4. This meeting was also notable for the fact that it paved the way for UK membership of the European Communities.
5. In addition to the relevant legislation, and Butterwick and Neville-Rolfe (1968), the foregoing account has been gleaned from Muller (1970) and European Communities—Information (1975).
6. Even then West Germany, Ireland, and Luxembourg had not yet applied the provisions. On 1 January 1978 only the United Kingdom and Belgium had passed the necessary legislation (Commission, 1979).
7. Of which it is estimated £79 million was paid on fresh and processed fruit and vegetables: evidence to the House of Lords Select Committee on the European Communities (House of Lords, 1981, p. 105). £188 million, about 300 million ecu depending upon the exchange rate used, represented about 22 per cent of all customs duties collected by the UK in 1980.
8. The relevant legislation, on the financing of the CAP, replacing Regulation No. 25 is Regulation 729/70.
9. The terms 'obligatory' and 'non-obligatory expenditure' are also used. For further details, see Wallace (1980) or Strasser (1981).
10. Further details of the operation and role of FEOGA are given in its first annual report (Commission, 1973). The annual reports provide detailed data on both the guarantee and guidance sections.
11. For a discussion of the politics of the Community Budget, see Wallace (1980).
12. There were further complications in that in 1977 the FEOGA guarantee estimates and expenditures were written into the Budget as if the green conversion rates of the unit of account had been the budget unit. A correction, labelled the 'dual exchange rate', had subsequently to be added back in. To extend the numerical example given above, suppose that the green conversion rate for the UK was £1 = 1.80 ua and that for Germany 3.4 D-Mark = 1 ua. The £1 spent in the UK would still be entered into the FEOGA budget headings as 2.40 ua; but split 1.80 ua against the particular action and 0.60 ua against 'dual rate'. The equivalent sum of 4 D-Mark would still amount to 1.09 ua; but split 1.18 ua against the particular action and −0.09 ua against 'dual rate'. This 'dual rate' expenditure—amounting to 509 mua in 1977—was, however, included within the overall FEOGA total. (See Commission, 1978c, pp. 18, 85.)
13. For a discussion of possible additional sources of revenue see the Commission document 'The Way Ahead' (Commission, 1978b) and House of Lords (1979).
14. For a description of the financial mechanism, prior to its modifications in May 1980, see House of Lords (1979, Annex 3).
15. A further rebate to Britain had, however, been agreed in May 1982 to cover the year 1982. This settlement followed the Falklands Islands' crisis, and the clash over majority voting in the Agriculture Council (see Chapter 2). Under the circumstances it is understandable, yet regrettable, that decisions on the future funding of the Community were delayed for another year.

REFERENCES

Butterwick, M., and Neville-Rolfe, E. (1968) *Food, Farming and the Common Market*, Oxford, University Press.

Commission of the European Communities (1973) *First Financial Report Concerning the European Agricultural Guidance and Guarantee Fund—Year 1971*, SEC (73) 1259, Brussels.

Commission of the European Communities (1978b) *Financing the Community Budget—The Way Ahead*, COM (78) 531, Brussels.

Commission of the European Communities (1978c) *Seventh Financial Report on the European Agricultural Guidance and Guarantee Fund Year 1977 Part I: Guarantee Section*, COM (78) 633, Brussels.

Commission of the European Communities, (1979) *Twelfth General Report on the Activities of the European Communities in 1978*, Brussels.

Commission of the European Communities (1981) *Commission Report on the Mandate of 30 May 1980*, COM (81) 300, Brussels.

Commission of the European Communities (1982) *Preliminary Draft General Budget of the European Communities for the Financial Year 1983*, 7 volumes, COM (82) 200, Brussels.

Customs and Excise (1982) *72nd Report of the Commissioners of Her Majesty's Customs and Excise for the Year Ending 31 March 1981*, Cmnd. 8521, HMSO: London.

European Communities—Information (1975) *The European Community's Financial System*, Brussels.

Harris, S. A., and Josling, T. E. (1977) *A Preliminary Look at the Food Industry and the CAP*, an Agra-Europe research document, Agra Europe: Tunbridge Wells.

House of Lords Select Committee on the European Communities (1979) *EEC Budget*, 2nd Report Session 1979–80, HL17, HMSO: London.

House of Lords Select Committee on the European Communities (1980) *1980 Budget*, 57th Report Session 1979–80, HL 301, HMSO: London.

House of Lords Select Committee on the European Communities (1981) *Fruit and Vegetables*, 22nd Report Session 1980–81, HL 147, HMSO: London.

Intervention Board for Agricultural Produce (1974) *Report for the Calendar Year 1973*, Cmnd 5699, HMSO: London.

Intervention Board for Agricultural Produce (1981) *Report for the Calendar Year 1980*, Cmnd 8283, HMSO: London.

Muller, F. (1970) *FEOGA—The Agricultural Guidance and Guarantee Fund of the EEC*, Agricultural Adjustment Unit, University of Newcastle-upon-Tyne.

Strasser, D. (1981) *The Finances of Europe*, revised and enlarged edition, Office for Official Publications of the European Communities, Luxembourg.

Wallace, H. (1980) *Budgetary Politics: The finances of the European Communities*, George Allen and Unwin: London.

The United Kingdom and the European Communities, (1971) Cmnd 4715, HMSO: London.

Chapter 14

Whither the CAP?

In Chapter 3 the slow process of assembling a common agricultural policy from the building blocks of six national policies, and the political compromises that were inevitably involved, was outlined as a necessary prelude to a clearer understanding of why the CAP displays certain features today. The negotiations were often prolonged, and rarely was a common solution obvious to all. As a result, it would be surprising if the CAP were to fully meet the aspirations of all Community citizens. This is particularly so as the CAP is the main EC policy and thus subject to the full glare of public scrutiny. Over the years, there have been many critics of the CAP: consumers, taxpayers, foreign suppliers (notably the USA and Australia), and even farmers themselves.

Almost all policies involve 'costs' in the sense that they impose burdens on society at large, or some groups in society, in attempting to achieve certain objectives. The 'benefits' that arise from full or partial attainment of the policy objectives are presumed to outweigh—at least in the minds of the policy makers—the 'costs', for otherwise the policy would not be implemented. The benefits that accrue from agricultural policies are assumed to be basically social in nature—maintenance of a viable population in marginal areas, the social stability and 'values' implicit in a prosperous rural community, the peace of mind associated with self-sufficiency, and others elaborated in Chapter 1—though economic factors are also important. Society's evaluation of the benefits of attaining those objectives may be coloured by the views and political allegiances of those in power,[1] and may differ markedly from any individual's perception, but they are none the less the substance of decision making. Equally the 'costs' may involve social and economic aspects, and these will not receive equal weighting by all citizens. Thus agricultural policy, as any other policy, is likely to generate conflicting views as to whether it is 'good' or 'bad'; and the CAP is certainly no exception.

The literature tends to discuss the 'cost' of the CAP at three levels. First in terms of economic efficiency; second in terms of the immediately recognizable symptoms of any malaise, notably of butter 'mountains' and wine 'lakes'; and finally in terms of transfers between individuals, Member States and, less commonly, in terms of the burdens imposed on Third Countries. The effect of the CAP on Third Countries—particularly with respect to the level and stability of world market prices—was discussed in Chapter 11, but the other issues have only been touched upon on earlier pages. Thus the first part of this chapter takes a brief look at some of the criticisms directed at the CAP, because these views have implications for the future development of policy.

The politics of change in the CAP are, however, complex. Decisions are not, in the main, made to reflect the abstract views of economists; nor even—in the EC context—in response to the majority view of a particular country's citizens; they are more likely to be the consequence of defensive reactions to pressures the EC's institutions cannot ignore. A particular example, or so at least it seems to many observers at the time of writing, is the inexorable pressure that the exhaustion of Budget funds is expected to bring to the CAP. This problem was examined in Chapter 13.

An issue with budgetary implications, but with other facets as well, is that of the problems associated with the Iberian Enlargement (if indeed Spain ever does join).[2] The Third Enlargement will have implications for the political balance within the EC's institutions, and the changed volumes of production and consumption of agricultural and horticultural products that are expected to emerge will have implications for Third Countries, particularly in the Mediterranean basin.[3] Thus, it is expected that in the 1980s, pressures for change will continue to come from the international Community as well as from internal sources.

The latter part of this chapter will review some of the ideas that have been put forward for change, or 'reform', of the CAP.[4] The purpose is to clarify the issues involved: for the different perceptions of what is to be reformed, and how that reform is to be undertaken are myriad. No attempt will be made to survey all the literature, though most of the important ideas will be discussed; nor to forecast how the CAP will, in fact, respond to the pressures of the 1980s.

THE 'COST' OF THE CAP[5]

Efficiency, 'lakes', and 'mountains'

The theme of economic 'efficiency' is one that has emerged in several places in this book. It was implicit, for example, in the analysis of policy mechanisms in Chapter 3; and it also emerged in the discussion on 'green money' and MCAs in Chapter 8, though there it was pointed out that many economists had reservations about fully embracing the theme.

A central assumption is that the cost of producing a product accurately reflects the value that society places on the alternative goods that could be produced with those inputs. Thus, if the total cost of producing a good is greater than the price at which it can be purchased elsewhere or at which it can be sold, a loss is necessarily borne by society. Evidence for this loss is provided when goods can be obtained more cheaply on world markets than from domestic producers, and consequently import barriers are necessary to protect the viability of domestic industry; when subsidies have to be paid to enable domestic producers to compete in the face of cheaper imports; and when domestic production goes unsold at the support price and has to be bought into intervention or sold, with the aid of export subsidies, on world markets. Thus intervention stocks—the butter 'mountains' of the popular press—and high budgetary expenditure on subsidies, are merely aspects of a policy mechanism which imposes an economic cost upon society.

Two problems arise in trying to assess the economic costs outlined in the previous paragraph. First there is by no means a consensus of view amongst economists that market prices do reflect society's valuation of the alternative uses to which inputs into the farming sector could be put: not only might other policies of government distort input prices, in the same way as price support policies have distorted the price of agricultural products, but also the price paid by individuals for an input could be greater than the price society would have to pay. Thus with high unemployment a farmer would still have to pay the going wage rate to hire an additional man from the ranks of the unemployed, but from society's point of view this additional cost would be much less because alternative production elsewhere in the economy would not be foregone. Hence the proposition that, under certain circumstances, an increase in agricultural protection might lead to an increase in national income, rather than the reverse.

The second problem is the misconception that budgetary expenditures and the size of intervention stocks gives a measure of the economic cost of a policy. This is not the case. It is possible, for example, to imagine the production of a product within Europe at twice the cost, in terms of inputs, that it could be obtained on the world market. The necessary protection from cheap imports might be provided by the variable import levy policy described in previous chapters. If domestic producers are unable, even then, to meet domestic demand at the artificially inflated support price imports will be necessary; there will be budget revenue, not expenditure; and no stocks will accumulate. The policy will none the less impose a cost upon society: hence the budgetary costs of CAP price support are not a good indication of the costs of the policy. Despite this the Commission (1981b, p. 11) has tried to compare levels of agricultural support in developed countries by expressing Budget expenditure on price and income support as a proportion of agricultural value added. This approach is highly misleading for the EC, where the major part of agricultural support comes from the higher prices consumers pay for their food than would be the case if a different policy were adopted.

The excess of domestic production over consumption at the support price is sometimes referred to as a 'surplus': and CAP 'surpluses' attract a particularly bad press. As indicated in the previous paragraph a support policy might be imposing severe costs upon society even though 'surpluses'—as defined above—do not appear. There are essentially three methods of disposing of 'surpluses', all discussed in Chapter 3, if one of the policy constraints is that the production side of the equation is not to be tampered with. One way would be to reduce the price to consumers, with the aid of a 'consumer' subsidy, to the point that demand absorbed the available supply; another would be to export on to world markets, as is the case with sugar in the EC; and a third would be to add to intervention stores. Thus intervention stocks are not a measure of EC 'surpluses': the stocks will increase as 'surpluses' are bought, leaving smaller quantities to be exported; and will be reduced as intervention stocks are sold for subsidized export, resulting in increased budgetary expenditure. When, as in recent years, the Commission has increasingly relied on export refunds to dispose of the Community's 'surpluses', and consequently intervention stocks have been reduced, it is wrong to suggest—as some commentators have done—that the problem of 'surpluses' has been brought under control.

Income distribution

Potentially of far more importance to policy makers is the extent that these policies distribute gains and losses amongst members of society. For example, an export tax, as applied by the EC to sugar exports in 1980, would have several distributional effects. It would ease the burden on the authorities to raise tax revenue elsewhere; there would be a reduction in potential income for the farm sector which would be borne in an undisclosed fashion by landowners, farm labourers, and farmers; and the price of the farm product to the food industry would be lower than it otherwise might have been, a saving which might be passed on direct to the consumer or retained as higher profits to industry. There would be other distributional impacts, as well, although they would not all have to be considered by policy makers as some of the effects would be very diffuse.

A number of themes have been introduced in the previous paragraph, none of which have been adequately dealt with in the literature dealing with the CAP. No attempt can be made in this text to make good the deficiency; rather some of the issues will be expanded briefly in the following paragraphs.

It is believed by economists that increases in the degree of price support will tend to increase the price of land; work by Traill (1980) supports this view. But there is little evidence to suggest that policy makers have any clear idea of the likely impact of their policies on even farm business profits, let alone other variables such as land prices, wage rates, and fertilizer usage.

On the other hand, there is a growing concern in policy making circles that the CAP might have an undesirable regional impact.[6] This belief has four elements. First, that low income regions have poor resource endowment, hence low levels of output, and gain less from the CAP price support mechanisms than do high output regions. Second, is the belief that the CAP is biased in favour of cereal production rather than grass-fed livestock. The latter is concentrated in marginal hill lands, whereas the former is located on the better land with good agricultural potential. As commented in Chapter 5, the dependence of many small low income farmers on milk production places considerable constraints on any reform proposals. A third problem arises from the fact that, with the exception of aids under the hill farming directive and the other regionally specific aids discussed in Chapter 9, the marginal farming areas have gained relatively little from CAP structural measures. The fourth, and by no means least important, regional 'issue' is the belief in France, Italy, and Greece that the CAP is biased in favour of 'Northern' agriculture, rather than 'Mediterranean' agriculture. One consequence of this 'North–South' confrontation was the Mediterranean package of 1977, discussed in Chapter 7; but in addition the Community institutions are likely to have embarked upon an agonizing consideration of a second, much larger, Mediterranean package—as a prelude to the Iberian Enlargement—soon after this book has gone to press.

Chapter 10 was devoted to the theme that the CAP has direct implications for the profitability and level of employment of the food industry; but too many studies tend to assume a direct link between farmers and consumers. Thus it is assumed that one group's benefit is automatically another group's loss; to a certain extent—though not always—policy makers have concurred with this view. For example, in 1976 the Labour government in Britain resisted a 'devaluation' of the then overvalued 'green pound' because it was believed that this would lead to a rise in food prices and thus fuel inflation; whereas in 1981 the Conservative government resisted a 'revaluation' of the then undervalued 'green pound' because it was said that this would not result in a fall in food prices. Undoubtedly market circumstances do change, but the role of the food industries in price formation has yet to be systematically analysed.

The CAP is also said to have a distributional impact across income classes.[7] CAP support mechanisms that increase the farm gate price of agricultural products are of greater benefit to the large scale than the small scale producer and thus tend to be biased in favour of the high income producer. If the farm gate price is maintained by a government subsidy paid directly to the producer, then the progressive[8] nature of the tax system means that low income households are spared the burden of farm support; whereas a CAP type system means that low income households are called upon, in the form of higher food prices, to support the farm sector.

'Costs' and 'benefits' of the CAP to the Member States

All the distributional considerations discussed above, and the implications for Third Countries discussed in Chapter 11, are as relevant to national agricultural policies as they are to the CAP. The CAP is different, however, in that it is a policy applied with common rules across national boundaries and consequently it has distributional implications for the Member States. The Member States' contributions, in the form of own resources, to the budgetary expenditures of the CAP, and their receipts of FEOGA funds, form only a part of the calculation.

The common agricultural policy involves each Member State adopting common funding through the Community Budget for agricultural support, as well as the same method of price support and (in theory at least) the same level of support. Compared to the domestic policy that was previously pursued (or the policy the analyst would prefer) there will undoubtedly be a difference in the level of domestic output and consumption, and hence in traded quantities and the level of the world market price. Calculating the 'cost' of the CAP to the European Community of these effects is, however, fraught with difficulties. Not only can disagreement ensue over what should be the 'correct' reference policy, but also over the various supply and demand elasticities used in the analysis.

However, the problem is more clearly specified, and more closely corresponds to the concept of 'cost' or 'benefit' of the CAP to Member State economies, if the 'reference' policy is taken to be a set of national policies with the same impact on prices as the CAP, but without common funding or free trade between the Member States. As explained in Chapter 13, the revenue and expenditure occasioned by the CAP become part of the Community Budget and thus involve net transfers across the foreign exchanges, and not just transfer payments within the Member States. In addition to this, trade between the Community countries takes place at Community prices, not world prices. Thus the total economic cost or benefit of the CAP for an individual country includes not only the net budget transfers, occasioned by the policy, but also the net financial surplus or deficit on the internally traded quantities, valued first at Community prices and then at world prices. In this instance world prices are a valid benchmark because the question posed deals not with price levels and traded quantities—which remain constant—but with the common financing of the Community system.

A number of such studies have been made,[9] but in general they all display features common to the results presented in Table 14.1. Britain, West Germany, Italy, and Belgium—the four net food importers of the then nine Member States—emerge with a net burden imposed by the CAP; whereas the other Member States, and in particular Ireland and Denmark in relation to their size, emerge as beneficiaries. This result is hardly surprising, but it does explain why certain Member States do not wish to modify the CAP

Table 14.1　CAP induced transfers across the foreign exchanges—1979. £million

	CAP transfers through the Budget	Estimate of trade transfers	Total
Belgium/Luxembourg	−49	+300	+250
Denmark	−336	−375	−710
West Germany	+465	+125	+590
France	−255	−600	−850
Ireland	−339	−275	−610
Italy	−4	+700	+700
Netherlands	−329	−325	−650
United Kingdom	+882	+225	+1110

Notes: +ve implies a *cost* to a Member State, −ve implies a *receipt* by a Member State.

Only CAP-induced transfers through the Budget are considered; all other budgetary transactions are ignored.

The arithmetical oddities were present in the original source.

SOURCE　Calculations by the British Ministry of Agriculture, Fisheries and Food, following the methodology of Rollo and Warwick (1979). Published in House of Lords (1981), Volume II, p. 194.

mechanisms. One interesting feature of the table is the extent to which the Budget transfers, particularly for Italy and Belgium, fail to give a reliable indication of the total impact of the CAP on their national economies. Even so, politicians concentrate their attention on the Budget transfers.

THE 'BENEFITS' OF THE CAP?

The first part of this chapter has examined a number of the 'costs' that are said to be associated with the CAP, the most significant politically being the burden imposed upon certain Member States because of the common funding of the policy. The last part of the chapter takes a look at some of the ideas for 'reform' which have been put forward. It would, nevertheless, be misleading if some of the arguments in favour of the CAP were not voiced in the chapter, however briefly, because the policy does have its supporters; and, while there are pressures which indicate change is on the way, there are strong political forces which seek to bolster the status quo.

The Commission, in its *Reflections on the Common Agricultural Policy*, has advanced a number of achievements:

(a) That the quantity and quality of foodstuffs in consumption has improved 'to an extent never before known' and that this was helped by the 'spectacular development of agriculture and of intra-community trade in agricultural produce';

(b) That the CAP has 'encouraged the modernization of European agriculture';

(c) That the growth in productivity, 'supported by the common policy, contributed in the sixties and seventies to the remarkable boom in the industrial and tertiary sectors by providing them with the necessary labour';

(d) That 'the common policy has enabled agricultural income to keep on growing and at the same time it has protected the sector from the recessions which have affected the economy since 1974';

(e) 'That the CAP has facilitated the export of agricultural products both within the Community and to non-member countries and has thus had important consequences for the trade balance of the Member States';

(f) That 'as regards security of supply, Europe has not only been shielded from any physical shortage of foodstuffs, but it has also been protected from the speculative movements which sometimes affect the world markets in raw materials';

(g) And finally, the Commission comments, that 'we should not forget the contribution of European agriculture to satisfying world demand for food, including demand from those parts of the world unable to pay for it. If the FAO's forecasts are correct, the world will need all its available resources in order to meet its future food requirements'. (Commission, 1980, pp. 4–5.)

Agriculture has certainly shared in the rapid technological changes that have taken place since the Second World War; labour has been released from the land and—until recent years—been absorbed into other growing sectors; and as incomes have risen so have living standards with a concomitant rise in the range, quality, and—in some cases—quantity of food consumed. The extent to which the CAP has contributed towards these changes is, however, uncertain. The views credited to the Commission in the previous paragraph imply that the CAP has fostered change: however, an alternative view is that one advantage of the CAP is that it has slowed the rate of exodus from the land and, hence, made the adjustment problems (discussed in Chapter 1) easier to bear. For example, Villain, the Director-General for Agriculture in the Commission, pointing to the high levels of unemployment characterizing the European economy in 1979, asked whether it was sensible to accelerate the departure of farmers from the land (Villain, 1979, p. 17).

The view that, in a hungry world, European agriculture should produce an abundance of food, not only to secure supplies to European consumers but also to feed the hungry elsewhere, is one that has a lot of support. It is evident, for example, in the writings of Cayre who comments 'it must never be forgotten that the ancient craft of agriculture, rejuvenated by the 1973 crisis, is never noticed except during a period of shortage!' (Cayre, 1980, p. 149).

During the period of high world commodity prices, associated with the first increase in energy costs in 1973 to which Cayre refers, European consumers were indeed shielded by the CAP from high prices, but very few could have been in danger of suffering physical shortages of food—though many consumers in low income countries were. The stability that the CAP has brought to European food prices is, no doubt, prized by consumers; although as argued in Chapter 11 stability in Europe has been purchased at the expense of greater price instability elsewhere. The apparent success of the OPEC oil cartel, the US soya embargo of July 1973, and food shortages in Poland, the USSR and other Eastern bloc countries have undoubtedly convinced many Europeans of the need for bountiful European harvests, and this will understandably influence the EC's agricultural policy for many years to come. Alternative policies—involving internationally co-ordinated grain stocks and the freeing of international trade—are less intuitively appealing.

Many people are appalled at the contrast between starvation and malnutrition in many parts of the world and at the surpluses and obesity of the West. Many countries, including the EC, have responded to this and enacted food aid programmes (see Chapter 11 for a discussion of the EC's food aid activities). Some 70 per cent of all food aid given or sold to less developed countries is marketed in the recipient country, and so is a form of budgetary support to those governments. The remaining 30 per cent 'is designed to be distributed free of charge to the poor, either through long-term development projects or in relief operations after disasters and for refugee feeding' (Jackson and Eade, 1982, p. 1).

This project food aid is probably what the European taxpayer has in mind when the Commission argues that European agriculture has a contribution to satisfying 'demand from those parts of the world unable to pay for it'. But food aid is not without its problems. Jackson and Eade have commented:

> On the surface project food aid seems to provide a morally and politically acceptable way of sharing the fruits of over-production in the North with those in need in the South. Because of its appeal at this simple level, *and because of governments' interests in supporting their own rural economies,* food aid's inherent weaknesses have been largely overlooked. But donors must recognise its ineffectiveness and the damage it can cause. (Jackson and Eade, 1982, p. 91, emphasis added)

The Commission's comment that 'The CAP has facilitated the export of agricultural products ... and has thus had important consequences for the trade balance of the Member States' is rather disingenuous. Undoubtedly the trade balance of France, Ireland, and Denmark has been aided but, as was pointed out at the end of the preceding section, this has been at the expense of countries such as Italy, West Germany, and the UK. Therein lies the CAP's greatest success; the most powerful arguments for maintaining the status quo; and the main benefit that the EC derives.

The success is the fact that the CAP has survived despite the tensions it has generated between the Member States. The fact that the policy has been so resilient when other European initiatives have been less successful means that the CAP is the Community's major achievement—without the CAP the EC would seem less secure. Because of this those countries that are disadvantaged by the policy have not been willing to press their criticisms too far and, recognizing this, those that gain have stood their ground. This was the implicit compromise between Germany and France; the United Kingdom sits less securely in the picture.

'REFORM' OF THE CAP

It will be clear from the foregoing discussion that there are many pressures for change, or 'reform' of the CAP. Consequently, it is important that those discussing reform clarify in their own minds what it is they want to reform, and that all parties to the discussion are conscious of the objectives of their fellows. Otherwise a dialogue of the deaf can quickly result. In the following paragraphs various viewpoints are outlined: it is not intended that these caricatures accurately represent the views of any single individual or organization. The position of most commentators is an amalgam, in varying proportions, of the opinions discussed.

The 'free-trader', for example, recognizes no justification for state intervention in any sector of the economy and thus reform in his eyes would entail the wholesale dismantling of the CAP. This stance would probably also result in the break-up of the EC because in a free trading world there would be no need for a customs union.

At the other extreme is the view that the problems of the CAP largely stem from imperfections in its protectionist nature. Thus if manioc from Thailand, soya from the USA, sugar from various ACP (African, Caribbean, Pacific) countries, and New Zealand dairy produce were not permitted such liberal access, then the market imbalance evident within the CAP would be greatly diminished and the Budget costs of CAP support reduced. The Commission (1981b, p. 68) has estimated that the cost to the Budget in increased export refunds, of the EC's import concessions on sugar, butter, beef, and cereal substitutes was equivalent to about $11\frac{1}{2}$ per cent of Budget spending on CAP market support.

The EC's trading partners throughout the world complain not only that high CAP prices reduce the market share for foreign supplies (by encouraging EC production and discouraging consumption), but also that the EC's system of variable import levies and export refunds represents a particularly pernicious form of protectionism. Given the degree of acrimony in recent disputes between Australia and the USA, and the EC, it is not inconceivable that EC industrialists, anxious to safeguard their export markets, could seek to 'reform' the CAP in a fashion satisfactory to major exporters of agricultural produce throughout the world.

Ministers of Finance, aware of the difficulties of raising tax revenue and now concerned about a possible linkage between the rate of inflation and the level of government expenditure, have typically been concerned about the budgetary costs of agricultural policies, regardless of other consequences. In the EC, with its common system of financing, the situation is infinitely more complex for the interests of Ministers naturally lie in minimizing *national* exchequer costs of *common* policies. 'Reform', in the sense of minimizing national exchequer costs, can be sought in reducing the overall budget cost of the CAP; in modifying the rules on national contributions to the budget; or—for the individual Member State—in seeking to maximize those aspects of the CAP which yield a high national return.

The farming interest tends to lie in maintaining, or even increasing, the current level of farm income whilst avoiding the political embarrassment of unwanted stocks. Ritson has pointed out that it is not the stocks themselves which are embarrassing, but rather the cost of their disposal (Ritson, 1980, p. 107). Indeed, few would object to the production of an abundance of competitively priced products. Equally, stocks of food are sometimes welcome—unfortunately, however, it is not always clear which stocks, or what level of stocks are required.

The consumer interest on the other hand is taken to be the continuing availability of foodstuffs at the lowest possible price. There are other criteria which are possibly of equal (though less quantifiable) importance: stable prices, for example, through both normal seasonal variations and abnormal famine and glut situations.[10] However, the fact that much of our food is processed, packed, and otherwise prepared before sale does mean that there is no simple link between farm gate and retail prices.

Besides the interests outlined above there are many other lobbies in a modern economy which could legitimately claim a hearing in any reform discussion. They would include agricultural suppliers, the food industry, forestry, other rural dwellers, environmentalists, animal welfare groups, and probably many others.[11] Each would have views on 'reform of the CAP'.

Proposals for reform of the CAP

In selecting the reform proposals discussed in this section the following criteria have been used: that the proposal should seek to reduce the cost of surpluses, or that it should seek to reduce the price to consumers, or both. Clearly such schemes cannot meet all the objectives outlined in previous paragraphs, but it is believed that they are sufficiently wide ranging to cover most realizable schemes.

All the possible policies involve advantages and disadvantages: there is no perfect solution. As Josling has succinctly remarked:

> The problem for the reformer is basically that no scheme can at the same time cost less, relieve the burden on consumers, be consistent with trading interests, and preserve the present income position of EC agriculture. (Josling, 1980, p. 98)

Equally all schemes must be administered, at a greater or lesser cost; but there is a danger that administrators might overestimate the logistical difficulties, and costs, of administering a new scheme and so bolster the status quo.

Diversion of resources from agricultural production

To many observers in many countries it has often seemed that too many resources are devoted to food production and that governments should act to limit resource use in agriculture. Many mechanisms could be devised, some somewhat indistinguishable from quotas discussed below, and many offering considerable financial rewards to unscrupulous practitioners.

In the EC it has been suggested that forestry should receive additional state support such that it bids away considerable tracts of land from food production.[12] This would tend to raise the price of land to the benefit of land-owners, but not tenant farmers. In the United States farmers are paid to hold their land in fallow. In the EC farmers have been paid to slaughter dairy cows and grub up orchards—but the problem with such schemes is that they tend to subsidize individuals who would have abandoned that particular activity even without subsidy, and do nothing to stop the remaining participants in the industry expanding to make up the potential loss of supply; nor do they prevent new entrants from coming into the industry with the consequent potential for an increase in supply.

In the past many observers have believed that if European agriculture could be helped to modernize and shed labour then ultimately a smaller farm population could produce a smaller quantity of produce, at lower cost, and with higher incomes.[13] Unfortunately, the fabric of farming is slow to change—involving as it does the critical factor of land ownership—and, as Tangermann has pointed out, 'structural policies' have often tended to increase the productive capacity of agriculture rather than encourage the outmigration of labour from the sector (Tangermann, 1980, pp. 111–112).

Other policies would seek to curb the use of resources in agriculture by acting directly on the profitability of farming. In the first instance various government subsidies (e.g. reduced interest rates) or concessions (e.g. reduced tax rates on fuels) could be stopped. As a second stage various inputs into agriculture (e.g. soya meal, manioc) could be taxed. All such measures raise political and moral questions as to whether or not farmers should receive some form of compensation (income supplements—discussed below), and none reduce the price of the final product to the consumer.

Quotas

Quotas come in a whole series of guises, and they are frequently used in Western economies. Most towns for instance limit the number of taxi cabs that can ply in their area, and international air travel displays similar features. In farming, quotas can apply to individual resources or to final output. Both systems have their disadvantages—if for instance the quota specifies the number of hectares planted to potatoes per farm, or the number of milk cows per dairy, there will be an incentive to maximize output per unit of permitted input and consequently the impact on total output might be less than expected. If the quota seeks to control the volume or proportion of output that can legally be sold, it is quite easy to imagine severe public relations difficulties. Ritson conjures up the image of a dairy farmer, told that he can not sell his entire milk production, pouring the remainder down the drain in front of a battery of television cameras (Ritson, 1980, p. 106).

Quotas are synonymous with high prices. Indeed, the quota is necessary to maintain price: if the quota were relaxed output would expand and prices would fall. To the farming community this can be presented as a distinct advantage: if quotas are reduced to remove 'surpluses' then prices can be simultaneously raised to maintain income. The more effective is the quota in controlling supply then the higher the price is likely to be, to the disadvantage of consumers.

Most economists dislike quotas because, unless saleable, they tend to ossify production patterns. The essence of a growing economy is that less efficient producers should be replaced by more efficient producers; but with unsaleable quotas the less efficient producer is protected and the more efficient is not permitted to expand.

If quotas are transferable, and a market develops, then some of these disadvantages can be reduced. The less efficient producer, in ceding his quota to the more efficient, receives a capital sum to ease his transition from the industry. Indeed, this mechanism could be used to reduce the overall size of an industry and yet not increase prices in compensation. The government itself could purchase quotas in the open market, which would then be liquidated. It is unclear what the market value of quotas would be and thus it is difficult to estimate the budgetary costs of the policy—but it would provide retirement incentives to some producers, discourage expansion by others (because the market value of the quotas would be bid-up by the government activity), and in conjunction with some other measures might be the only feasible method of tackling the EC's dairy surplus in the short term. As with many other schemes an army of inspectors would be required.

Quantums

There is much confusion over the difference between quotas and quantums, indeed both words mean many things to different people. However, what most authors (e.g. Bergmann, 1980, p. 5) seem to have in mind is that a Community, or national, guaranteed quantity should be established and that if production exceeds this specified amount then a fall in price would be triggered. In some schemes the fall in price is supposed to apply retrospectively in the current marketing period (to intervention prices and export refunds for example) and in some to the next marketing period. In any event it is the price mechanism which is expected to eliminate 'surpluses'; the quantum merely specifies the decision-making rules. It was proposals on these lines that the EC implemented in 1982 for some commodities.

Other schemes envisage differential pricing, even for the individual farmer. As output expands each successive slice would receive a lower guaranteed price, in the same way as an income tax applies on a progressive basis to each additional slice of income. Such schemes, it is said, could be tailored to give aid to the small farmer as well as to restrict supply.

On the basis of the—rather arbitrary—difference established here between quotas and quantums the EC's sugar policy (see Chapter 6) might be termed a quantum policy. Sugar factories receive a lower price for 'B' sugar than for 'A' sugar, and (usually) an even lower one for 'C' sugar. There is not an absolute limit on production, as with a pure quota system, but once the 'A' quota is filled any extra production reduces the average price that will be received by beet growers.

Co-responsibility levies

Since 1977 a co-responsibility levy has been applied in the milk sector, and the Commission favours extension of the co-responsibility principle to other CAP products in surplus.[14] Essentially two schemes have been used, or proposed, so far.

The original co-responsibility levy on milk imposed a tax on all production (except as discussed below); thus the price paid by the purchaser exceeded that received by the producer by the extent of the tax. It was originally proposed that the tax revenue be used to promote the marketing of the product—though no evidence was produced to suggest that generic advertising is a cost effective activity. More recently the levy has been seen as a mechanism for reducing the price to producers whilst generating revenue to finance the EC budget. However, as with most of these schemes, it is unrealistic to expect that Ministers will reduce the price received by producers unless there is some offsetting compensation; and it is more likely that the levy will be used to tax consumers and so evade the Budget ceiling.

The various exemptions concern small farmers and producers in disadvantaged regions. This two-tier pricing system is an attempt to emulate the concept of giving income supplements to low income producers. However, it suffers two disadvantages: first to benefit from the scheme the small producer must continue producing milk; and second it is a difficult idea to 'sell' to large and articulate producers that they should receive a lower price for their product.

The second scheme that was proposed was that any dairy that increased output would be subject to a super levy. The super levy would be equal to the marginal cost, to the Budget, of disposing of an additional unit of output. This tax on extra production would have been so heavy that no dairy would have wished to increase output: it was in fact a disguised form of quota.

Deficiency payments

The term 'deficiency payment' is not acceptable to CAP purists and yet deficiency payments (or similar) have in fact been a permanent feature of several CAP market mechanisms (e.g. oilseeds, olive oil, and tobacco). The essential feature of such schemes is that the market price is allowed to freely react to changing market circumstances (usually linked to the world market) whereas producers, in addition to revenue from sales, also receive a subsidy which is directly linked to their volume of production.

Under a 'pure' system the deficiency payment would be finely calculated on each transaction such that the total revenue from a sale was never less than the 'guaranteed price'. In practice such a scheme would be impossibly costly to administer, and payments are, in fact, usually made on the basis of an estimated, or predicted, price gap during a specified time interval which to a greater or lesser extent compensates the producer for the deficiency.

The price to the consumer is reduced, to the level of the world market price if required, and 'surpluses' magically disappear because all production is sold at the prevailing market price. Thus both the objectives of the 'reform' specified earlier, would be satisfied. There is of course a substantial budgetary cost (the deficiency payment) and national authorities require adequate administrations to make the payments.[15] With the current preoccupation with the budgetary costs of policies, deficiency payments schemes are, politically, unacceptable.

The price mechanism

Prices operate in the markets for farm inputs and farm products; the former was briefly discussed under the first category of reform measures and it is the latter that shall be dealt with here. The price mechanism is a chimera to most policy analysts. On the one hand it seems the obvious answer to the CAP's problem of surplus disposal, and yet on the other it seems that a price cut of the required magnitude would be impossible to sustain politically unless producers are in some way sheltered from the consequences. Income supplements are usually suggested as the most suitable form of compensation (e.g. Bergmann, 1980; Marsh, 1980; Tangermann, 1980).

The dilemma is as follows. For many products, and in particular milk, the difference between EC and world prices is so great that any politically feasible price cut would do little to bridge the gap and—with the constant adoption by farmers of new technology—it might not even stop the growth of surpluses.

The Commission has consistently urged that a prudent price policy be pursued such that, through inflation, the real level of prices would be eroded. But at most price reviews there will be at least one Minister who for domestic political reasons, will wish to see that higher prices are agreed. Politics will always intervene to ensure that 'prudent' pricing policies are overthrown[16]—it would seem that the only alternative is a major change in policy.

Income supplements

There is no consensus that the farm sector should be compensated for an income loss brought about by a reduction in support prices: some would argue that this is a risk comparable to that faced by any other businessman and that plenty of warning signals have been given. On the other hand, given the degree of state involvement in agriculture, it is, many believe, unrealistic to suppose that substantial price cuts could be achieved and sustained without some degree of income compensation. But again there is some difficulty in clarifying what is meant.

An economist has only one stipulation—that the payment of the supplement to an individual should not be dependent upon that individual's future contribution to farm output. But, that being said, there are an endless variety of schemes that can be visualized. The costs of the schemes would also vary widely: ranging from rather limited payments over, say, a five-year period, to much more substantial sums with some payments continuing for forty or fifty years. As an alternative all the beneficiaries could receive a single lump sum; but the magnitude of this is unlikely to endear the scheme to Ministers of Finance.

All the programmes have in common the fact that a register of interests would have to be established on day one of the scheme (a formidable administrative task) and all would suffer from the fact that a great deal of advance warning (in the form of lengthy Ministerial meetings) might encourage individuals to enter farming specifically to take advantage of the income supplements.

The principle underlying the scheme is that those who have suffered an income loss because of the change in policy should be compensated. But how is the target group to be defined, how is the income loss to be measured, how long are the payments to continue, how are the payments to be adjusted for inflation, and is there to be a maximum annual payment per person (or family)? These are immensely difficult questions to answer and in practice some rather arbitrary distinctions are liable to be drawn.

Farm workers, landowners, and farm machinery suppliers are likely to suffer some loss of income for instance; but it is unlikely that those groups will receive assistance. Some farmers will have been in business thirty years and will have no overdraft or mortgage payments outstanding. Others will have been in business for three months and will be heavily indebted. Are they all to receive the same treatment? Some farmers will be nearing retirement age—should they receive compensation until the end of their lives (and their dependants thereafter) as with a retirement pension, or is there a presumption that national social security schemes take over at 65?

The catalogue of questions recited in the preceding paragraphs is by no means exhaustive. Nor does it attempt to deal with the intricate questions of EC finance: budget ceilings and national contributions. However, it is included to emphasize the point that the cost of a policy of income supplementation will be dependent upon the form the policy takes; and equally its acceptability to all participants—farmers, consumers, the food industries, and taxpayers—will depend upon the generosity of its provisions, and upon its cost.

Re-nationalization of the CAP?

Chapter 14 has been concerned with a recitation of the problems faced by the CAP, and a brief discussion of some of the proposals for reform that have been put forward. Some EC citizens are satisfied with the CAP, others are not and lobby for change. In addition to issues specific to the farm and food sectors other major policy issues have a direct bearing on agricultural policy. It is not possible to predict how the CAP will respond to the emerging pressures: whether or not the Community will impose a tax on vegetable oils for example, as a precondition for Spanish accession, and the reactions of the USA to such a move. One prediction does seem possible none the less: that the future existence of the Community could be threatened if the budgetary problems are not resolved in a satisfactory fashion. This is so for two reasons: first, the threat of British withdrawal cannot, at the time of writing, be discounted completely,[17] and second, the possibility that the Community Budget might exhaust its funds.

There is current the idea that 'debudgetization'—that is the national funding of EC policies—involves reform of the CAP. This is true only in a limited sense. What is likely to happen if the Community runs out of funds is that Member States—rather than let the CAP support mechanisms come to a halt—will meet out of national funds the shortfall. The theory is that by making the Member States bear the marginal costs of CAP price support they will quickly come to realize that the CAP must be reformed. It seems more likely that the Member States will seek to ensure that their partners bear the marginal costs. By delaying payments, and generally making life difficult for traders, it would be perfectly feasible to make sure that fewer products were bought into domestic intervention stores, or exported from home ports, whilst more favourable treatment was available from the authorities in another Member State. Even now large quantities of products cross boundaries to take advantage of small differences in market conditions. Thus in 1978 30 per cent of all skim milk powder bought into intervention in Germany originated in other Member States.[18]

It would not be long before Member States would raise objections to the import of CAP products from other Member States, particularly if it was believed that they operated the EC's intervention mechanisms more liberally than their partners. It is difficult to see how a CAP involving Community preference and common support mechanisms can long survive without common financing. This conclusion was supported by the Commission (1980, p. 16) when it asked the rhetorical questions 'Can one imagine Ireland accepting high prices for beef if it had to bear the consequencies, or France backing high prices for cereals or sugar. . .?'.

NOTES

1. See, for example, the attempt by Grant (1981) to explain the British government's policy on the green pound according to the political party, and personalities, in power at the time.
2. These issues have been explored by Josling and Pearson (1982).
3. See, for example, the discussion in Chapter IV of FAO (1979).
4. As noted in Chapter 3 the Commission itself has put forward several proposals to 'reform' the CAP. They include the Mansholt Plan (Commission, 1968), the Improvement document (Commission, 1973), and the Stocktaking (Commission, 1975). In addition to that there have been specific policy initiatives for many products, including milk, wine, cereals, and sugar, some of which are referred to in the commodity chapters. More recent pronouncements of interest include the Reflections (Commission, 1980), the Mandate (Commission, 1981a), and the detailed proposals arising from the Mandate as outlined in the Guidelines document (Commission, 1981b).
5. As explained above, the 'cost' to Third Countries was explored in Chapter 11, and consequently that discussion is not repeated here.
6. The Commission has been studying the regional impact of the CAP, on the basis of national reports from commissioned experts. The national studies have not been published, but a summary has (Henry, 1981).
7. See, for example, the now rather dated study by Josling and Hamway (1976), and the more recent work by Dilnot and Morris (1982).
8. A progressive tax system is one in which the proportion of income deducted as tax rises, as income rises.
9. See Bacon, Godley, and McFarquhar (1978), Blancus (1978), Cambridge Economic Policy Group (1979), Rollo and Warwick (1979), Morris (1980), and Buckwell et al. (1982). Some studies have attempted to identify the budget transfers occasioned by the CAP; others take total budget transfers as a proxy for CAP induced flows. Some studies are based on actual budget transfers, and others calculate budget flows. Consequently care is necessary in looking at different sources.
10. This, as noted above, has been claimed as a beneficial consequence of the CAP. For a discussion of the issues raised by consumer security as against stable prices, see Federal Trust (1975).

340

11. See, for example, the book by Shoard (1980).
12. Notably in the Mansholt Plan and the Vedel Commission's report—see Chapter 3.
13. This was the motivating force behind many of the structural policy schemes outlined in Chapter 9.
14. See, for example, the Commission's Reflections (Commission, 1980) where the concept is introduced as the fourth pillar of the CAP along with market unity, Community preference, and financial solidarity (discussed in Chapter 3). For some products (e.g. cereals) the Commission's views on how 'co-responsibility' would be applied involve a quantum policy rather than a co-responsibility levy.
15. One of the arguments put forward to resist the widespread use of deficiency payments in the EC is the administrative consideration of the number of farmers to whom payments would have to be made (over 5 million). When the UK ran a deficiency payments support system, prior to EC entry the number of farmers involved was comparatively small at some three hundred thousand.
16. Indeed, domestic political considerations will militate against the effectiveness of quotas, quantums, and co-responsibility levies, if decisions have to be taken on an annual basis.
17. Though the policy issues also cover topics other than agriculture and the budget.
18. See European Parliament, 1980, p. 7.

REFERENCES

Bacon, R., Godley, W., and McFarquhar, A. (1978) 'The direct costs to Britain of belonging to the EEC', *Economic Policy Review*, No. 4.

Bergmann, D. (1980) *Possible Alternatives to the CAP and Their Economic Consequences*, unpublished paper presented to the Agricultural Economics Society Conference 'The CAP in the 1980s'; London, 2 December 1980.

Blancus, P. (1978) 'The Common Agricultural Policy and the Balance of Payments of the EEC Member Countries', *Banca Nazionale del Lavoro Quarterly Review* **127**, pp. 355–370.

Buckwell, A. E., Harvey, D. R., Thomson, K. J., and Parton, K. A. (1982) *The Costs of the Common Agricultural Policy*, Croom Helm: London.

Cambridge Economic Policy Group (1979) *Cambridge Economic Policy Review* No. 5.

Cayre, H. (1980) *Agricultural Plenty*, Gentry Books: London.

Commission of the European Communities (1968) *Memorandum on the Reform of Agriculture in the European Economic Community*, COM (68) 1000, Part A, Brussels.

Commission of the European Communities (1973) *Improvement of the Common Agricultural Policy*, COM (73) 1850, Brussels.

Commission of the European Communities (1975) *Stocktaking of the Common Agricultural Policy*, COM (75) 100, Brussels.

Commission of the European Communities (1980) *Reflections on the Common Agricultural Policy*, COM (80) 800, Brussels.

Commission of the European Communities (1981a) *Commission Report on the Mandate of 30 May 1980*, COM (81) 300, Brussels.

Commission of the European Communities (1981b) *Guidelines for European Agriculture*, COM (81) 608, Brussels.

Dilnot, A. W., and Morris, C. N. (1982) 'The Distributional Effects of the Common Agricultural Policy', *Fiscal Studies*, **3**, Institute of Fiscal Studies.

European Parliament (1980) Committee on Budgetary Control, *Notice to Members*, PE 64 131/Ann.

Federal Trust (1975) *The CAP and the British Consumer*, Report of a Study Group, London.

Food and Agriculture Organization (1979) *Commodity Review and Outlook: 1979–80*, FAO: Rome.

Grant, W. (1981) 'The politics of the green pound, 1974–79', *Journal of Common Market Studies*, **19**, 313–329.

Henry, P. (1981) *Study of the Regional Impact of The Common Agricultural Policy*, Regional Policy Series No. 21, Commission of The European Communities: Brussels.

House of Lords Select Committee on the European Communities (1980) *The Common Agricultural Policy*, Session 1979–80, 32nd Report, HL 156, HMSO: London.

House of Lords Select Committee on the European Communities (1981) *The Common Agricultural Policy—Directions of Future Development and Proposals for Prices and Related Measures*, Session 1980–81, 19th Report, 2 volumes, HL 126, HMSO: London.

Jackson, T. with Eade, D. (1982) *Against the Grain. The Dilemma of Project Food Aid*, Oxfam: Oxford.

Josling, T. E. (1980) 'Memorandum', in *House of Lords* (1980), pp. 95–98.

Josling, T. E., and Hamway, D. (1976) 'Income transfer effects of the Common Agricultural Policy', in B. Davey, T. E. Josling, and A. McFarquhar (eds.) *Agriculture and the State*, Macmillan for the Trade Policy Research Centre: London.

Josling, T. E. and Pearson, S. R. (1982) *Developments in the Common Agricultural Policy of the European Community*, Foreign Agricultural Economic Report 172, United States Department of Agriculture: Washington.

Marsh, J. S. (1980) 'Memorandum', in *House of Lords* (1980), pp. 98–107.

Morris, C. N. (1980) 'The Common Agricultural Policy', *Fiscal Studies* 1, Institute of Fiscal Studies.

Ritson, C. (1980) 'British interests and the common agricultural policy', in Wallace, W. (ed.), *Britain in Europe*, Heinemann: London, pp. 91–110.

Rollo, J. M. C., and Warwick, K. S. (1979) *The CAP and Resource Flows among EEC Member States*, Government Economic Service Working Paper No. 27, London.

Shoard, M. (1980) *The Theft of the Countryside*, Temple Smith: London.

Tangermann, S. (1980) 'Memorandum', in *House of Lords* (1980), pp. 107–112.

Traill, W. B. (1980) *Land Values and Rents: The Gains and Losses from Farm Price Support Programmes*, University of Manchester Department of Agricultural Economics, Bulletin No. 175.

Villain, C. (1979) 'L'Etat de la Politique Agricole Commune', in Tracy, M. and Hodac, I. (eds.), *Prospects for Agriculture in the European Economic Community*, College of Europe: Bruges.

Postscript

THE GUIDELINES AND THE 1983/84 PRICE FIXING

The 1983/84 price fixing made some progress in successfully applying two of the most important guidelines laid down in the Commission's 1981 Guidelines Report. This was unexpected as it had been widely assumed that the 'Guidelines' would turn out to be just another in the long line of CAP reform proposals which, after some initial impact, had been quietly forgotten. The guidelines applied were those covering the need to narrow the gap between support prices in the EC and in the principal Third Country agricultural exporters, and the need to penalise overproduction by adjusting the following year's support prices (the so-called 'modulation of guarantees').

The Commission, in its original 1983/84 price proposals, suggested a 'norm' price increase of 5.5 per cent. For cereals, however, the Commission reduced the 'norm' to 4 per cent as a gesture towards narrowing the gap with US support prices. Other products in surplus, and of importance in international trade, (milk products and sugar) were treated similarly. The Commission further reduced the 'norm' for milk and cereals to take into account 1982 production levels significantly exceeding the production thresholds set at the 1982/83 price fixing. For sugar an equivalent deduction was not made because of the obligation on producers to fund directly the cost of export refunds. The result of these factors was that there was a gradation in price increases by commodity:

	1983/84 price rises by commodity in ecu terms
— wine, olive oil, the meats	+5.5%
— sugar	+4.0%
— cereals	+3.0%
— milk products	+2.33%

342

The price fixing was unique in another respect also, in that for the first time since the late 1960s, the Council of Ministers adopted the average price increase proposed by the Commission (of 4.2 per cent in ecu terms) without raising it. However, the actual average rise in national currencies, taking account of green rate changes, was 6.9 per cent. The Council was constrained because in 1982 EC farmers did well financially, in part due to the generous 1982/83 price settlement: hence it could not be claimed that they were in need of especially favourable financial treatment. The impending exhaustion of Own Resources was a further major factor constraining the Council from demanding a higher level of CAP price settlement, while the third major factor was the need to show restraint in price setting as a means of defusing US criticisms of the CAP.

EMS RESHUFFLE BECAUSE OF CAP

An undesirable precedent at the 1983/84 price fixing was the CAP tail wagging the EMS dog. It was found expedient to realign the value of sterling within EMS *solely* in order to allow a successful conclusion to the CAP price fixing. This is the first time that EMS currencies have been realigned for CAP purposes, rather than for the need for realistic currency parities within EMS. Essentially the problem was that in the previous realignment (on 22 March 1983), the DM was revalued by 5.5 per cent so increasing the German MCA. At the 1983/84 price fixing Italy and France were adamant that the German MCA should be reduced; Germany was equally adamant that this should not mean a reduction in support prices in DM terms, and the Commission refused to raise its original proposal of a 4.2 per cent average price rise in ecu terms. The outcome was a further EMS reshuffle on 18 May 1983 taking into account sterling's appreciation since the previous reshuffle, but not affecting the *cross* exchange rates of the other EMS currencies. As a result the ecu was revalued by 1.2 per cent, hence reducing all positive MCA's and increasing all negative ones. Thus part of the German MCA reduction came from the EMS reshuffle rather than from the revaluation of the green mark.

THE BUDGET

The 1984 Preliminary Draft Budget put forward by the Commission showed that the exhaustion of Own Resources, which had been feared toward the end of the 1970s, was imminent. This was principally due to the need to provide for the UK's Budget refunds, and Greece's accession, together with a slowing in the rate of increase in Own Resources due to the recession. Furthermore, at the beginning of the 1980s Agriculture Ministers had felt able to be generous in their 1981/82 and 1982/83 price settlements (after having adopted low rates of price increase in the late 1970s), while on the other hand the European Parliament successfully increased expenditure in non-CAP areas to strengthen other EC policies. The end result is that the 1984 Preliminary Draft Budget involves a VAT rate of 0.956 per cent, leaving uncommitted only about $2\frac{1}{2}$ per cent (667 million ecu) of the estimated Own Resources total.

As a consequence of the difficult Budget position and the need to come to a long term settlement of the UK Budget problem, the Commission put forward in early 1983 new proposals for financing the Budget. These involved:

(a) raising the maximum ceiling on the rate of VAT chargeable for the Community Budget from its current 1 per cent to 1.4 per cent in the first instance;

(b) making it easier to raise the VAT ceiling in the future by allowing the Council of Ministers and the European Parliament (acting together as the Budget Authority) to take the decision, rather than the national parliaments as at present;

(c) part of each country's VAT contribution would be 'modulated' to take account of its share in final agricultural production, its gdp per head and its share in the EC's net operating surplus. The 'modulated' VAT contributions would pay for that proportion of agricultural spending (excluding food aid and the Lome sugar protocol) which exceeded 33 per cent of total Budget spending. The effect of this change would be to shift some of the burden of financing the Budget onto the major recipients of CAP expenditure;

(d) the reimbursement to the EC countries of 10 per cent of the revenue collected as customs duties and agricultural levies would no longer be automatic;

(e) customs duties on coal and steel products should form part of Own Resources.

AGRICULTURAL TRADE MATTERS

In 1982 the US adopted a more aggressive stand against the EC's use of export refunds which result, in its view, in the EC taking an unfair share of world markets and depressing world prices. The US, faced with large agricultural surpluses of its own, threatened to indulge in an export subsidy war to take markets from the EC. It made a large sale of wheat flour to Egypt at subsidised rates (a 'traditional' EC market) as a warning shot.

Both the EC and the US recognized, however, the ultimate futility of such developments and both faced Budget problems in increasing spending on agricultural export subsidies. Consequently a series of bilateral meetings occurred in the first half of 1983 concerned with US/EC agricultural trade tensions. The EC, for its part, limited the amount of wheat it exported to the world market and continued, for the second year running, its restraint on sugar exports. The US, for its part, forbore from dumping its dairy surpluses on the world market while adopting domestic programmes designed to cut back its grain and dairy stocks.

Some of the US/EC discussions occurred under the auspices of GATT where, it is understood, a deal was being formulated as this book went to press which would resolve some of the specific US/EC trade disagreements and may well involve some commitment towards 'managed' world trade. On this latter point an agreement to respect each other's traditional markets for cereals appears to be in prospect, while the EC would like the US to be involved in its dairy agreement with New Zealand. (It should be remembered that it is through the GATT Dairy Council that the EC and New Zealand have co-operated to stabilise and raise some world milk product prices). It is also noteworthy that the EC's proposals for a successor to the 1977 International Sugar Agreement involve a degree of international market management by the world's 10 largest exporters.

GATT AND THE PASTA CASE

As part of the US offensive against the EC it initiated six cases concerning agricultural products in GATT alleging that the EC was using its export refunds to obtain an unfair share of world markets. One of these cases concerned pasta. Under the EC's system for processed food products, including pasta, export refunds are available for their export to the world market.

The GATT Panel of Inquiry ruled, in May 1983, that pasta was a processed food product. The GATT exemption for agricultural export subsidies applies only for primary products. Consequently, by ruling that pasta was a processed product, the Panel found it did not come within the scope of the GATT agricultural exemption.

The implication of the GATT Panel ruling, if upheld, is that the EC's use of export refunds for processed food products in general is not permissible under GATT. The consequence may be a need to revamp the EC's export refund system for processed products (e.g. by adopting a production refund system) unless the US withdraws its pasta complaint as part of a wider deal on US/EC agricultural trade issues.

THE CENTRAL DAIRY ISSUE

The Council in its decisions on the 1983/84 price proposals accepted with surprisingly little difficulty the Commission's new approach to intervention prices for dairy products. The threshold system reduced the intervention price to a 2.33 per cent increase in ecu terms. At the same time the Council accepted that the base threshold for 1983 should be 1981 plus 1 per cent. In other words, should milk deliveries rise by more than 1 per cent above the 1981 figure, then a one to one reduction in the 1984/85 intervention price will operate.

This poses in an acute form the central problem of surplus control in the dairy sector: the refusal of a number of Member States to accept absolute reductions in the intervention price. On present trends, the potential cut in the 1984/85 intervention price should be of the order of 7 per cent. In view of present inflationery trends it is unlikely that intervention prices in general will need to be raised by this amount as an offset, and consequently the dairy intervention price will have to be cut in practice. Combined with a continuing need to revalue the DM, the Commission must decide whether artificially to raise the intervention price to a level which avoids the need for an absolute reduction, or whether to face the Council with this central issue. In earlier years, with the co-responsibility levy the Council has tended to increase support prices to offset any increase in the levy. It remains to be seen whether the Commission and the Council will follow the same easy route for 1984/85 with the threshold arrangements.

Index

347